AF324862

Media, Propaganda and the
Politics of Intervention

This book is part of the Peter Lang Media and Communication list.
Every volume is peer reviewed and meets
the highest quality standards for content and production.

PETER LANG
New York • Bern • Frankfurt • Berlin
Brussels • Vienna • Oxford • Warsaw

Florian Zollmann

Media, Propaganda and the Politics of Intervention

PETER LANG

New York • Bern • Frankfurt • Berlin
Brussels • Vienna • Oxford • Warsaw

Library of Congress Cataloging-in-Publication Data
Names: Zollmann, Florian, author.
Title: Media, propaganda and the politics of intervention / Florian Zollmann.
Description: New York: Peter Lang, 2017.
Includes bibliographical references and index.
Identifiers: LCCN 2017017969 (print) | LCCN 2016057752 (ebook)
ISBN 978-1-4331-2824-0 (hardcover: alk. paper)
ISBN 978-1-4331-2823-3 (paperback: alk. paper) | ISBN 978-1-4331-3940-6 (ebook pdf)
ISBN 978-1-4331-3941-3 (epub) | ISBN 978-1-4331-3942-0 (mobi)
Subjects: LCSH: War—Middle East—Press coverage. | War—Africa, North—Press coverage.
Kosovo War, 1998–1999—Press coverage. | Human rights—Press coverage.
Mass media and propaganda. | Journalism—Objectivity—United States.
Journalism—Objectivity—Great Britain. | Journalism—Objectivity—Germany (West)
Classification: LCC PN4784.W37 (print) | LCC PN4784.W37 Z65 2017 (ebook)
DDC 070.4/333—dc23
LC record available at https://lccn.loc.gov/2017017969
DOI 10.3726/b11346

Bibliographic information published by **Die Deutsche Nationalbibliothek**.
Die Deutsche Nationalbibliothek lists this publication in the "Deutsche
Nationalbibliografie"; detailed bibliographic data are available
on the Internet at http://dnb.d-nb.de/.

The paper in this book meets the guidelines for permanence and durability
of the Committee on Production Guidelines for Book Longevity
of the Council of Library Resources.

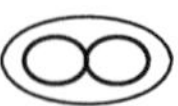

TABLE OF CONTENTS

ACKNOWLEDGEMENTS

There are many people who supported me in various ways during the time I conducted this research. I would like to especially thank my former doctoral supervisor, colleague and friend Richard Lance Keeble for his tremendous support and kindness. Richard's help was invaluable and his work has served as an inspiration. My sincere gratitude goes to my other former doctoral supervisor Ann Gray. I am indebted to my colleague and friend the late John Tulloch. Very special thanks to John Pilger for his generous support and for being a role model throughout his enormous journalistic career. Very special thanks to Piers Robinson for his support, advise and the highly informative discussions we had (cheers to Keiths). Very special thanks to Edward S. Herman and Noam Chomsky for sharing their busy schedules to answering some of my questions as well as providing insightful help. Many thanks to David Edwards and David Cromwell for their inspiring work and support. Many thanks to Mary Savigar for acting as my editor with Peter Lang. Many thanks to Michael Doub and Kat Harrison from Peter Lang for all their help during the production of this book. A special thanks go to the following colleagues and friends who supported me in various ways: Jefferey Klaehn, Daniel Broudy, Andy Mullen, Joan Pedro, Katharina Nötzold, Ben O'Loughlin, Muhamad Al-Darraji, Sylvia Harvey, Lena Jayyusi, Donald Matheson, David Miller,

Lydia Sargent, Michael Albert, Paul Street, Stephen Roblin, Uwe Krüger, Tobias Eberwein and Richard Bähr. Special thanks to Gerard de Zeeuw and Martha Vahl. Thanks to my former colleagues at Liverpool Hope University, particularly Jacqui Miller and Nick Rees, as well as the university for supporting some of my conference travels. I would particularly like to thank my mother Doris and my parental friend Werner for always believing in me, for supporting me and for teaching me how to write. The biggest thanks goes to my wife and love of my life Stefanie for always being at my side, for caring about and looking after me. Stefanie's brilliant mind has been a great source of inspiration during many fruitful discussions.

Durham, May 2017

LIST OF ABBREVIATIONS

BBC	British Broadcasting Corporation
CPA	Coalition Provisional Authority
DT	Daily Telegraph/Sunday Telegraph
ECA	Ethnographic Content Analysis
EWG	Emergency Working Group
FAZ	Frankfurter Allgemeine Zeitung/Frankfurter Allgemeine Sonntagszeitung
FR	Frankfurter Rundschau
FRY/Serbia	Federal Republic of Yugoslavia
G	Guardian/Observer
I	Independent/Independent on Sunday
IBC	Iraq Body Count
ICC	International Criminal Court
IDP	Internally Displaced Person
IGC	Iraqi Governing Council
IIG	Iraqi Interim Government
IPS	Inter Press Service
IRCS	Iraq Red Crescent Society
IRIN	Integrated Regional Information Networks

NATO	North Atlantic Treaty Organization
NYT	New York Times
OSCE	Organisation for Security and Co-operation in Europe
R2P	Responsibility to Protect
SCHRD	Study Centre for Human Rights and Democracy
SZ	Süddeutsche Zeitung
T	The Times/Sunday Times
TAZ	Die Tageszeitung
W	Die Welt/Welt am Sonntag
WP	Washington Post

LIST OF ILLUSTRATIONS

FOREWORD

As I write, highly civilised men and women sitting at desks in London and Washington are approving sales to Saudi Arabia of billions of dollars' worth of weapons which are being used to attack hospitals, schools and other civilian centres in Yemen. An appalling humanitarian crisis mounts in that country where a ruthlessly imposed blockade is leading to mass poverty and famine. Fleet Street and the broadcasting companies refer to it from time to time as the 'forgotten war'.[1] And yet it remains 'forgotten' simply because the mainstream media has chosen not to highlight in any consistent way the horrors being inflicted on Yemen. There is no hysterical, sustained, highly personalised demonisation of the leaders of Saudi Arabia – as applied in the past to dictators such as Saddam Hussein, of Iraq, Col Gaddafi, of Libya, and Slobodan Milošević, of Serbia. Can you imagine the *Sun* carrying the headline: 'Evil Saudi King Salman blamed for massacre of innocents in Yemen.' Dream on.

Western politicians, business leaders, arms sellers, royals, intelligence officials all suck up to the Saudi dynasty. One person is executed every two days there, women endure severe repression, the state's funding of its extremist Sunni Wahhabi sect fuels terror across the globe. And yet both the US and UK back the election of Saudi Arabia to head a human rights panel at the UN. The occasional editorial or think-piece on Fleet Street expresses dismay – but there is no sustained outrage.

The complex operation of Fleet Street's consensus (such as over Saudi Arabia) is one of the many subjects analysed in Florian Zollmann's pioneering study. Here his focus is on the reporting of human rights violations by the FRY/Serbs in Racak/Kosovo, Gaddafi's forces in Libya/Benghazi, the Syrian army in Syria/Houla, US/Coalition forces in Fallujah/Iraq and the Egyptian security forces in Cairo/Egypt. But in extending the study beyond Fleet Street to take in the leading corporate press in both the US and Germany, Florian Zollmann is able to argue that this consensus operates internationally. This is a particularly original and important finding of this study. Moreover, the research (which incorporates meticulously detailed qualitative and quantitative analysis) shows how campaigns in the international news media consistently shame 'enemy' while exempting 'allied' countries for their human rights violations.

Let us return for a moment to the US-led Desert Storm attack on Iraq in 1991. The hyper-coverage of this conflict in the global corporate media gave the appearance of transparency. Indeed, following the rapid assaults by the Western powers against puny, Third World states (Falklands 1982; Grenada 1983; Libya 1986; Panama 1989) a Big Victory needed to be *seen to be won* against a Big Enemy – if only to help 'kick the Vietnam syndrome' and (with the Soviet Union in terminal decline) provide a *raison d'être* for the rapidly expanding military/industrial/intelligence/media complex. Hence the manufacture of 'Saddam' as a global threat and credible enemy. But, in fact, the spectacle of the conflict mostly served to hide (and, effectively, keep secret) the reality in which up to 250,000 Iraqi soldiers were eliminated in a 42-day assault. One slaughter followed another. In 2016, the 25th anniversary of the conflict passed by unnoticed in the corporate media. Strange how such horrors can be quietly forgotten.

Indeed, the value of Florian Zollmann's study is that it is refusing to let the horrors committed in our names by our governments and armed forces sink into the dustbin of history. Academics studying the coverage of conflicts may bury themselves in the documents, in the archives and in libraries – and spend hours searching the web. But all this hard graft is meaningless unless it is fired by a moral and political passion to expose the lies and myths on which obscenely costly military adventures are too often based. Florian is clearly fired by that passion – and so this text moves me profoundly.

Richard Lance Keeble
Professor of Journalism
University of Lincoln

. 1 .

INTRODUCTION

Propaganda, New Militarism and Intervention

Analysis of news media's double standards

The news media in liberal democracies operates as a propaganda system on behalf of state-corporate elite interests. This propaganda function becomes most evident if news reporting on relatively similar human rights violations is compared. If countries designated to be 'enemy' states of the West conduct human rights violations, the news media highlights these abuses and conveys demands for action to stop human rights breaches. If, on the other hand, Western states or their 'allies' are the perpetrators of human rights violations, the news media employs significantly less investigatory zeal in its reporting and virtually no measures to stop abuses are conveyed. A radically dichotomised news media treatment of human rights violations can particularly be observed when human rights breaches are instrumentalised in the pursuit of narrow agendas. Take the following example:

In February 2011, Libyan security forces crushed a revolt against state authorities. Several cities in Eastern Libya had slipped out of government control as an opposition movement attempted to overthrow the regime of Muammar al-Gaddafi. Libyan security forces consequently clashed with protestors in a range of cities from Benghazi in the East, where the uprising initially started, to the capital in Tripoli. It is estimated that between 500 and 700 people were killed during these incidents in February 2011 (ICC 2011: 4). The Western news media depicted actions of the Libyan security forces as indiscriminate attacks against protestors. Furthermore, the news media framed the events as atrocious crimes, ordered from the highest levels of the regime. Also at this time, powerful spokespersons from US, UK and EU governments as well as partisan think-tanks demanded political and military measures to stop the actions of the Libyan government. Such policies ranged from official inquiries and proceedings by the International Criminal Court (ICC) to sanctions and military actions in line with the responsibility to protect (R2P) doctrine (see further context on R2P below). The news media highlighted this discourse emphasising that Western forces needed to intervene in Libya. The United Nations Security Council eventually authorised procedures to end the violence, including sanctions, criminal proceedings and military means. On 19 March 2011, the North Atlantic Treaty Organisation (NATO) launched military operations in Libya. During the course of this intervention, the regime of Gaddafi was dismantled.

In 2004, US military forces were fighting a national resistance movement against the US/Coalition occupation authorities in Iraq. A range of Iraqi cities in the Sunni dominated regions of the country had defied the US/Coalition authority after the 2003 Iraq War. As a result, US forces started operations to root out resistance forces in a range of cities and municipalities where fighters were embedded with the local population. In April 2004, about 600 Iraqi civilians were killed when US forces clashed with fighters in Fallujah (IBC 2004b). During similar incidents in Iraq, civilians were killed on a large scale. A cluster sample survey, published in the British medicine journal the *Lancet* in October 2004, found that 98,000 excess deaths had occurred in Iraq between 19 March 2003 and mid-September 2004. The authors of the study wrote that the deaths 'were mainly attributed to coalition forces' and 'most individuals reportedly killed by coalition forces were women and children' (Roberts *et al.* 2004: 1857). The *Lancet* study was published several days before US/Coalition forces attacked Fallujah for the second time, on 8 November 2004. During this assault, between 800 and 6,000 civilians were killed, depending on estimates (see Jamail 2004b; Marqusee 2005). In its reporting on Iraq, the Western news media largely failed to highlight the casualty figures outlined above. Events in Iraq were framed as legitimate warfare conducted by US/Coalition forces with the aim to bring democracy and stability to Iraq. When civilian deaths piled up, Western government and other spokespersons did not demand any serious counter-measures to stop the attacks by the US military that evidently harmed Iraqi civilians. Investigations into the nature and effects of US/Coalition warfare were prescribed by human rights organisations. However, these measures were hardly comparable with those sanctioned and institutionalised in Libya. The news media remained cautious as well and its investigatory zeal in regard to US/Coalition actions was hardly on the scale as in Libya. In fact, the US/Coalition occupation could go on for several years without serious challenge from the Western diplomatic, human rights and intellectual community.

It is of further significance that the carnage inflicted by Gaddafi's security forces in Libya undercut the carnage inflicted by US/Coalition forces in Iraq by large margins in terms of casualty numbers. Moreover, there were some important differences: Libyan security forces were legally policing their country. It turned out that Libyan government installations and personnel had initially been attacked by violent protestors (see Kuperman 2013: 109–110). The documentary record further suggested that Libyan security forces had *not* indiscriminately targeted protestors during the clashes (for a detailed review of the evidence see *ibid*: 108–113). Yet, Libya was earmarked for military intervention. This so-called 'humanitarian intervention' was far more deadly than the clashes that had preceded it and which were used as a pretext to intervene. According to one scholarly estimate, 'NATO intervention magnified the death toll in Libya by about seven to ten times' (*ibid*: 123).

In contrast, the documentary record for Iraq shows a different picture: The US/Coalition had invaded Iraq in violation of the United Nations Charter (UN Charter), according to Mandel (2005). US/Coalition forces did not have, then, the legal mandate to police the country. Moreover, it is well established that the Iraqi resistance was instigated by heavy-handed military tactics and radical economic policies enforced by US/Coalition authorities (see Schwartz 2008). Ample evidence exists that US/Coalition forces resorted to indiscriminate force during their assaults against the Iraqi resistance (see e.g. Amnesty International 2004; Human Rights Watch 2003a, b, c). Yet, the US/Coalition occupation would go on for years. Over this period, Iraq's well-developed and secular society was destroyed. One estimate suggests that the Iraq War and occupation 'triggered an episode more deadly than the Rwandan genocide' (Roberts 2007: 32).

In liberal democracies, the news media is assumed to follow ethical standards enshrined in the 'objectivity' norm such as accuracy, fairness and impartiality (see Keeble 2006). However, the news media's framing of the cases outlined above does indicate a double standard: in the light of the actual casualty data and evidence, it was not accurate to depict Libyan actions as indiscriminate and US/Coalition actions as diligent. Similarly, the news media did not apply the same standards of fairness and impartiality: the Libyan government was often labeled as nefarious on the one hand whereas the US/Coalition authorities were depicted as legitimate on the other. In fact, Libyan forces were rather engaged in legitimate operations with limited effects on the populace if compared to the effects of US/Coalition operations. This journalistic performance suggests that the news media followed a partisan agenda: In the case of Libya, news media highlighted a propagandistic narrative that emphasised the necessity for an intervention to stop human rights violations. In the case of Iraq, news media highlighted a propagandistic narrative that suggested the necessity for the US/Coalition to remain and police the country. This case comparison, which will be further elaborated in this study, demonstrates that the news media supports a militaristic agenda. In fact, the pretext for the intervention in Libya was manufactured, with terrible consequences for the country. In Iraq, on the other hand, civilian carnage and the virtual destruction of a society did not evoke much outrage in the West and there were not many calls for protective measures.

There has been a strong emphasis in recent years that the international community has to protect populations from international crimes. During the last two decades, Western governments have conducted various interventions (at times coined 'humanitarian interventions') with the declared aim of stopping human rights violations. This so called 'ethical' foreign policy obtained institutional support by the R2P doctrine, which was affirmed by the members of the United Nations (UN) at the World Summit in 2005 and re-affirmed by the UN-Security Council in 2006 (see Bellamy 2008; Cunliffe 2011). R2P spells out several measures that may be enforced by the international community to protect human rights and prevent international crimes including diplomatic, coercive and military means (see Bellamy 2008; Cunliffe 2011; Evans 2006). According to Evans (2006: 713) R2P could 'become the primary frame of reference within which catastrophic human rights violations [will be] assessed and responded to in the future'. Research by Risse and Sikkink (1999: 5) indicates that 'the diffusion of international norms in the human rights area crucially depends on the establishment and the sustainability of networks among domestic and transnational actors who manage to link up with international regimes, to alert Western public opinion and Western governments'.

Main aim of the study

What if this process of shaming and intervening is selective and biased towards the interests of powerful states? What if the news media has ignored mass atrocities if they occurred during military and/or police operations of the US and their allies? What if the cases in which 'humanitarian interventions' have been evoked in the news media involved the inflation of casualties and enemy atrocities? What if the news media has been supporting military interventions, which were actually designed to crush states that acted independent of Western powers?

The aim of this study is to investigate US, UK and German elite news media coverage of a range of cases that involved human rights violations during military or police operations including Kosovo (1999), Iraq (2004), Libya (2011), Syria (2012) and Egypt (2013). The study assesses 1,911 news, editorial and comment items from the national press. It will be demonstrated that 'humanitarian intervention' and R2P as well as criminal proceedings are evoked against so called 'enemy' countries of Western states. The Western news media and intellectual community show less concern for human rights violations, if they were carried out by Western states and their 'allies'.

The news media is supposed to scrutinise governments particularly during times of war. Yet, this study demonstrates that the news media plays a crucial role in facilitating a selective process of shaming during the build-up towards military interventions. News media discourses serve powerful states to realise narrow elite goals such as to secure a positive investment climate. These processes have led to an erosion of internationally-agreed norms of non-intervention, as enshrined in the UN Charter, with terrible consequences for the target countries. In fact, the massive refugee crisis of 2015 and the rise of ISIS are crucially linked to Western military interventions, which have been accompanied by a policy of state-ending (see Baker, Ismael and Ismael 2010: 3–7). Intervention has led to massive destruction of state owned industries and was used to institute neo-liberal 'reconstruction'. Furthermore, divide-and-rule policies have been applied in multi-ethnic states like the former Yugoslavia, Iraq, Libya and Syria. Intervention has thus led to state-disintegration along sectarian lines and internal conflict (see *ibid*; also Zollmann 2014b).

New militarism

Military intervention is the most dangerous policy tool at the disposal of states. The UN Charter, which came into effect on 24 October 1945, strictly prohibits the use of military force in international affairs. According to the UN Charter, which is binding law for all signatory states including the US and UK, the only legal conditions that allow states to intervene militarily are Security Council authorisation or self-defence. This high threshold was instituted after World War II with the aim 'to save succeeding generations from the scourge of war' (Preamble of the UN Charter).[1] The UN Charter's outlook is in alignment with the seminal legal precedent, the Judgment of the Nuremberg Tribunal, which convicted the German Nazis. The Tribunal concluded that Germany had undertaken a 'war of aggression' which 'contains within itself the accumulated evil of the whole' (cited in Gerhart 1998: 1109). This court verdict regards initiators of unlawful wars as responsible for all of their wars' outcomes. The judges established this legal rationale because the destruction caused by Nazi Germany, including the Holocaust, mass civilian deaths and displacement, wanton destruction of rural areas, cities and countries, as well as famines and starvation, had effectively accrued from Germany's initial military interventions (see Mandel 2005). That is why the UN Charter regards military intervention as a last resort only to be applied in exceptional cases and with a high burden of proof. It could thus be argued that military intervention as a policy tool was *de jure* outlawed after World War II.

Additionally, traditional militarism of the type seen during World War II and the Vietnam War posed various problems for Western elites. During World War II the centralisation of the economy and mass conscript participation helped to advance the power of organised labour. As a consequence, the 'free-enterprise' economic model preferred by corporate business elites came under challenge from progressive working class activism (Fones-Wolf 1994: 2; Keeble 1997: 6). During the Vietnam War, broad mass movements exposed the aims and effects of US-militarism and challenged the foundations of the social order. The 'New Left' exposed the US as an aggressor who was defeated by a disadvantaged enemy. For Western elites, this became to be known as the 'Vietnam syndrome'. As a counter measure, new militarist strategies were implemented in order to avoid extensive military adventures and their socio-political repercussions (*ibid*: 6–7, 42–43).

At the heart of what Keeble (*ibid*) terms 'new militarism' has been the Low Intensity Conflict (LIC) strategy (*ibid*: 16–17). LIC involves the use of special-forces, secret services, proxy armies, air raids and modernised war technology together with diplomatic, economic, trade, social and cultural forms of warfare which are largely applied in secrecy (*ibid*: 7, 16–17). According to Keeble (*ibid*: 17), LIC was 'developed in response to the perceived threats to vulnerable US strategic interests', to avoid unpopular 'mass participatory warfare' and act without declaring war in order to keep political aspects and gruesome details about conflicts off the public agenda.

A second strategy of new militarism has involved 'occasional manufactured, media-hyped "operations"' (or media centric 'wars') against vulnerable enemy states or movements who were depicted as existential threats (Keeble 2011: 188). According to Keeble (*ibid*) 'these "operations" are then spectacular, essentially PR, events providing the theatre in which the US and its allies can claim their so-called "victories"'.

Yet significantly, the secrecy and propaganda surrounding new militarism has been shielding the fact that we are currently experiencing an age of military intervention that defies any serious legal reasoning and accountability. The US and UK have been engaged in a range of LIC style covert military interventions using proxy armies, special-forces, and secret services as well as unmanned vehicles (drones). For instance, in 2015, US Special Operations were deployed in 135 countries worldwide including Iraq and Syria (Turse 2015).

In the last three decades, US and UK-led coalitions (often under the umbrella of NATO) have conducted overt, media-hyped military interventions in Bosnia (1992–1995), Kosovo (1999), Afghanistan (2001), Iraq (1991, 2003, post 2003), Libya (2011) and Syria (2012–2017). Many of these incursions into sovereign states *de facto* violated the UN Charter.

The classic contemporary case constitutes the 2003 Iraq War, which, in accord with the reasoning established at Nuremberg, triggered a devastating chain of events: the death of more than one million Iraqis, mass displacement, radioactive contamination, sectarian war and spill-over effects into surrounding countries as well as the creation of the terrorist entity ISIS. Yet, the dominant intellectual and media culture has not been able to take cause and effect into account. In the most critical liberal spectrum of intellectual debate, the Iraq War is referred to as a mistake, failure, policy blunder or quagmire. State managers tend to be criticised in the news media for their failures when it comes to the execution of the Iraq War or the reconstruction of Iraq. It is rarely stated in the news media, however, that the Iraq War constituted a 'war of aggression' which 'contains within itself the accumulated evil of the whole' (Judgment of the Nuremberg Tribunal of 1947 cited in Gerhart 1998: 1109).

This study will demonstrate how selective news media reporting on human rights violations has contributed towards undermining the UN Charter and the threshold it places on the use of military violence. Moreover, the study highlights how atrocities have been instrumentalised to incite 'humanitarian interventions' by powerful states in order to punish 'enemy' countries of the West. The fallacy of the 'humanitarian intervention' doctrine can best be revealed on the basis of comparative studies, which clearly demonstrate that human rights violations by Western states and their 'allies' remain underexplored in the news media and consequently exempt from conflict resolution and international punishment.

Chapter outline

The book is further structured in seven chapters: Chapter 2 critically reviews the literature on news media performance. The first part introduces the two major academic positions in the field, the liberal-pluralist and hegemonic perspectives. The second part reviews empirical and theoretical studies in order to assess the validity of the two theoretical paradigms. It will be demonstrated that a large body of media scholarship has produced findings confirming the assumption of the hegemonic model that news media content is aligned with state-corporate elite interests. Chapter 3 introduces and updates Herman and Chomsky's propaganda model, the leading analytical tool to assess hegemonic news media performance. In this chapter, the propaganda model's main predictions will be highlighted and the model will be elaborated in terms of its international scope. Chapter 4 delineates the research method and case study selection choices. The chapter reflects on the study's application of quantitative and qualitative content analysis of 1,911 news, editorial and commentary items to assess how similar human rights violations by 'enemy' and 'allied' countries were reported in the US, UK and German national press. Chapter 5 presents the first set of findings on news media reporting of human rights violations by the FRY/Serbs in Racak/Kosovo, Gaddafi's forces in Libya/Benghazi, the Syrian army in Syria/Houla, US/Coalition forces in Fallujah/Iraq and the Egyptian security forces in Cairo/Egypt. This chapter reveals how indignant campaigns in the international news media consistently shame 'enemy' while exempt 'allied' countries for their human rights violations. Chapter 6 presents further findings on the case studies looking at the news media's framing of the details of and responsibility for violence. Chapter 7 concludes the study by confirming the main predictions of the propaganda model.[2]

· 2 ·

LIBERAL, HEGEMONIC AND GATEKEEPER THEORIES

A Reassessment

Introduction

There is broad agreement in the literature that the news media is one of the most important institutions for opinion-making in Western liberal democracies (see e.g. Curran and Seaton 2010: 370; Eilders 2002: 25–27; Jarren and Donges 2002: 31–32; Lichtenberg 1990c; Nacos *et al.* 2000: 42; Page 1996: 1–13). Representative democracy is largely operated by professionals detached from the citizenry: political decisions are formed and decided by elected officials during parliamentary debates and implemented by an elected executive. Political officials are assumed to act in accord with the policy preferences of their constituency. Citizens, it is argued, thus need to be sufficiently informed in order to evaluate the policies conducted on their behalf and weigh their possible political choices – a process which can be described as public deliberation (see Page 1996). Because citizens do not directly participate in the political process they depend on mediated information. The news media is thus regarded as the institution situated as an intermediary between the political and public sub-systems: it monitors and mediates the political process and provides the information on which citizens base their political choices upon (see Jarren and Donges 2002: 143–145). Hence, Sparks (1999: 41) sets out a general research priority: 'Today, no theory of democracy could possibly be taken seriously if it did not discuss the mass media in general, and the newspaper press in particular, as key elements in the constitution of political life.'

It could be argued that the societal function of the news media becomes even more important in consideration of war, conflict and foreign policy events (see Löffelholz 2004: 55; Nichols and McChesney 2005: 37). News media performance during times of war can be regarded as essential for democracy. Nichols and McChesney (2005: 37) argue, that to assess the performance of a media system (and journalism) it is necessary to analyse 'how the press system enables the citizens to monitor the government's war-making powers' because 'war is the most serious use of state power: organised, sanctioned violence'. Therefore, it is important to evaluate 'how well [war] is under citizen review and control' which 'is not only a litmus test for the media but for society as a whole' (*ibid*).

Consequently, it would evidence a deep systemic flaw of our democracies, if the news media constituted a propaganda system that operates on behalf of elite interests during times of war and international conflict. In fact, only a minority of scholars actually describe the news media as a propagandistic institution and many researchers are hesitant to conflate news and propaganda. However, this does not mean that the propaganda perspective is invalid. The following discussion will demonstrate that mainstream academic research basically supports the assumption that the commercial news media is embedded in and supportive to state-corporate elite sectors. Empirical research has demonstrated that the news media has been highly constrained by elite power. Yet significantly, for ideological reasons, scholars have neglected to apply the propaganda concept on the news media despite the fact that the empirical literature supports the conflation of both terms. This will be illustrated on the basis of the following review of the literature, which pulls together the findings of major works in the field. Before I review the critical empirical literature, I will broadly discuss the main theoretical perspectives.

The news media

In modern Western democracies, with the exception of public broadcasting, most journalists work in commercial news organisations that follow profit maximising principles. News organisations operate in two markets (advertising and reader markets) and have to rely on advertising support for their survival. Moreover, they belong to larger corporations that have multiple links with other corporations via joint ventures, interlocking boards and social circles. Like non-media corporations, media firms and conglomerates have striven to expand within and beyond industries and national borders (Herman and McChesney 1997: 1–9; Schiller 1982). Hence, the media is heavily concentrated in ownership and market shares, a tendency which has globally increased during the last decades (Albarran 2002: 188; Albarran and Chan-Olmsted 1998: 332–333; Doyle 2002b: 1–4; Trappel 2008: 147). Capital exchange has also fostered the integration of media and traditional industries leading to multisectoral concentration (Leidinger 2003: 175). As a result, the news media is integrated in a 'Euro-North American' corporate network that dominates the global capitalist economy (*cf.* Carroll 2010: 224; Herman and McChesney 1997). Finally, it should be noted that there is a statist component: the development of the news media into a corporate-capitalist conglomerate was not the result of evolutionary processes but has actively been encouraged by state interventions (see McChesney 2004). How can this structure allow for independent journalistic reporting?

Liberal theories: social responsibility and free market perspectives

The news media's corporate organisation and commercial orientation has been a major concern for academics, journalists, publics and policy makers. In 1956, Siebert, Peterson and Schramm (1984 [1956]) published *Four Theories of the Press*, which is still regarded as a landmark work of liberal media scholarship.[1] In their study, Siebert, Peterson and Schramm (*ibid:* 78) summarise the 'general' findings of 20th century press assessments. One of the major findings warned that 'the press is controlled by one socioeconomic class, loosely the "business class," and access to the industry is difficult for the newcomer; therefore, the free and open market of ideas is endangered' (*ibid:* 78–79).

As a remedy, Siebert, Peterson and Schramm (*ibid*) suggested the implementation of *The Social Responsibility Theory of the Press*. Social responsibility theory proposes a set of regulatory mechanisms that consists of two main elements: state and professional regulation (*ibid:* 92–96). It does not question the basic organisational structure and funding model of the news media (*ibid:* 93).[2] Following World War II, policies in accord with social responsibility theory were encouraged in the US, UK, Germany and other parts of Western Europe where its implementation grade can be measured in terms of the levels of institutionalised media regulation and professionalisation (see McQuail 2010: 171; also Hallin and Mancini 2005: 220).[3] Scholars who assume the news media to be independent from state-economic power basically argue that anti-trust state regulation and professional codes of conduct safeguard journalistic autonomy. This constitutes the critical liberal spectrum of scholarship. Indeed, today, the liberal-pluralist perspective constitutes the dominant approach in the Anglo-American and European media studies. Scholars within this tradition argue that the media is independent from other societal sectors and reflects rather than shapes society although there are significant differences (Curran 2002: 127; see also McQuail 2010: 63; for various liberal perspectives see the collection by Lichtenberg 1990a).

Historically, liberal theorists see the media's development as an independent institution free from the influence of other social forces (i.e. religious, social, economic and political) in conjunction with similar developments in the political (i.e. representative democracy, party formation, constitutionalism), religious (i.e. freedom of religion) and economic (i.e. free market) spheres, and as a result of emerging legal freedoms and, more significantly, self-governing regulatory mechanisms (Alexander 1981: 24).

At the heart of the liberal discourse is a political component: In *On Liberty* Mill (2009 [1859]: 19) asserted that 'the "liberty of the press"' was 'one of the securities against corrupt or tyrannical governments'. This argument was translated in the requirement that the media and its personnel had to be independent from the state. Hence, similar to other institutions, the press became legally protected from government and other social forces, as codified, for example, in the First Amendment of the US Constitution, Article 5 of the German Basic Law or through several British court cases (Keane 1991: 9; Keeble 2009: 9; Meyn 2001: 49). This was regarded as a guarantor for freedom enabling the media to monitor the state and reflect society.

In its purest interpretation, liberal press theory suggests that contemporary news media actually hold the government to account (i.e. performs as a watchdog) and mirrors and informs all sectors of society. The media is seen as an independent intermediary (i.e. Fourth Estate)[4] between the political system and the electorate providing the crucial information upon which people base their political choices upon (see Alexander 1981; Kovach and Rosenstiel 2003: 18; Ungar 1990).[5] This is regarded as necessary by liberal democratic theorists because governments have to 'derive their just powers from the consent of the governed' (Meiklejohn 1960: 9). Thus, free competition of the voices represented in society is regarded as a necessary condition for the functioning of a democratic system which is governed by representatives because public discussion can be regarded as an extension 'for freedom of parliamentary debate' (Kelley and Donway 1990: 70).[6] Theorists claim that when different viewpoints are freely accessible to the people and compete in a market place of ideas the most reasoned arguments win and become mutually-agreed principles (see Siebert, Peterson and Schramm 1984 [1956]: 44). The market liberal perspective is a minority view in academia. There is almost a consensus among scholars that the media should not simply be left to the market.

The social responsibility theory, then, can best be understood as a modification of liberal press theories (Siebert, Peterson and Schramm 1984 [1956]: 2). It differs from classic liberal and market-liberal theory in that it strengthens the role of the state and suggests regulatory mechanisms in order to enable the news media to better function in accord with liberal expectations. This was seen as necessary due to the multiple problems associated with ownership concentration and news media operating in the corporate capitalist market system (*ibid*: 78–79).

It could be argued that, since the end of World War II, liberal media scholarship has regarded the social responsibility approach as the model for Western media systems and media research. This is suggested by the great variety of critical liberal scholarship proposing cosmetic regulatory remedies for problems within the news media.[7]

The emphasis on regulatory remedies reflects a general belief in the ability to preserve journalistic autonomy within corporate media organisations that operate in a corporate-capitalist market system. It also reflects a positive belief in the functioning of Western liberal democracy. Both are the most common denominators of the contemporary liberal school of thought.

Hegemonic theories: Marxist, political economy and functionalist approaches

Critical political economy and functionalist perspectives (henceforth also hegemonic approaches) are in opposition to liberal press theories. Approaches within this tradition argue that the media are controlled by dominant forces and thus shape rather than reflect society although there are significant differences (see Curran 2002: 108–110; also Curran, Gurevitch and Woollacott 1982; McChesney 2008; Meier 2003; Mosco 2009; Murdock and Golding 1973, 1977, 2005).

Historically, critical political economy and functionalist theories regard the media and other sectors of society not as mutual social forces. Rather, this approach identifies imbalances of power in the political economy of society and how, subsequently, dominant sectors and/or actors are able to control other spheres of society – in our case the production of news (Mosco 2009: 24).[8] Contrary to liberalism, which situates the different relations in society as coequal, hegemonic theories see economic (or material) relations as determining, as highlighted in the works of Karl Marx.[9] The major difference between approaches in this category can be seen in how they theorise possibilities of 'control, conflict and contradiction' (Hesmondhalgh 2010: 151) and thus the media's ability to reinforce the status quo in favour of the powerful. For instance, a pure interpretation of hegemonic theories assumes that the structure of the media industry (concentration of private property ownership, hierarchical workplace relations, etc.) uniformly determines its immaterial output (Adorno 1991). Hence, Adorno and Horkheimer's (1997 [1944]: 121) claim in their essay on the culture industry: '[…] the basis on which technology acquires power over society is the power of those whose economic hold over society is greatest.' Accordingly, Adorno and Horkheimer argue that the integration of the news media within other capitalist industries has led to a 'system which is uniform as a whole and in every part' (*ibid*: 120).

Contesting Adorno and Horkheimer's rigid Marxism, Murdock and Golding (1977: 16) stress that Marx had used the notion of determination 'in a much looser sense of setting limits, exerting pressures and closing off options' thus allowing 'a good deal of room for intellectual autonomy and innovation' (see also Murdock and Golding 2005: 63). Furthermore, they highlight Marx's emphasis on the different manifestations of capitalism during specific historical circumstances (1977: 17). Thus, Murdock and Golding (*ibid*: 19–20) claim that the economic base is the most powerful but not the only lever in cultural production. Hence, they argue, an important task of Marxist analysis is to show 'in detail how economic relations structure both the overall strategies of the cultural entrepreneurs and the concrete activities of the people who actually make the products' of the media (*ibid*: 18) in order to avoid the mistake of simply relating the properties of media output to media structures (*ibid*: 17). In general, Murdock and Golding's perspective leaves room for media openness: 'Owners, advertisers and key political personnel cannot always do as they would wish. They operate within structures that constrain as well as facilitate, imposing limits as well as offering opportunities.' (2005: 63)

Similarly, other critical scholars have identified 'countervailing influences that pull against the magnetic field of power' suggesting the media's inability to perpetuate continuously a dominant framework (Curran 2002: 148; see also Gitlin 1980: 273–274; Habermas 1992: 437–438; Hallin 1994: 36).

Building on work by scholars such as Marx and Engels, Althusser, Gramsci and Williams, Hall's (1977) early work emphasised the media's 'ideological effect' (for an overview see also Hall 1982).[10] Elsewhere, Hall *et al.* (1978) conceptualise how the routines of news production and professional practice 'combine to produce a systematically structured *over-accessing* to the media of those in powerful and privileged institutional positions' leading the media 'to reproduce symbolically the existing structure of power' in society and thus '*the dominant field of the ruling ideologies* [emphasis in the original]' (*ibid*: 58–60). This is explained by the claim that powerful spokesperson are the '*primary definers*' of news who 'establish the initial definition [emphasis in the original]' of events (*ibid*: 58). It is perhaps important for this perspective that secondary definitions are also able to become part of the news discourse (*ibid*). However, they do not equally balance the primary discourse. As Hall further argues, secondary definitions are embedded within 'the larger ideological syntagms' and thus subordinated to the 'fundamental agreements' which bind opposing fractions of elites 'into a complex unity' by setting 'the limits to the argument' (1977: 345–346). Hence, the 'areas for negotiation within the hegemonic codes' combined with the media's 'relative autonomy' provide the media a 'popular basis' of legitimacy (*ibid*: 345).

The concept of hegemony was derived from the work of the Marxist scholar Gramsci who, in Hall's words, delineated how 'the agencies of the superstructure' the 'family, education system, the Church, the media and cultural institutions' including the coercive state sectors (i.e. law, police, army) disseminate ideology in order to cement hegemony over subordinate classes (Hall 1977: 333).[11] According to Gramsci, hegemony is based on economic power and becomes evident when alliances with similar class interests direct politics through 'cultural, moral and ideological' headship (cited in Forgacs 1988: 423; see *ibid* 211–212 for 'economic power'). In liberal democracies, Gramsci claims, hegemony is sustained rather by consent and direction than coercion and domination (as in totalitarian states) although it may contain all of these elements (*ibid*: 423–424). Moreover, hegemony is achieved when a single ideology or combination of them 'propagate [...] throughout society – bringing about not only a unison of economic and political aims, but also intellectual and moral unity' (Gramsci 1971: 181). Significantly, hegemonic ideology is not one-dimensional: it includes elements of other ideologies. But by presenting different concerns under the umbrella 'of a universal expansion, of a development of all the "national" energies', dominant ideology subverts the 'general interests of subordinate groups' and thus becomes hegemonic (*ibid*: 182; see also Hall

1977: 333). That does not imply that ideological hegemony is total. It has to be sustained and can be challenged and overcome. Thus, ideological hegemony depends on the organisational ability of ruling blocks to achieve '*complementarity* between hegemonic and subordinated classes and their cultures [emphasis in the original]' (Hall 1977: 334).

Miller and Dinan build upon Gramsci's notion of hegemony, which they understand 'as the possibilities of ruling class unity' (2008: 180). In neoliberal societies, contrary to social democracy, hegemony does not necessarily need public consent because elite unity may 'bypass public opinion' (*ibid*).[12] Hence, 'the only constituency' corporations 'need to satisfy' in an elite managed society 'are closely related fractions of their own side – in politics, the media and civil society' (*ibid*). This seems to be an expansion of Hall's concept (which as discussed above included the ideology of subordinate classes) suggesting that ideology targets corporate, political and professional elites who have important decision-making powers (see also DiMaggio 2009: 233). Miller and Dinan have also connected the economic with the ideological perspectives:

> We [...] think that it is social and economic interests which are embodied in the institutions created and operated by real humans which provide the link between the economic and the ideological. Ideas are produced and fight their fight only in the context of the material circumstances in which all – economy, polity, ideology – operate. (2008: 173)

Adding to the work outlined above, various scholars have alleged a propaganda function of the media as a purveyor of ideology (see Curtis 1995: 165; DiMaggio 2009; Edwards and Cromwell 2006, 2009; Herman 1986; Herman and Chomsky 1988a, 2008; Keeble 1997; Lazarsfeld and Merton 1957 [1948]: 457–458; Miliband 1987 [1973]: 197–198; 211; Smythe 1981: 39; Winter 1997, 2007).

Herman and Chomsky (1988a, b, 2008) propose a propaganda model which describes a set of institutional constraints or news 'filters' that guide news selection processes and lead to propagandistic and hegemonic media output (see 2008: 1–29).[13] A similar argument was put forward by Lazarsfeld and Merton (1957 [1948]: 461) who abstracted social functions 'from the social structure' of the media. One concern of Lazarsfeld and Merton was how 'chief power groups, among which organised business occupies the most spectacular place' in society converted 'economic power' to 'psychological exploitation, achieved largely by disseminating propaganda through the mass media of communication' (*ibid*: 457–458).

These researchers do not suggest that dissemination of propaganda is the only activity the media engage in. Moreover, they do not specifically analyse how effective media propaganda actually is (Herman 2000: 102–103; Herman and Chomsky 2008: IL; Lazarsfeld and Merton 1957 [1948]: 461, 465, 467).[14]

Whether the liberal or hegemonic perspective is accurate is still contested in the scholarly community. In fact, the emergences of the Internet and the so-called new media environment has further strengthened the liberal perspective as scholars emphasise the deliberative potential of participatory media technology (for an overview see Zollmann 2015b). Yet significantly, as will be further discussed below, a review of the major empirical literature on news-room performance points to the applicability of hegemonic models.

Closing the gap: how the findings of empirical and conceptual studies match with theory

One of the main assumptions of liberal press theories is that the news media somehow mirrors society. This position was already questioned over half a decade ago. In a pioneering work, Lang and Lang (1953) compared the coverage of an event by different actors including the news media. Lang and Lang (*ibid*: 4) highlighted how the media's 'selection, emphasis, and suggested inference' constructed a specific reality of an event, which was in conflict with the perception of other observers of the same event. Lang and Lang regarded this as evidence that the news media produced a particular 'image' which overshadowed 'immediate reality' (*ibid*: 11). This finding basically pointed out that media coverage was a social construct (*cf.* Epstein 2000 [1973]: 25; Glasgow University Media Group 1976: 10). Nonetheless, it was still to be clarified by later researchers how news was re-constructed and what kind of an image it produced.

Hence, a large body of research has analysed the context, mechanics and output of news production to assess how news is manufactured. This research is important for this study because it enables us to further clarify the general applicability of the theoretical approaches discussed above.

Enquiries within the field have often been classified as gatekeeper studies.[15] Generally, these studies assess the media production process in relation to journalists, the organisational context, properties of news output and other factors such as external events and technology. Being grounded in empirical research, gatekeeper studies rely on observations and/or questionnaires. Later research has increasingly used content analyses to underpin theory-building studies. Some studies are purely theoretical.[16] Because researchers have applied varying designs, results can be tentative and hard to generalise. Furthermore, researchers have interpreted findings differently and placed them within liberal or Marxist/functionalist paradigms depending on their individual categorisations (*cf*. Bennett 1990: 103; Epstein 2000 [1973]: 269). Yet, this comprehensive review points to the fact that the gatekeeper studies provide extensive support for the applicability of hegemonic theories. In the following, I will combine a discussion of empirical and theoretical work in order to highlight the major issues and findings in the field.

The early gatekeeper studies

Two early studies by White (1950) and Snider (1967) analysed how one editor ('Mr. Gates') who worked at a midsized US-morning newspaper selected news from wire services. Both studies concluded that news selection processes were primarily based on the journalist's subjective experiences, attitudes, and expectations.[17] Such findings highlighted, in accord with liberal theories, the importance of individual journalistic conduct over other factors in the news selection process. In contrast, Gieber's (1956: 432) study of 16 wire editors using the Associated Press (AP) services demonstrated how the selection of material was determined by a 'mechanical process' which Gieber described as 'wire-copy fixing'. Due to time constraints editors were confined to copy reading and editing while news was pre-selected by AP (*ibid*). Such findings were supported by later studies with a broader scope whose findings suggested the influence of organisational over individual contexts. The general findings of these studies were summarised by Epstein (2000 [1973]: 41):

> While any given news decision, when taken alone, may seem idiosyncratic, it is still possible, paradoxically, for the total news output of an organisation to be largely determined by general rules, routines and policies.

A similar finding had already been established in a foundational study by Breed (1955) who interviewed 120 journalists at a mid-sized US newspaper.[18] Breed assessed if newsroom policies, which had been identified as a source of media bias in the report of the Commission on the Freedom of the Press (1947), influenced journalistic routine procedures.

Breed's (1955: 328) work provides evidence for journalistic conformism: journalists are socialised into the newsroom where they learn 'to anticipate what is expected [...] so as to win rewards and avoid punishment' from executives and veteran staffers (*ibid*: 328, 332).

Breed consistently found the existence of a 'covert nature of policy' which was learned as a 'pattern of control through reprimand' (*ibid*: 328–329). According to Breed, policy norms to which journalists conform are manifest so that they override 'personal beliefs' and 'ethical ideals' (*ibid*: 332). The newsroom policy is established by the publisher and executed by a 'reference group' whose centre comprised the elite of executives and experienced staffers (*ibid*).

Such findings provided evidence to contradict studies emphasising the importance of individual conduct. Then again, Breed's study also suggested reporters' ability to deviate and bypass policy, albeit in exceptional circumstances. For example, ambiguous stories, which could not easily be classified within standard frameworks enabled journalist to include individual angles. Breed also found that specialist reporters working on beats had more autonomy than editorial staffers. Finally, 'star' reporters were observed to have more privileges and leeway (*ibid*: 333–334).

In conclusion, Breed (*ibid*: 334) suggested that journalists' adherence to newsroom policy enables the newspaper to keep 'publishing smoothly'. On the opposite side, the following of policy norms had negative consequences:

> For the society as a whole, the existing system of power relation-ships [sic] is maintained. Policy usually protects property and class interests, and thus the strata and groups holding these interests are better able to retain them. For the larger community, much news is printed objectively, allowing for opinions to form openly, but policy news may be slanted or buried so that some important information is denied the citizenry. (This is the dysfunction widely scored by critics.). (*ibid*: 334)

Breed also highlighted how performance results from the problem that 'the news-man's [sic] source of rewards is located not among the readers, who are manifestly his clients, but among his colleagues and superiors' (*ibid*: 335).

A similar study by Warner (1971: 292), which looked at US television reporters, came to comparable findings: 'The action of the reference-group – as in the press – cements allegiance and identification in TV news, especially in the well-established news shows' thus forging conformity.

Sigelman (1973), who questioned reporters at two metropolitan newspapers in the US, found an even less overt policy in newsrooms. Deviating from previous studies, Siegelman observed a more subtle process of socialisation during which reporters voluntarily altered their behaviour to fit within the institution (*ibid*: 140). Siegelman's findings indicate that socialisation led to a situation in which journalists avoided conflicts in the newsroom and rationalised editorial bias via their adherence to professional norms (*ibid*: 149).

The early work of the Glasgow University Media Group (1976), which analysed BBC and ITN television news of industrial disputes, identified how ideological assumptions were transported via professional routine procedures and how news coverage consequently reinforced 'certain stratified cultural perceptions of society and how it should, ought, and does, work' (*ibid*: 2). According to the Glasgow University Media Group (1980: 400–402) studies, dominant notions such as 'neutrality', 'impartiality' and 'balance' when embedded in practice enabled a consistent style which hid ideological elements although coverage was, on closer examination, weighed against organised labour and the working class.

Gatekeeper studies

During the 1970s, 1980s and 1990s, a large body of literature followed the early gatekeeper research looking at the organisational context of news production, routine mechanisms and/or the interplay between journalists and sources via participant observations, interviews and/or content analysis. This work further pointed to the applicability of hegemonic models.

One of the most consistent findings of these studies has been that official administration sources gain preferential access to journalists and dominant space in the news because they are regarded as authoritative, legitimate and newsworthy (e.g. Bennett 1990; Cohen 1963; Gans 1980; Hallin 1989; Hallin, Manoff and Weddle 1993; Sigal 1973; Tuchman 1978). Gans (1980: 119) stressed in a seminal study of broadcasting news which was based on participant observation and content analysis that, 'while, in theory, sources can come from anywhere, in practice, their recruitment and their access to journalists reflect the hierarchies of nation and society'. This happened because journalists subscribed to the liberal ideal of representative democracy which assumed that power is relegated from the electorate to officials thus making it 'a prime journalistic norm [...] to inform citizens of the actions of their government officials' (Bennett 1996: 375). The conventional search for news beats even unites journalists from various national news organisations around these same sources and stories (*ibid*: 373). Hence, if journalists had a liberal bias as claimed by some critics it could be argued that this contributed to permitting powerful actors access to the news. Indeed, as the Glasgow University Media Group (1985: 5) observed, journalists believed they were 'independent and critical' but at the same time studies on television coverage demonstrated that news tended largely to 'follow "official" explanations and to justify these in reporting'.

Gatekeeper studies also highlighted how the drift towards officialdom was reinforced by economic imperatives: considerations of efficiency led news organisations to rely on 'routine channels for newsgathering' (Sigal 1973: 187; also Gans 1980: 128, 282–283) and 'routinized events' such as press conferences, official hearings and speeches by authoritative persons (Epstein 2000 [1973]: 32). Such media performance is steadily encouraged due to limitations in personal, time and economic resources (see Gans 1980: 283; Tuchman 1973: 118). Hence, the news organisation had virtually become dependent on news subsidies because it has a 'continued need for anticipated stories' (Gans 1980: 122). As a result, the same public institutions and elite agencies which are sourced in the news further attempt to accommodate pre-packaged information via 'various techniques of strategic communications' (Bennett 1994: 29). As Bennett, Lawrence and Livingston (2007: 59) argue, news media 'are regularly fed, monitored, and targeted with spin by influential elites'. The ability to plant messages in the media is related to an institution's status and economic might (Herman and Chomsky 2008: 18–24).

Similar patterns occur when journalists cover non-routine or 'unexpected events': in such cases, journalists follow 'typifications' to allow for the 'routine processing and dissemination' of news (Tuchman 1973: 125, 129). Furthermore, due to economic considerations and fear of government and business *flak* investigative reporting proves to be the exception rather than the rule (Epstein 2000 [1973]: 260; Bennett, Lawrence and Livingston 2007: 67; Bennett and Serrin 2005) and cases which are regarded as triumphs of investigative reporting, such as the Watergate scandal, would not have gone far without support by elite sources who instigated such coverage (Hallin 1994: 54).

Moreover, journalists follow professional conventions of 'objectivity' in order to minimise their vulnerability to outside pressures, such as libel suits or denial of access, and inside pressures, such as sanctions by chief editors and publishers (Tuchman 1972: 662–664; see also Gans 1980: 120). Thereby, a major 'strategic ritual' of journalistic conventions is to present conflicting possibilities as 'objective' facts (Tuchman 1972). However, as Tuchman (1972: 665–666) points out in her news room study, journalists often do not verify the substance of such 'truth-claims' and are only able to provide some 'sides of a story' – particularly those emerging from official sources who are regarded as authoritative.[19]

Generally, the gatekeeper studies demonstrated that journalistic behaviour is constrained by organisational structures and hierarchies, economic realities, routine procedures, time constraints, news values and outside pressures (i.e. government and business). Individual journalistic conduct may at best serve as a secondary variable for an explanation of media performance (Epstein 2000 [1973]: 43, 73; Molotch and Lester 1974; see also Shoemaker *et al.* 2001).

These findings lend support to the assumption made by hegemonic theorists that the news media tends to be driven towards the power centres of society. As Gans (1980: 277) writes:

> [...] my observations support the structural analyses of the news media proposed more often by activists or social scientists on the Left than on the Right: that journalists are restrained by systemic mechanisms that keep out some news.[20]

Main gates: news media and the 'indexing' of official power blocs

The US media scholar Bennett built on the insights of gatekeeper researchers when he proposed and applied the widely cited 'indexing' norm (1990: 103).[21] As Bennett (1990: 106) claims, professional journalists 'tend to "index" the range of voices and viewpoints in both news and editorials according to the range of views expressed in mainstream government debate' (see also Bennett 1994, 1996; Bennett, Lawrence and Livingston 2007). According to the 'indexing' norm, non-official sources are only incorporated in news and editorials if they convey judgements already expressed in political officialdom (Bennett 1990: 106). Furthermore, the media displays critical viewpoints if there is political elite opposition whereas media marginalises critical perspectives if there is bipartisan agreement over policies (Mermin 1996: 181; see also Bennett 1990: 106). The press is thus virtually dependent on 'power blocs' within the government nexus whose perceived challenge or lack thereof to the leading institutional actors determines whether the press opens or closes its news gates (Bennett, Lawrence and Livingston 2007: 48–49).

Critical liberal scholars such as Bennett (1996: 377) see 'indexing' as a legitimate process if 'the range of debate among powerful decision-makers results in a fairly good approximation of representative democracy in action'. In such cases it is seen as democratically viable if criticism in the media increases in correlation with criticism raised inside the government because official conflict is seen as legitimate and newsworthy (Mermin 1999: 5–6).

On the other hand, 'evidence supporting the indexing hypothesis' has implications, Bennett writes (1990: 106), because it 'would suggest that the news industry has ceded to government the tasks of policing itself and striking the democratic balance'. Such performance is regarded as problematic because the media's critical potential is dependent on elite conflict and there might be important areas in which the media displays 'official consensus forged with little regard to either public interest or expressed public opinion' (*ibid*). Similarly, Mermin (1999: 6) argues if critical views in society are ignored or marginalised when they have not been articulated in official government circles 'indexing' has profound significance because then press performance contradicts 'the First Amendment ideal of a press independent of government'. Mermin (*ibid*: 6) describes this as the '*marginalisation* version of the indexing hypothesis [emphasis in the original]'.

Elite 'indexing' also suggests criticism in the media to deal with tactical/procedural and not fundamental/substantive issues because officials tend to agree on 'first principles [i.e. fundamental/substantive issues] even if they disagree on how to translate those principles into policy [i.e. tactical/procedural issues]' (Althaus 2003: 383; see also Hallin 1989: 110; Hertog 2000: 613; Robinson *et al.* 2009: 538).[22]

A variety of studies has generally confirmed the 'indexing' norm or provided evidence for similar pattern when assessing how war and foreign policy have been represented in the media of the US, UK and Germany (see Bennett 1990; Bennett, Lawrence and Livingston 2007; Eilders and Hagen 2005; Eilders and Lüter 2000; Entman and Page 1994; Hallin 1989; Mermin 1999; Zaller and Chiu 1996).

For instance, in the major study of US media coverage of the Vietnam War, Hallin highlighted how critical voices only entered media discourses when leading political elites spoke out against the war thus refuting the thesis that popular dissent emerging from the anti-war movement encouraged critical reporting (1989: 99, 1994: 54–55).[23]

Zaller and Chiu (1996: 388–389) analysed coverage of 39 foreign policy crises from 1945 to 1991 in the US news magazines *Time* and *Newsweek* which are less confined to neutral reporting than newspapers and could thus potentially carry a broader range of views. Zaller and Chiu (1996: 385) conclude: 'The single most important rule was that reporters, as Lance Bennett has maintained, tended to "index" their coverage to reflect the range of views that exists within the government.'

Entman and Page (1994: 84) looked at how the *New York Times* and *Washington Post* covered two crucial periods in the 1990–1991 Gulf War during which unusual elite conflict in Congress was existent providing 'nearly ideal conditions' for greater media independence (*ibid*: 96). While the authors found a 'substantial amount of critical reporting' this finding was in harmony with 'indexing' because reprimand 'depended crucially upon the existence of divisions among elites' (*ibid*: 96–97). Henceforth, criticisms were overwhelmingly procedural and effectively all published views in the '"great debate" over peace or war with Iraq shared certain basic assumptions with the Bush administration' such as that '*Iraq must be unconditionally dislodged from Kuwait by force, if necessary* [emphasis in the original]' (*ibid*: 95; see also Entman 2004: chapter 4). *Times* and *Post* coverage of the pre-war phase and US television coverage of the Gulf War had similar reporting pattern (see Dorman and Livingston 1994; Hallin and Gitlin 1994).

Similar patterns were evident in UK coverage of the Iraq War: during the actual war period, and 'at an aggregate level', coverage turned out to be more supportive to the US/Coalition and was generally 'elite-driven' (Robinson *et al.* 2010: 162). In the major study on UK television and press news coverage of the Iraq War, Robinson *et al.* (*ibid*: 172–173) also found an element of conflict. However, as the scholars note, 'much of the criticism occurred at a procedural rather than a substantial level' (*ibid*: 163). In the same fashion, Tumber and Palmer (2004: 164–165) suggested that British news media coverage of the Iraq War (including the pre-invasion phase) did, in general, not transgress the sphere of legitimate elite controversy (*cf*. Lewis *et al.* 2006: 197).

As discussed above, the prevalence of procedural and the absence of substantial criticism generally indicate performance in accord with 'indexing'. This is substantiated because a strong anti-war movement, which placed fundamental issues on its agenda, was present during the time of reporting but marginalised by the British media (Robinson *et al.* 2010: 154, 158).

As the findings of these studies suggest, 'indexing' should generally be regarded as a norm which leads the news to stay 'within the sphere of official consensus and conflict displayed in the public statements' of elite officials 'who manage the policy areas and decision-making processes that make the news' (Bennett, Lawrence and Livingston 2007: 49). Nonetheless, because of changing levels of conflict within and between power blocs there can be great variations in news coverage of different issues (Bennett 1994: 24). However, for individual actors and groups who deviate from the official spheres of debate it is extremely difficult to get sustained news coverage of their view points (Gitlin 1980; Hallin 1989; Robinson *et al.* 2010).[24]

Third factors (I): professional working routines

Other factors that determine coverage may be rooted in professional ideological realms (see Robinson *et al.* 2010: 166–170). This is suggested by studies whose findings amend the 'indexing' norm. Journalists attempt to operate in accordance with norms of 'objectivity' and 'balance' that are rooted in the professional ideology and guide them to cover different sides of a story and remain impartial. However, during the Cold War, virtually any foreign policy crisis was placed within an anti-communist framework. Military interventions were legitimised by labelling actors hostile to Western administrations as communist and thus problematic (Entman 2004; Robinson *et al.* 2010: 37). The applicability of professional norms of 'objectivity' and 'balance' was significantly inhibited by such schemas which can be related to the ideological device of anti-communism (Hallin 1989). With the fall of the former Soviet Union, Entman argues, foreign policy events, issues and actors became ambiguous making one-dimensional framing of enemy states more difficult (2000, 2004: 95–97). Entman generally identified more space for 'balanced' media coverage after the breakdown of the Cold War consensus in 1990 (2004: 95).

However, such shifts to more nuanced coverage have largely occurred in procedural areas such as 'costs and risks', 'problem definitions', or 'policy options' (Entman 2004: 97). Nonetheless, it can be seen that next to 'indexing' other factors may determine news output.

For instance, Entman's (2004: 50–52) study of *New York Times* coverage of US actions in Grenada (1983), Libya (1986), and Panama (1989–1990) identified a media-elite consensus in regard to the problem definition provided by the administration on the one hand and procedural media criticism of the administration's remedies (i.e. strategies to reach set goals) on the other. Because there was a near-absence of Congressional elite opposition in these cases, Entman regards the critical dimension of media content as a deviation from 'indexing' encouraged by the media's commitment to 'provide some degree of balance in their coverage of ambiguous issues' (*ibid*: 56). Entman also identified 'counterframing that emphasised cost and risk' in the cases of (possible) US interventions in Somalia (1993), Haiti (1994), the Balkans (1992–1999), and Afghanistan (2001) (*ibid*: 97).

Pohr (2005) examined editorial coverage of the preparation and execution of the 2001 invasion of Afghanistan in the five leading German nationals. The study generally confirmed the 'indexing' norm: there was a broad parliamentary consensus in Germany supporting the war and media coverage included 'considerably more favourable than sceptical voices' (*ibid*: 274). On the other hand, there was also a significant element of criticism in coverage (particularly in the left-leaning press) arguably in accord with public sentiments, a finding which Pohr relates to several caveats: an incomplete elite consensus, the secondary role of German forces in Afghanistan, and the German's press's expected critical stance towards militarism (*ibid*). Nonetheless, with the exception of the left-leaning *tageszeitung*, criticism was overwhelmingly tactical suggesting the applicability of the amended 'indexing' norm (*ibid*).

These studies suggest a variation to the 'indexing' norm related to journalistic conduct. Yet, as a caveat, these studies did not identify significant amounts of substantial criticisms – a fact which would still suggest consistency with hegemonic models.

Third factors (II): uncontrolled events and technology

Literature on public crises points to unexpected changes in patterns of reporting, findings which scholars also regard as evidence for a more independent media (e.g. Cottle 2006). It has been argued that in the case of accidents, differing accounts are likely to emerge during the initial stages of such events because officials are not able to impose their views on the media allowing for more independent and conflicting coverage (Molotch and Lester 1974: 109). Hence, scholars found that after the unfolding of sudden, dramatic and uncontrollable non-routine events, political institutions were not able to set the agenda (Bennett and Lawrence 1995; Bennett, Lawrence and Livingston 2007: 10–11; Lawrence 1996, 2000; Livingston and Bennett 2003; Molotch and Lester 1974).

Bennett and Lawrence's (1995: 26) research into such event-driven news suggests that symbolic events or news icons have the potential to reshape 'political culture and public policy'. According to Bennett and Lawrence (*ibid*: 23), a news icon 'emerges when an ongoing news story is crystallised in a dramatic event'. Bennett and Lawrence (*ibid*: 29) studied the *New York Times* and *Los Angeles Times* reporting of the *Mobro* garbage barge between 1987–1989.[25] During this period, the *Mobro* became a 'powerful symbol' of a 'waste disposal crisis' (*ibid*). Significantly, coverage linked the barge with other events thus publicising and legitimising ideas from the environmental movement (*ibid*: 33). During this process, the news icon was used by nonmainstream sources in their attempts to voice concerns and 'direct journalistic and public attention' to issues such as garbage, waste, consumption and consumerism (*ibid*: 35). As a consequence, 'recycling became elevated from countercultural trend to broadly endorsed public policy' (*ibid*: 33).

Lawrence (1996: 438–439) assessed the interaction of icons and indexing in the *Los Angeles Times* coverage of police use of force from 1987 through 1992 – a time frame which included the 1991 Rodney King beating.[26] According to Lawrence's (*ibid*: 450) study, dramatic events may cause news media to open up the range of debate: Lawrence found a high amount of non-official voices in coverage regardless of elite conflict. Furthermore, the proportions of non-official voices and challenging views were not strictly 'indexed' to elite conflict (*ibid*: 441–443).

Event-driven news is facilitated by new technologies, such as the Internet and mobile devices, which enable journalists to abandon their conventional working routines and may thus be evident in coverage of international affairs with their 'steady stream of wars, terrorist incidents, famines, and humanitarian crises' (Livingston and Bennett 2003: 367). For example, Robinson *et al.* (2010: 125–126) found evidence for event-driven news during the Iraq War of 2003 in areas which were beyond the control of US/Coalition officials such as civilian and military casualties, humanitarian operations, and law and order. Vietnam war reporting after the Tet offensive in 1968, with its focus on negative news and bloody battles, can also be placed in this category and later government news management strategies (pooling and embedding systems, etc.) have been identified as an official strategy to counter the effects of event-driven news (Livingston and Eachus 1995: 414).

Contemporary scholars have described processes during which elites lose policy control as a result of real-time news as the 'CNN effect' (e.g. Robinson 2006; also Livingston and Eachus 1995). For instance, there is evidence that media coverage contributed to triggering military intervention during the 1991 Kurdish crisis in Iraq, the 1992–1995 Bosnian War and the 1999 Kosovo War and it is assumed that policy uncertainty was a major cause for the CNN effect (Robinson 2000a, 2006).

Some scholars go so far as to proclaim revolutionary changes in media pattern as a result of rapid technological developments and the digitalisation of communication infrastructure. Hoskins and O'Loughlin (2010: 2) see 'a new media ecology' in 'the emergence of networked, diffuse communication and participatory media' undermining the validity of traditional concepts in media research (*ibid*: 185). New technologies, it is argued, enable multidimensional communication flows and as a result media performance can hardly be explained in terms of rather linear models such as gatekeeping and 'indexing' much less hegemony (*ibid*: 10, 185; see also Castells 2010: 12).

However, research on event- and technology-driven news suggests several caveats for the media independence thesis: for instance, elite conflict has been identified as a co-variable which boosted the 'dynamics of icon making' (Lawrence 1996: 448; see also Bennett and Lawrence 1995: 35; Molotch and Lester 1974: 109).

Without elite conflict and after time it can be expected that routine procedures increasingly come into play thus inhibiting event- and technology-driven news (see Bennett and Lawrence 1995: 38; Molotch and Lester 1974: 109). There is also evidence for official news management of icon-driven news thus channelling its critical potential (see Lawrence 1996: 446). For example, the Abu-Ghraib torture scandal of 2004, which revealed how US/Coalition forces had engaged in appalling torture in Iraq, had the potential for critical event-driven news coverage because of the existence of photographic evidence. However, due to the absence of official conflict, the Bush administration was able to impose its frames on the media which consequently portrayed Abu-Ghraib as a story of 'abuse' despite of the existence of evidence indicating 'a possible policy of torture laid bare' (Bennett, Lawrence and Livingston 2007: 107).

The general applicability of the CNN effect has also been questioned by scholars who re-examined coverage on humanitarian crises during the 1990s and similar work during which technology-driven news had been found (Livingston and Eachus 1995; Robinson 2000b, 2006). Scholars identified other variables, such as geo-strategic interests, which were influential at the time when CNN effects had seemingly occurred. Furthermore, so-called 'humanitarian interventions' could be shown to appear in highly selective pattern. In fact, 'humanitarian' arguments have been used by Western governments to justify interventions in strategically important regions (see Hammond 2007; Herman and Peterson 2010). After 9/11 the 'war on terror' framework increased policy certainty thus further diminishing the prevalence of CNN effects (see Robinson 2006: 345–348).

Thus, Bennett, Lawrence and Livingston (2007: 10) describe event-driven news as 'the exception that proves the rule of the press being largely dependent on the government to filter, define, and accent the news'.

There is also not much evidence for the media independence thesis built upon the assumption that a new media ecology has broken up traditional pattern of reporting (e.g. Castells 2010; Hoskins and O'Loughlin 2010), in regard to coverage of political news and high intensity conflict (i.e. warfare) but also in consideration of Internet access and consumption patterns (see the discussion in Robinson *et al.* 2010: 167–170; for the Internet see Curran 2012; Hindman 2009; McChesney 2013; Zollmann 2015b). For instance, the major studies on British news coverage of the Iraq War of 2003 point to the news media's heavy inclusion of official at the expense of other societal actors in accord with traditional gatekeeping pattern (Robinson *et al.* 2010: 78–80; also Lewis *et al.* 2006; Tumber and Palmer 2004). Curran (2012: 21) further points to a substantial movement of advertising revenues from traditional media to the Internet which forced the former to cut budgets and downsize news rooms. As a consequence journalists are even more encouraged to rely on 'tried-and-tested' mainstream sources and content replications (*ibid*).

The Internet provides space for a range of alternative news providers and forms potentially breaking up traditional news media dominance. However, as yet, the large majority of online news carriers are subsets of traditional news providers. Furthermore, traffic is heavily concentrated and users largely rely on online news syndicated by the same legacy news media (*ibid*: 19–20).[27] Curran (*ibid*: 19) thus argues the Internet 'has not undermined leading news organisations' but 'enabled them to extend their hegemony across technology'.

Hindman (2009: 40) assessed the number of hyperlinks pointing to political information websites because linkage correlates with a site's search engine ranking and visits. According to the study, link distribution 'approximates a power law, where a small set of hyper-successful sites receives most of the links' (*ibid*). In conclusion, Hindman's (*ibid*: 56) work provides 'little support' to the argument that the Internet enables 'an epochal shift from broadcasting to narrowcasting' because the prospect of establishing a political website 'is usually equivalent to hosting a talk show on public access television at 3:30 in the morning'.

Lockmasters: news media and corporate-market constraints

While the previously discussed work highlights the media's proximity to the state whose official proclamations have virtually been able to flood the media gates, Herman focused on the corporate-market dimension of gatekeeping. Herman (1986: 173) criticised gatekeeper researchers for their focus on micro issues at the expense of assessing 'the main drift, the net social outcome' of news media. Gatekeeper studies, Herman claimed, lack any discussion on how news media 'mobilise public opinion, or are manipulated (or co-operate) in mobilisation by others' (*ibid*: 174). Furthermore, despite their important findings on official co-option of the media during the Cold War, gatekeeper studies provided 'no systematic analysis of government management of the media and joint ventures by media and government, or by media and other power groups like business and its various components' (*ibid*). Herman referred to one of the prominent gatekeeper researchers, Gans, who had stated at the end of his study that he had 'largely ignored the intriguing possibility that journalists and their firms are pawns of larger and more basic social processes to which they unwittingly respond' (Gans 1980: 290). Gans had also referred to a major function of journalists, which was 'to manage, with others, the symbolic arena, the public stage on which national, societal, and other messages are made available to everyone who can become an audience member' (*ibid*: 298). However, these processes remained largely unexplored in Gans's work and that of other gatekeeper researchers (Herman 1986: 174–175). The same, it could be argued, applies for the 'indexing' scholars who focus on government officials at the exclusion of wider societal processes. Thus, while previous researchers had explored individual, routine or organisational news gates, Herman located the further variables of gatekeeping on the levels of corporate, market and government control as well as ideology (*ibid*: 174–176).

There is considerable literature relying on empirical, historical and/or anecdotal evidence, which supports the assumption that journalistic conduct is guided by structural-institutional imperatives and outside pressures. Research has focused on how the interaction of market forces and advertising dependency, in conjunction with political and technological developments, has led to national and international media concentration and conglomeration and, consequently, on how this media structure has colluded with news and/or culture production in particular and the power structure of society in more general (e.g. Bagdikian 2004; Curran 1977, 2002; Curran and Seaton 2010; Hackett and Uzelman 2003; Hall 1977, 1982; Hall *et al.* 1978; Hardy 2010; Herman 1986, 1995, 1999; Herman and Chomsky 1988a, 2008; Herman and McChesney 1997; Hindman 2009; McChesney 1997, 2004, 2007, 2008; Murdock 1982; Murdock and Golding 1973, 1977, 2005; Parenti 1993; Schiller 1973, 1982, 1986, 1989; Shoemaker and Reese 1996; Smythe 1981; Winter 1997, 2007).

Nevertheless, commercial and market-structural influences on gatekeeping processes are hard to measure because such research ideally requires the triangulation of participant observation of sensitive media operations, questionnaires and content analyses. Hence, studies have often relied on anecdotal evidence, observations or inferential content analyses.

For instance, anecdotal research suggests that journalists are driven out of the system if they do not internalise commercial values or self-censor (Borjesson 2002). A Pew Research Center survey of 300 US journalists in 2000 found that about 50 per cent admitted they sometimes consciously censored themselves to serve the commercial interests of their company or advertisers, only 25 per cent stated that this would never happen (McChesney 2003: 310). Liberal gatekeeper researchers also observed systemic self-censorship in the newsrooms they studied (Epstein 2000 [1973]: 57, 76; Gans 1980: 277).

Furthermore, scholars highlight that organisational interests are often executed through owners and managements who appoint 'key personal' who 'become the proprietor's "voice" within the newsroom, ensuring that journalistic "independence" conforms to the preferred editorial line' (McNair 2003: 57). Research by Curran and Seaton suggests that interventionist owners and managers are prevalent in the newspaper industries in the UK (2003: 101). Other studies indicate how top-down interferences influence working routines (see Winter 2007: 45–46).[28] Significantly, managers and owners do not simply intervene on political or ideological grounds, they are themselves exposed to economic pressures and may merely interfere upon them (McChesney 2003: 306; also *cf.* Bakan 2005). For instance, owners and managers operating in media conglomerates have to respond to pressures from interlocking boards which are related to other corporations and groups. As Soontae and Jin (2004: 579) write, corporate interlocks are a widespread feature of capitalist institutions and 'are established as a means to facilitate inter-firm collusion and cooperation'.

Influences by advertisers on the press have also been highlighted (see e.g. Franklin 1997: 92–95; Keeble 2006: 44–45; McNair 2003: 58–59).[29] The crucial power of advertisers is inherent in their position 'to choose among stations and programs [sic]' according to their ideological preferences (Herman 1995: 169). Hence, Curran (2002: 96) stressed advertisers' '*de facto* licensing authority since, without their support, newspapers ceased to be economically viable [emphasis in the original]'. For example, despite high reader demands until well into the mid-20th century, a vibrant political working class press virtually disappeared from the British market (*ibid:* 103). This can be explained by the fact that in media markets, organisations have to follow the demands of the advertising industry, which largely funds their products (which constitutes of wealthier audiences) (Barnouw 2006 [1978]; Smythe 1981). If news media attempt to serve other target groups, they cannot expect sufficient advertising revenues. These mechanisms also influence the content production: news media are inclined to favour those messages which are in accord with the preferences of advertisers and the rather wealthier audience groups targeted by advertisers. This can be regarded as a market-structural barrier, which filters out an unknown but likely important variety of messages. Because this suggests a closed system, Curran even went so far to claim that 'market forces succeeded where legal repression had failed in establishing the press as an instrument of social control' (2002: 81). Liberal scholars have held comparable views. Owen, one of the founders of media economics, argued:

> [...] the Miltonian process [i.e. the marketplace of ideas] may not work properly, and ideas that are not the truth may come to dominate the intellectual market as a result of the systemic exclusion of messages that do not suit the economic or political interests of those who control access to the media of transmission. (1975: 5)

Media economists highlight how specific characteristics of media products – they are sold on two markets (to advertisers and readers), they are so called public goods, and they produce important externalities – lead to systemic market failures (Doyle 2002a: 10–13, 161–163). Economists who are generally in favour of market regulated media systems have pointed out that markets are inadequate to enable a variety of normative arrays which are usually ascribed to the news media: 'the mass medial reconstruction of reality to manufacture public', 'the production of diversity of opinion', 'the production of truth', and 'the formation of societal norms' (Heinrich 2002: 46; see also Karmasin 1998: 114–119; Kiefer 2001: 146–148). Heinrich (2002: 46), one of the leading German media economists, argues that if society wishes the manufacture of the 'merit goods' described above, 'one cannot leave their production to the market' (*ibid*). This results from the fact that merit goods are not rateable via cost-benefit analysis (*ibid*).[30] In other words: moments held dear by liberal press theorists – such as public representation, truthfulness, diversity of views and values – are, if we follow classic economic theory, not sufficiently produced by media even if operating under the ideal market condition of perfect competition.[31] Moreover, such competition has never existed. Scholars point to the prevalence of media concentration which has globally increased during the last decades (Albarran 2002: 188; Albarran and Chan-Olmsted 1998: 332–333; Doyle 2002b: 1–4; Trappel 2008: 147).[32] There is a vast body of literature dealing with the multi-dimensional and widespread adverse effects of economic and journalistic concentration on media performance which augment the general problems which have already been associated with markets (for an overview of the literature see Leidinger 2003).[33]

The following characteristics of media performance are likely linked to market-structural imperatives: empirical findings on media content point to significant cooperation between news media and the state-corporate-military-industrial complex (e.g. Bennett 1990; Bennett, Lawrence and Livingston 2007; Bennett and Paletz 1994; Boyd-Barrett 2004; DiMaggio 2009; Eilders and Lüter 2000; Hallin 1989; Herman and Chomsky 2008; Keeble 1997, 2004; Mermin 1999). Content analyses in the US, UK and Canada suggest a tendency of bias in favour of the business industries (Edwards and Cromwell 2006, 2009; Hackett and Uzelman 2003; Herman and Chomsky 2008).[34]

Topics, which according to polls, are important for the civil sector such as universal healthcare, the reduction of military spending, and opposition to 'free trade' agreements are marginalised in US media coverage (Herman and Chomsky 2008: xl–xli). Page describes such phenomena, where the news media takes the sides of elites at the expense of the population, as 'elite-mass gaps' (1996: 118). Elite-mass gaps constitute cases when news media excludes issues which are favoured by the population – which is indicated by trends in opinion polls. According to Page:

> On some issues these gaps are so great that public discourse, as articulated by officials, experts and journalists, may be quite distant from the values and concerns of ordinary citizens. (*ibid*: 118–119)

Such phenomena are quite frequent, Page (*ibid*: 118) further argues, particularly in regard to foreign policy. An unknown but likely important amount of facts and perspectives is thus generally suppressed by the news media. Keeble describes this phenomenon as the media's 'silencing function' (1997: 200).

There is also extensive evidence that news media apply a double standard in coverage of foreign events which is related to political-economic relations. Various scholars in the US, UK and Canada have analysed a range of different cases identifying media pattern that display dichotomised media choices (e.g. Chomsky and Herman 1979a, b; DiMaggio 2009; Edwards and Cromwell 2006, 2009; Herman 1986, 1995; Herman and Chomsky 2008; Herman and Peterson 2007, 2010).

So far, I have identified news routines, the 'indexing' of political elites, ideology, self-censorship, state-corporate propaganda and organisational as well as corporate-market structures as constraining elements during the production of news. As a consequence, news content on foreign policy, war and economic issues closely corresponds with elite discourses and interests.

Diversity largely occurs in the tactical sphere: media critic procedural choices and outcomes without discussing the underlying principles of policy. In many cases, such kinds of criticism occurred when elites were in disagreement about issues. And if journalists more autonomously followed professional standards of 'objectivity' and 'balance' (also during periods of elite consensuses) they still largely focused on procedural and not substantial issues when being critical. And it has been well established that such kinds of patterns provide evidence of hegemonic news media performance. The complementarity of some approaches also seems noteworthy: the 'indexing' norm (Bennett 1990) strikingly resembles Hall *et al.*'s (1978) primary definer model as well as the third 'filter' of Herman and Chomsky's (2008) propaganda model. Furthermore, treatises within classic media economics support the assumptions of a hegemonic model.

Concurrently, however, empirical studies also suggest a degree of openness. The question remains if the conflicting element in coverage can be incorporated in a hegemonic model or if it provides evidence for a semi-liberal press?

Discussion and synthesis: liberal vs. hegemonic models

Liberal models emphasis dynamic media performance as a result of the contest between official authorities and challengers over influencing news media coverage (e.g. Wolfsfeld 1997). Wolfsfeld (*ibid*: 4) postulates that when:

> [...] authorities lack or lose control it provides the news media with a much greater array of sources and perspectives from which to choose. This offers important opportunities for challengers to promote their own frames to the press.

Scholars claim that the breakdown of the Cold War consensus has made it difficult for Western authorities to impose their preferred frames on the Anglo-American media during international conflicts suggesting a shift to more nuanced coverage in the fashion described by Wolfsfeld (e.g. Althaus 2003; Entman 2000, 2004; Zaller and Chiu 1996). The professional autonomy of journalists, media system characteristics, technological changes, and uncontrolled events have been identified as variables which permit 'plural pattern of war reporting' (Robinson *et al.* 2010: 177). And finally, the media have been identified as more diverse before and after the outbreak of conflicts because war constitutes an exceptional state leading to the closure of debate around patriotic discourses (i.e. rallying effects) (*ibid*: 122–123).

Hence, some of the leading scholars do not accept the validity of a hegemonic model (e.g. Entman 2004; Hallin 1994; Wolfsfeld 1997). It could be argued that there is a general tendency to see the media in the fashion of Wolfsfeld's (1997: 210) 'semi-honest brokers' who 'depend on their "preferred customers" for most of their business, but are open to offers from any challengers who can come up with a reasonable bid'. Thus, critical liberal scholars seem to be inclined, like Bennett, Lawrence and Livingston (2007: 46), to refer to the news media as 'semi-independent'.

But yet, these same scholars have consistently suggested that news media are largely subordinate to political officials and perform accordingly. It is argued that news operate within the spheres of elites (Entman 2004: 154; Hallin 1989), are 'gleaned from' official statements (Bennett, Lawrence and Livingston 2007: 50), and do not provide sufficient space for those in need of being heard because media access is related to monetary power (Wolfsfeld 1997: 24). Isn't this evidence for hegemonic performance?

Moreover, the accounts of the liberal scholars discussed above, most of which build upon or refine the 'indexing' norm, suffer from theoretical shortfalls.[35] Their studies shed light on important dimensions of the news production process: the relationship between government officials and journalist. In addition, they accurately explain variations in media coverage as a result of political elite agreement/disagreement or the changing political consensus. With an increase in political elite conflict, it is argued, the media becomes more open and democratic. Hence, the reference to the media's semi-independence, meaning: a dependent media during elite consensuses and a more diverse and open media during elite conflict. And here is my point of disagreement: such a perspective regards political elite diversions as an indicator for democratic vigour as if, in the classic fashion of liberal press theories, differences in official political opinion represent similar differences in public opinion. While this can technically be the case, there are two problems with such an argument:

(1) Many issues of public concern are neither discussed nor resolved by political elites if they affect corporate interests (see Ferguson 1995; Herman and Chomsky 2008: XL–XLVII). This can be explained by the power which the corporate business sector has attained over the democratic decision-making processes in Western democracies (see Balanyá *et al.* 2000; Dinan and Miller 2007; Domhoff 2002; Domhof and Dye 1987; Ferguson 1995; Kolko 1976; Miller and Dinan 2000, 2008; Mills 1956).

(2) Diversions within the political class often express diversions within the elite constituencies which politicians represent. Ferguson's (1995) investment

theory of political parties sheds light on this process. According to Ferguson, the major impetus for political parties in Western democracies is not to maximise votes but to satisfy investors (*ibid*: 27–28). This results from the logic of money-driven political systems which can be described as follows: whenever '*money matters importantly to mounting campaigns* [emphasis in the original]' (*ibid*: 382) the market for political parties is not voters but large investors (*ibid*: 22). Hence, investor blocs determine the centre of political parties and can be seen as 'responsible for most of the signals the party sends to the electorate' (*ibid*: 22). The dominant investor blocs usually stem from the corporate sector because business firms have the largest resources to invest in political candidates.[36]

Ferguson's theory does not rule out that parties do pay attention to voters or that masses of voters can become investors (*ibid*: 28–29). Rather, investment theory suggests that whenever entry and information costs are high (which is usually the case in money-driven systems) parties 'dominated by large investors' try to gather votes by making 'limited appeals to particular segments of the potential electorate' (*ibid*: 28). Ferguson (*ibid*: 28) describes the political manifestation of such a system as follows:

> If it pays some other bloc of major investors to advertise and mobilise, these appeals can be vigorously contested, but [...] on all issues affecting the vital interests that major investors have in common, no party competition will take place. [...] and if all major investors happen to share an interest in ignoring issues vital to the electorate, such as social welfare, hours of work, or collective bargaining, so much the worse for the electorate.

As a consequence, foreign policy issues such as the Washington Consensus, the peace dividend and the use of force may not be questioned if they fall within the bi-partisan consensus.[37] Even if majority preferences in public opinion prefer alternative policies such proposals cannot be transported in the political arena because publics do not tend to have the resources to invest in candidates to represent their interests.[38] Thus, issues which are debated by public officials tend to represent topics on which investor blocs disagree upon.

Hence, an assessment of the news media has to consider this class bias in democratic societies and how conflict and consent in media coverage can be related to agreed and disagreed aims of various upper class fractions (i.e. the state, corporate and managerial elites) who usually constitute major investors for political parties (*cf.* Mullen 2010: 674).

Liberal scholars classify the political elite as consisting of the executive branch and oppositional actors usually stemming from the opposition parties (Althaus *et al.* 1996: 408). Applying the investment theory it could be expected that the political elite, whether under conditions of political conflict or not, advances the interests of various investor groups.

Yet, liberal media scholars largely neglect this perspective. As a result, they over-emphasise media openness: Wolfsfeld, for example, fails to link 'the extent to which the news media can break away from the authorities and become independent' (1997: 198) to how different elite factions evaluate policies by authorities.[39] Like other liberal scholars who overstate the role of political conflict (e.g. Althaus 2003; Bennett 1990; Bennett, Lawrence and Livingston 2007; Entman 2004; Hallin 1989), Wolfsfeld classifies media freedom as 'independence from the authorities' (1997: 29; see also Entman and Page 1994: 83). From this it follows that tactical challenges of official administration/government/military policies are regarded as evidence for media independence (in the classic liberal sense of a government 'watchdog') as in major recent studies by Althaus (2003), Entman (2004), and Wolfsfeld (1997).[40] Such a scholarly rationale accepts what Richard Keeble (1997: 193) describes as the 'myth' that press 'freedom' means 'autonomy from the state'. In contrast, a hegemonic model expects the prevalence of government/military criticism because it 'argues, from its foundations, that the media will protect the interests of the powerful [i.e. the corporate sector], not that it will protect state managers from their criticisms' (Chomsky 1989: 149). Similarly, Ferguson (1995: 401), argues the news media can be highly critical of government officials or the state. But such criticism is flawed because the critical range of opinion represents 'diversity among large investor blocs' (*ibid*) and not among the various contesting views of a society.

It should also be noted that the same sectors, which invest in political parties also have a stake in the media as they comprise media owners and shareholders as well as the advertising industry.

In conclusion, liberal scholars focus on the interplay between journalists, political officials and government authorities thereby neglecting the media's corporate integration and subjugation to market and investor pressures. A hegemonic model, on the other hand, emphasises the sovereignty of corporate investors over the political system and media (see Herman 2000). Ferguson (1995: 400) describes the resulting implications:

> Just as large profit-maximising investors in parties do not pay to undermine themselves, major media [...] controlled by large profit-maximising investors [i.e. owners, advertisers, share holders] do not encourage the dissemination of news and analyses that are likely to lead to popular indignation and, perhaps, government action hostile to all large investors, themselves included.

Such a perspective is seriously at odds with the liberal approach which assumes news media to operate as a mirror of society and a watchdog of the powerful. If investors can regularly determine news media to align with their interests this evidences a hegemonic system. Accordingly, this study assumes hegemonic news media performance.

· 3 ·
THE PROPAGANDA MODEL
OF MEDIA PERFORMANCE

Overview

Herman and Chomsky's (1988a, b, 2008) propaganda model of media performance describes, on a macro level, the categories that explain why the news media operates as a hegemonic system. The propaganda model hypothesises that state-corporate-capitalist interests are in disagreement with broader societal interests. Because of state-corporate-capitalist control and funding, the news media operate as a propaganda system. Thus, Herman and Chomsky (2008: 1) argue that it is the media's

> [...] function to amuse, entertain, and inform, and to inculcate individuals with the values, beliefs, and codes of behavior [sic] that will integrate them into the institutional structures of the larger society. In a world of concentrated wealth and major conflicts of class interest, to fulfil this role requires systematic propaganda.

The propaganda model constitutes a structural model based on industrial organisation analysis. Its analytical categories focus on the institutional composition and environment of the media (Herman 1981, 1986, 2000). The propaganda model situates the news media in a market system guided by a set of five interacting and reinforcing news 'filters'. These operating principles (two institutional and two outer institutional as well as ideology) largely shape media performance.[1] The first and second 'filters' point to the news media's market logic, concentration, corporate organisation, advertising dependency as well as links with external institutions. These institutional realities have significant implications: (1) Market dependencies encourage the news media to produce cost effective and thus surrender journalistic over profit imperatives. (2) Heavy market and ownership concentration encourage the recycling of information at the expense of original inquiries, the ideological abuse of market power and product homogenisation. (3) Corporate organisation further leads to the prioritisation of profits over other motifs. (4) Advertising dependency cedes organisational autonomy to the sponsor of media products, and this can be factored in direct relation to the amount of advertising revenue that is required. (5) Links to external organisations like banks and other shareholders further increase the dependency on outside actors.

As a consequence of these institutional constraints, the news media can reflect audience demands only as long as their media messages do not violate the interests of their corporate affiliates.

Owners and media managers, who constitute part of the elite business community via interlocking boards and social circles, are sufficiently able to impact on journalistic behaviour through the selection and appointment of personnel as well as rewards and reprimands. Journalists tend to adhere to such pressures via internalisation of dominant values and self-censorship in the same fashion as identified by the gatekeeper studies.

Because of these constraints a propaganda model assumes formally autonomous news media organisations to operate on the basis of 'common outlooks' (Herman 2000: 105).

The third 'filter' of the propaganda model stresses the media's reliance on elite sources stemming from government as well as to other powerful institutions. Journalists establish source relationship with these institutions in order to obtain a 'reliable flow of the raw material of news' (Herman and Chomsky 2008: 17).

The third 'filter' is in agreement with the findings of the scholars researching the evident prevalence of the 'indexing' norm that suggests heavy inclusion of official at the expense of societal perspectives. Additionally, the propaganda model focuses on the relationship between market logic and the news media's sourcing. Herman and Chomsky found that economic considerations encourage journalists to frequent a narrow range of news beats in order to account for their daily demand for news and information. Furthermore, these elite sources are regarded as more credible because of their 'status and prestige' in society. Additionally, elite actors can sanction media organisations with access denials in cases of unfavourable coverage. Following other, less credible sources enhances the costs of research and fact-checking, in particular if media organisations anticipate 'criticism of bias and the threat of libel suits' (*ibid*: 18).

Herman and Chomsky (*ibid*: 18–21) also highlight the ability of the corporate community and state institutions to produce massive PR campaigns which by far exceed the resources that can be spent by the cumulative effort of non-governmental or grassroots organisations and are often used by the media for their cost effectiveness. In sum:

> [...] the large bureaucracies of the powerful *subsidise* the mass media, and gain special access by their contribution to reducing the media's costs of acquiring the raw materials of, and producing, news [emphasis in the original]. (*ibid*: 21)[2]

Finally, the fourth and fifth 'filters' of the propaganda model incorporate *flak* and 'anti-communism'. So-called *flak* campaigns constitute a 'negative response to a media statement or program' (*ibid*: 24). *Flak* puts pressure on news media organisations to abide by or follow a specific agenda. The impact of *flak* is usually related to the power of the originator. Due to their economic might, governments, corporations and state-corporate sponsored think-tanks are the dominant providers of *flak* (*ibid*: 24–27).

The ideology of 'anti-communism', as Herman and Chomsky (*ibid*: 27–29) argue, was applied to mobilise the population against those who threaten US state-corporate interests. For instance, the media has in the past often adopted 'anti-communist' rhetoric in order to gain support in favour of foreign interventions or to weaken domestic working-class organization (*ibid*). After the disintegration of the Soviet Union, anti-communism has declined as an ideological imperative and been replaced by other devices such as a belief in the 'market' (Herman 2000: 109), the 'war on terrorism' after 9/11, or 'a liberal "humanitarian" discourse', which have become powerful notions to understand political events (Robinson 2004: 107). Curtis (2003: 380) suggests another ideological concept, the idea of 'basic benevolence' of the West. News media coverage, Curtis (*ibid*) argues, virtually underwrites that foreign policy is driven by noble goals such as to promote 'democracy, peace, human rights, and development'.

Generally, these 'filters' can be used as categories to illuminate the 'basis and operations of what amount to propaganda campaigns'; they define news worthy items and set the parameters of discourse (Herman and Chomsky 2008: 2). Journalists tend to work under these constraints mostly with integrity and commitment, and formally adhere to professional news values, because 'the operation of these filters occurs so naturally [...] that alternative bases of news choices are hardly imaginable' (*ibid*).

The impact of the propaganda model's 'filters' on news media performance can vary during different time/space contexts leaving room for variations in coverage. Yet, Herman and Chomsky's model suggests that, as a result of the net workings of the 'filters', news media systematically serve state-corporate elite interests in important domains. Hence, their claim that one of the news media's functions is to produce propaganda.

First order predictions of the propaganda model[3]

The propaganda model's 'filters' were deduced from earlier work within the political economy and gatekeeper traditions as well as functional analysis (see Herman 1986, 1999). The novelty of Herman and Chomsky's study was to verify empirically the 'filters' in a US context and to integrate them in one model. Moreover, Herman and Chomsky derived predictions for media coverage that were verified with content studies (see Chomsky 1989; Herman and Chomsky 2008; Klaehn 2005). Thus, the propaganda model, as applied by Herman and Chomsky, incorporates a two-tiered research approach:

(1) Theoretical postulation and empirical verification of the news 'filters' (independent variable = 'filters').
(2) Theoretical deduction and empirical verification of predictions on media content pattern via content analysis (dependent variables = predictions or media content) (see also Thompson 2009: 76).

This section will discuss a propaganda model's predictions on media content pattern. And it will demonstrate that there is alignment between the predictions and concepts of major news media and propaganda scholars.

Generally, a propaganda model predicts the news media to approve the established socio political and economic order in a system-reinforcing fashion (see Chomsky 1997) as observed by Curran and Seaton (2003: 103). In the propaganda literature, such performance has been described as propaganda of integration, which subjects the public to certain ideological premises about the nature and character of that society (see Bussemer 2005: 34; Ellul 1973: 74; Silverstein 1987: 50).

Secondly, there are more limited elite agendas reflected in economic (e.g. 'free trade' agreements, labour, welfare, or health care policies) or foreign (e.g. military interventions, human rights violations, war, foreign elections, support for 'client' and opposition towards 'enemy' regimes) policies. In such cases, the propaganda model predicts media 'to effectively legitimise and facilitate the (geo)political-economic interests of dominant elites' (Klaehn 2002: 166). These processes further depend on how different elite blocs position towards an issue. For example, in cases when political parties and the corporate elite are united on an issue but the public takes a different position or disagrees the model 'predicts that media will exemplify tendencies towards ideological closure and [...] media coverage will be aligned with elite interests' (Klaehn 2002: 165; see also Herman and Chomsky 1988a: 171–172). Examples constitute elite-mass gaps when issues of public importance, such as public health care in the US, were entirely ignored by media (for references see Chapter 2). Different examples constitute coverage in approval of administration policies such as during the first phase of the overt Vietnam War (early until mid 1960s) when the US media supported the war effort almost like a monolith (see Hallin 1989). These examples may also be defined as ideological media content pattern when, as Philo and Berry (2011: 174) argue, 'interest-linked perspective' dominate the news agenda. Or in other words: these constitute instances when propaganda acts 'as a purveyor of ideology' (Jowett and O'Donnell 1992: 1; see also Ellul 1973: 63–64).

Thirdly, the propaganda model does not rule out diversity and critique. On the contrary, the model predicts that there is a range of permissible opinion which 'is bounded by the consensus of powerful elites while encouraging tactical debate within it' (Chomsky 1989: 59). The media may also take 'an "adversarial stance" with regards to those holding office' when elites are not satisfied with specific policies or are in conflict over certain issues (Herman and Chomsky 1988a: 171). Chomsky further argued that the news media 'must present a picture of the world that is tolerably close to reality, even if only a selective version' so that 'investors', 'state managers' and other 'politically active elites' are enabled to 'make judgements based on the facts of the real world' particularly 'if they are to serve their own interests effectively and play their social roles' (1989: 151). This is also important because it suggests that the news media presents a large amount of information which is factually accurate. However, this information tends to be embedded in ideological structures or weighted according to elite priorities. Indeed, an important aspect, which often tends to be ignored by critiques, is the model's emphasis on *how* the news media carries facts as opposed to omitting them. As Herman and Chomsky (1988b: 15) have argued elsewhere: more significant than the suppression of information are the ways the press 'present a particular fact – its placement, tone, and frequency of repetition – and the framework in which it is placed'. This is also useful for elites as propaganda is assumed to be more effective when it is grounded in verifiable facts and occurrences. Accordingly, Ellul (1973: 85) has argued that today it is unusual to find propaganda 'composed solely of claims without relation to reality'. Ellul (*ibid*) thus pointed out that propaganda's 'content increasingly resembles information'. And this might be even more so the case during war, Ellul further wrote, when 'successful propaganda is that based directly on obvious facts' (*ibid*: 84). Similarly, the sociologist Merton (1968: 578) differentiated between an argumentative type of propaganda and a rather crude incendiary type. With view towards earlier studies of propaganda, Merton argued that individuals were more willing to accept propaganda if it was based on facts (*ibid*: 579).

Generally, the propaganda model predicts a restrained range of diversity, which emerges as a result of divisions within the elite rather than societal dissent (see Chomsky 1989: 59). This prediction gains further support from Hall *et al.*'s (1978: 58) primary definer thesis (i.e. elite definition of events) and the findings of the 'indexing' scholars who observed a large amount of tactical/procedural criticism (i.e. the spectrum of allowed expression indexed from elite circles) and the absence of fundamental/substantial criticism (i.e. elite consensus areas which are not scrutinised). For instance, media has displayed administration criticism about the justification, execution, cost or achievement of military interventions while substantial foreign policy issues such as economic priorities and nefarious intent largely remained unquestioned (Herman and Chomsky 1988a: 172; Klaehn 2002: 166–167).

Fourthly, the model predicts the existence of parochial journalistic autonomy and influence of professional news values (Herman and Chomsky 2008: XII). Deviant elements, Herman and Chomsky argue (*ibid*), constitute 'the beauty of the system' because 'dissent and inconvenient information are kept within bounds and at the margins' unable 'to interfere unduly with the domination of the official agenda' while, at the same time, demonstrating that the media 'is not monolithic' (*ibid*). Thus, the propaganda model predicts the punctual inclusion of dissent and inconvenient facts at the bottom of the inverted pyramid or in the back and comment pages. This prediction further corresponds with Hall's notion of secondary definitions, which are embedded in coverage albeit in a subordinated position (Hall 1977: 345–346). Similarly, a range of studies found evidence for marginalised dissent in coverage but, at the same time, approved the media's general tendency to be elite-driven (e.g. Althaus 2003; Entman 2004; Robinson *et al.* 2010).

And fifthly, the model predicts dichotomised media choices when news media cover 'similar events which differ primarily in their political implications' (Herman 1986: 175). The media is predicted to act as an agenda setter and how stories are framed is assumed to be based on elite utility and not on an independent standard (*cf. ibid*). Thus, Herman and Chomsky (2008: 33) write that 'the modes of handling favored and inconvenient materials (placement, tone, context, fullness of treatment) differ in ways that serve political ends'. Herman and Chomsky (2008) compared coverage of victims of state-violence by so called 'enemy' countries of the West (such as the former Soviet Union, Poland, North Vietnam, Cambodia and the former Republic of Yugoslavia) with coverage of victims of comparable state-violence by the US or 'allied' client-states (such as Guatemala, Chile, El Salvador, Turkey and Indonesia) (see also Chomsky and Herman 1979a, b). They concluded (2008: 34) that 'differential treatment occurs on a large scale' and 'that the US mass media's practical definitions of worth are political in the extreme and fit well the expectations of a propaganda model' which assumes news media to 'consistently portray people abused in enemy states as *worthy* victims, whereas those treated with equal or greater severity by its own government or clients will be *unworthy* [emphasis in the original]'. These findings, they argued, result from dichotomised media selection choices: casualties of state-violence are only worthy to be covered by news media if victimisation meets 'the test of utility to elite interests [emphasis in the original]' (*ibid*: 31). As a result, Western states and their 'allies' are shielded from public scrutiny, whereas so called 'enemy' states are shamed until they (are forced to) integrate into the dominant order.[4] The findings of this study will mainly relate to this fifth prediction (and its various components) of the propaganda model (see concluding chapter).

It is important to note that the propaganda model does not predict total closure. If reporting on 'enemy' and 'allied' countries is compared, the model predicts the representation of human rights violations to differ if the overall quantity of coverage as well as the amount of indignation, details and recrimination featured in coverage is factored. Hence, media may cover Western human rights violations particularly if a country has a high baseline coverage. However, if 'enemy' countries engage in similar violations the model predicts coverage to differ significantly (see generally Chomsky 1989: 151–153). Such differences in news media treatment can, of course, be identified in the ways that the news media emphasises and de-emphasises facts and ideological perspectives. Comparing cases of human rights violations of 'enemy' and 'allied' countries sheds a revealing light on the news media's weighting of facts and frameworks which, as will be shown in this study, is based on political convenience and not on an independent standard.

An international propaganda model

The propaganda model was developed with the US context in mind. However, several scholars argue the media systems in Britain and Europe differ from the American in several ways: they have more competitive, less consolidated media markets, a broader newspaper spectrum, alternate professional norms, and feature public service providers which do not operate under corporate-market constraints. This, it could be argued, enables greater spaces for media diversity in sources and opinions (see DiMaggio 2009: 52–55; Hallin and Mancini 2010; Robinson *et al.* 2010: 177; Sparks 2007: 77). Sparks (2007: 73–74) further identifies a broader political spectrum in European countries, which could enlarge the range of debate. Moreover, DiMaggio (2009: 55) points out how differences in economic and military investments can impact on foreign policy reporting. For instance, the US has larger economic and military stakes in the Middle East than Britain and this might increase elite pressure on the news media (*ibid*). Several studies on the Iraq War of 2003, indeed, found more critical and diverse coverage in the UK and Germany than in the US (see Eilders 2005: 640–641; Kegel 2003; Krüger 2003; Robinson *et al.* 2010; Sparks 2007).

On the other hand, the US, UK and German media are integrated into the corporate power structure which overlaps these three core states of the world capitalist system (see Herman and McChesney 1997). Gramsci termed this structure 'the combinations of States in hegemonic systems' (1971: 176). As William K. Carroll (2010: 224) mapped out in an empirical study:

> The global corporate network is overwhelmingly a Euro-North American configuration. This shows the enduring influence of a North Atlantic ruling class, which has long been at the centre of global corporate power.

More specifically, Wallerstein's (1974: 390; also 2004) 'world-system' approach for comparative analyses views states as part of the 'world capitalist economy' (1974: 391). Wallerstein (*ibid*: 401) identifies three structural positions in the world-system: core, periphery, and semi-periphery. While the status of a state can change over time, the stronger, core states aim at enforcing relations of asymmetrical exchange on weaker, peripheral countries because corporate-capitalist elites use nation states to enhance their economic power (see *ibid*: 401–402). In the words of Wallerstein (*ibid*: 401): '[...] capitalism involves not only appropriation of the surplus-value by an owner from a laborer [sic], but an appropriation of surplus of the whole world-economy by core areas.' Within the world-system, DiMaggio (2009: 169) further argues that 'poorer states [...] exist primarily to enhance the wealth of core states, not to develop into major challenges to the power of those states'. Hence, core states connect with peripheral states, which are forced to provide cheap access to their resources. In many cases, such relationships can only be upheld if the peripheral states oppress their populations. Thus, core states support tyrannical elites in peripheral states in order to undermine national currents, which claim resources for their population's benefit (see *ibid*: 169).

The Iraq War of 2003 and subsequent occupation constitutes a case in which core states (mainly the US and UK) attempted at imposing a typical core-peripheral state relationship on a country (Iraq) that has otherwise the potential to develop into a core state (see Schwartz 2008: chapter 3). To subjugate peripheral states is part of the foreign policy consensus among elites in Western core states: this rationale is implicit in the neoliberal 'Washington Consensus' which most core governments in the world endorse (for evidence see Chossudovsky 2002).

In accordance with the propaganda model, it would make sense to relate news media content to consensual and conflicting interests within the Euro-North American state-corporate axis of the world system. Coverage is expected to be homogenous in areas were interests overlap, whereas differences, as Nacos *et al.* (2000: 41) postulate, 'reflect distinct national and regional interests, policies, and politics'. Accordingly, DiMaggio (2009: 186) provides the following working hypothesis for hegemonic reporting:

> [...] national media coverage [...] should be distinguished by each country's economic and political position in relation to the [conflict]. Wealthy core countries that are directly involved in the conflict, or closely allied with countries involved, should [...] be the least open to moral [i.e. fundamental/strategic/substantial] criticisms.

Evidence suggests that US, UK and German press discourses followed national political and economic elite priorities during coverage of the Iraq War and other military interventions:

Couldry and Downey found that during the Iraq War build-up, 'elite media and political discourse concerning the waging of a war against Iraq in the UK was deeply divided' (2004: 280). For an understanding of why critical coverage was prevalent, it is crucial that the 'war option' attracted a significant degree of opposition from political and economic elites. As was already discussed during the actual war period Iraq War coverage was generally 'elite-driven' (Robinson *et al.* 2010: 162–163).

The Iraq War is useful to compare with the 1956 invasion of Egypt by the British and French during the Suez Crisis: In both conflicts parts of the British press were critical of the authorities and questioned the rationales for going to war (see Tulloch 2007: 45–46). And the crises share another common denominator: misgivings towards military action were voiced from within the British oil industry. Considering Iraq, Sampson (2002: 17) described in December 2002 how 'BP is worried about being displaced by US companies'. Moreover, Sampson (*ibid*) suggested:

> Many oil executives now fear a war against Iraq could have more dangerous repercussions; if it goes wrong, they will be among the first to blame the governments that launched it.[5]

The invasion of Egypt, Sampson (*ibid*) further writes, was conducted 'without consulting the oil companies which' were 'opposed' to it.

In contrast, during cases without similar elite divisions, such as the 1991 Gulf War, the 1999 NATO onslaught on FRY/Serbia, the 2001 attacks on Afghanistan, and the 2011 military intervention in Libya, Fleet Street news coverage largely backed Western militarism (Keeble 2004: 51; for Libya see Edwards and Cromwell 2011; for coverage see generally Hammond and Herman 2000; Hammond 2007; Keeble 1997; Lanine, Edwards and Cromwell 2007; Lewis *et al.* 2006).

If the Suez Crisis and the Iraq War constitute exceptional periods 'when the confrontational stance of the media reached its peak' the 'answer is clear and precise: powerful groups are capable of defending themselves' (Herman and Chomsky 2008: 281).[6]

In the US, a considerable body of literature suggests similar elite-driven pattern of coverage in the conflicts mentioned above (see e.g. Bennett and Paletz 1994; Bennett, Lawrence and Livingston 2007; DiMaggio 2009;

Hammond and Herman 2000; Hart 2011; Herman and Chomsky 2008; Mermin 1999; Moeller 2004; Nichols and McChesney 2005).[7] Furthermore, studies on coverage of nefarious actions (i.e. aggressive wars and/or human rights violations) in peripheral states have identified a connection between press performance and elite interests: if the US government or one of its 'clients' was responsible for violations, victims of violence were 'unworthy' of being covered. If, on the other hand, so called 'enemy' state were the perpetrators of comparable violence, coverage remarkably differed in its 'quantity' and 'quality'. Thus, suppression of human rights violations shielded the US and its 'clients' from public outrage. Then again, indignant coverage of 'enemy' states prepared Western audiences for military action or other policies useful to Western elite interests (see Chomsky and Herman 1979a, b; Herman and Peterson 2007, 2010; Herman and Chomsky 2008).

As noted above, since the end of the Cold War, some studies have found evidence for more diverse coverage in the US. However, as in the case of the UK, diversity has usually been identified in the tactical sphere and evidence for media independency has thus not been impressive.

In Germany, a large section of the political class was critical of military intervention in Iraq in 2003 (Harnisch 2004). Scholars who found critical Iraq War coverage in Germany (e.g. Krüger 2003; Szukala 2003) did not assess the implications of the fact that performance actually related to elite discontent. But as Eilders (2005: 642) states, the 'critical attitude of the German media' reflected 'a mechanism referred to as the "indexing theory"' and not 'a sudden spread of pacifism in Germany'. Thus, if Iraq War criticism was 'indexed' from elite circles it was likely procedural expressing discontent with Bush's unilateral policies. Such a finding would lend support to a hegemonic model.

By February 2004, Germany had realigned with the US when then-Foreign Minister Joschka Fischer, at the Munich Security Conference, 'called for a new transatlantic Middle East initiative structured around NATO, thereby embracing the US position that the status quo in the region entails a security risk' (Harnisch 2004: 22).[8] In further accord with 'indexing', such policy changes could explain a shift in coverage to more sympathetic reporting during the occupation. Indeed, the German media has applied the 'indexing' norm quite consistently: an earlier study by Eilders and Lüter (2000: 426) found that the German press closely followed political elite discourses during the 1999 Kosovo war thus legitimising the first German military intervention since the Second World War. Moreover, other studies on German media coverage of the 1991 Gulf War and the Kosovo war, during which military actions had elite support, found that coverage was also supportive to the war efforts (Eilders 2005: 639–640; see also Krüger 2013 for an assessment of the connections between the media and powerful in Germany).

Considering the world-system approach, it seems plausible to assume that the differences of US, UK and German press coverage within the tactical sphere express elite diversions about when and in whose interest resource rich areas are to be subdued. Indeed, the European Union (EU) has started to pursue a strategy in the Middle East, which challenges 'America's monopoly in regional arbitration' (Brzezinski 2003/2004). Moreover, European and British oil companies were concerned about unilateral US policies towards Iraq (Sampson 2002: 17).

On the other hand, consensual aspects of coverage suggest the existence of shared elite aims, for example the general acceptance of the necessity to subordinate resource-rich regions.

In conclusion it can be added to the propaganda model's predictions that the distinctness of media propaganda in coverage of different countries is dependent on the factors outlined in this section.

$$\cdot\ 4\ \cdot$$

METHOD OF RESEARCH AND CASE SELECTION

Content analysis

There has been disagreement among researchers over how news media performance should be classified because such assessments depend on contested models of bias and individual scholarly judgements (see Bennett 1990: 103–104; Herman 1986: 171–172). Herman (1986: 175), therefore, suggests applying a method which compares news media's 'treatment of similar events which differ primarily in their political implications'. Such an approach, as Herman (*ibid*: 179) further writes, avoids normative ambiguities because its focus on 'pairing, [provides] a basis for the evaluation of objectivity and bias without resort to the explanations and rationalisations of the participants [i.e. the researchers]'.[1] Methodologically, it is further useful to conduct comparative case studies in order to enhance the validity of content analysis.[2] Findings suggesting different news media treatment of comparable events constitute powerful evidence for double standards in news reporting because the news media is supposed to report on events in an 'objective' and balanced way.

In their comparative analyses, Herman and Chomsky studied quantitative and qualitative representations of human rights violations conducted by 'enemy/non-allied' and 'allied' states in order to measure how events, which primarily differed in their political implications, were reported by the news media (see 2008: 37–40). Herman and Chomsky placed news media content in three categories: indignation, details of slaughter and responsibility. Herman and Chomsky's (*ibid*: 34) predicted that 'the extent and character of attention' given to each of the outlined categories differs significantly if 'enemy/non-allied' and 'allied' states engage in relatively similar human rights violations.

This content analysis, therefore, uses the outlined content categories to compare coverage of six different incidents, involving human rights violations by 'enemy/non-allied' and 'allied' states. Building on Herman and Chomsky's work, the categories mentioned above were refined and detailed coding definitions were elaborated. The content categories are outlined below.

1) Indignation

Indignation refers to aspects of coverage that carry resentments or calls for actions against perpetrators of possible crimes and human rights violations. Indignation was divided into four sub-categories which included (1) direct references of outrage, (2) demand for, discussion or consideration of investigations or inquiries as well as court proceedings, (3) demand for, discussion or consideration of sanctions (in a broad sense) including political sanctions, policies by outside states to put pressure on a target country as well as demand for, discussion or consideration of regime change, and (4) demand for, discussion or consideration of military intervention including use of air and/or ground forces, establishment of no-fly zones and or humanitarian corridors, and/or the support of militant anti-regime forces.

2) Details of slaughter

Details of slaughter refers to humanising elements of victims of violence. Details include any reference with literal, attributive or evaluative descriptions of civilian casualties and/or suffering.

3) Responsibility

Finally, responsibility refers to assignments of guilt and criminal liability. This category includes any direct allegation that someone might be or is responsible for a (possible) crime.

Coding

Each category was consecutively examined in sentences or paragraphs of news, editorial and commentary items. If one categorical attribute was found, an article was coded in the relevant category. Hence, the unit of analysis was the article. Only the indignation category was quantified.[3] All categories were subjected to qualitative content analysis. A total of 1,911 items were coded.

Qualitative coding

For the coding, I relied on a procedure established by Altheide (1996) who blends 'the traditional notion of *objective content analysis* with *participant observation* to form *ethnographic content analysis* [all emphasis in the original]'. Ethnographic content analysis (ECA) refers to the researcher's approach of interacting with multiple documents (*ibid*) and is a specific way of structuring the research process.

ECA uses a research protocol to identify 'questions, items, categories, or variables' in order to structure the data collection process (*ibid*: 26). ECA, therefore, relies on 'qualitative' categories that include 'text, narrative and descriptions' and can additionally incorporate 'quantitative' categories that count certain attributes of the text (*ibid*: 27). That is why ECA is suitable to be used in conjunction with quantitative procedures if content analysis.

This method was chosen because the protocol approach enables the researcher to systematically structure and analyse the data using word documents or PDFs of news items as protocols. I used Word documents for an initial study of all the items on the Fallujah 1 and 2 as well as Račak cases (the discussion of the case selection follows further below). For the other cases I annotated the PDF of each news items. The protocol approach was suitable for propaganda analysis to identify content pattern as well as punctual specifics.

ECA aims at 'capturing definitions, meanings, process, and types' (*ibid*: 26–27). In contrast to quantitative content analysis, ECA is recursive and reflexive. A researcher is engaged in an interactive process, constantly comparing and contrasting data (*ibid*: 16–17). The circular research process puts emphasis on validity, discovery and verification at the expense of reliability because the categories of the protocol allow for the inclusion of descriptive data and are less precise and strict than those in quantitative content analysis (*ibid*: 15, 27). Nevertheless, rereading (every data set was at least coded twice, at different points in time) and correcting of codes resemble stability testing, which enhances reliability (see Krippendorff 1980: 130).

When conducting ECA, each news item has its own protocol sheet or an annotated PDF of a news item (Altheide 1996: 28). At the start of the research, the initial research problem should be covered by the chosen categories. During the research process, the categories can be adjusted or changed; new categories are allowed to emerge (*ibid*: 16, 27). This study rested on already pre-determined content categories that were not adjusted during the research. The protocol approach allows for a 'reflective segment' or space enabling the researcher to indicate how an article differs from previously researched items (*ibid*: 27). At a later stage of the research, the data within each category is compared to identify similarities and differences in order to establish typical and extreme cases (*ibid*: 41). These types or clusters can then be displayed in case study analysis (*ibid*: 42). Furthermore, the structured codifying of data allows the researcher to grasp the general thrust of coverage and also to identify important specifics.

More generally, ECA can be used with a specific 'theoretical focus' (*ibid*: 44). Hence, the categories were theorised and adopted in accord with my framework and the content indicators described above. Because ECA is 'orientated to documenting and understanding the communication of meaning, as well as verifying theoretical relationships' (*ibid*: 16) it is suitable for my research purpose.

To further assess quantitative differences between cases the number of articles identified for a relevant category was related to the overall amount of deaths per theatre and the baseline coverage (see generally Chomsky 1989: 151–153; Herman and Peterson 2010: 35).

It should be noted that the quantitative assessment of coverage was used to establish the general thrust of coverage. This analysis was complemented by a detailed qualitative analysis of the different topical clusters that were identified for each category. Because of the large amount of data that was assessed, drawing on the full text of 1,911 items (including news, editorials and comments), I focused on displaying the overall tenor of coverage in the international press. This was conducted at the expense of a more detailed analysis of the specifics of national news coverage. I was more interested in exploring the striking similarities of US, UK and German coverage rather than the differences. Notwithstanding, I highlighted deviating examples of coverage in order to account for extremes in coverage.

Framing

The study was underpinned by a framing analysis. There is a large body of literature on framing and the various approaches that have been applied can differ considerably (see Entman 1993, 2004).[4] Framing analysis broadly assesses how causal, treatment, and/or moral categories in regard to issues, events and/ or actors are featured in coverage (see Entman 1993, 2004: 5, 24; Hammond 2007: 17–19; Iyengar and Simon 1994: 171). Moreover, framing confines media content by setting boundaries. Accordingly, Entman (2004: 5), defined framing as '*selecting and highlighting some facets of events or issues, and making connections among them so as to promote a particular interpretation, evaluation, and/or solution* [emphasis in the original]'. Hammond adds (2007: 19):

> In order to appreciate the significance of how a particular event was framed, it is important to consider the range of other possible interpretations: both those which were available at the time and those which have become established since.

Framing analysis should rely on quantitative and qualitative analyses (see Hammond 2007: 17). The former sheds light on the 'extent and persistence of a given frame' whereas the latter enables a holistic analysis by identifying nuances and contradictions within the text, which can consist of differing frames (*ibid*).

According to Entman (1993: 52), in media texts frames 'are manifested by the presence or absence of certain keywords, stock phrases, stereotyped images, sources of information, and sentences that provide thematically reinforcing clusters of facts or judgments [sic]'. Hence, the quantitative assessment uses words as the unit of analysis and counts the keywords applied to classify/ describe the different incidents under study (for a discussion of the case selection of the incidents see further below).

It is assumed 'that the most frequently appearing words reflect the greatest concerns' (Weber 1990: 51). However, to ensure the validity of keyword analysis it has to be considered that a word can have different meanings and can be placed in various contexts (*ibid*: 51–52). That is why this content analysis was underpinned by a qualitative study. Moreover, keywords were counted together with a close reading of every newspaper item. This helped in considering the contexts in which words were placed and thus strengthened the validity of the study. In a second step, manual counting was used to exclude instances that were invalid. For example, keywords used to describe other events but which would have been counted by a database search could be excluded.

During the keyword analysis, every reference to the main incident under study was counted. References to aspects or facets of the incidents were not counted. For the framing analysis, the words were categorised as either martial (i.e. military-linked) or atrocious (i.e. atrocity-linked). Words were placed in the former category when they indicated that the incident constituted a military endeavour. Words were placed in the latter category when they indicated that the incident constituted an atrocity. Generally, martial descriptions included words such as operation, offensive, battle, assault, invasion, siege, attack, fighting, etc; atrocious descriptions included words such as carnage, massacre, atrocity, war crime, collective punishment, crackdown, bloodbath, genocide, devastation, violent attack, bloody assault, pyrrhic victory, etc. Together with the qualitative content study, this analysis helped to identify whether the incidents were framed as martial or atrocious and whether this was accurate in light of the factual record. There are some validity and reliability limitations to this kind of analysis: keywords are small units of the text and keyword analysis thus needs to be underpinned by a more holistic qualitative study. Moreover, it can be difficult to identify to which incidents certain descriptions may apply. This is the case when news reporting assesses a range of events that unfold during the same time and it may lead to counting errors. In order to mitigate these shortfalls, news items were re-read and keywords re-classified, if necessary.

Case selection

This study investigates six incidents when military and/or security forces conducted human rights violations. They include three cases in which 'enemy/non-allied' and three cases in which 'allied' countries were engaged in relatively similar human rights violations arising from the use of military and/or police force. Human rights violations were primarily determined on the basis of civilian deaths per theatre, as documented by human rights organisations and governmental/non-governmental reports. The right to be free from extrajudicial execution can be regarded as a basic human right (see Risse and Sikkink 1999: 2). Civilian deaths thus constitute important indicators for human rights violations. Secondly, reports by human rights organisations and other bodies as well as academic studies were considered in order to assess the context of human rights violations. In the findings section, such reports were used to further substantiate the factual record of each case.

The following list provides an overview of the selected cases. The list headlines show the countries that were designated as the perpetrators of human rights violations as well as their status as 'enemy/non-allied' or 'allied' states. Moreover, the headlines depict the municipal location of the incident, which was also used as its label. Additionally, the headlines include a date that refers to the start of the study period. This date was usually congruent with the unfolding of the incident. Finally, the headlines display the amount of civilian deaths per incident as well as the civilian and combatant casualties per nationwide theatre in order to indicate the overall level of violence in a given conflict. Under the headlines, the context of the incidents is briefly documented. A more detailed elaboration of the context of human rights violations for each case and further sources of the respective casualty figures is provided in Chapter 5.

I: 'Enemy/non-allied':
1) Federal Republic of Yugoslavia ('enemy/non-allied'): Račak incident, Kosovo, 15/01/1999
Civilian deaths per theatre: 45, nationwide deaths: 2,000

The Račak incident refers to a police/military operation conducted by Serbian forces in the Kosovo-Albanian village Račak on 15 January 1999. The event occurred during the 1998/1999 Kosovo War between the Federal Republic of Yugoslavia (FRY/Serbia), consisting of Serbia and Montenegro, and Kosovo Albanian separatists. Kosovo was a province inhabited by an Albanian Muslim majority (about 90 per cent of the population) and a Serbian Christian Orthodox minority (about several hundred thousand people) (see Mandel 2005: 114). The conflict proceeded between the priorities of the Kosovo Albanian's drive for independence and FRY/Serbian claims to uphold the status quo. Being in the large majority, the Kosovo Albanians aspired for statehood. On the other hand, Kosovo was part of the FRY/Serbia, its historical, cultural and religious heritage was important for the Serbs. Furthermore, Kosovo was rich in resources with the Trepča mines a major source of export revenue for the FRY (*ibid*: 114–115). Violence in Kosovo escalated when the Albanian independent movement started a militant uprising, which was spearheaded by the Kosovo Liberation Army (KLA). In February 1998, an Albanian insurgency triggered the Kosovo War and this event culminated in a NATO military intervention in March 1999 (*ibid*: 116–117). During the Kosovo War, between March 1998 and March 1999, about 2,000 people were killed with an equal distribution among Serbian and Kosovo Albanian victims (*ibid*: 116, see also Chapter 5 for further discussion). On 15 January 1999, FRY/Serbian forces attacked the Kosovo Albanian village Račak. The operation was officially conducted against Račak and three further villages in order to detect a KLA group that had killed four Serbian police (*ibid*: 120). Later, during the trial of Slobodan Milošević, former President of the Federal Republic of Yugoslavia, it was confirmed by the Organisation for Security and Co-Operation in Europe (OSCE) observers, who were monitoring Račak at the time, that KLA fighters were killed during the police operation (*ibid*: 120, 387).[5] During the Račak incident, 45 people were killed (see *ibid*: 119; see also Herman and Peterson 2010: 95).

2) Libya ('enemy/non-allied'): First Benghazi incident, Libya, 17/02/2011
Civilian deaths per theatre: 228, nationwide deaths: 500–700

The first Benghazi incident refers to the attempt by Libyan security forces to quell a militant uprising in the city. Clashes between Libyan forces and protestors took place in Benghazi on 17 February 2011 and lasted for several days. On 15 February, the uprising had initially erupted in Benghazi and further cities in Eastern Libya where protestors and rebels aimed to topple the regime of Muammar al-Gaddafi. The rebellion then further spread to other areas of the country, including Libya's capital Tripoli. It is estimated that between 500 and 700 people were killed across Libya during February 2011 (ICC 2011: 4).[6] In March 2011, a medical committee from Benghazi estimated that 228 residents were killed in Benghazi alone (Kuperman 2013: 119; see also AP 2013). Also in March 2011, NATO led a military intervention with the official aim to establish a no-fly zone and stop human rights violations in Libya.

3) Syria ('enemy/non-allied'): Houla incident, Syria, 25/05/2012
Civilian deaths per theatre: 116, nationwide deaths: 6,000–15,000

The Houla incident refers to the killing of about 116 civilians in the Syrian village of Taldou, which is located in the Houla region in western Homs. The Syrian civil war had erupted in 2011. The conflict placed the Syrian Armed Forces, headed by President Bashar al-Assad, against an amorphous collection of insurgent groups that had largely united under the banner of the Free Syrian Army (FSA). The Houla incident took place on 25 May 2012, at the same time when clashes between the Syrian Armed Forces and the FSA had occurred in the region. Overall, between 6,000 and 15,000 people were killed during the Syrian civil war until May 2012, depending on estimates (see Khera 2012). In March 2012, the UN had estimated that more than 8,000 people had been killed in the conflict (see CBS/AP 2012). According to Khera (2012) 'as of 29 May, the Syrian Observatory for Human Rights had put the number of civilian dead at 9,183, with 3,821 dead from the security forces.'

II: 'Allied':
1) US ('allied'): First Fallujah incident, Iraq, 06/04/2004
Civilian deaths per theatre: 600, nationwide deaths: 6,990–55,000

The first Fallujah incident refers to the attempt by US/Coalition forces to crush the Iraqi resistance movement, which had its base in the city.[7] A several weeks long military operation started on 5 April 2004, about one year after US President George W. Bush had proclaimed the end of the Iraq War at a speech on the aircraft carrier USS Abraham Lincoln. The US/Coalition halted the operation on 29 April because civilian deaths had provoked widespread outrage among the Iraqi populace. Moreover, the Iraqi political elite, which had collaborated with US/Coalition authorities, threatened to abandon its assistance. The Fallujah incident took place in the context of extensive US 'counter-insurgency' operations conducted against Sunni and Shiite resistance forces throughout Iraq in 2004. It is estimated that about 600 Iraqi civilians were killed during the incident (IBC 2004b). According to passive surveillance data by Iraq Body Count (IBC), which provides a conservative estimate, 14,007 Civilians were killed in Iraq between 20 March 2003 and 19 March 2004 (IBC 2013). If the period after the invasion phase from May 2003 to March 2004 is considered, still 6,990 civilians were killed in Iraq (see IBC n.d. for the IBC database). A passive survey by Medact (2003: 1) estimated between 22,000 and 55,000 civilian and combatant deaths by October 2003.

2) US ('allied'): Second Fallujah incident, Iraq, 07/11/2004
Civilian deaths per theatre: 800–6,000, nationwide deaths: 13,644–98,000

The second Fallujah incident refers to the attempt by US/Coalition forces to crush the Iraqi resistance movement for the second time. On 8 November 2004, US/Coalition forces launched a military operation in Fallujah that lasted for about one week and is considered to be the largest military operation during the occupation phase. Some 15,000 US/Coalition soldiers (10,000 of which comprised the attacking force) took part in the overall operation which had been planned since early September and which the US named 'Operation Phantom Fury' (Camp 2009: 123, 131, 169; US Department of Defence 2004). The battle plan provided a frontal attack with six battalions entering Fallujah from the north then pushing southwards on a three mile line accompanied by tank platoons as well as artillery and air support (Camp 2009: 128; West 2005: 268).[8] Various estimates by doctors and human rights organisations suggest that between 800 to 6,000 civilians were killed in Fallujah (see Jamail 2004a, b; Marqusee 2005). If we look at the period after the invasion phase from May 2003 to October 2004, IBC estimated that 13,644 civilians were killed in Iraq during that time (see IBC n.d. for the IBC database). It might be worth mentioning that this conservative assessment puts civilian deaths in Iraq on a higher level than during a similar period in Syria. Moreover, assessments based on the use of sample surveys find significantly higher numbers in Iraq. The British medicine journal *The Lancet* estimated 98,000 excess deaths in Iraq between 19 March 2003 and mid-September 2004 (Roberts *et al.* 2004: 1857).

3) Egypt ('allied') First Egyptian raid/Cairo incident, Cairo, Egypt, 08/07/2013
Civilian deaths per theatre: 51, nationwide deaths: +1,000

The first Egyptian raid incident refers to a military and police operation conducted by Egyptian security forces and the military in Eastern Cairo, Egypt, on 8 July 2013. Egyptian security forces attempted to quell protest gatherings by Muslim Brotherhood supporters. During the incident, 51 protestors were killed (Human Rights Watch 2013). Protests by the Muslim Brotherhood increased after the military overthrew Mohamed Morsi of the Muslim Brotherhood, the first democratically elected President of Egypt, on 3 July 2013. Egypt's security and military forces were led by General Abd al-Fatah as-Sisi, who would later become president of Egypt after dubious elections held in May 2014. The Cairo incident took place in the context of wider clashes between protestors and security forces that had occurred in Egypt since the emergence of the so called 'Egyptian Revolution' of 2011. In the early phase of the revolution, about 846 people were killed in Egypt and investigations suggests that Egyptian security forces had used 'excessive' force (AP cited in BBC News 2011). Further evidence for civilian deaths during clashes with security and/or military forces in 2011, 2012 and 2013 (until 8 July) is scattered. Between October and November 2011, about 96 protestors were killed (Amnesty International 2012a: 136). During several events in 2012, about 99 people were killed (Amnesty International 2013: 87). In January and February 2013 about 60 people were killed (BBC News 2013). It is further estimated, that 117 people were killed between 23 June and 8 July 2013 (Chalabi 2013).

Rationale for case selection

For the case selection it is important that in each incident, military and/or police tactics involved the use of indiscriminate force against adversaries embedded in populated areas leading to civilian deaths. Entman, who applied a comparative approach in one of his studies, argues that comparing cases does not require that they are 'analogous to a fine degree' (2004: 30). Rather, each event should be regarded as a complex case open to differing interpretations (see *ibid*). In fact, the incidents described above are still contested in the literature and different narratives exist in relation to certain facets of each incident. Nonetheless, there is no ethical reason why the news media should apply different standards when reporting on civilian deaths in the outlined incidents, if such occurrences accrued from the use of indiscriminate force (see Chapter 5 for further evidence in this regard). In further agreement with Entman, it could thus be argued that in the light of the available evidence, 'there is no way to establish as a factual matter' that the perpetrators of certain human rights violations are 'less morally responsible' for the fate of civilians than the perpetrators of other, similar human rights violations (*ibid*).

Notwithstanding, to strengthen the design of the study, the chosen incidents of human rights violations conducted by 'allied' states in Fallujah and Iraq include higher levels of civilian deaths than those of 'enemy/non-allied' actors. It should be further noted that the calculation of civilian deaths relies on conservative estimates by mainstream organisations. Even under consideration of such data, the body counts in Fallujah/Iraq were the highest. This case selection should thus provide a strong test for a critical hypothesis that expects atrocities in 'enemy/non-allied' states to be featured more prominently in the news media.

There are some further details that are of interest in relation to the case selections: Two of the cases (Račak, Benghazi) were chosen because they incited 'humanitarian interventions' in accord with R2P. One case (Houla) was chosen because it was regarded as a threshold event, which evoked extensive discussions about intervention and related policies without actually leading to a large-scale military intervention. All three cases relating to 'enemy/non-allied' states were major incident featured prominently on the news agenda and in official political discussions. The US cases (Fallujah 1+2) were chosen because they included the most comprehensive military operations during the occupation of Iraq and can be regarded as major human rights issue due to their impact on civilians. News media coverage about both cases was extensive and the incidents occurred at a time when the US/Coalition occupation was the subject of bi-partisan political discussions about the Iraq occupation regime in the US and UK. The Egyptian case (first Egyptian raid/ Cairo incident) was chosen because, like the US cases, it constituted a major human rights issue and fell within a time frame during which R2P had been discussed in relation to Libya and Syria.

Research period

The content studies survey the first two weeks after each incident unfolded. A two-week period incorporates the significant peak coverage (Esser, Schwabe and Wilke 2005: 320; Mermin 1999: 42) and is sufficiently long to feature critical perspectives that might develop later (Mermin 1999: 42).

Population: the US, UK and German national press

The study compares US, UK and German national elite press news coverage. Comparative, international research grounded in content analysis is considered to be an important research area (see Alexseev and Bennett 1995: 396) and such studies are desiderata in the field (Hallin and Mancini 2010: 103–104; Löffelholz 2004: 38, 54). As Hallin and Mancini (2010: 104) write: 'Most of the literature on the media is highly ethnocentric, in the sense that it refers only to the experience of a single country, yet it is written in general terms, as though the model that prevailed in that country were universal.' This research contributes to filling this gap by expanding the scope to three countries.

For practical reasons, the work provides an assessment of national newspaper reporting. The amount of data did not warrant an additional evaluation of television or online coverage. Despite the societal importance of television and online news, there are compelling reasons for studying newspaper coverage of the national elite press: Such a design is in line with a 'best-case approach' which assesses the most critical news media in society that are regarded as having 'large foreign news staffs, high prestige and sophistication, and a record of willingness to take on the government' (Entman 2004: 77). A best-case approach limits the sample to those news media that are expected to carry the most extensive and comprehensive coverage in society. These usually include the major agenda-setting elite media: the newspapers of record and the liberal press. Hence, while findings of such a study are limited, they can still be regarded as an indicator for the general performance of a media system. In fact, while such a kind of newspaper analysis will not provide insight about television, online or 'conservative-right' discourses, it can provide crucial findings about the nature of mainstream discourse and the boundaries of acceptable debate in mainstream intellectual culture.[9] This stems from the fact that the national elite press constitutes an inter-media agenda-setter and its total news output approximates the political spectrum of information in society (see Eilders 2002: 29; Herman and Chomsky 2009: 16; Tunstall 1996: 1). Consequently, an analysis of national press news coverage is indicative of news coverage as a whole. It can thus be assumed that perspectives not featured in the national elite press will also be absent from television and mainstream online news. That is why, despite the larger societal penetration and trustworthiness of television news among audiences as well as the increasing importance of online news, it still makes sense to focus on the national elite press.

For this study it is finally important that the national elite press is largely read by professionals occupying those positions in society that enable them to manage economic, political and/or educational affairs – the professional elites, who constitute the main target of propaganda.

The US sample

The content analysis investigates coverage in the *New York Times* and *Washington Post*. Both constitute the leading agenda-setting news media in the US and can be regarded as the newspapers most widely read by American elites (Friel and Falk 2007a: 2; Gans 1980: 180; Mermin 1999: 12–13; Sparrow 1999: 22).[10] Furthermore, the significance of the *New York Times* should be highlighted: According to Howard Friel and Richard Falk (2007a: 2), the *Times* inherits 'an exalted place in the political and moral imagination of influential Americans and others as the most authoritative source of information' which 'has acquired its special status as the newspaper of record in the United States'.

The UK sample

The UK sample features the national newspapers the *Guardian*, the *Independent*, *The Times*, and the *Daily Telegraph* as well as their respective Sunday papers the *Observer*, the *Independent on Sunday*, the *Sunday Times* and the *Sunday Telegraph*. These newspapers are part of 'the "top end" of British journalism' (Lewis *et al.* 2008: 3) and arguably constitute the major agenda-setting news media in the UK whose main target audiences are the professional elites (Tunstall 1996: 9; also Keeble 2009: 57; Sparks 1999).

The German sample

The German sample includes the five so-called 'German national prestige newspapers' who are regarded as representative for the full political spectrum in Germany (Eilders 1999: 304, 308; Eilders and Lüter 2000: 418). They include, on the very left-hand side, the *tageszeitung* and, on the opposite right-hand side, *Die Welt*. Between them, located from left to right, are the *Frankfurter Rundschau, Süddeutsche Zeitung*, and *Frankfurter Allgemeine Zeitung* (Eilders 1999: 304). These newspapers are regarded as inter-media agenda-setters (Pohr 2005: 267). They are the newspapers most widely read by German journalists and have the widest distribution among German national quality papers. While the *Süddeutsche Zeitung* ('left-liberal') and *Frankfurter Allgemeine Zeitung* ('conservative') differ in their political slant both focus on foreign news coverage (Meyn 2001: 105; Weischenberg, Malik and Scholl 2006).

Data selection

The content studies apply a full-text analysis of a total of 1,911 newspaper items (news, editorial and commentaries). For this study, all items that included at least one paragraph relating to the chosen incidents were selected. Items that focused on other issues than the chosen incident or conflict, but mentioned the incident in passing, were excluded. Items which mainly dealt with other facets of a main conflict but also mention the incident were kept as part of the sample.

To obtain all relevant items, digital databases were approached. All US newspaper items were downloaded from the *Factiva* database. The British newspaper items were downloaded from the *Factiva or LexisNexis* databases with exception of the *Telegraph's* items on the Račak incident which were bought as hard copies from the British Library archive in Colindale, London. The German newspaper items were downloaded from the *Factiva* database with the only exception of the *Frankfurter Allgemeine Zeitung* whose articles were bought and downloaded from the newspaper's digital archive. Most newspaper items were stored as PDFs.

Because digital databases can be incomplete, several measures were employed to ensure that all relevant newspaper articles were obtained. Some of the Anglo-American newspapers were cross-searched by using the *LexisNexis* and *Factiva* databases. Articles missing in one database were added from the other.

With regard to the German press, it turned out that the *Factiva* database was incomplete. Therefore, access to all newspaper online archives was bought and missing items were obtained assuming that the databases of the newspapers are complete.

In the *Factiva* database, double and triple versions of some items existed depending on whether newspapers publish regional or other editions. Because the editions were not specified in all cases I had to choose between different versions of the same article. Sometimes, the texts of these versions differed slightly as well.

At times, the original page numbers of the newspaper articles were not clearly labelled on the items from the databases. The author tried to verify the page numbers via online and database searches but this was not always possible. That is why some of the page numbers may not be accurate.

Finally, it should be noted that all cited German newspaper items and secondary references were translated by the author.

· 5 ·

THE POLITICS OF INTERVENTION

Selective intervention

If dominant Western[1] elite interests favour intervention – whether through military or other means – then this will be communicated through the news media. In contemporary affairs, the threshold for intervention in 'enemy' countries is low. Military interventions may be advocated through the news media by policy makers, human rights practitioners and journalists, even if evidence about human rights violations is murky and the responsibility of perpetrators is far from clear. The Western news media allows for ad-hoc vilification of states, which have been designated as nefarious. The news reporting model works as follows: campaigns of shaming are facilitated by Western government spokespersons and pro-Western interest groups. 'Facts' and supporting data are initially manufactured on the basis of hearsay or unsubstantiated evidence. Once a dominant narrative is established, perspectives that serve this party line receive dominant attention in the news media. Counter facts that question the party line or cast doubt about specific facets of events or actions allegedly conducted by 'enemy' states tend to be marginalised.

During this process, the news media prominently carries calls for actions against the designated target countries. These statements include emotional outbursts that may incite wider public indignation. More importantly, the news media provides a platform for the deliberation about policies including investigations, criminal proceedings, diplomatic actions, sanctions and military means. These measures are largely raised and implemented with reference to 'enemy' states. If Western states and their 'allies' conduct human rights violations that are similar or in excess of those conducted by 'enemy' countries, then this model does not apply. This dichotomised treatment of events, actors and actions accrues from the fact that the news media over-emphasises the public discussions by Western governments and their aides. The news media thus provides a relatively accurate picture of the deliberations by Western governments and their supporters who comprise the 'international community'.

However, the government nexus operates like a filter advantaging facts, perspectives and events whose transmission has utility for domestic power centres. This is also true for the international sphere of governance. The UN has been dominated by Western powers and their allies who have the ability to implement policies that target their adversaries. Nonetheless, a careful reading of the news also reveals a range of alternative perspectives that tend to be relegated to secondary spaces. These facts may be included in the news media because they stem from statements by dissidents and/or foreign policy makers. For instance, domestic political elite disagreements or deliberations at the UN level are prominently featured in the news media. Counter perspectives raised by powerful domestic actors or non-Western countries will be taken into account. At times, Russia and China may block Western policy initiatives and this will be reported in the news media. Moreover, journalistic professionalism allows for some leeway to publish alternative evidence. Overall, though, a dominant perspective emerges in the news. The outlined dynamics will be demonstrated on the basis of the following case studies.

Indignation and dichotomised news media campaigns

Herman and Chomsky (2008: 34) argued that a

> propaganda system will consistently portray people abused in enemy states as *worthy* victims, whereas those treated with equal or greater severity by its own government or clients will be *unworthy*. The evidence of worth may be read from the extent and character of attention and indignation. [emphasis in the original]

Accordingly, indignation constitutes the news media content category that was used to analyse the politics of intervention. If states conduct human rights violations, the news media produces a range of indignant statements. To follow but also refine the approach by Herman and Chomsky, indignant statements were further elaborated and differentiated in terms of their character. Therefore, indignation was separated into the following character dimensions:

1) Military policy
2) Sanctions or other actions/policies
3) Investigation and/or criminal proceedings
4) Outrage, concern and mourning

Indignant statements may be produced by the news organisation's journalists or by sources that are referenced in news items. Because indignant statements are reactive to human rights violations they either convey indignation in the literal sense of the term and with reference to category (4) or they entail calls for specific actions to end the violence in the sense of categories (1), (2) and (3). Indignation may also refer to the discussion of policies that are already implemented. For instance, in the case of Syria, the Annan peace plan (see also the discussion in the section on Syria below) specified certain rules of behaviour for the Syrian government. If the news media discussed these policies in relation to the actions of the Syrian government and its forces, they were coded as indignation 2. It is important to note that the ability to enforce measures like UN sanctions or peace plans on other countries is crucially dependent on power struggles that take place on the international level. Generally, such policies may be warranted and important. However, indignant policies are applied and reported in a highly selective fashion that is independent of the magnitude of actual human rights violations. Furthermore, ad-hoc inflation of human rights violations may lead to the implementation of policies that are inappropriate and/or unjustified. The aim of this study is to reveal this double standard in foreign policy making and news media coverage.

This chapter firstly discusses quantitative findings of content studies to account for the extent, attention and character relegated to indignation. Secondly, I will review qualitative findings of content studies to further investigate the properties of indignation in relation to the context of the chosen cases.

Selective shaming: quantitative evidence (I)

Table 1 below shows the quantity of news items carrying indignation in US, UK and German national press coverage of the six cases under review. The first three entries show coverage given to civilian victims killed by 'enemy' countries: (1) the FRY/Serbia (Račak), (2) Libya (Benghazi) and (3) Syria (Houla). The further three entries show coverage given to civilian victims killed by 'allied' countries: (4) the US/Coalition in Iraq (Fallujah 1), (5) the US/Coalition in Iraq (Fallujah 2) and (6) Egypt (Cairo).

Each case study heading depicts the name of the incident and theatre as well as the casualty estimates for the incident and theatre as derived from mainstream sources.[2] Row 1, under each case study heading, depicts the amount of items produced per newspaper on the case (N Articles). Row 2 depicts the amount of items that carried indignant statements (N Indignation). Rows 3–6 specify the character of indignant statements (Military policy, Sanctions, Investigation, and/or Outrage). Rows 3–6 allow for multiple mentions. This means that if one news item carried two indignant statements that matched different categories of indignation, they were both counted. For instance, if a news item carried one indignant statement that fit in the 'Military policy' category and a second indignant statement that fit in the 'Outrage' category both were included respectively in rows 3 and 6. However, in the overall indignation category (N Indignation) only one entry was codified.

As is evident from the data displayed in Table 1, the coverage on 'enemy' countries displays remarkably different quantitative reporting pattern in comparison to coverage on 'allied' countries. And this remains consistent for all newspapers under review independent of their national affiliation.

Firstly, the intensity of indignation differed sharply. Consider the ratio of N Articles/N Indignation: In reporting on 'enemy' countries, the amount of items that carried indignation was far higher in relation to the total amount of published articles. In reporting on 'allied' countries, on the other hand, the amount of items that carried indignation was much lower in this regard (with some exceptions to be further discussed below). This means that indignation in coverage on 'enemy' countries was published repetitive and in a sustained fashion. Indignation in coverage on 'allied' countries was published intermittently and rather scattered. The reading of news items further indicated that a similar pattern was reproduced on the level of individual news items. Thus, in reporting on 'enemy' countries, news items included a larger amount of indignant statements than news items on 'allied' countries (this finding is based on the author's reading and was not quantified).

Secondly, quantitative findings on the character of indignation differed remarkably. Only in coverage on 'enemy' countries did the press carry statements relating to Military policy. Similarly, Sanctions policies were more often included in indignant items if newspapers reported on the actions of 'enemy' countries. This finding is of further importance: indignant statements that included deliberations about Military policy and/or Sanctions would produce, if translated into actual policy, significant effects on the target countries. And none of the items included in Table 1 substantially questioned Military or Sanctions policies. Hence, when including discourses about Military or Sanctions policies, the press operated as a facilitator for intervention in 'enemy' countries. This does not mean that the newspapers were uncritical. At times, indignant statements entailed procedural criticisms of the policy measure. For instance, in the Syrian case, military intervention was not favoured by the US President Obama administration and thus many of the indignant statements questioned military intervention on tactical grounds. However, this finding additionally demonstrates that the news media is highly attentive to political elite discourses and not intrinsically a conveyor of peaceful measures.

It should be further noted that the Sanctions category included a range of policies that differed on a qualitative level. For example, in reporting on 'enemy' countries, Sanctions included punitive measures like economic sanctions, the expulsion of ambassadors or regime change. In the case of 'allied' states, Sanctions included rather benign measures such as considerations about the revocation of financial aid or demands to cease military actions. This means that even in cases when Sanctions were discussed in relation to 'allied' countries such as Egypt, the actual quality of the policies differed substantially if compared to 'enemy' countries.

Overall, 'enemy' countries also tended to receive more indignant items that carried statements in the Investigation and/or Outrage categories (with some exceptions to be further discussed below). However, the Fallujah 2 and Cairo incidents carried a large amount of statements in relation to deliberations about investigations. In fact, Fallujah 2 and Cairo carried more indignant statements in these categories than some of the 'enemy' cases. For instance, the *New York Times* included more statements carrying discussions about investigations in its reporting on Fallujah 2 than in its reporting on Houla and Benghazi. Yet, as will be demonstrated in a detailed discussion in later sections of this chapter, in their reporting on Fallujah 2, the *New York Times* (and the other newspapers as well) largely focused on investigations set in motion by the US-military. Again, this was a relatively benign discourse. The military had launched its own investigation to interrogate individual soldiers for alleged abuses and this was highlighted by the press. Because this constituted an investigation conducted by the military of an 'allied' state, the proceedings were reported in a rather neutral or appreciative fashion (the same applied to reporting on an investigation by the Egyptian regime). If newspapers focused on investigations in 'enemy' countries, such statements did relate to the deliberations about independent investigations in pursuit of personnel from higher ranks who had allegedly conducted major war crimes. Furthermore, such investigations tended to be reported with greater investigatory zeal and higher levels of outrage. These examples thus also demonstrate dichotomised media reporting even though the quantitative pattern may have suggested otherwise.

It should be further noted that overall the Cairo case received a relatively high amount of items carrying statements of indignation. A qualitative discussion of this case will reveal, however, that Outrage and other forms of indignation in relation to Cairo operated on different qualitative levels than in cases featuring 'allied' countries. In fact, the newspapers rationalised and at times explained sympathetically the actions of the Egyptian military. Moreover, as will be shown, the discourse on the Cairo incident was hardly comparable with that on the Benghazi or Račak incidents.

Outrage constituted the category which was most evenly distributed across cases if the total amount of published items is considered. As a matter of fact, newspapers carried a relatively large amount of items featuring Outrage in their reporting on 'allied' countries. Yet, as already discussed above, this picture changes, if relative figures are considered. If the ratio of total articles (N Articles) versus articles carrying Indignation (N Indignation) is factored, then 'enemy' countries received more Outrage than 'allied' countries. Moreover, if the amount of civilian deaths per case and theatre were further factored then the Fallujah 1 and 2 cases received even less indignation as the number of casualties was the highest.

Finally, the data in Table 1 suggests that the US, UK and German press featured relatively similar reporting patterns. The main difference constitutes the amount of coverage. Particularly the German press tended to include a smaller number of items. Overall, the US press included the largest amount of items on Fallujah 1 + 2 as well as Cairo. The UK press included more items in their reporting on Houla and Benghazi than the US and German press. Fallujah 1 + 2 constituted operations led by the US-military and this may explain the prominence in the US news media. Moreover, the US contingent in Iraq was larger than the British one and mainly US personnel was engaged in the Fallujah operations. In regard to Cairo, it could be argued that US relations

Table 1: News items carrying indignation during two week period/dimensions of indignation as mentioned in items (multiple mentions possible).

Newspaper	NYT	WP	G	I	T	DT	FR	SZ	TAZ	FAZ	W
N Total	232	204	247	194	205	194	122	133	104	163	113
1. Račak/Kosovo (01/1999): Civilian deaths: 45/nationwide deaths: 2,000											
N Articles	24	18	25	25	18	24	16	16	12	22	15
N Indignation	20	17	23	24	16	21	14	16	12	22	12
Military policy	19	15	19	20	7	13	12	14	7	18	9
Sanctions	18	15	17	22	8	11	11	12	8	14	7
Investigation	20	9	15	19	11	13	9	7	9	14	8
Outrage	13	13	17	18	10	14	6	10	6	9	7
2. Benghazi/Libya (02–03/2011): Civilian deaths: 228/nationwide deaths: 500–700											
N Articles	35	30	63	38	49	50	23	28	22	38	18
N Indignation	24	20	39	25	36	31	14	21	17	30	14
Military policy	7	7	11	5	9	12	1	4	2	8	3
Sanctions	13	11	27	14	15	18	7	6	4	12	8
Investigation	2	5	8	1	7	7	2	2	1	6	0
Outrage	18	13	33	21	28	24	10	17	15	27	11
3. Houla/Syria (05–06/2012): Civilian deaths: 116/nationwide deaths: 6,000–15,000											
N Articles	18	23	35	31	35	29	16	15	16	19	25
N Indignation	17	22	32	28	30	28	16	15	16	18	22
Military policy	13	9	15	13	18	11	10	12	7	11	14
Sanctions	15	20	25	20	27	21	14	15	11	14	18
Investigation	6	5	10	7	10	13	5	4	7	7	3
Outrage	15	14	24	18	19	21	13	8	8	12	14
4. Fallujah 1/Iraq (04/2004): Civilian deaths: 600/nationwide deaths: 6,990–55,000											
N Articles	48	62	43	37	39	40	23	25	17	21	17
N Indignation	8	21	16	11	11	10	3	2	5	3	3
Military policy	0	0	0	0	0	0	0	0	0	0	0
Sanctions	0	1	2	1	1	0	0	0	0	1	1
Investigation	0	0	2	0	0	0	1	1	0	0	0
Outrage	8	21	15	10	11	10	2	1	5	3	2
5. Fallujah 2/Iraq (08/2004): Civilian deaths: 800–6,000/nationwide deaths: 13,644–98,000											
N Articles	82	45	52	47	45	34	25	24	20	25	19
N Indignation	25	12	22	19	12	5	12	9	10	9	6
Military policy	0	0	0	0	0	0	0	0	0	0	0
Sanctions	0	0	0	0	0	0	1	1	1	0	0
Investigation	9	2	6	6	2	1	3	4	2	2	5
Outrage	21	12	20	20	12	5	11	9	10	9	6

Newspaper	NYT	WP	G	I	T	DT	FR	SZ	TAZ	FAZ	W
6. Cairo/Egypt (07/2013): Civilian deaths: 51/nationwide deaths: +1,000											
N Articles	25	26	29	16	19	17	19	25	17	38	19
N Indignation	13	20	21	11	15	13	8	18	13	20	15
Military policy	0	0	0	0	0	0	0	0	0	0	0
Sanctions	9	14	6	6	6	7	6	10	3	12	8
Investigation	3	0	5	3	0	1	0	1	3	3	2
Outrage	7	18	15	9	14	7	5	12	13	14	11

to Egypt were exceptional and this explains the prominence of the case in the US news media. With respect to Houla and Benghazi, it could be argued that British interests have historically been more deeply involved in Syria and Libya and this might explain the greater number of articles.

In conclusion, the quantitative findings shown in Table 1 validate a propaganda model that predicts a dichotomised treatment in terms of the quantitative relegation of indignation in news media coverage of 'enemy' and 'allied' states.

The dynamics of indignant media campaigns: quantitative evidence (II)

Tables 2a and 2b depict the distribution of indignation over the two-week period of study for each case. Table 2a shows data for 'enemy' countries and Table 2b data for 'allied' countries.

Each case study heading depicts the name of the incident and theatre as well as the casualty range of the incident and theatre as derived from mainstream sources.[3] For both Tables, columns 1–14 under each case study heading show whether a newspaper carried statements including Outrage (O), Investigation (I), Sanctions (S) and/or Military policy (M). That means, for instance, if on a given day a newspaper published one item including two statements that were respectively coded as Military policy and Outrage, then the data entry for that day was (M O). Similarly, if a newspaper published the same statements in two different items on a given day than this was equally coded as (M O). Tables 2a and 2b thus indicate the range of indignant statements published per day in the specified newspaper. On a given day, newspapers could publish more than one news item including a statement that fit in a certain category. For example, on one day, a newspaper may have published three individual items each of which included one statement that was coded as Sanctions and one statement that was coded as Military policy. In such instances, the data was displayed as (S M). Thus, the table displays a conservative estimate because it does not account for mentions of the same category in multiple items per day.

A comparison of Tables 2a and 2b further reveals dichotomised news media selection choices. Only in coverage of 'enemy' countries did the press regularly feature statements about Military policy and Sanctions. In coverage of 'allied' countries, the newspapers largely relied on statements of Outrage although at times further including statements relating to Investigation and Sanctions (particularly in reporting on Cairo).

Furthermore, the tables show that in reporting on 'enemy' countries, the news media regularly covered statements in a range of categories. This finding suggests that indignant news media patterns during the shaming process of 'enemy' countries were repetitive and intense. Indeed, in coverage of 'enemy' countries, campaigns largely unfolded over several days and consistently included the full spectrum of indignant statements. News media pattern during the shaming of 'allied' countries, on the other hand, were sporadic and moderate. This means in reporting on 'allied' countries, campaigns appeared to be interrupted and largely included only one and at times two or three categories of indignation on the same day. As a consequence, news coverage on 'enemy' countries appeared to have a vigorous character. Statements about interventionist policies underpinned by outrage were frequent and high up on the news agenda. In the case of 'allied' countries, reporting was muted and did not generate similar levels even so the magnitude of human rights violations was equal or even greater.

If we look more closely at the different cases, there are some further striking findings. In reporting on Račak and Houla, news coverage quickly featured indignant statements in all categories. In the second week of reporting, the intensity and repetition would decrease. The German press tended to publish statements later than the Anglo-American newspapers and over a shorter period in time. These gaps spoke to the lower amount of coverage featured in the German press.

The Benghazi case indicated a build-up of a campaign that increasingly gained momentum. This demonstrates that the news media is able to mobilise indignation quickly. In the case of Cairo, the campaign developed in an opposite direction. Initially, coverage appeared to be intense. Then, towards the second week, the amount of indignant statements decreased in terms of frequency and intensity. This evidences that the news media rationalised the human rights abuses by 'allied' state Egypt.

Table 2a: Days when newspaper carried: Outrage (O), Investigation (I), Sanctions (S) and/or Military policy (M) ('enemy' states).

Newspaper	NYT	WP	G	I	T	DT	FR	SZ	TAZ	FAZ	W
1. Račak/Kosovo (01/1999): Civilian deaths: 45/nationwide deaths: 2,000											
Day 1	OISM	OISM	OISM	OISM	OI	OIS	–	–	–	OI	OI
Day 2	OIM	OISM	OISM	OSM	OISM	OISM	OISM	OISM	OIS	OISM	OM
Day 3	OIS	OSM	OISM	OISM	OISM	OISM	OISM	OISM	ISM	OISM	OISM
Day 4	OISM	OISM	OISM	OISM	ISM	OISM	OISM	ISM	OISM	OISM	ISM
Day 5	ISM	–	OISM	OISM	–	ISM	ISM	OISM	ISM	OISM	M
Day 6	OISM	OSM	OISM	OISM	OI	OISM	OISM	SM	OISM	ISM	–
Day 7	OISM	O	OISM	–	OISM	–	ISM	–	ISM	ISM	IS
Day 8	–	OSM	OIM	OISM	–	OISM	–	–	–	–	OISM
Day 9	OISM	–	–	–	OISM	O	–	–	–	–	–
Day 10	–	SM	–	–	–	–	–	OSM	OISM	ISM	I
Day 11	ISM	OISM	–	SM	–	I	SM	–	ISM	OISM	–
Day 12	–	OISM	–	OSM	–	–	–	M	–	–	–
Day 13	OISM	SM	OSM	OISM	O	–	OSM	OI	OI	ISM	–
Day 14	OSM	OSM	–	ISM	–	ISM	–	–	–	SM	–
2. Benghazi/Libya (02–03/2011): Civilian deaths: 228/nationwide deaths: 500–700											
Day 1	O	–	OS	O	OS	–	–	–	–	O	–
Day 2	OS	–	O	–	–	S	–	–	–	O	–
Day 3	OS	O	OS	OS	OIS	–	O	–	O	O	OS
Day 4	O	O	OS	O	O	OI	–	–	–	–	–
Day 5	O	O	OS	OS	O	OS	O	O	O	O	–
Day 6	OS	OIS	OS	OS	OI	OS	OS	OS	OS	O	O

Day 7	O	OSM	OISM	–	OSM	OM	OS	OS	–	OIS	OSM
Day 8	OISM	ISM	OISM	OSM	OSM	OSM	OS	O	OS	OIS	OS
Day 9	OS	OIS	OSM	OS	OSM	OISM	M	OM	O	OSM	OS
Day 10	OISM	OISM	OISM	OISM	OISM	OISM	O	OS	O	OISM	O
Day 11	OM	–	OISM	OS	OIS	OISM	–	–	–	OSM	–
Day 12	OSM	OISM	OISM	O	–	OISM	OIS	OISM	OIS	OISM	SM
Day 13	SM	O	SM	OSM	–	OSM	IS	M	OSM	SM	O
Day 14	OSM	OSM	–	OSM	–	–	OS	M	–	OSM	O

3. Houla/Syria (05–06/2012): Civilian deaths: 116/nationwide deaths: 6,000–15,000

Day 1	O	–	O	–	S	S	–	–	–	–	–
Day 2	OIS	OIS	OIS	OISM	OIS	OISM	–	–	–	OI	–
Day 3	OISM	OIS	OSM	OISM	OISM	OISM	–	–	–	–	–
Day 4	OSM	OSM	OISM	OSM	OSM	OSM	OISM	OSM	OISM	OISM	OISM
Day 5	OSM	OSM	OISM	OSM	OISM	OSM	OISM	OISM	OISM	OISM	OS
Day 6	OISM	OISM	ISM	OISM	OISM	OIS	OISM	OISM	ISM	ISM	OSM
Day 7	OSM	OSM	OIS	ISM	OISM	OSM	OSM	SM	–	OSM	OSM
Day 8	OISM	OIS	OISM	OISM	OIS	OI	OISM	OISM	I	OISM	OSM
Day 9	O	OISM	OSM	OS	OISM	O	–	–	–	OISM	SM
Day 10	OSM	OSM	IS	–	–	OISM	ISM	–	OSM	OSM	OSM
Day 11	–	SM	SM	SM	OSM	IS	OSM	–	IS	OISM	SM
Day 12	OSM	S	SM	OSM	S	OISM	OS	OS	OSM	–	–
Day 13	ISM	S	OSM	I	S	IS	–	–	–	–	SM
Day 14	OISM	OS	OSM	OSM	OSM	OISM	–	OISM	I	OSM	OIS

Table 2b: Days when newspaper carried: Outrage (O), Investigation (I), Sanctions (S) and/or Military policy (M) ('allied' states).

Newspa-per	NYT	WP	G	I	T	DT	FR	SZ	TAZ	FAZ	W
4. Fallujah 1/Iraq (04/2004): Civilian deaths: 600/nationwide deaths: 6,990–55,000											
Day 1	–	–	–	–	–	–	–	–	–	–	–
Day 2	–	O	–	–	–	O	–	–	–	–	–
Day 3	–	O	OIS	–	O	O	–	I	–	OS	–
Day 4	O	O	–	O	O	O	–	–	–	–	–
Day 5	O	O	OS	O	OS	O	–	–	O	O	–
Day 6	–	O	O	O	O	O	–	–	–	–	O
Day 7	O	O	O	O	O	O	–	–	–	–	–
Day 8	O	O	O	O	O	–	O	–	O	–	–
Day 9	O	–	–	–	–	–	I	–	O	–	O
Day 10	–	OS	OI	O	–	–	–	–	–	–	–
Day 11	–	–	–	O	–	–	–	O	–	–	–
Day 12	–	O	O	–	O	–	O	–	O	–	–
Day 13	–	O	O	O	O	–	–	–	–	–	S
Day 14	–	–	–	–	–	–	–	–	–	–	–
5. Fallujah 2/Iraq (08/2004): Civilian deaths: 800–6,000/nationwide deaths: 13,644–98,000											
Day 1	–	–	–	–	–	–	–	O	–	–	–
Day 2	O	–	–	O	O	O	–	O	–	–	O
Day 3	O	O	O	O	O	O	O	O	O	O	O
Day 4	O	O	O	O	O	–	OIS	–	O	O	–
Day 5	O	–	O	–	–	–	–	–	–	–	–

Day 6	O	–	O	O	O	–	O	O	O	O	–
Day 7	O	–	O	O	O	O	–	–	–	O	–
Day 8	OI	O	–	O	–	–	–	–	O	O	–
Day 9	I	OI	I	OI	I	–	–	–	O	–	–
Day 10	OI	OI	OI	OI	OI	OI	OI	OI	O	OI	OI
Day 11	OI	O	OI	O	–	–	OI	OI	OI	–	OI
Day 12	–	O	–	–	–	–	–	–	O	–	–
Day 13	OI	O	O	O	O	–	O	OIS	OIS	O	–
Day 14	O	O	OI	OI	O	O	–	–	–	OI	–

6. Cairo/Egypt (07/2013): Civilian deaths: 51/nationwide deaths: +1,000

Day 1	IS	O	O	OS	OS	S	–	OS	O	OS	O
Day 2	OIS	OS	OIS	OIS	OS	OIS	OS	OIS	OIS	OIS	OI
Day 3	OIS	OS	OI	O	O	OS	–	O	OI	OS	O
Day 4	S	OS	O	OIS	O	–	S	O	O	OI	OS
Day 5	–	O	S	O	–	S	O	–	O	OS	–
Day 6	OS	OS	–	S	O	O	OS	S	O	OIS	OIS
Day 7	S	OS	O	–	OS	–	–	–	–	OS	OS
Day 8	–	OS	O	–	O	S	–	OS	–	S	OS
Day 9	OS	OS	S	S	OS	–	OS	S	–	OS	–
Day 10	–	OS	S	–	O	S	–	–	OS	S	S
Day 11	–	OS	O	–	O	–	–	OS	O	–	S
Day 12	O	–	OI	–	–	–	S	–	–	–	S
Day 13	–	OS	S	–	OS	–	–	S	O	OS	O
Day 14	–	–	–	–	–	O	–	–	–	–	–

Dichotomised news media campaigns: further findings

The following section will discuss the six case studies in more detail and on the basis of a qualitative content analysis. During this course, each case study will be reviewed in relation to the character of indignation. For an assessment of the politics of intervention, it is of further importance to look at the factual record in relation to each event. This will be conducted at the beginning of each case study.

'Enemy' countries

Račak

In January 1999, 45 Albanian civilians were allegedly killed in close-range executions by FRY/Serbian forces in the Kosovo-Albanian village Račak. This event received great news media attention. Račak served as a symbol for Serbian villainy and was highlighted as a justification for 'humanitarian intervention'. The incident can thus be regarded a threshold event that played an important role during the build-up towards NATO air strikes against FRY/Serbia in March 1999.

Yet significantly, the factual picture of the Kosovo War raging between March 1998 and March 1999 did not suggest a clear-cut aggressor-victim scenario. While Western news media and interest groups had pointed to Serbian genocide and ethnic cleansing in Kosovo, not much evidence in support of this narrative was found (see Chomsky 2003; Pearl and Block 1999). For instance, the UN Security Council (1998) had expressed concerns about 'excessive and indiscriminate use of force by Serbian Security forces and the Yugoslav Army' in its Resolution 1199 from 23 September 1998. But the council did not indicate the existence of ethnically motivated violence by FRY/Serbian forces (see *ibid*).[4]

An investigation by the *Wall Street Journal* suggested that FRY/Serbian killings largely occurred in areas dominated by the KLA (see Pearl and Block 1999). This pointed to the existence of a FRY/Serbian 'counter-insurgency' programme. Furthermore, casualty ratios amounted to major conflict in Kosovo with many FRY/Serbian victims. As already indicated in the previous chapter, about 2,000 people were killed during the Kosovo War, with an equal distribution among FRY/Serbian and Kosovo Albanian victims (Chomsky 2003: 72; Mandel 2005: 116).[5] This evenly distributed casualty ratio evidences fighting rather than ethnic cleansing. In line with such a rationale, OSCE monitors and other observers identified Račak as an 'isolated event' and not part of a wider pattern (Chomsky 2012: 99).

In terms of the amount of casualties, Mandel pointed to reports by Amnesty International according to which a thousand or more people were killed in the same time period during conflicts in Congo, Rwanda, Algeria, Afghanistan, Indonesia and Colombia (2005: 116, 386). In none of these cases did the West apparently seek to intervene on humanitarian grounds (see *ibid*). In fact, Chomsky (2012: 99–100) documented how the US and their 'allies' even shielded Indonesia from 'international interference' after it had conducted several massacres in East Timor shortly after Račak took place. The rationale for 'humanitarian intervention' in Kosovo, thus, did not rest on firm grounds if casualty figures are used as a benchmark. Moreover, the news media could have questioned intervention under consideration of standards like universality. The press could have asked why NATO aimed at intervention in Kosovo while, at the same time, not reprimanding Indonesia. Yet, when it came to the Račak incident, the Western news media emphasised policies of intervention.

News media coverage

The Račak case produced the largest amount of indignant news items in which military interventionist strategies were discussed if compared with the other cases under review (see Table 1). In further consideration of the contextual evidence provided above, this suggested a partisan and militarist agenda. After all, actual casualty figures in Kosovo were relatively low and on that basis the rationale for military intervention on humanitarian grounds could have been disputed.

The issue of NATO strikes in Kosovo was a major topic in the Western press, which highlighted different intervention scenarios including the use of air power and ground troops. While the military approach was not necessarily endorsed at all times, it was virtually not denied on principle in the newspapers under review. Moreover, there appeared to be a consensus that some kind of action was necessary.

Many articles placed in the indignation category featured content discussing military action. For instance, on 20 January, the *New York Times* (1999: 30) argued in its editorial: 'NATO should give Mr. Milosevic a short deadline to comply with all his promises' and in case he does not it should 'bomb selected Serbian military targets'. A lead article in the *Independent* (1999: 3) of the same day argued that 'if we do not wish to see more innocent people die, the only solution is to intervene in force'. The *Independent's* editorial was seconded by a comment from Paddy Ashdown (1999: 4), then member of the British Parliament, saying: 'Air strikes may be used to prevent further instances of the use of excessive force and heavy weapons against defenceless Albanian villages, and to force Milosevic to return to compliance if Serbia uses heavy weapons against Albanian civilians in contravention of the Geneva Convention.' Münch (1999: 4) demanded in the German *Süddeutsche Zeitung* a day earlier that the West needed to be prepared for 'a long-term engagement in Kosovo, also involving ground troops'.

NATO's threatening posture was sustained as indicated by items that appeared several days after Račak had occurred. For instance, on 29 January, the *Guardian* (1999a: 1) reported that 'the six contact group countries – the US, Russia, Britain, France, Germany and Italy – meet in Paris and will tell the Serbian government and ethnic Albanian leaders to negotiate a political settlement or face military action'. If accurate, this statement evidenced full Western support for military intervention. While Russia is included in the list as well, it should later oppose NATO intervention and together with China block an UN Resolution calling for such action. The *Guardian* article further depicted how the warning was 'backed by the United Nations secretary-general, Kofi Annan, who said that force would be used if necessary' (*ibid*). Doesn't the UN Charter outlaw the use or the threat of force in international relations? Again, this question was not further pursued by the Western press in relation to the statement by the UN's then-Secretary General. In fact, NATO had already prepared for intervention in Kosovo several months before the Račak incident took place. A news item in the *Guardian* highlighted how in October 1999, NATO had adopted a threatening posture – 'to prepare a short, sharp air strike as a response to future Serb atrocities' (Walker, Bird and Black 1999: 3). While this policy was to be enforced in reaction to Račak, the statement above could have indicated that the NATO intervention was pre-mediated. But the newspapers under review hardly investigated NATO's role and whether its goals could have been strategic rather than humanitarian. For instance, air strikes against the FRY/Serbia could have symbolically served to re-establish NATO as a credible force after the end of the Cold War. Moreover, the US, UK and Germany needed to cement their dominance in the region (see Keeble 2000: 69).

On a second level, indignant statements included the discussion of a diverse set of measures that were coded in the Sanctions category. Sanctions entailed policies to be enforced by the 'international community' largely against the FRY/Serbs.

For instance, statements coded as Sanctions incorporated calls for an 'internationalisation of the conflict', as demanded by Bujar Bukoshi, the then-exiled Prime Minister of Kosovo, in an interview with the German *tageszeitung* (Rathfelder 1999). In fact, most aspects of internationalisation short of military action described policies in the Sanctions category. It is, of course, significant, that 'internationalisation of the conflict' is not at the top of the agenda when the US and their 'allies' are engaged in human rights violations. In such instances, the powerful states remain largely unconstrained by such measures.

More specifically, Sanctions related to the following measures (some of which are stated in Drozdiak 1999; Moniac 1999; Rathfelder 1999; The Guardian 1999b; The New York Times 1999):

- Retreat military forces, cease operations and otherwise comply with a US/NATO-brokered ceasefire.
- Comply with the demands of the UN Security Council and/or its Resolution 1199.
- Accept specific policy designs for the governance of Kosovo.
- Cooperate with the Kosovo Verification Mission, which was established under the auspices of the UN Security Council and OSCE, and other international agencies.
- UN and other deliberations about potential and actual 'reactive' policies by powerful states and their representatives, such as discussed in relation to the January 1999 visit by NATO's chief military commander, US General Wesley Clark, and the chairman of its military committee, German General Klaus Naumann, to Slobodan Milošević, then-President of the Federal Republic of Yugoslavia.

Sanctions were extensively discussed in the news media (see Table 1). Furthermore, calls for Sanctions were coupled with military threats. Thus, an exemplary item in the *Washington Post* (Drozdiak 1999: A 17) related to NATO's activation order as well as a range of Sanctions policies:

'Secretary Albright is encouraged by the strong statement [of NATO's activation order] and the strong message in the statement that NATO has just approved,' said her spokesman, James P. Rubin. 'She believes it appropriate to continue to marshal diplomatic pressure to convince President Milosevic and the Serbs to comply with obligations they have assumed, and she hopes that the gravity of the situation will be understood when General Clark and General Naumann of NATO go to Belgrade this week.'

Hence, NATO sent a message that if Sanctions in the form of diplomatic measures were not leading the FRY/Serbs to comply with the designs enforced by NATO governments, military intervention could happen. The newspapers transmitted these discourses and did not challenge them on substantial grounds. Demonisation of the FRY/Serbs was so pronounced that a critical evaluation of the role of NATO in the conflict appeared to be excluded from reporting.

On a third level, there were multiple items in the indignation category discussing the launching of investigations into Račak or the demand for FRY/Serbian cooperation with the International Criminal Tribunal for the former Yugoslavia (ICTY), whose prosecutor Louise Arbour also attempted to investigate the incident (for this category see Table 1).

The Investigation and Sanctions categories were related. The demand 'to allow the chief prosecutor of the international war crimes tribunal, Louise Arbour of Canada, to investigate the killings' (Erlanger 1999: 4) in Račak, was actually enforced by Western states. Accordingly, Perlez (1999c: 6), of the *New York Times*, reported how the State Department spokesman, James P. Rubin, had 'said Mr. Milosevic was being asked to identify and "take action" against those who had ordered the massacre and to allow the International War Crimes Tribunal for the Former Yugoslavia, sitting at The Hague, into Kosovo to investigate'. Similarly, Bird (1999b: 1) reported in the *Guardian* how 'the West, including Foreign Secretary Robin Cook', had demanded 'that the international war crimes tribunal investigator, Louise Arbour, be given unfettered access to the massacre site'.

Calls for independent investigations also emerged from demands by Western spokespersons. For instance, the *Washington Post's* Smith (1999: A1) further reported how 'a senior Clinton administration official told staff writer Dana Priest in Washington,' that 'We have to have a full, independent investigation of this to get to the bottom of it [...]. Those responsible have to be brought to justice.' (cited in *ibid*) Calls for investigations were substantive and widely reported by the press. A Finish forensic expert mission team of the

EU, together with pathologists from the Federal Republic of Yugoslavia and Belarus, should later conduct an inquiry into the incident. Forensic evidence could not corroborate the Western version of the incident (see Mandel 2005: 121–125; also Herman and Peterson 2010).

Some Western actors had already formed an opinion about the incident before any investigation had taken place. In the *Independent*, Sarah Schaefer (1999: 8) provided another quote by then British Foreign Secretary Robin Cook who argued: '[…] In any common sense understanding of the term, this was a war crime' (cited in *ibid*). The quotation was published on 19 January and thus preceded any outcome of an investigation or tribunal. At this point in time, evidence about the event was hardly conclusive. But Cook's statements were reported without challenge. The overall tenor in the press was that the Račak incident constituted a massacre for which the FRY/Serbs were responsible.

Yet, the FRY/Serbs put forward a different narrative about the incident: As Paul Wood (1999: 2) reported on 17 January in the *Independent*, the FRY/Serbs claimed 'they had been on a search operation when they had encountered hostile fire. Those killed, they maintained, were in uniform: members of the Kosovo Liberation Army (KLA)'. While this perspective was mentioned in many reports it was marginalised or appeared in a negative context.

Louise Arbour, who incidentally would be the UN commissioner for human rights in 2004 during the Fallujah November operation, was also cited in coverage on Račak. In the *Süddeutsche Zeitung* Roser (1999: 2) quoted Arbour as saying that '"in the interest of truth and justice" evidence related to the massacre had to be secured and eye-witnesses had to be interrogated'. According to Roser (*ibid*), Arbour also welcomed that a Finnish expert team would start an enquiry in Račak saying she 'hopes they would get free access to the material they need for their work' (cited in *ibid*). The press did not cite Arbour with a similar statement during the Fallujah November operation when specific, such as forensic investigations, were neither demanded nor set in motion. There are only sporadic calls for independent investigations by spokespersons from the 'international community' when Western states and their 'allies' conduct human rights violations.

Generally, the tenor of indignant statements during coverage of Račak was that action was necessary. Statements demanding specific policies were often underpinned by a range of emotional sentiments that were coded as Outrage. They included expressions of anger, mourning or concern, which were raised by local actors and international politicians. For example, on

17 January, two days after the incident took place, a story by Chris Bird (1999a: 1) in the *Observer* provided the following context:

> A KLA guerrilla squatted, crying. 'It was an execution – all of them were shot in the head,' said British army officer Chris Cobb-Smith, in Kosovo with the OSCE. 'It is about as horrendous an event as I have seen, and I have been in some nasty situations,' said William Walker, head of the Kosovo verification mission, talking to reporters after being shown a ditch full of corpses.

In an item published on the same day, Perlez of the *New York Times* (1999c: 6) referred to 'President Clinton' who 'issued a written statement condemning the killings in the "strongest possible terms" and calling them a "clear violation" of the Serbs' cease-fire agreement with NATO three months ago.' The *Independent's* Wood (1999: 2) quoted William Walker saying: 'It's hard to find words when I see bodies like this, shot execution-style [...]. It looks like it was done by people who have no value for human life' (cited in *ibid*). On 18 January, the London *Times'* Bremner (1999) wrote that Javier Solana, the NATO Secretary General, 'condemned the massacre as a "flagrant violation of international humanitarian law"' saying: 'President Milosevic must name those who carried out the killings.' On 19 January, a report by Evans and Webster (1999) in the London *Times* again referred to Robin Cook calling 'on Yugoslavia to allow international war crimes investigators into Kosovo to conduct an inquiry into the "appalling massacre", and he warned President Milosovic that the threat of Nato airstrikes remained'.

Overall, the Western press was flooded with indignant statements by a range of international political actors who condemned the incident or demanded reactive counter measures. The list included US President Bill Clinton and US Foreign Secretary Madeleine Albright, former US Ambassador and American head of the Kosovo Verification Mission (KVM) William Walker, British Prime Minister Tony Blair and Foreign Secretary Robin Cook, NATO General Secretary Javier Solana, German Chancellor Gerhard Schröder and Foreign Secretary Joschka Fischer and French President Jacques Chirac (see Butler 1999: 1; Cornwell 1999: 1; Süddeutsche Zeitung 1999: 7; Walker, Bird and Black 1999: 3).

Support from this power collective, it could be argued, facilitated the Western press's frequent inclusion of actors who called for intervention as well as local and elite sources voicing strong concerns. Indignation about the Račak incident thus paved the way for NATO military intervention in March 1999. On the importance of Račak, a subsequent OSCE report commented that it 'provoked an international outcry' and 'altered the perspective of the international community towards the [Federal Republic of Yugslavia] and Serbian authorities in Belgrade' (cited in Herman and Peterson 2000: 117).

Yet, the press hardly questioned the strategic goals underpinning NATO intervention. There was a significant political interest involved as the US and Germany, in accord with the priorities of the global financial system, aimed to dissolve the FRY/Serbia in order to transform the Balkans 'into a safe haven for free enterprise' (Chossudovsky 2002: 280). Hence, NATO military intervention was followed by 'market reforms' (*ibid*: 296).

Benghazi

In February 2011, Libyan security forces attempted to quell an uprising in Benghazi. As in the case of Račak, the Benghazi incident generated extensive news media attention. The actions by Libyan security forces, led by Muammar Gaddafi, were met with great indignation. It was quickly argued that Gaddafi's military, particularly the Libyan air force, had indiscriminately killed civilians and that the people in Benghazi would face further massacres. Benghazi was consequently used as an example to advocate military measures against Libya including 'humanitarian intervention' in line with the 'Responsibility to Protect (R2P)' doctrine. A UN authorised NATO intervention aiming to implement a no-fly zone was quickly on the agenda of the news media and would later be enforced. Calls for intervention emerged from the rebel movement that received support by Libyan expats and interest groups. Western powers would lend their backing to this ambiguous network.

The rebellion in Libya received public support and was driven by genuine concerns. Large segments of the Libyan population did not gain from the oil-riches of the country, unemployment rates were high and this was coupled with corruption and political repression (see Achcar 2013: 199–209). But the situation was more complex. Evidence suggested that Gaddafi's regime still retained significant support among the Libyan population (see Zollmann 2014a). Secondly, the uprising was split along tribal lines. Laura Pitel (2011: 6, 7) argued in *The Times* newspaper: 'The Cyrenaica region, at the centre of much of the recent unrest [and where Benghazi is located], is home to several tribes whose members are fiercely opposed to the government, and the area has long harboured ill-feeling towards the ruling family.' This opposition, as the article further discussed, resulted from traditional clan rivalries as well as Gaddafi's patronage system, which had disadvantaged the tribes of the eastern regions (see *ibid*). The divide was further grounded in the fact that the eastern tribes had been associated with the former King Idris, who had ruled the country and was overthrown by Gaddafi in 1969 (see *ibid*). As a consequence, the region was not only prone to rebellion but also to a 'rise in Islamic extremism in the Nineties' (*ibid*). A study by the Combating Terrorism Centre of West Point, published in 2007, argued that the eastern region of Libya (particularly Darnah and Benghazi) 'has long been associated with Islamic militancy' (Felter and Fishman 2007: 12). These were the forces that also played a role in the 2011 uprising. As Kuperman (2013: 116) commented: 'Contrary to the portrayal by Western media of a nationwide peaceful protest against a dictatorial regime, the conflict started as an armed rebellion by regional, tribal, and Islamist opponents of the regime.'

These facts about the uprising in Libya could have cautioned the West towards intervention and support for the rebels, which were not a monolithic and uniformly popular movement. Incidentally, it appeared that during the build-up for intervention, Western governments were not fully aware of the nature of the rebellion. On 2 March 2011, when the campaign against the Gaddafi regime was already in full swing, US officials appeared to have no clear picture about who was leading the Libyan opposition. As the *Washington Post*'s DeYoung and Whitlock (2011: A08) reported:

> As it seeks to calibrate its message, the [US-] administration is also trying to determine who is in charge of the opposition. With few direct contacts in Libya, U.S. officials have queried those with business and other non-governmental ties for names, phone numbers and assessments of those who appear to be in charge.

A second issue concerned the framing of violence in Libya. It is estimated that about 228 people were killed in Benghazi during several weeks of clashes (Kuperman 2013: 119; see also AP 2013). The ICC estimated that up to 700 people were killed across Libya in February 2011, after the uprising had spread in various cities (ICC 2011: 4). Overall, casualties in Libya were thus arguably not in excess of 1,000, a number which constitutes about 50 per cent of the killings estimated for the Kosovo War (for a review of casualty data in Libya see Kuperman 2013). The factual record thus suggested that the threshold for military intervention against 'enemy' countries had decreased, if casualty numbers for Libya and Kosovo are compared. Indeed, justifications for 'humanitarian intervention' in Libya rested on weak grounds in terms of the amount of casualties. I have already shown that other countries, which had not been targeted for 'humanitarian intervention', were inflicted by conflicts with similar or higher casualty numbers. Just further consider that three of Israel's military operations in the Gaza Strip, conducted between 2008 and 2014, have all in all killed about 3,700 Palestinians (and 90 Israelis were killed) (see Finkelstein 2014).

A third problem with Libya is that much of the evidence that was provided about human rights violations as well as indiscriminate fighting tactics by Libyan forces had been contested or falsified. Take the following examples.

The Office of the Prosecutor in The Hague found in its first report on the incidents in Libyan cities, published on 4 May 2011, 'a consistent pattern of Security Forces firing live ammunition at civilians' (ICC 2011: 6). The report also noted that there have been 'allegations of war crimes committed, including the use of imprecise weaponry such as cluster munitions, multiple rocket launchers and mortars, and other forms of heavy weaponry, in crowded urban areas.' (*ibid*) Similarly, a report by Amnesty International (2011a: 7), published in May 2011, found that Libyan security forces 'greeted the peaceful protests in the eastern cities of Benghazi, Libya's second city, and al-Bayda with excessive and at times lethal force, leading to the deaths of scores of protesters and bystanders'. The report further argued that Libyan forces had contravened 'not only international standards on the use of force and firearms, but also Libya's own legislation on the policing of public gatherings' (*ibid*).

The findings by the ICC and Amnesty International support the official Western narrative depicting Libyan security forces as the aggressors. Yet, Kuperman's review of the factual record of the incidents in Libya suggested an alternative narrative (2013). Kuperman argued that while 'the government did respond forcefully to the rebels, it never targeted civilians or resorted to "indiscriminate" force' (2013: 110). Kuperman collected factual evidence from mainstream sources indicating that (1) Libyan protestors tended to be armed and violent from the start of the uprising; (2) in the main cities of the uprising violence was initiated by the protestors; (3) government forces initially relied on nonlethal force to counter the protests but resorted to heavier tactics when the uprising spread violently; (4) government forces largely targeted combatants and (5) government forces did not engage in revenge killings or bloodbaths after retaking rebel-held cities (see Kuperman 2013: 108–112).

Kuperman's perspective is also supported by Forte's (2012) discussion of the factual record and his critical review of the work by Western human rights organisations including Amnesty International. Forte collected evidence for a range of inconsistencies in the dominant narrative including the inflation of atrocity stories. Forte (2012: 12) concluded that leading human rights organisations 'supported foreign intervention, and until the very late stages of the war they persistently magnified their criticism of "Gaddafi forces" while somewhat minimizing any direct criticism of insurgent action'.

Kuperman and Forte's assessments were broadly confirmed by a report of the UK Parliament's House of Common's Foreign Affairs Committee, published on 9 September 2016. Amongst other things, the report examined the March 2011 NATO intervention in terms of the conduct of Gaddafi' forces. According to the report:

> Despite his rhetoric, the proposition that Muammar Gaddafi would have ordered the massacre of civilians in Benghazi was not supported by the available evidence. The Gaddafi regime had retaken towns from the rebels without attacking civilians in early February 2011. [...] The disparity between male and female casualties suggested that Gaddafi regime forces targeted male combatants in a civil war and did not indiscriminately attack civilians. More widely, Muammar Gaddafi's 40-year record of appalling human rights abuses did not include large-scale attacks on Libyan civilians. (Foreign Affairs Committee 2016; see also Edwards 2016)

Finally, in early March 2011, it had already been acknowledged by the US high command that there was no evidence that Gaddafi's air force had attacked protestors (see the discussion in the next section). One of the major justifications for 'humanitarian intervention' had thus quickly collapsed. Yet, as we shall see in the next section, intervention was high up on the agenda of the news media, which had largely sided with the elements challenging the Gaddafi regime.

News media coverage

The Benghazi case produced the least amount of indignant news items with statements about military interventionist strategies, if the data is compared with the other 'enemy' cases under review (see Table 1). The main reason for the lower amount of items on Military policy in the case of Libya is that a novel campaign for intervention was constructed by various interest-parties in February 2011. In contrast, the Kosovo War as well as the Syrian conflict had started about a year before the time period under review in this study. Thus, in the Kosovo and Syria cases, military intervention had already been on the Western agenda for some time. The lower amount of articles including Military policy in the Benghazi case thus resulted from the fact that the issue emerged on the news agenda during the study period.

Conflict in Libya actually erupted on 15 February 2011. Since my study looked at news items published between 17 February and 2 March 2011, Benghazi constituted a rather sudden event at the early stages of the violent conflict. How did indignation feature in news coverage of Benghazi? In this section, we will again look at the different character dimensions of the category.

The first calls for Military policy were embedded in news items published on 23 February 2011. This date constituted day seven in the study period. From that day onwards, calls for intervention were part of the international news agenda. Aside from the German *tageszeitung*, all newspapers under review started carrying Military policy statements between 23 and 25 February. The issue then remained on the news agenda (see Table 2a).[6] Viewed in this light, the data attests to an impressive propaganda campaign. In effect, the news media displayed calls for intervention just about eight days after the conflict had erupted. In terms of the quantity, the German press included less items featuring Military policy than the US and UK press (see Tables 1 and 2a).

First calls for intervention focused on the implementation of a no-fly zone, which was contingent on some kind of military supervision. The news media further discussed a range of military scenarios including the use of air power and ground troops as well as active support for the militant elements of the uprising. Some items included statements contesting procedural aspects of Military policy, a reflection of political and military elite deliberations. Substantive criticisms were virtually absent from coverage.

On 23 February, the *Washington Post's* Tara Bahrampour (2011: A 9) reported how a loose group of Libyan exiles living in the Washington area has been organising rallies and meetings with senatorial aides. According to the article the group 'urged the United States [including Senator John F. Kerry (D-Mass.)] to impose a no-fly zone over Libya to prevent the regime from using planes to attack protesters.' (*ibid*) Similarly, Richard Spencer (2011: 14), of the *Daily Telegraph*, described in a news item how protestors and defectors from the Gaddafi regime 'were calling for the UN to impose a no-fly zone to prevent a repeat of the air attacks ordered by the regime on Monday night.' A news item by Dietrich Alexander und Alfred Hackensberger (2011: 7), published in *Die Welt*, referred to Libya's Ambassador to India, Ali al-Essawi, who had resigned from his post and now demanded the UN to enforce a no-fly zone. Soon, the issue was to be debated on the international stage. *The Times'* Martin Fletcher (2011a: 1, 8) summarised the discussion of the day as follows:

> The UN Security Council met in emergency session last night amid growing international outrage at the carnage, demands for the imposition a no-fly zone over Libya

and calls for sanctions. Navi Pillay, the UN High Commissioner for Human Rights, said the regime's 'reported use of machine guns, snipers and military warplanes against civilians' may constitute crimes against humanity.

Note how a range of indignant measures including sanctions were also on the order of the day and how quickly the Gaddafi regime was shamed for nefarious actions it had allegedly conducted. Calls for Military policy were further included in news items published during the following days and it would soon become evident that the Western-led 'international community' was supporting intervention.

On 24 February, Nicholas D. Kristof (2011: 27) demanded in an op-ed published in the *New York Times* to impose 'a no-fly zone, as Libya's deputy ambassador to the United Nations proposed after he defected, to prevent the government from bombing or strafing its own people'. David Usborne (2011: 4, 5), writing for the *Independent* on the same day, quoted Lord Owen, a former Foreign Secretary, saying: 'At any moment this man [Colonel Gaddafi] could order an air force officer to bomb a crowd of protesters. It is vital we act now to prevent this before it is too late.' As Usborne further wrote, preventive actions may have included proposals ranging 'from re-imposing economic and trade sanctions on Libya to establishing a no-fly zone over the country to prevent air strikes against protesters or cities such as Benghazi that have fallen out of Colonel Gaddafi's control' (*ibid*).

First calls from Western governments to implement a no-fly zone apparently emerged from France. The *Guardian's* MacAskill, Wintour and Watt (2011: 6) reported on 24 February that Nicolas Sarkozy, the French President, was leading the calls for a NATO-imposed no-fly zone to be enforced over Libya to 'prevent the use of that country's warplanes against [its] population.' (cited in *ibid*) At this point in time, the US was still considering its options. Accordingly, the article (*ibid*) further highlighted how US President Barack Obama 'is sending Hillary Clinton, the secretary of state, to Europe to discuss with allies what actions can be taken to stop the violence'. But on 26 February the *New York Times'* Cooper and Landler (2011: 1) referred to 'American officials' who were 'discussing a no-flight zone over Libya to prevent Colonel Qaddafi from using military aircraft against demonstrators'. On the same day, a lead article in the *Frankfurter Allgemeine Zeitung* referred to diplomats who had said the European Union would 'participate in the enforcement of a no-fly zone sanctioned by the UN Security Council' (FAZ 2011: 1). Moreover, the article mentioned German Minister for Foreign Affairs Guido Westerwelle, who would not preclude a no-fly zone as an option if the policy was aligned with Article VII of the UN Charter (*ibid*).

There were also critical voices in the news media. Particularly the German left-liberal newspapers tended to include statements and commentaries opposing a new-fly zone on procedural grounds or critically evaluating the policy. In an item published on 25 February, the *Frankfurter Rundschau's* Knuf mentioned NATO Secretary Anders Fogh Rasmussen, who said that NATO had not been authorised to intervene and that such a policy would need to be covered by the UN (Knuf 2011: 4). On 1 March, Damir Fras, from the *Frankfurter Rundschau*, wrote that particularly the US were in favour of a no-fly zone (Fras 2011: 7). Fras (*ibid*) also transmitted tactical criticisms raised by German Minister for Foreign Affairs Westerwelle who had said that the UN authorisation of military policy could encourage Gaddafi to take foreign nationals into captivity. On the same date, a commentary by Stefan Kornelius (2011: 4) of the *Süddeutsche Zeitung* provided a set of arguments against military intervention. Kornelius (*ibid*) stated that a no-fly zone was not practical and could 'escalate the war'. Reflecting on other military options, Kornelius pointed out that sending ground troops into Libya would be dangerous and also meet opposition from the so-called Libyan transitional government as well as from Western publics (*ibid*). Kornelius further wrote that the UN Security Council would not be able to authorise a broader NATO air war due to misgivings by China towards such policies (*ibid*). Finally, Kornelius pointed out that an intervention in accord with the R2P doctrine was not appropriate as the sufficient threshold of violence had not reached the levels of the Balkan-Wars (*ibid*). It should be noted that in Iraq, the violence had reached (if not exceeded) the levels of the Balkan-Wars but R2P was not evoked in the press (see discussion in the Fallujah sections below). Nonetheless, such criticisms in the German press were not substantive and coincided with German elite disagreement about Military policy. Yet, they made the Germany news media appear to be less zealous about Military policy than the US and UK press. Indeed, Germany should later belong to the countries not taking part in the NATO intervention.

If we look again at the Anglo-American press, substantial announcements about Military policy were made in news items published on 1 and 2 March. On these days, actual strategies materialised in Western government circles. The US and UK press highlighted these deliberations that further included a range of tactical considerations.

On 1 March, the *Guardian's* Borger, Wintour and Chulov reported that British Prime Minister David Cameron had initiated preparations for a no-fly zone: 'Cameron said he had told the Ministry of Defence and the chief of the defence staff to draw up plans for a no-fly zone in coordination with Britain's Nato allies' (2011: 1). The article went on adding that such policy 'would be designed principally to prevent attacks on Libyan people by the Gaddafi regime – mainly by his helicopter gunships' (*ibid*). The journalists further highlighted that 'discussions on a range of military options' had begun 'last week between British and US officials at the Pentagon' (*ibid*). Policies that were mentioned in the article included the armament of Libyan rebels as well as the establishment of protected humanitarian corridors (see *ibid*). Apparently, Cameron was also coordinating the approach with President Nicolas Sarkozy of France (*ibid*). The *Guardian* journalists failed to further question the chosen military strategy (or cite sources critical of the military response) yet made use of the humanitarian terminology. The journalists pointed to some tactical concerns, namely that Russia and China could raise their veto in the UN Security Council: 'Resistance in the security council and within Nato would leave Washington and London to draw on a "coalition of the willing" to carry out a humanitarian intervention, something both are extremely reluctant to do.' (*ibid*)

In this particular context, it was important for Western powers not to appear as acting unilaterally against Libya. Accordingly, an item in the *Washington Post* published on 2 March stated that 'U.S. defence leaders expressed caution Tuesday about military intervention in Libya, warning that enforcement of a no-fly zone would require scarce air assets, domestic political approval and international authorization' (DeYoung and Whitlock 2011: A 08). Yet, on the other hand, the article reported that foreign leaders and some US officials had also stated that a no-fly zone was under consideration and 'Defense Secretary Robert M. Gates said the Pentagon was preparing "a lot of options and contingencies" for President Obama' (*ibid*).

It was thus useful for the NATO powers that local actors demanded 'humanitarian intervention'. Rebel leaders were 'debating whether to ask for Western airstrikes under the United Nations banner', Fahim and Kirkpatrick (2011a: 11) reported on 2 March in the *New York Times*. The rebel council was apparently 'seeking to draw a distinction between such airstrikes and foreign intervention which the rebels said they emphatically opposed' (*ibid*). And the US government was well aware of this fact. Thus, Fahim and Kirkpatrick (*ibid*) added: 'Secretary of State Hillary Rodham Clinton told the House Foreign Affairs Committee on Tuesday that the Obama administration knew that the Libyan opposition was eager to be seen "as doing this by themselves on behalf of the Libyan people – that there not be outside intervention by any external force.'" The news media did not further elaborate on this approach and whether it was appropriate for Western governments to officially side with the rebels in Libya.

On 17 March 2011, the UN Security Council authorised military intervention (exempting the use of foreign occupation forces) in Libya on the basis of Resolution 1973 (2011). One clause of the resolution provided for 'a ban on all flights in the airspace of the Libyan Arab Jamahiriya in order to help protect civilians' and authorised member states 'to take all necessary measures to enforce compliance with the ban on flights' (*ibid*: 3).

As is apparent from many the statements cited above as well as the text from Resolution 1973, the imposition of a no-fly zone in Libya was demanded to prevent Gaddafi's troops from targeting civilians with air forces. Hence, what might be termed an 'aerial slaughter story' (see Roberts 2011) was a crucial component of the shaming campaign for military intervention. The substance and evidence for this story initially appeared to have rested on statements provided by Libyan defectors and interest-party sources who had alerted Western politicians. Significantly, the narrative that Gaddafi's air force was shooting demonstrators could not be verified on the basis of first-hand evidence because virtually no Western journalists were reporting from the scene. As Stewart and Sengupta (2011: 1, 2), from the *Independent*, acknowledged in a report on 21 February: 'The picture in Libya is at times confused. Foreign reporters have been barred from the country, and the authorities have periodically blocked access to the internet.' Yet, many allegations against the Libyan regime appeared to be presented as if based on verifiable facts rather than hearsay.

Hugh Roberts (2011), former Director of the International Crisis Group's North Africa Project, would later write that there was 'no evidence for the aerial slaughter story'. In early March 2011, then-US Secretary of Defense Robert Gates and Admiral Mike Mullen, then chairman of the Joint Chiefs of Staff, testified in hearings of US Congress that 'they had no confirmation of reports of aircraft controlled by Gaddafi firing on citizens' (*ibid*). This episode was even mentioned in my newspaper sample. The *Washington Post's* Karen DeYoung and Craig Whitlock (2011: A 08) reported on 2 March 2011 how Gates and Mullen 'told reporters that they had no confirmed reports that Libyan leader Moammar Gaddafi had used airstrikes against civilians or opposition forces that occupy the eastern half of the country'. But this did not lead the news media to challenge the discourse of intervention.

The 'aerial slaughter story' had striking propaganda value. The propaganda motif was indirectly acknowledged by some of the newspapers under review. 'Russia and China have made it clear they are opposed in principle to' plans for a no-fly zone, Black and Borger (2011: 16) wrote in the *Guardian*, 'but they would be under heavy pressure to relent if the Gaddafi regime committed an atrocity with mass casualties using warplanes or helicopters' (*ibid*). There is no evidence that Russia and China would later lend support to the UN sanctioned no-fly zone due to Western news media reporting. Nonetheless, the news media did highlight the no-fly zone angle without substantive criticism. Furthermore, the news media transmitted atrocity stories although they could hardly be thoroughly verified. News reporting thus produced an image of 'aerial slaughter' that was not sufficiently supported by evidence.

Let us now look at the other dimensions of indignation. Firstly, I will review policies that were coded in the Sanctions category. Sanctions broadly entailed deliberations about measures to be applied by outside powers against the Gaddafi regime and its forces. Table 1 shows the extent to which Sanctions were mentioned in the news media in relation to Benghazi: the amount of items including Sanctions was less pronounced than in the other 'enemy' cases under review (if the ration N Articles/N Sanctions is considered). In fact, the discourse about Sanctions policies built up over time. Early calls for Sanctions were voiced by Libyan defectors, lobby groups and Libyan expats as well as human rights organisations. Western government spokespersons were further cited in support of Sanctions. The upward trajectory of the Sanctions (and overall indignation) campaign was related to the unexpected nature of the incident. Moreover, the quotations provided below indicated that interest parties quickly demanded various forms of intervention. Indeed, the Sanctions discourse was connected to a range of news management activities.

On 19 February, the London *Times*' Fletcher (2011b: 9) cited Oliver Sprague, Director of Amnesty UK's arms programme saying: 'Ministers here must immediately suspend any further transfers of arms, security equipment and training programmes to Libya [...].' The *New York Times* quoted Issa Abdel Majeed Mansour, an opposition member based in Oslo, saying: 'The international community is watching [...]. Why isn't anyone helping us?' (cited in Shadid 2011: 1). Similarly, on 22 February, the *Guardian* published a commentary by Mohamed Abdul Malek (2011: 30), chairman of the London based Libya Watch group, urging the West 'to exert pressure on Gaddafi to follow the leaders of Egypt and Tunisia and relinquish control of' Libya. This was essentially an early call for 'regime change'. On 25 February, *The*

Times referred to Downing Street and the Foreign and Commonwealth Office, which had 'said that a British-led lobby had secured enough signatures to hold a special session of the UN Human Rights Council' and demanded 'that British representatives would call for Libya to be suspended from the council' (Coates, Asthana and Savage 2011: 10, 11).

These statements by interest group representatives were in alignment with Western governments who pressed for further action in Libya. Correspondingly, on 24 February, Leila Fadel and Sudarsan Raghavan (2011: A 01), of the *Washington Post*, quoted US President Obama who had said 'the United States was developing a "full range of options" and would intensify discussions with other nations to address the violent unraveling [sic] of Gaddafi's regime'. A report published in the German *tageszeitung* (TAZ/RTR/AFP 2011: 1) of the same day wrote that 'EU states consulted about sanctions yesterday'. Pressure further tightened when it became apparent that, as the London *Times'* Fletcher and Haynes (2011: 1) reported: 'Western leaders were plotting last night to bring an end to Colonel Muammar Gaddafi's 41-year regime [...].' The article also referred to President Obama, David Cameron, President Sarkozy of France and Italy's Prime Minister, Silvio Berlusconi who had 'discussed ways to remove the Libyan dictator' and coordinate multilateral measures against Libya (*ibid*). As was the case in Račak, a Western state collective, comprising the traditional colonial powers, had set path towards intervening in Libya.

Overall, the following policies were discussed/mentioned in press coverage and coded as Sanctions (for exemplary items see Cooper and Landler 2011; DeYoung and Whitlock 2011; Fadel and Faiola 2011; Kristof 2011; RTR/DPA/AP/TAZ 2011; The Washington Post 2011):

- Halt the violence in Libya.
- International action and/or intervention short of military means by states and/or human rights bodies.
- Demotion of diplomatic relations and treaties with Libya.
- Bring the Libya case to the UN Security Council.
- Exclude Libya from UN Human Rights Council.
- Remove Gaddafi from power (i.e. 'regime change').
- Outreach to opposition forces.
- A variety of sanctions policies including, economic, financial and military sanctions; asset and export freezes as well as travel bans for the Gaddafi regime and members of the government.

Many of the outlined measures, including a variety of sanctions policies, were actually implemented against the Gaddafi regime.

As part of the efforts to 'isolate' the Libyan regime via sanctions, the news media also carried calls for investigations and demands to bring Gaddafi 'before a war crimes tribunal' (Cooper and Landler 2011: 1). Table 1 shows the amount of items carrying such statements.

For instance, on 23 February, Ian Black (2011a: 1) of the *Guardian*, referred to Navi Pillay, the UN human rights chief, calling for 'an independent international investigation into the killings'. On 24 February, the *Guardian* reported that the EU had 'pushed for an independent, UN-led investigation' and that British Foreign Secretary William Hague, had 'stressed he wanted an international inquiry into possible war crimes, saying this represented the best chance to stop murder and atrocities by the regime' (MacAskill, Wintour and Watt 2011: 6). Note how the Libyan regime was already implicated in 'murder and atrocities' (*ibid*) although it should be the task of a tribunal to establish such matters. Furthermore, statements that suggested the need for investigations or the referral to the ICC appeared to further implicate regime responsibility rather than leaving it open for the prosecutors to investigate the liability of all sides of the conflict. For instance, a news item based on agency material and published in the German *tageszeitung* said, with reference to a vote in the UN Security Council, 'the International Criminal Court in Den Haag shall investigate against the Gaddafi clan for crimes against humanity' (RTR/DPA/AP/TAZ 2011: 1). Similarly, on 28 February, legal scholar Kai Ambos (2011: 2) appeared to welcome, in an op-ed for the *Süddeutsche Zeitung*, the UN Security Council's decision, codified in Resolution 1970, to refer the Libya situation to the International Criminal Court without questioning the substance of the allegations.

On a fourth layer, news media reporting carried multiple statements classified as Outrage (see Table 1). Strong language statements signalling emotive reactions to the incident were coded in this category. Reporting pattern on Benghazi virtually mirrored coverage of the other 'enemy' cases. Statements of Outrage were widely disseminated. Accordingly, Fletcher (2011b: 9) of *The Times* described the actions of Libyan forces as 'the most ruthless response of any regime to the popular uprisings sweeping the Arab world'. Fletcher also quoted Sarah Leah Whitson, Middle East and North Africa Director of Human Rights Watch, saying that the security forces '[…] "vicious attacks on peaceful demonstrators lay bare the reality of Muammar Gaddafi's brutality when faced with any internal dissent"' (cited in *ibid*). Ian Black (2011b: 1), of the *Guardian*, summarised the wave of Outrage saying: 'Libya is defying growing international condemnation of a bloody crackdown [...].' Sudarsan Raghavan (2011a: A 01), of the *Washington Post*, described how 'U.S. and European Union officials on Sunday condemned Libya's crackdown' adding that State Department spokesman P.J. Crowley said the United States was 'gravely concerned' and had received 'multiple credible reports that hundreds of people have been killed and injured' (cited in *ibid*). The *Washington Post's* (2011: A 12) editorial argued that 'Gaddafi was waging war against its own people'. Statements of Outrage carried emotive phrases and further signalled the responsibility of the Gaddafi regime.

Another set of articles in this category carried statements of Outrage voiced by Libyan defectors who had resigned from their diplomatic posts. Accordingly, *Die Welt* reported in a title story on 23 February that 'in protest at the violence [...] several members of the Libyan section of the UN in New York had also quit their allegiance with Gaddafi' (2011: 1). Fahim and Kirkpatrick (2011b: 1), of the *New York Times*, referred to 'high-profile aides and diplomats' who 'continued to defect, among them Libya's interior minister and the country's ambassadors to the United States, India and Bangladesh'. In the London *Times*, Fletcher and Haynes (2011: 1) reported indignant statements by a range of defectors:

> Ahmed Gadhaf al-Dam, a cousin of Colonel Gaddafi, defected to Egypt, denouncing the Libyan regime's 'grave violations of human rights'. Another defector, the former justice minister Mustafa Abdel Galil, said the dictator still had biological and chemical weapons and would not hesitate to use them. 'At the end when he's really pressured, he can do anything. I think Gaddafi will burn everything left behind him.'

The 'defector angle' lent credibility to the Western discourse. After all, these were powerful statements by Libyan diplomats who appeared to be in sync with Western spokespersons condemning the Gaddafi government. Hence, on 24 February, the *Independent* cited John Kerry, chairman of the Senate Foreign Relations Committee, praising the defectors: '[...] "Libya's mission to the UN bravely condemned their own government. Now UN action is critical"' (cited in Usborne 2011: 4, 5).

But how genuine were the Libyan defections? The Western press provided some indications that Libyan defections could have been encouraged by the coordinated campaign of the US government to isolate the Gaddafi regime. For example, DeYoung and Whitlock (2011: A08) wrote on 2 March in the *Washington Post*:

> The [US-]administration has sharply increased both its rhetoric and actions against
> Gaddafi in recent days, hoping to persuade senior Libyan military and regime leaders
> to decide that his cause is lost and that they should turn against him. At the same
> time, it is coordinating possible military actions with European allies in case they
> become necessary.

It seems plausible to assume that Western pressures including the prospect of military and other forms of intervention had encouraged the defections as Libyan diplomats tried to cover their backs. A reading of many of the news items in the sample would suggest, however, that Libyan defections were conducted in response to the actions of the Libyan government.

In conclusion, the narrative emphasised in the newspapers under review was partial and driven by the forces opposing the Libyan regime. The shape of this power collective will now be further outlined. As already indicated by the source attribution of indignant statements, news media coverage was flooded by Western government announcements. Hence, the demonisation campaign was driven by officials. Furthermore, the discourse of shaming can be related to a range of partisan think tanks and actors. For instance, an early call for the establishment of a no-fly-zone was made by affiliates of the Brookings Institution (see Shaik 2011), which, according to scholars Mearsheimer and Walt (2006) was 'part of the pro-Israel chorus'. Moreover, as early as 21 February, an appeal supported by 70 NGOs, demanding the implementation of R2P, was publicised by the organization *UN Watch*, a pro-Israel NGO, together with the National Endowment for Democracy (see Forte 2012: 247; for the petition see UN Watch 2011). Dr. Sliman Bouchuiguir, of the Libyan League for Human Rights (LLHR), was one of the most prominent signatories of the petition. Bouchuiguir had been a leading campaigner for the implementation of R2P in Libya. As such, Bouchuiguir and the LLHR provided documentation about crimes allegedly committed by the Libyan government. This was part of the documentation used by the International Criminal Court, the Human Rights Council and the UN Security Council to form opinion on Libya (Cartalucci and Bowie 2012: 50–52; see also Forte 2012: 247–248). The validity of the evidence provided by Bouchuiguir was questioned in the documentary, *The Humanitarian War*, by French journalist Julien Teil (see *ibid*). According to Teil, resolutions implemented against Libya, which included its suspension from the Human Rights Council, were largely based 'on the statement claiming that Gaddafi had led jet attacks on his own people and engaged in violent repression against the uprising' (cited in Forte 2012: 247). Teil further found that these statements 'were spread before they could have been verified' (cited in *ibid*). Forte commented on the policy process depicted in Teil's documentary, which also featured an interview with Bouchuiguir (2012: 248):

> Bouchuguir [sic] was careful to note the sequence of events in his interview with Teil: all of the NGOs that signed the UN Watch petition were acquainted with one another, and it was the UN Human Rights Council that brought them to Geneva to present their case. That was when they signed the petition. In his presentation at the UNHRC, Bouchuguir [sic] further added the allegation that the Libyan government was using planes to bomb its own people, and using indiscriminate violence against all civilians. Bouchuguir's [sic] testimony also ended up 'informing' the International Criminal Court's indictment of Muammar Gaddafi, Saif al-Islam Gaddafi, and Abdullah Senussi.

As demonstrated in this section, Western newspapers were largely not able to critically examine what effectively constituted a partisan network. Quite to the contrary, the international press would feature many of the indignant allegations that this faction had produced – without substantial scrutiny.

Houla

In May 2015, about 116 civilians were killed in the Syrian village of Taldou, which is located in the Houla region in western Homs. The so-called Houla incident constituted a 'tipping point' (Fletcher 2012: 1, 6, 7) and paved the way for sanctions against Syria. Because Russia and China would not agree to UN Security Council authorisation of military measures, Western states shied away from direct military intervention. Like Račak and Benghazi, the Houla incident generated extensive news media attention and indignation. Houla had quickly served as a symbol for Syrian villainy. Yet again, the factual record of Houla does not suggest a monolithic picture.

The dominant Western narrative alleged that the Assad regime constituted the sole aggressor in the conflict. The Assad government's use of indiscriminate force is well documented. Thus, Human Rights Watch stated in a March 2012 report that it 'has repeatedly documented and condemned widespread violations by Syrian government forces, including disappearances, rampant use of torture, arbitrary detentions, and indiscriminate shelling of neighborhoods'. The organisation also found evidence for abuses conducted by armed opposition groups including kidnappings, torture and executions (*ibid*). Thus, according to Human Rights Watch (*ibid*), 'certain armed attacks by opposition groups were motivated by anti-Shia or anti-Alawite sentiments arising from the association of these communities with government policies'. Nonetheless, reports by Western human rights organisations broadly suggested that the Syrian government was responsible for more killings than the opposition (see Lynch 2016). Yet, many of the organisations that provide casualty figures, such as the Syrian Observatory for Human Rights, appear to be associated with the Syrian opposition and/or use methodologies that cannot be verified (see e.g. Christensen 2016). Thus, it has been difficult to establish the proportion of casualties in terms of civilians and combatants as well as Syrian regime and opposition forces. Looking at the casualty figures in Syria, by May 2012, between 6,000 and 15,000 people were killed (see Khera 2012). The Syrian Observatory for Human Rights had put the number of civilian dead at 9,183, and 3,821 dead from security services by May 2012 (*ibid*). While these figures should be used with caution, the ratios indicated that Syrian forces had received significant casualties and were not necessarily engaged in a one-sided killing spree against defenceless opposition groups. Casualty figures from the Syrian Observatory for Human Rights, incorporating the years 2011, 2012, and 2013 suggested that about 52,000 pro-government forces, 46,000 civilians and 29,000 anti-government forces were killed (see Wikiwand n.d.; also Reuters 2013). If we further consider these data, casualty estimates did not warrant the conclusion that pro-government forces were responsible for most of the violence. In fact, the high casualty figures on the side of the regime attested to the fact that the opposition applied significant offensive capabilities. While the Syrian army was arguably in the possession of superior fire-power, including air forces, these ratios point to a scenario in which both sides engaged in the use of heavy weaponry. A significant number of civilians was thus likely killed as a result of indiscriminate attacks by both sides and during fighting in urban theatres. These facts, of course, do not mitigate the responsibility of the Syrian army for the crimes it may have conducted when using force indiscriminately. But the same reasoning should then also apply to the opposition and its supporters who equally used weaponry in an indiscriminate fashion.

Secondly, already by the time the Houla incident took place, it was well established that the Syrian opposition had received support by outside powers. Diplomatic cables disclosed by *Wikileaks* show that between 2006 and at least until 2010 the US State Department had 'secretly financed Syrian political opposition groups' (Whitlock 2011). When the Syrian civil war eventually erupted, Western powers and their allies prepared to aid the Syrian opposition. In November 2011, the *Daily Telegraph* reported that members of the new Libyan regime met with the Syrian opposition and Turkish officials in Istanbul, Turkey, and declared they were ready to send arms and fighters to Syria (Sherlock 2011). On 9 March 2012, the website *Examiner.com* (Tilford 2012) reported a statement by Russian Ambassador to the UN, Vitaly Churkin, who 'accused Libya of training and arming rebels fighting against the Syrian government of President Bashar al-Assad': 'We have information that in Libya, with support from the "authorities", there is a special training center for Syrian rebels, and groups are sent from there to Syria, to attack the legal government,' Churkin said. The article also claimed that Libyan fighters were funnelled through Turkey and received 'military training from Western, Turkish and Arab army instructors, as well as civilian security consultants and ex-special forces trainers from the US, Britain, France, Italy, Saudi Arabia, Jordan and Qatar' (*ibid*).[7] On 19 March 2012, the *Australian* (Lyons 2012) referred to 'reports that Saudi Arabia, one of the key powerbrokers in the Middle East, had begun supplying rebels with "military equipment"'. The article further referenced Agence France Press quoting 'an Arab diplomat as saying: "Saudi military equipment is on its way to Jordan to arm the Free Syrian Army."' (*ibid*). Similarly, a critical commentary in the *Guardian* by Patrick Seale (2012: 27), published on 28 May 2012, stated:

> The Gulf states have pledged $100m to the opposition, to enable it to pay its fighters and buy arms. The US has no intention of getting involved in a war in Syria itself, but it is said to be co-ordinating the flow of weapons and intelligence to the rebels. Although its says it supports the Annan plan, it is unashamedly undermining it by helping to arm the rebels.

The *Washington Post's* DeYoung and Sly (2012: A 01) also reflected on such policies in an article published on 30 May: 'Some regional powers, led by Saudi Arabia, see deposing Assad as a way to damage arch enemy Iran. The Saudis and others in the region are funding arms shipments to the rebels and have called for outside military intervention.' In an 3 June op-ed for the *Post*, Danielle Pletka (2012: B 02), vice president of foreign and defense policy studies at the American Enterprise Institute, would even argue that word throughout the region was 'that Obama is comfortable subcontracting U.S. Middle East policy to Qatar and Saudi Arabia'.

Gulf state and Western proxy support for the opposition in Syria should further accelerate from 2012 onwards (for an overview and sources see Sinclair 2015).

In terms of the political designs that Western powers seek to implement in Syria, an essay by John Pilger, published on the journalist's website johnpilger.

com, provided evidence from leaked UK-US intelligence files suggesting that intervention in Syria had already been on the agenda in 1957 (2015). Pilger also reported of high level planning meetings about intervention in Syria that apparently had taken place before the start of the uprising in Syria:

> In 2013, the former French Foreign Minister Roland Dumas revealed that 'two years before the Arab spring', he was told in London that a war on Syria was planned. 'I am going to tell you something,' he said in an interview with the French TV channel LPC, 'I was in England two years before the violence in Syria on other business. I met top British officials, who confessed to me that they were preparing something in Syria [...]. Britain was organising an invasion of rebels into Syria. They even asked me, although I was no longer Minister for Foreign Affairs, if I would like to participate [...]. This operation goes way back. It was prepared, preconceived and planned.' (*ibid*)

In conclusion, these dimensions of the Syrian civil war appeared to have been reported in passing. Furthermore, the evidence suggested that the traditional colonial powers and their Arab allies were involved in a proxy war in Syria. Many of the proxy fighters thus in fact constituted terrorists. Yet, indignation in news media coverage, as the next section reveals, pointed mainly towards Syrian government culpability.

News media coverage

The Houla case produced a large quantity of indignant news items featuring statements about military intervention, only slightly undercutting Račak (see Table 1). Such treatment attested to the news media's propaganda function as a conveyor of interventionist strategies. In comparison with the other 'enemy' cases under review, Houla/Syria had most intensively been affected by violence. The high levels of violence may further explain the large volume of indignant statements demanding actions to stop human rights violations. On the other hand, and as we shall see in the next section, such indignant calls are far less pronounced in reporting about violent conflicts involving 'allied' countries (see also Table 1). In this section below, I will look more closely at the properties of news media reporting on Houla. Before presenting the findings of the indignation category, I will review important contextual evidence that suggested that the Syrian regime and not the opposition had attempted to reduce the violence during a ceasefire period. Significantly, while this evidence was reported in the news, it did not significantly alter the indignant discourse, as I will demonstrate further below.

On 27 May, two days after the Houla incident had occurred, the *Independent's* Patrick Cockburn (2012a: 36, 37) pointed out that 'the Houla slaughter makes Syria once again the centre of international attention and a possible target for some form of foreign intervention'. Indeed, the Syrian opposition had long been inviting foreign intervention. Already in November 2011, Colonel Riyadh al-Assad, chief of the Free Syrian Army, had demanded intervention including logistic support, protection, the establishment of no-fly- and buffer zones as well as strikes against targets with strategic value for the Syrian regime (see Zenko 2011). Houla was useful for the opposition because, as Michael Stephens, researcher at the Royal United Services Institute's branch in Qatar, argued, it 'changed the game completely in terms of what people were willing to accept and what they were not' (cited in Reuters Beirut 2012: 18).

Before Houla, foreign military intervention had arguably been complicated by a UN-authorised peace plan. The UN had established a supervision mission in Syria on 21 April 2012 to monitor a ceasefire between government and opposition forces as well as to implement a six-point peace plan to end the Syrian conflict. The peace plan was initially put forward by the then-Special Envoy to Syria Kofi Annan (see UNSMIS n.d.). Annan's peace plan constituted an important element of the policies that the 'international community' had enforced against the Assad regime and its adversaries. The Annan initiative was extensively featured in news media coverage. The plan was also important in that it could have halted the violence without changing the status quo in Syria. But the Houla incident contributed towards undermining the peace plan. Accordingly, Cockburn (2012b: 2, 3) stated in a further news item that the Houla 'massacre could mark a crucial stage in the war in Syria because it will energise the insurgents inside and outside the country' and will also 'underline that the ceasefire arranged by the UN-Arab League envoy Kofi Annan is foundering' (*ibid*). Yet, in the other news item by Cockburn (2012a: 36, 37) discussed above, the journalist provided crucial context about how the peace plan and the ceasefire agreement related to the war parties as well as the Houla event:

> The ceasefire was only sporadically implemented from the beginning. The government has always had more interest in its successful implementation, which would stabilise its authority, than the insurgents, who need to keep the pot of rebellion boiling. The UN monitoring team says that during the ceasefire 'the levels of offensive military operations by the government significantly decreased' while there has been 'an increase in militant attacks and targeted killings'. But any credit the Syrian

government might be hoping for showing restraint will disappear if the latest atrocities are confirmed.

If Cockburn's statements are accurate, then the Syrian government had no rational motif to commit an atrocity in Houla because this could jeopardise its outlook under the Annan plan and incite the opposition. Furthermore, as acknowledged by Cockburn and indicated by the cited statement of the UN monitoring team, the Syrian government benefited from the ceasefire and had even restrained its use of force. The opposition, on the other hand, had not much to gain from the ceasefire and actually increased its targeted killings during the period, as also suggested by the UN team quoted by Cockburn (see *ibid*). It is also important to note that Houla was partly a targeted killing and thus resembled similar actions reportedly conducted by the militants (see *ibid*). The *Guardian's* Milne (2012: 30) similarly reported that, according to estimates by human rights groups, lethal violence had decreased by 36 per cent since the Annan plan came into effect. Milne further highlighted how government casualties had 'increased sharply over the same period' with 953 killed since mid-March (*ibid*).

Significantly, Houla was useful for those factions within the opposition who demanded intervention by blaming the Assad regime for the violence. That is because if the Houla killings could be associated with the Assad regime they would, as Cockburn further argued, diminish 'any credit' it may 'be hoping' to obtain 'for showing restraint' and thus make Syria 'a possible target for some form of foreign intervention' (2012a: 36, 37). The critical op-ed comment by Seale (2012: 27) in the *Guardian* on 28 May argued just that: 'The strategy of the armed opposition is to seek to trigger a foreign armed intervention by staging lethal clashes and blaming the resulting carnage on the regime'. Additionally, the opposition could use the incident as an excuse not to adhere to the Annan plan. Again, this was indirectly acknowledged in an item by the *New York Times'* MacFarquhar and Saad (2012: 1) who wrote that the Free Syrian Army 'the loose federation of armed militias across the country, issued a statement saying it was no longer committed to the United Nations truce because the plan was merely buying time for the government to kill civilians and destroy cities and villages'. But if the UN monitors referred to by Cockburn were accurate, then it was the opposition, which had increased its violent attacks during the ceasefire period and not the Syrian regime. Overall, these dots were not connected in the news media, which highlighted statements discussing intervention rather than investigating the validity not only of the claims provided by the Syrian government but also of Western officials and the Syrian opposition. This further demonstrates an assessment of the news media's use of statements that could be classified as indignation.

I will firstly look at the Military policy category (for quantitative evidence see Table 1). On 28 May, the London *Times'* editorial (2012a: 2) referred to 'Anne-Marie Slaughter, a Princeton academic and former State Department official' who 'has proposed that the Friends of Syria group of nations establish "nokill zones" near the Turkish, Lebanese and Jordanian borders, with rebels armed with anti-tank and anti-aircraft weapons'. On the same day, the *New York Times* MacFarquhar (2012a: 1) provided space for Mitt Romney, then the designated Republican presidential candidate, demanding the armament of the opposition. 'The United States should work with partners to organize and arm opposition groups so they can fund themselves,' Romney was quoted (cited in *ibid*). Note that such armament policies were already taking place. MacFarquhar (*ibid*) also provided a tactical assessment of military policies towards Syria: 'Russia has typically rejected any international effort to support the opposition in a way that might repeat the NATO military intervention in Libya, and despite strong statements, the West has avoided getting further embroiled in the Syria fighting out of fear of the long-term, consequences.' The Russians had supported the UN authorised no-fly zone in Libya but did not agree with its actual implementation. A 29 May article by the *Guardian's* Black and Elder (2012: 16) elaborated on this issue near the bottom of the news story: 'Russia felt duped by the west after giving its support to a UN security council resolution that was phrased to support a no-fly zone but used to authorise armed Nato intervention.' This statement appeared to be an acknowledgement that the NATO intervention in Libya was conducted under false pretexts: rather than securing the air space, NATO had actively supported the opposition in Libya. It could thus be asked whether the news media should have investigated the justifications for intervention in Syria more thoroughly. Yet, substantial criticisms were not part of news coverage although a range of newspapers highlighted further Russian (and also Chinese) opposition to a UN-sanctioned military intervention in Syria. For example, David Blair (2012a: 21) argued in a feature for the *Daily Telegraph* on 29 May:

> [...] UN authority would be the essential prerequisite for intervention – and any attempt to win a vote in the Security Council would fall foul on Russia and China. Both countries may, in their own ways, be embarrassed by Mr Assad; Beijing may even, sotto voce, wish for his departure. Yet, neither Russia nor China will lift their vetoes on intervention.

According to Blair (*ibid*), Russian opposition lent itself to 'vital strategic interests' because 'Syria serves as the Kremlin's only base for influence in the Middle East, as well as providing a port for warships and a market for arms exports'. China, as Blair (*ibid*) further pointed out, 'has an ideological aversion to any interference in the "internal affairs" of sovereign countries'. But, as Blair (*ibid*) also conceded, both countries 'officially support the peace plan devised by Kofi Annan'. Accordingly, it could be argued that Western designs such as arming the opposition and other forms of military intervention posed a threat to Russian and Chinese interests. From a geo-strategic position, it was in fact understandable that Russia objected to intervention because this would undermine the Russian position in Syria. Similarly, the US would hardly accept a Russian-led campaign to implement such policies in Mexico or Colombia, two countries located in the American hemisphere, which have been afflicted by internal conflict and human rights abuses. Yet, the news media would provide space for actors who discussed the feasibility of precisely such interventionist policies in Syria, albeit under consideration of tactical concerns.

Thus, also on 29 May, the *Washington Post's* Liz Sly (2012a: A 06) reported a statement by General Martin Dempsey, the Chairman of the US Joint Chiefs of Staff, warning 'that such "atrocities" could trigger international military intervention' although 'he would like to see the global community exert greater diplomatic pressure on Assad before exploring military options'. Chris McGreal (2012: 1), of the *Guardian*, similarly reported Dempsey's statement in a front-page article titled: 'US threatens use of force after Syria massacre.' The article also provided tactical criticism by Mitt Romney and Republican Senator John McCain the latter calling 'the White House "feckless" for not doing more to stop Syria' (*ibid*). Ansgar Graw (2012: 7), of the German newspaper *Die Welt*, further elaborated on US deliberations about policy options indicating that the US would be hesitant to intervene militarily because it had not much to gain from intervention. Similarly, the *New York Times'* Landler (2012: 6) reported that Tom Malinowski, head of the Washington office of Human Rights Watch, said that even 'if the White House has valid reasons to avoid intervening' it would be 'useful to raise the possibility of military action' (2012: 6). Yet, the article went on, this might not translate into real policy because, as Landler further mentioned, 'there is little support in either party for military intervention' (*ibid*). On the other hand, the *Washington Post's* Pincus (2012: A 13) reported on 31 May how a 'group of Americans has been pressing for U.S. military involvement' in Syria. According to Pincus (*ibid*), the policy-makers included Senators John McCain (R-Ariz.), Lindsey O. Graham (R-S.C.), Joseph I. Lieberman (I-Conn.) and Mitt Romney and they demand to 'start with the supplying of arms to the Assad opposition with the implied promise that there would be additional support, starting with the application of air power'. The same policy was also advocated by France. On 30 May, Blair (2012b: 17), of the *Daily Telegraph*, referred to an interview by Francois Hollande, the then newly elected President of France, saying 'the use of armed force could be possible following Houla, but that it had to be carried out under UN auspices'. Hollande's statement was also reported in the German *Süddeutsche Zeitung* on 31 May (see Fried and Ulrich 2012: 1). The article added a reference to the German position. A spokesperson of the German foreign office was stated saying that 'there would be no reason to speculate about military options in relation to the Syrian situation' as it was important at the moment to implement the Annan peace plan (*ibid*). However, in other instances, the German position towards military policy appeared to be more sympathetic. The *New York Times* Kulish and MacFarquhar (2012: 8) wrote on 2 June:

> Russia's objection to any effort by the United States and its allies that could lead to a forceful United Nations Security Council intervention in Syria and the ouster of Mr. Assad has been a major source of contention. But Mr. Putin showed no sign of yielding to pressure from either Angela Merkel, Germany's chancellor, or later with Francois Hollande, the new president of France.

In the light of this statement, military intervention appeared to be disputed by Russia whereas major European powers like Germany and France appeared to attempt to influence Russia to agree to such a policy.

On 4 June, an item in the *Washington Post* by Liz Sly (2012b: A 01) reported that 'Secretary of State Hillary Rodham Clinton's public pronouncements on Syria took on a sharper tone as she signalled impatience with the U.N. peace plan, which has clearly failed to halt the violence, and with diplomatic efforts to push for tougher sanctions against Syria in the Security Council'. The UN monitors findings that the Syrian regime had actually reduced its offensive activities, whereas the opposition had expanded its attacks, was not mentioned in the article (for the UN findings see Cockburn 2012a: 36, 37). Rather than discussing ways to reduce the violence on both sides, Sly (2012b: A 01) mentioned how Clinton 'appeared to edge closer to endorsing a military option for Syria', saying, 'Every day that goes by makes the argument for it stronger' (cited in *ibid*).

Nonetheless, a range of procedural criticisms against military intervention were reported in some of the newspapers. For instance, Ian Black (2012a: 21), of the *Guardian*, summarised these tactical concerns on 8 June:

> After Iraq, Afghanistan and Libya, and with a presidential election looming in the US and the EU in deep crisis, Nato forces will not be deploying to Syria any time soon, by land, sea or air. No-fly zones, humanitarian corridors or no-kill zones – strategies that have been mooted to help the opposition – would all require offensive action against Assad's armed forces.

The *Guardian's* editorial even spoke out against military intervention because this could lead to 'a long war with an inconclusive outcome, possibly even the breakup of Syria' (The Guardian 2012: 36). However, such criticisms were largely tactical. In principle, the newspapers consistently depicted the Syrian regime as the sole nefarious actor without scrutinising the role of the opposition and its Arab and Western state supporters. Hence, while displaying a range of critiques and at times even procedurally opposing intervention, the newspapers did not seriously scrutinise the fact that the US was already intervening in Syria via proxies. Thus, the article by Black (2012a: 21) described a range of covert military activities already implemented in Syria, without noting that these policies could be part of the problem or could further undermine the Annan peace plan, which aimed to forestall a reduction in violence:

> External involvement is already a reality though: Arab support for the fighters of the Free Syrian Army appears to be growing, and there are signs they are acquiring anti-tank missiles, with the US playing some kind of covert co-ordinating role. Jihadi-type groups are also in evidence, Syrian opposition sources report – though their role is exaggerated by the regime. Russia and Iran, by contrast, openly support Assad, providing not just loyal political cover but arms, technology and advice.

A crucial point was not mentioned by Black: outside support for Syrian fighters is hardly compatible with international law. Yet, the overall tenor of news media coverage was that the 'international community' needed to act in Syria to stop the actions of the Assad government. In fact, on 7 June it was reported by the *Guardian's* (2012c: 2) Black that 'ministers and officials from 15 countries and the EU agreed at a meeting hosted by Turkey to convene a new "co-ordination group" to provide support to the Syrian opposition'. Hence, the international newspapers quite coherently provided a platform for Western politicians and other interest group sources to elaborate on interventionist policies. It was hardly a concern that the pro-posed interventionist strategies violated Syrian state sovereignty and could have further fuelled the conflict.

I will now look at the next categorical level of indignation, which dis-plays calls for action that were coded as Sanctions. The Sanctions category included a broad set of measures that were discussed in the news. The amount of news items carrying statements that were coded in this category was com-parable with Račak (see Table 1).

On 27 May, MacFarquhar and Saad (2012: 1), of the *New York Times*, ref-erenced British Foreign Secretary William Hague saying: 'Britain was looking for a strong international response and hoped to convene an "urgent" ses-sion of the United Nations Security Council "in the coming days."' The UN Security Council would actually condemn the Syrian government, as the *Post's* Sly reported on 29 May (2012a: A 06). Sly also referred to a statement by Salman Shaikh, director of the Brookings Doha Center, arguing that the UN statement 'contained no threat of new measures against the Syrian gov-ernment, and the international community is too divided to come up with effective ways of putting pressure on the regime' (*ibid*). According to the arti-cle, Shaikh also said: 'This gruesome incident could give real momentum to diplomatic efforts, but so far it's not had much effect' (cited in *ibid*). Note that intervention was again on the agenda of the pro-Israel Brookings Institution.

In fact, as highlighted above, concrete interventionist policies would soon be discussed. Furthermore, several sanctions measures had already been imposed by the US and EU. Hence, the *Guardian's* Black (2012b: 16) high-lighted on 29 May: '[…] on top of a non-binding UN statement, there is talk of yet more EU sanctions; another meeting of the large and unwieldy Friends of Syria group; a frosty few minutes at the Foreign Office for the Syrian charge d'affaires in London.' As in the case of Libya, diplomatic penalties were part of the Sanctions catalogue. On 30 May, Jagger and Boyes (2012: 6), of the London *Times* reported on how 'European Union countries, the United States, Australia and Canada expelled more than 20 Syrian diplomats'. 'The initiative', the article went on, 'appears to have been co-ordinated by Britain and William Hague […] said it was part of a strategy, including a tightening of EU sanctions, to squeeze the Syrian leader' (*ibid*). Thorsten Knuf (2012: 7), of the German *Frankfurter Rundschau*, similarly reported on 30 May that Syrian ambassadors had to leave several countries and this 'was part of a coordinated action'. Knuf further reported how German Minister for Foreign Affairs Westerwelle had called for Assad's removal: 'He has to clear the way for peaceful change in Syria' (cited in *ibid*). An item in *Die Welt* by Gabriela Keller (2012: 8), published on 30 May, similarly cited Westerwelle denouncing Syria for '[…] "using heavy weapons against civilians in defiance of Security Council Resolutions"' and arguing that this should lead to 'serious diplomatic and political consequences'. Yet, due to the Russian veto, the UN Security Council could not agree to a further sanctions packet (see The Times 2012b).

Significantly, the controversy over Sanctions remained on the news media agenda – often coupled with threats of military intervention. For instance, on 7 June, Gladstone and Lowrey (2012: 8), of the *New York Times*, reproduced statements by US Treasury Secretary Timothy F. Geithner, 'who hosted the so-called Friends of the Syrian People International Working Group on Sanctions', saying 'he hoped that "all responsible countries will soon join in taking appropriate economic actions against the Syrian regime"'. The journalists further wrote that Geithner's 'remarks did not rule out the possibility that military action could also be invoked because sanctions could include, "if necessary, Chapter 7 action in the U.N. Security Council […]"' (*ibid*).

Overall, the following policies were discussed in the news media and codified as Sanctions:

- Demand an end to violence and/or change of policies and/or action against and/or intervention short of military policies in Syria.
- Demand international action against Syria by states such as the US, Saudi-Arabia and/or Qatar.
- UN Security Council special sessions or other meetings by Western states to consider policies.
- Obama should act outside of UN and without Russia and/or do more.
- Discuss or demand sanctions and/or UN actions and/or an UN arms embargo and/or political, diplomatic and/or economic sanctions and/or to bypass UN Security Council to impose sanctions.
- Demilitarise both sides in the conflict.
- Support the opposition and/or provide funds to the opposition.
- Intensify pressure and/or urge Russia and/or China to put pressure on Syria.
- Implement Annan plan and/or criticise flaws of the plan and/or lose faith in it and/or declare it as a failure.
- Blame UN observers for not acting properly and/or demand withdrawal of observers and/or demand expansion of mandate.
- Discuss expulsion of Syrian diplomats.

- Discuss suspension of Syria from Arab League.
- Isolate and/or push out/remove Assad and/or end his regime and/or implement Yemen style solution and/or demand Assad's resignation and/or demand penalty for Assad (i.e. 'regime change').

The Sanctions outlined above framed the policy deliberations about Syria. Issues were centred on the Syrian government and largely exempted the opposition as well as its state supporters from substantial scrutiny. In fact, Western governments and their 'allies', like Saudi-Arabia and Qatar, appeared to be regarded as honest brokers.

On a third level, newspapers carried calls for Investigations into the Houla incident (for the quantitative amount of coverage see Table 1). Thus, on 27 May, MacFarquhar and Saad of the *New York Times* quoted Hillary Clinton demanding: 'Those who perpetrated this atrocity must be identified and held to account' (cited in MacFarquhar and Saad 2012: 1). Similarly, in the *Observer* of the same day, Chulov provided space for then-British Foreign Secretary William Hague saying: 'Our urgent priority is to establish a full account of this appalling crime and to move swiftly to ensure that those responsible are identified and held to account' (cited in Chulov 2012a: 1). The *Die Welt* newspaper's Keller and Smirnova referred to the German UN Ambassador Peter Wittig 'demanding that the incidents in Houla ought to be independently investigated' (Keller and Smirnova 2012: 6). On 28 May, MacFarquhar, of the *New York Times*, quoted Navi Pillay, the UN High Commissioner for Human Rights, calling 'for Syrian cooperation with an independent, international investigation to determine what happened' (MacFarquhar 2012a: 1). On 31 May, the *Washington Post* carried an op-ed by Donatella Rovera (2012: A 15), Amnesty International's senior adviser on crisis response, criticising the UN observer mission for 'the absence of a mandate to monitor and investigate human rights abuses, including war crimes and crimes against humanity' demanding that the body 'must investigate allegations of abuse by both sides'. Such an authorisation for an investigation was, as the *New York Times* reported on 2 June, voted in by the 'main United Nations human rights body' and could according to top UN rights official Navi Pillay 'lead to war-crimes charges' (Kulish and MacFarquhar 2012: 8). In this context, an article by Jordans in the *Washington Post* mentioned on 2 June that the UN had already conducted 'preliminary U.N. investigation' but a US and Arab-led resolution would instruct 'an expert panel to conduct an "international, transparent, independent and prompt investigation"' thus echoing 'calls by U.N. rights chief Navi Pillay for the U.N. Security Council to consider referring Syria to the International Criminal Court' (Jordans 2012: A 06). Yet, as Black in the *Guardian* wrote, Russian Foreign Minister Sergei Lavrov was expected to veto 'moves to refer Syria to the international criminal court for war crimes' (Black 2012b: 16). In fact, the resolution by the UN Human Rights Council that called for an international criminal inquiry was not approved by Russia, China and Cuba (Chulov 2012b: 35). Thus, the *Guardian's* Borger (2012: 12) wrote on 4 June that the International Criminal Court (ICC) in The Hague was 'unable to begin an investigation into the killing without a mandate from the UN security council'. As in the other 'enemy' cases under review, calls for Investigations highlighted the fact that the Houla incident was a terrible crime and that legal accountability should be established. In comparison, there were no calls for referrals to the ICC when 'allied' countries were the perpetrators of human rights violations (see discussion in next section).

On a fourth layer, indignant statements included Outrage (for the extensive quantitative findings see Table 1). Like the calls for Investigations, statements of Outrage contributed to the demonising campaign and indicated regime responsibility for crimes. Take the following examples: MacFarquhar and Saad (2012: 1), of the *New York Times*, said on 27 May that international officials 'largely blamed the government' for the incident. Furthermore, Ban Ki-moon, the United Nations Secretary General, and Kofi Annan, his predecessor and envoy to Syria, issued a 'scathing condemnation' saying this '[...] appalling and brutal crime involving indiscriminate and disproportionate use of force is a flagrant violation of international law and of the commitments of the Syrian government to cease the use of heavy weapons in population centers and violence in all its forms' (cited in *ibid*). The same article cited further statements of Outrage by the White House, saying the incident was 'a vile testament to an illegitimate regime that responds to peaceful political protest with unspeakable and inhuman brutality,' Hillary Clinton, who described the event as a 'vicious assault that involved a regime artillery and tank barrage on a residential neighbourhood,' Laurent Fabius, the French Foreign Minister, accusing the Syrian regime of 'new massacres' (cited in *ibid*) William Hague, who said 'Britain was looking for a strong international response' and the Syrian National Council, the umbrella opposition organisation in exile, condemning 'the killing' and calling 'for three days of mourning' (*ibid*). An article by Brössler (2012: 1) in the *Süddeutsche Zeitung* of 30 May referred to a statement by German Minister for Foreign Affairs Westerwelle who denounced

Syria: 'The Syrian regime is responsible for the horrible events in Houla' arguing that Syria had to face consequences because 'it applied heavy weapons against its own people in defiance of resolutions of the security council' (cited in *ibid*). An item by Jagger (2012: 6, 7), of the London *Times*, re-produced indignant statements by several actors including General Mood, William Hague, Ban Ki Moon, Kofi Annan, Hillary Clinton, the Free Syrian Army, EU foreign policy chief Baroness Ashton of Upholland, Nabil Elaraby, Secretary-General of the Arab League, Justin Forsyth of Save the Children, Deputy Prime Minister of the UK Nick Clegg, and Sheikh Abdullah bin Zayed al-Nahyan, UAE Foreign Minister. General Mood was also cited with the following words: 'In any scenario, I have never been able to anticipate this kind of violence. It is beyond the imagination. […]' (cited in *ibid*).

In the light of the Houla event, Outrage was certainly warranted. The problem of news media reporting rested in its inability to assess critically the role of Western powers and the actions of the Syrian opposition. Indignation mainly pointed one way: towards the Syrian government and its forces. Thus, while Houla would not directly lead to military intervention, indignant news reporting contributed towards outlawing the Syrian government and preparing the ground for future intervention. Moreover, the news media hardly scrutinised the Syrian opposition, which had increased its use of force during the period when the Annan peace plan was supposed to be implemented. It was largely not scrutinised how Western and Gulf state support might have encouraged the Syrian opposition to escalate the violence and thus undermine the Annan plan. Finally, it was not further investigated by the newspapers that the Houla incident could even have been carried out by the opposition with the aim of inviting foreign military intervention. In his book on Syria, Anderson (2016: 71) provided the following context:

> The killings at Houla deserve close attention. However, because of NATO's abuse of the 'no fly zone' authorisation for Libya and the wider geo-politics of Syria, Russia and China would not allow a similar UN Security Council authorisation of force. As the US did not want another prolonged ground war, big power intervention remained indirect, through proxy militias. While the Syrian army attacked those armed groups, those groups carried out public executions and constantly tried to blame the Syrian Army for attacks on civilians.

The blaming of the Syrian army apparently worked well: as my study reveals, the US, UK and German press had orientated its indignation mainly towards the Syrian government and its forces.

'Allied' countries

Fallujah 1

On 5 April, the US Marines' First Expeditionary Force was ordered with a full-scale attack on Fallujah to 'root out the insurgents who had turned the city into their stronghold' (Allawi 2007: 276; see also Herring and Rangwala 2006: 29). This operation was part of the wider US strategy to attack the Sunni resistance in Iraq and coincided with a Shiite uprising in Najaf, Baghdad and other Iraqi cities led by the cleric Muqtada al-Sadr. In early 2004, about one year after the official ending of the Iraq War had been proclaimed by then-US President George W. Bush (see CNN 2003), US/Coalition forces were confronted with two resistance movements. At this point in time, Fallujah 1 constituted the most comprehensive military operation by US/Coalition forces. But it was by no means the only one. Between May 2003 and November 2004, the US/Coalition had engaged in about 115 operations each of which could last up to several weeks and included dozens of raids against suspected targets (GlobalSecurity.org n.d.a).

The Fallujah 1 incident generated extensive news media coverage and indignation. In fact, the US/Coalition had to halt its operation on 29 April because the use of military force in civilian areas had provoked outrage among the Iraqi populace. Moreover, the Iraqi political elite, which had collaborated with US/Coalition authorities, threatened to abandon its assistance. Political repercussions were fuelled by an 'unembedded' Al-Jazeera crew, led by the reporter and talk show host Ahmed Mansour, which was the only news team to broadcast graphic footage from Fallujah depicting US actions as a horrific atrocity (see discussion in Mansour 2009). Yet, Fallujah 1 generated nowhere near as much indignation as the already reviewed incidents involving 'enemy' countries. Indignation was mainly relegated to statements of Outrage by Iraqi actors and did not incorporate calls for 'internationalisation' of the conflict or more specific political actions to be implemented against the US/Coalition. As my study reveals, the news media largely followed the official narrative according to which the US/Coalition engaged in legitimate counter-insurgency operations.

The factual record suggests, however, that the levels of violence in Fallujah were at least comparable with those identified in the 'enemy' case studies under review. Furthermore, evidence suggested that the US/Coalition had used indiscriminate force: Fallujah was reportedly treated like a free-fire zone with snipers being engaged in random killings (see Jamail 2007: 130–142; Mansour 2009; Schwartz 2008: 94–97).

The Fallujah 1 incident comprised an intensive military operation involving artillery, ground and air forces. The sociologist Schwartz (2008: 95–96) described the US/Coalition military strategy in April as follows:

> The invasion of Fallujah started with air attacks on electrical power plants and other public services, a standard shock-and-awe technique designed to deprive the resistance of needed resources and undermine the morale of the insurgents and their supporters. Ground forces then assaulted the three neighborhoods [sic] that marines believed were most supportive of the guerrillas. [...]

> The occupation brought the full strength of its technological superiority to bear: armored [sic] vehicles that could blast holes in any cover used by the guerrillas, automatic salvos from helicopters and C-130 gunships that could shoot through the walls of most buildings, and–when the return fire was not silenced by these weapons–air strikes featuring bombs (some as large as two thousand pounds) that annihilated large structures in a few seconds.

Fallujah has a population of 250,000–300,000 inhabitants, of which about 60,000 had fled during the military operation (GlobalSecurity.org n.d.a. for Operation Vigilant Resolve; Zollmann 2008). Additionally, Fallujah constituted a densely populated area. The US/Coalition was attacking an urban area with a size of roughly 20 km^2 encompassing 50,000 buildings arranged in 2,000 blocks each averaging 100 × 200 m (Camp 2009: 13).[8] Camp (*ibid*) cited Marine Major Christeon Griffin commenting on the environment: '[The houses] are so close together that there's only a two-foot gap between them [...] literally your house is touching your neighbour's house [...] minimal wasted space. It is the most densely built-up place I've ever seen.' Similarly, Amir Taheri (2004), of Arab News, argued that Fallujah had 'one of the highest rates of demographic density in Iraq'.

The use of heavy weaponry in urban Fallujah was thus questionable under the Geneva Conventions because it expectedly generated civilian casualties. In fact, NGOs and local medical facilities reported a heavy toll on the civilian population (for evidence see Holmes 2007; Jamail 2007). According to the organisation Iraq Body Count (IBC) (IBC 2004b), during the Fallujah 1 incident, about 600 civilians were killed 'with over 300 of these being women and children'. IBC claimed it derived its figures from 'multiply-cited reports from doctors and eyewitnesses' (*ibid*). According to IBC (*ibid*), the number of civilian deaths 'demonstrates the huge impact of US attacks on civilian areas, and allows the conclusion to be drawn that many of the males killed must also have been non-combatants'. Furthermore, IBC assumed that most of the dead were 'killed before US forces began to permit women and children to be evacuated from the town' (*ibid*). According to IBC's Principal Researcher, Hamit Dardagan, the US/Coalition aimed to '"pacify" Falluja via "overwhelming" military means' and this 'was first and foremost a disaster for its civilian population'. Moreover, as Dardagan observed, the incident comprised 'attacks on ambulances and sniper fire at children as well as the aerial bombardment of residential areas' (*ibid*).

Why did the US/Coalition apply what is termed overwhelming force in Fallujah? It is well documented that the US was determined to rebuild Iraq as a Western asset and military launch pad in the Middle East, which included the privatisation of the Iraqi economy (see Jamail 2007; Klein 2007; Schwartz 2008: Part II). When Iraqi acceptance for this strategy failed to materialise, the US/Coalition resorted to force. On 29 June 2003, US governor L. Paul Bremer III, then-head of the Coalition Provisional Authority (CPA),[9] explained to the BBC's Peter Sissons how the US/Coalition would handle the growing militancy of the Iraqis:

> [...] we are going to fight them and impose our will on them and we will capture or, if necessary, kill them until we have imposed law and order on this country [...]. (cited in BBC News 2003)

Looking at US/Coalition counter-insurgency operations in Iraq, Schwartz (2008) argued that rules of engagement permitted the use of military force whenever soldiers expected the presence of fighters, experienced enemy threats or found themselves under attack. Because counter-insurgency operations tended to take place in populated areas, the use of force routinely led to killings of civilians. Moreover, the rules of engagement were also enforced near check-points, during military escorts and demonstrations (for a detailed discussion see Schwartz 2008: 75–80).

The scale and effects of US/Coalition tactics during the Iraq occupation are well documented: Human Rights Watch (2003b) classified an incident in Fallujah in 2003, during which US forces shot 17 demonstrators, as 'excessive use of force by US troops'. In another study, Human Rights Watch (2003c) investigated civilian deaths caused by the US military in Baghdad. The organisation found 'a pattern' of 'over-aggressive tactics, indiscriminate shooting in residential areas and a quick reliance on lethal force' (*ibid*: 4). Likewise, a 2004 report by Amnesty International (2004: 4) on the first year of the occupation states: 'Scores of civilians have been killed apparently as a result of excessive use of force by US troops or have been shot dead in disputed circumstances.' In 2007, the *Nation* interviewed 50 US combat veterans from the Iraq War to inquire the effects of warfare on the civilian population. According to the report: 'Fighting in densely populated urban areas has led to the indiscriminate use of force and the deaths at the hands of occupation troops of thousands of innocents' (Hedges and Al-Arian 2007).

Moreover, an important element of military strategy was to rely on air force support. The majority of civilian deaths attributed to the US/Coalition during the first one and a half years of the occupation was according to surveys caused by aerial weaponry (see Roberts *et al.* 2004: 1863; also Hersh 2005).

US/Coalition dominance in military power found expression in casualty ratios. If we look at nationwide casualty figures, dating from March 2003 to March 2004, conservative estimates suggested that 6,990 to 14,007 civilians were killed in Iraq, the latter figure including the invasion phase (see IBC n.d., 2013 and sources in Chapter 4). A passive survey by Medact (2003: 1) estimated up to 55,000 civilian and combatant deaths by October 2003. About 1,315 US/Coalition forces were killed between May 2003 and December 2004 (CNN n.d.). According to stats by Jim Michaels (2007) of *USA Today*, resistance casualties for the same period were higher, with 597 fighters killed in 2003 (excluding Iraq army casualties during the Iraq War) and 6,801 fighters killed in 2004.

These ratios – low US/Coalition casualties, medium resistance casualties, and high civilian casualties – signal greater imbalances than identified in the ratios of the 'enemy' countries reviewed above. The data also indicates that in Iraq, the US/Coalition suffered the least amount of casualties due to superiority in technology and fire-power. Consistent with casualty ratios, contextual evidence suggested that US/Coalition forces were responsible for the largest segments of killings in Iraq. Accordingly, IBC claims that the 'majority of civilian deaths during the first year (at least 55%) were directly caused by US/Coalition forces' (IBC 2013). This means that the US/Coalition had arguably inflicted greater numbers of casualties in Iraq than the reviewed 'enemy' governments in their respective nationwide theatres. It seems plausible to assume that if we compare casualties for the periods that are assessed in this study, the US/Coalition had killed more civilians in Iraq than the Syrian army in Syria. However, this reality was not apparent from news reporting which framed US/Coalition actions in benign and Syrian army actions in nefarious terms. Similarly, the Western news media and 'humanitarian interventionists' in the intellectual community largely remained silent about these casualty figures and potential US/Coalition responsibility for civilian deaths.

It is also paradoxical that US/Coalition forces – in the same fashion as the Syrian army – had at times justified their actions in Iraq arguing that the resistance comprised foreign fighters and al-Qaeda terrorists (see Zollmann 2012 for an assessment of the classification of the resistance). Yet, while there was evidence that the Syrian rebellion had been fuelled by outside powers and included foreign mercenaries (see discussion in previous section), hardly any evidence to that effect materialised in Iraq in 2003 or 2004.[10] The Iraqi resistance in Fallujah was largely home-grown and acted in defiance of a foreign occupation power. Yet, in reversal of the facts, the news media depicted the actions of the Syrian regime as illegitimate and those of the US/Coalition as legitimate.

News media coverage

Western news media coverage would not treat US/Coalition actions in the same fashion as similar actions conducted by 'enemy' countries. This is clearly demonstrated by the data in Table 1, which shows lower levels of indignation during reporting of Fallujah 1. More specifically, the news media would not feature any statements coded as Military policy in the indignation category. Double standards in the intensity and distribution of indignation are so great that calls for no-fly zones, protected zones or humanitarian corridors are not featured in news coverage on human rights violations by 'allied' countries. This is particularly striking because Iraq suffered a significant number of civilian deaths due to air strikes, certainly more than Libya and Kosovo during the respective time frames (for casualty figures in Iraq see Roberts *et al.* 2004: 1863; see also Hersh 2005 for air power).

Air forces were also a major component of US/Coalition military strategy in Fallujah. On 8 April 2004, Patrick Cockburn (2004a: 1), of the *Independent*, depicted Fallujah under attack:

> AN AIRBORNE assault on a mosque killed at least 40 worshippers attending prayers in the city of Fallujah yesterday [...].
>
> The aircraft fired a rocket and a bomb into the compound of the Abdul-Aziz al-Samarrai mosque.
>
> Witnesses said the attack came as worshippers gathered for afternoon prayers. Improvised hospitals were set up in private homes to treat the wounded and prepare the dead for burial. [...]

> Overall civilian casualties in Fallujah are not known but 16 children and eight
> women were reported to have been killed when US aircraft hit four houses on Tues-
> day, according to Hatem Samir, an official at Fallujah hospital.

On 9 April, Cockburn cited the indignant Iraqi Hashim al-Jenabi, saying
about the strike against the Mosque: 'They talk about terrorism against the
twin towers in the US, but why is it not terrorism when American planes hit
a mosque and kill 40 people' (cited in Cockburn 2004d: 5).

While the newspapers carried such indignant statements of Outrage highlighting the effects of air strikes, this did not translate into calls for preventive
actions. Imagine how the news media would have reacted if evidence had
emerged that Gaddafi's air force had killed 40 prayers in a mosque in Benghazi.
Such evidence never materialised but Libya was marked for no-fly zones and
intervention.

Statements classified as Military policy could also have entailed strategies
of demilitarisation. Yet, such considerations hardly appeared in the reporting. Moreover, there were very few indignant statements demanding to constrain the US/Coalition forces' scope of operation – Sanctions were off the
agenda. Hence, there were no calls for UN resolutions to halt the violence
or for the implementation of peace plans specifying policy norms to mitigate
the conflict. No actor was quoted demanding the imposition of actual sanctions against the US/Coalition governments. This shows how powerful states
remain exempt from international punishment.

Rare examples of news items coded as Sanctions constituted the following: On 8 April, Julian Borger (2004b: 4), of the *Guardian*, mentioned Tom
Daschle, the then-Democratic leader in the US Senate, saying that 'reports
of civilian deaths should be investigated' and calling 'for greater international involvement in Iraq'. Rainer Hermann (2004b: 1), of the *Frankfurter
Allgemeine Zeitung*, mentioned Harith al Dhari, the General Secretary of the
Association of Muslim Scholars, asking 'the Arab world for help against the
occupation forces'. A critical comment by Zangana (2004b: 19), published
in the *Guardian* on 10 April, demanded that the role of the UN should be
re-defined, 'to work with Iraqis to rebuild their country, restore democracy
and regain their dignity' and to 'not to legitimise US-led occupation'. On 10
April, Hider and Bennett (2004: 1), of *The Times*, quoted Russia calling for
'an end to military operations, and restraint' (cited in *ibid*). Steele (2004b: 16)
suggested in a critical commentary putting 'foreign forces under an unambiguous UN mandate, name an early date for their full withdrawal that Iraqis can
believe, and immediately reduce the US contingent, which has shown it lacks

the training and enough commanders who are able to conduct intelligent peace-keeping'.

As mentioned above, such calls would not lead to more sustained discussions about Sanctions or other measures to constrain US/Coalition violence. There were tactical discussions about strengthening the role of the UN in Iraq. These were not coded as Sanctions because they emerged from US/Coalition government circles and largely not from actors belonging to foreign governments.

As Table 1 further shows, there were only seven items in the whole Fallujah 1 sample which were coded in the Sanctions category. It should be noted that there were intensive discussions in the news media about US/Coalition policies. Military tactics and the use of force were critically discussed and evaluated. However, such deliberations did not go so far as to prescribe the implementation of institutional policy measures, such as UN resolutions.

Similarly, only few items included discussions about investigations (see the article by Borger quoted above). For instance, the *Guardian* leader on 15 April stated:

> Now, the US military itself estimates that 600 Iraqis have been killed so far during the fighting in the Iraqi town, where many of Falluja's 300,000 civilians have been caught in the middle of a ring of US soldiers, and where fierce fighting still rages. The New York Times reported yesterday that US marines had orders to shoot any males who look of military age out after dark, whether armed or not. 'Sometimes the gunfire was so long and steady it sounded like rain,' the Times observed. This is a massacre in the making. The United Nations should investigate the deadly events in Falluja, as it did in Jenin, as soon as possible. (The Guardian 2004b: 25)

This appears to be a highly critical editorial reflecting on the indiscriminate nature of the operation in Fallujah. Yet, the allegation that civilians had been killed 'during the fighting' suggests that deaths were the tragic casualties of war. Note that when 'enemy' countries kill civilians on a comparable scale they are not depicted as casualties from 'fighting' but as 'murders'. Furthermore, it is important that the incidents depicted in the *Guardian* did not generate sustained indignation. There was virtually no hint in the newspaper sample as to whether the UN conducted any investigation in Fallujah. For instance, the *Süddeutsche Zeitung* mentioned in a short news items that 'the United Nations are discussing intervention' (2004a: 2). However, the context about these deliberations is neither explored nor highlighted in other news articles. Thus, propaganda in the news does not necessarily operate on the level of exclusion of inconvenient material. Rather, propaganda manifests as the selective emphasis of facts. Additionally, the press is able to describe nefarious behaviour, like the establishment of free fire zones in population centres or indiscriminate attacks, without further investigating these issues. If 'allied' countries conduct human rights violations, the press's motivation to conduct follow-up stories and investigations appears to be muted.

The largest amount of indignant news items was found in the Outrage category (see Table 1). The Fallujah 1 incident had enraged the Iraqi population and the Arab world. Thus, indignant statements by Arab actors were featured in news reporting.

For example, on 9 April 2004, Cockburn (2004d: 5) of the *Independent* indicated how Iraqis classified the nature of US military tactics: 'Many Iraqis say the Americans are killing people who have done nothing in an act of collective punishment [...].' Collective punishment constitutes a serious crime under the Geneva Convention. Again, this matter of fact was reported but no further context or follow-up investigations were featured in the newspapers aside from cursory mentioning (see examples below). Cockburn (*ibid*) further quoted a range of indignant Iraqis:

> 'It is barbaric what is happening at Fallujah,' said Abdul Rahman Khalil, an engineer working in the oil industry after he had given blood. 'The Americans don't see the difference between resistance and ordinary people.'

> Tariq Hamoudi, another engineer, said: 'We work for a company specialising in heavy equipment for the oil refining sector and both Shia and Sunni feel the same in our company. We are supporting Fallujah. It is not acceptable what the Americans are doing.'

In the *New York Times* of the same day, MacFarquhar (2004: 10) referred to Arab media reports describing how 'Falluja Is Burning' (Egyptian newspaper Al Ahrar) or decrying 'A Massacre Against Muslims in Falluja' (Al Wafd) (cited in *ibid*). On 10 April, McCarthy (2004d: 4), of the *Guardian*, argued that the 'ferocious fighting and huge loss of life has sparked fury among many Iraqis and has brought outright condemnation even from America's allies in Iraq'. This would even have led a member of 'the US-appointed Iraqi Governing Council' to suspend 'his membership and a second said he might resign'. McCarthy quoted a third member of the Council, Adnan Pachachi, saying that these '[...] operations were a mass punishment for the people of Falluja' and '[...] we consider these operations by the Americans unacceptable and illegal' (cited in *ibid*). Stephen Farrell (2004: 16), of *The Times*, summarised the Iraqi discourse as follows:

> But their anger is now fuelled by the daily scenes on their television screens of US troops attacking Fallujah, the mounting casualty figures from helicopter gunship attacks on that town and protests from Sunni clerics and hospital workers that aid convoys are being denied access by US forces.

On 12 April, Cockburn (2004c: 4) lamented how the 'US army's trigger-happy use of its massive fire power, regardless of how many civilians are killed infuriates Iraqis'. On 14 April, the German *tageszeitung* highlighted 'sharp criticisms of the US occupation forces' siege of Fallujah' by the US human rights organisation Occupation Watch (GB 2004: 1). According to the newspaper, Iman Ahmed Khammas, a representative of the organisation, had called the situation of people in the city 'catastrophic' (cited in *ibid*). 'Hospitals in Fallujah lack blood reserves and medication,' said Khammas who called the siege 'illegal' and a violation of the Geneva Conventions (cited in *ibid*). There was also some international concern. On 15 April, the *Guardian's* Jonathan Steele (2004a: 14) quoted Lakhdar Brahimi 'a highly respected veteran diplomat' who 'serves as the special adviser on Iraq to the UN secretary general, Kofi Annan'. Accordingly, Brahimi criticised the US/Coalition saying: 'The cordoning off and siege of a city is not acceptable. Collective punishment is not acceptable' (cited in *ibid*). And finally, on 17 April, the *Guardian* published a guest article by Jo Wilding (2004: 13), a UK human rights campaigner who stayed in Fallujah during the siege. Wilding (*ibid*) wrote that nowhere in Fallujah was safe and reported of the following incidents:

> The times I have been shot at – once in an ambulance and once on foot trying to deliver medical supplies – it was US snipers in both cases. It is so unacceptable to stop medical aid getting through. They could have just asked to search us. (*ibid*)

These examples of Outrage demonstrate that newspaper coverage was not monolithic. A careful reading of a large newspaper sample pointed to a range of indignant statements, which shamed the US/Coalition for their actions. But if compared with the 'enemy' cases, the standard of reporting was different. Outrage was largely confined to Iraqi and Arab actors and such statements were included in an irregular and rather scattered fashion. The news certainly carried a large amount of tactical criticisms. Yet, such deliberations did not seriously question the right of US/Coalition forces to use military might in Fallujah.

There was also an ideological dimension. Even highly critical writers appeared to accept the US/Coalition as a legitimate force in Iraq. Take for instance the comment by Steele, who represented the critical spectrum of Western journalists. Steel rhetorically asked as to whether the US/Coalition could 'find a path back to stability and acceptance' suggesting that the 'key task' was 'to make the occupation invisible' (2004b: 16). 'Enemy' countries would not receive such generous media treatment. Imagine a journalist writing after the Račak incident: 'Can the FRY/Serbs find a path back to stability and acceptance? The key task is to make the occupation of Kosovo invisible.' Such benign news media treatment is only granted to 'allied' countries.

Moreover, in coverage on the Fallujah 1 incident, criticism largely focused on occupation policies. While this included substantial criticisms about the US/Coalition's handling of the 'insurgency' the press did not establish an independent narrative about broader occupation policies. The latter were largely critiqued from a tactical point of view. This is evidenced by Cockburn (2004b: 10), who also represents the critical spectrum in the British press, and who stressted that the US had made 'a series of unforced errors' in Iraq thus evoking a Vietnam-like quagmire scenario. Cockburn (*ibid*) relegates these errors to 'hardline civilians in the Pentagon' who 'retain their control of the' CPA 'which they have staffed with fellow neo-conservatives who share their over-simplistic agendas for Iraq'. As a consequence, Cockburn (*ibid*) further argues: '[...] the US is reduced to playing its only remaining card in Iraq, which is its overwhelming military strength.' This example of heated administration criticism is illustrative for a broader 'quagmire' discourse featured in all newspapers under review but particularly in the UK press. Such reprimands echoed elite criticism towards unilateral US policies in Iraq. As British Tory leader Michael Howard argued, the UK is 'actually punching below our weight politically and diplomatically because we don't have a real say in the policy-making which takes place in Baghdad and the execution of that policy' (cited in Sparrow 2004: 5). Similarly, Watt and Norton-Taylor (2004: 1) reported how 'senior figures in diplomatic and military circles in Whitehall are exasperated by their [US forces] behaviour'.

The US/Coalition halted the first Fallujah operation on 29 April not least in reaction to the protest among ordinary Iraqis and the Iraqi elite, which threatened to abandon its assistance. US-General Conway resultantly authorised the formation of the 'Fallujah Brigades' an experiment to regain control of Fallujah through an Iraqi proxy-force. This project failed as the 'Fallujah Brigade' united with the resistance, which remained its base in Fallujah (Allawi 2007: 277ff.). Consequently, after intensive preparations, the US/Coalition would launch a second and larger operation in November 2004.

Fallujah 2

On 6 November 2004, after warplanes, helicopters and unmanned drones had repeatedly bombed areas in Fallujah throughout October, a US army cavalry unit (the Black Jack Brigade) established a 270 degree cordon around Fallujah to disallow anyone entering or leaving the city. Moreover, 850 soldiers of the British Black Watch regiment were ordered to patrol the driveways between Baghdad and Fallujah in order to cut the rebels' supply lines (Camp 2009: 128, 131; Lange 2006: 12).[11] Preparatory military operations started on 7 November and the main assault begun on the following day. About 15,000 US/Coalition soldiers took part in the operation which had been planned since early September and which the US named 'Operation Phantom Fury' (Camp 2009: 123, 131, 169; U.S. Department of Defence 2004). Six battalions entered Fallujah from the north then pushing southwards on a three-mile line together with tank platoons as well as artillery and air support to battle about 3,000 resistance fighters (Camp 2009: 128; U.S. Department of Defence 2004; West 2005: 268).

Fallujah 2 comprised the largest military operation conducted during the US/Coalition occupation of Iraq. The so-called Fallujah 2 incident generated extensive news media coverage and also indignation, particularly on the side of Iraqi actors.

Before looking at newspaper coverage, I will assess evidence on civilian deaths in Iraq and Fallujah. This context is important because in terms of 'humanitarian intervention' and Responsibility to Protect (R2P), Fallujah 2 could have provided several entry points to demand action to mitigate the violence.

On 29 October 2004, shortly before the Fallujah 2 incident unfolded, the British medicine journal the *Lancet* published a cluster sample survey titled 'Mortality Before and After the 2003 Invasion of Iraq'. The study found that 98,000 excess deaths – most of which caused by violence – had occurred in Iraq in the period spanning the invasion/occupation until mid-September 2004 (Roberts *et al.* 2004: 1857). According to the authors, violent deaths 'were mainly attributed to coalition forces' while most 'individuals reportedly killed by coalition forces were women and children' (Roberts *et al.* 2004: 1857). Assessing the findings of the study, Schwartz estimated that 60,000 of the deaths could actually be related to US/Coalition violence (Schwartz 2008: 120).

The *Lancet* figures should have no impact on news media reporting, if such impact is measured in terms of the frequency with which the *Lancet* study was reported. The *Lancet* study was hardly mentioned by any of the newspapers in my sample. Imagine how the news media would have reacted if the *Lancet*, one of the most respected medical journals in the Western hemisphere, had found similar mortality rates for Kosovo, Libya or Syria. Wouldn't the newspapers have focused on these findings? Note also that the *Lancet* study was published shortly before the start of a major military assault against a city that had already once been devastated by US/Coalition forces. How could the news media have failed to relate US/Coalition operations in Fallujah in November to the findings of the *Lancet*? This required systematic propaganda.

It is also remarkable that casualty rates in the Kosovo, Libya and Syria theatres undercut the casualty figures for Iraq by large margins (in the chosen time frames). This remained so even under consideration of conservative estimates for Iraq casualties. The IBC database, which certainly underestimated[12] the actual number of civilian deaths because its data is derived from passive surveillance, exceeded the casualty figures found in Kosovo, Libya and Syria. Excluding the invasion phase and looking at the period between May 2003 and October 2004, IBC estimated that 13,644 civilians were killed in Iraq during that time (see IBC n.d. for the IBC database). But news reporting hardly generated the impression of major carnage in Iraq. Again, this sharply contrasted with reporting on the Kosovo, Libya and Syria theatres.

Moreover, estimates for civilian deaths during the Fallujah 2 incident were high and exceeded figures for the other incidents under review. After the official ending of the Fallujah operation, a range of estimates on civilian deaths emerged: on 26 November 2004, an IRIN report referred to Muhammad al-Nuri, a spokesperson of the Iraq Red Crescent Society (IRCS), who had said 'that according to their information, they believe there could be more than 6,000 dead in Fallujah' (IRIN 2004d). This fact was reported on the BBC News website (2004) on 27 November and, in turn, in an Emergency Working Group (EWG) (2004d) bulletin on 30 November. On 4 January 2005, Dr Rafa'ah al-Iyssaue, the director of the main hospital in Fallujah, told IRIN (2005) that hospital emergency teams had recovered 700 bodies from the rubble of 1/3 of the city, of which 550 were women and children. An unknown number of bodies had already been buried and could not be counted by the doctors (*ibid*). The 700 deaths estimate was also cited in a 26 March 2005 report by the local human rights organisation Studies Centre of Human Rights and Democracy (SCHRD) (2005: 2) which was presented to the 61st session of the UN Commission on Human Rights (without making a larger impact at the UN). The researchers of the SCHRD noted that they 'definitely think that the number of' deaths 'is greater than that' because it is unclear where 1,300 people claimed to be killed by US/Coalition forces, of which the military had photographed 490 bodies, were buried (*ibid*). On 24 November 2005, the independent journalist Dahr Jamail (2005) referred to another estimate by the SCHRD according to which 4,000–6,000, most of them civilians, were killed in November and buried in mass graves at the outlying districts of Fallujah. An earlier casualty estimate by the Red Crescent assumed 800 civilian deaths and appears to be a credible approximation (see Jamail 2004b). Under consideration of the data provided by hospitals and the fact that casualty numbers tend to be corrected downwards after time, it seems appropriate to reckon the total amount of civilian deaths to be around 2,000. As we shall see, this number is consistent with US/Coalition military strategy and the civilian presence in Fallujah (see Chapter 6). But the numbers on civilian deaths presented above were almost entirely ignored by the Western press even until well after November 2004. This emerges from a *Factiva* and *LexisNexis* database survey in which all newspapers were searched for estimates on civilian deaths in Fallujah during the period from 8 November 2004 until 31 December 2005.[13] Only three items were obtained which featured one of the numbers discussed above.[14]

Finally, there were multiple reports pointing to the occurrences of potential war crimes in Fallujah, such as the use of phosphor as an incendiary weapon, the use of cluster bombs, thermobaric weapons and other heavy explosive weaponry in residential areas, the direct targeting of civilians and wounded combatants, the raid of a hospital, the harassment of doctors, hospital staff and patients, the prevention of civilians from leaving the city and the prevention of relief organisations from entering the city (see Holmes 2007; Jamail 2007; Zollmann 2010a, b, 2012, see Chapter 6 for a detailed discussion). Yet, these levels of civilian carnage would largely not be translated into indignant news reporting.

News media coverage

How did the press report indignant statements in relation to Fallujah? Despite the striking casualty figures for Iraq/Fallujah discussed above, the Western press consistently applied different standards in its reporting of the Fallujah 2 incident as opposed to its reporting of comparable incidents involving 'enemy' countries. This shows Table 1, which indicates low levels of indignation during reporting of Fallujah 2. The news media did not include any statements coded as Military policy. In fact, diplomatic or 'humanitarian' intervention was not on the agenda. While the news media transported humanitarian concerns in terms of Investigation and Outrage, there were virtually no statements that included Sanctions policy suggestions to mitigate the violence. Furthermore, the context about Fallujah could have provided entry points for a campaign of indignation that highlighted significant policy measures to stop the violence. As we shall see, such a campaign did not take place. It should be noted that the news media included critical angles about occupation policies and also highlighted the civilian plight in Fallujah to some extent. However, the scale of the violence was not accurately represented. Civilian deaths were mainly reported as tragic casualties of war. Humanitarian issues were framed in connection with reciprocal warfare rather than a military rationale that might have systematically led to civilian killings (for further discussions of evidence and the context of violence in Fallujah see Chapter 6).

If we look more closely at the indignation categories, on a few occasions, the German press provided statements classified as Sanctions. For example, on 11 November, the *Frankfurter Rundschau* reported about anti-war demonstrations in Germany (GUZ 2004: 33). According to the report, 'demonstrators appealed to the USA to withdraw their troops from Iraq and pay reparations for the damage causes'. Furthermore, the demonstrators 'called on the German government to immediately stop its political, economic and military support of the "crime" and pressure its allies to remove their troops from Iraq' (*ibid*). Such statements indicated how the Fallujah 2 incident could have facilitated substantive discussions about the occupation, its rationale and whether it was justified for the US/Coalition to remain in Iraq. Aside from the publication of a few news items, a comprehensive discourse on such matters did not materialise in the newspapers under review.

As Table 1 further shows, a larger set of news items featured calls for Investigations. Many of these items were produced in relation to the so-called mosque shooting. Towards the end of the operation, a US Marine had killed an unarmed, wounded resistance fighter in a mosque. The killing was filmed by NBC journalist Kevin Sites on 13 November and broadcasted by the NBC on 15 November (see AP 2004b: 12). Some later reports suggested in passing that Marines could have shot a further three wounded fighters (see e.g. Younge and Whitaker 2004: 15).

Generally, all newspapers covered the mosque shooting and it was reported that, as part of a military investigation, the Marine had been removed from duty. It was also widely reported in the newspapers sampled that the incident might have constituted a violation of the laws of armed conflict or a war crime. Furthermore, the actors of several humanitarian organisations including the United Nations, Human Rights Watch, Amnesty International and the Red Cross made an appearance in the news and it seemed as if, in the fashion of an uncontrolled event, the mosque shooting opened up coverage in regard to discussions on legal issues. For instance, the *Frankfurter Rundschau* (DPA/AP/RTR 2004b: 1) reported on the aim of the International Committee of the Red Cross's (ICRC) to investigate the incident. Moreover, there were demands to not only investigate the mosque shooting but other, similar occurrences. In the *Washington Post*, Shadid (2004c: A 15) cited an appeal by Amnesty:

> 'The deliberate shooting of unarmed and wounded fighters who pose no immediate threat is a war crime under international law, and there is therefore an obligation on the U.S. authorities to investigate all such reports and to hold perpetrators of such crimes accountable before the law' [...].

Similarly, in the *Guardian*, Younge and Whitaker (2004: 15) wrote: '[...] the protection of wounded combatants is a basic tenet of the Geneva conventions [sic] which govern the rules of war' highlighting how 'Louise Arbour, the UN high commissioner for human rights, said yesterday all those responsible for violations should be brought to justice'. Moreover, Andrew Buncombe's (2004c: 1) description in the *Independent* suggested that the shooting might not have been an isolated event: 'Other footage has shown troops shooting wounded fighters lying in open ground as well as attacks on Iraqis – some said to be civilians – by US aircraft and helicopters.' Buncombe (*ibid*) also quoted Kathy Kelly, a spokeswoman for the peace group Voices in the Wilderness, as saying she would not 'think the US is paying much attention to the Geneva Conventions any more – that is the problem' urging that 'this must be investigated'.

All newspapers provided evidence pointing to the accuracy of Kelly's statement. Yet, the Geneva Conventions were largely ignored and indignant comments, such as those displayed above, were cursory included without investigating their factual basis and the scope of possible violations.[15] Many of the discussions mainly centred on the individual Marine and even in this case it was disputed whether the episode actually constituted a war crime. All newspapers had also framed the event in the context of warfare as if the incident resulted from a 'military logic' (Festerling 2004: 3). It was off limits to, for example, suggest a criminal logic.

The press's general handling of the mosque shooting could partly be explained by the fact that the initial investigation was set up by the US military (see Goldenberg 2004: 2). The mosque issue was thus driven by US-officials who did not intend to broaden the investigation. Perhaps as a consequence, discussions in the press largely focused on the circumstances surrounding the mosque and the liability of the individual soldier. Thus, when General Casey claimed that '[…] "This whole operation was about the rule of law, and justice will be done"' (cited in Shadid 2004c: A 15) the substance of this statement was not further challenged in the newspapers under review. Hence, the press neglected to put the evidence it had provided in its own coverage, which suggested the systematic use of indiscriminate force not only against wounded soldiers but also the civilian population, in the context of the Geneva Conventions (the Geneva Conventions will be further discussed in Chapter 6).

Finally, as Table 1 shows, news coverage entailed a large amount of items, which were classified as Outrage. Comparable with reporting on Fallujah 1, the newspapers featured critical statements by Iraqi opposition groups suggesting that military actions were not justified and/or threatening their withdrawal from the interim government. On 9 November, the *Washington Post's* Spinner and Vick quoted the Association of Muslim Scholars, which represented Iraq's 3,000 Sunni Muslim clerics, demanding that Iraqi soldiers refuse to take part in the assault on Fallujah. Moreover, the Association urged Iraqis against

> 'being deceived that you are fighting terrorists from outside the country, because by God you are fighting the townspeople and targeting its men, women and children, and history will record every drop of blood you spill in oppressing the people of your nation'. (cited in Spinner and Vick 2004: A 1)

Similarly, in *The Times* of the same day, Richard Beeston (2004: 1) cited Muhammad Bashar al-Faidhi, of the Association of Muslim Scholars saying: 'The attack on Fallujah is illegal and illegitimate' (cited in *ibid*). Mohsen Abdel Hamid, the leader of the Iraqi Islamic Party, which had resigned from the interim government in protest at the offensive, had presented a similar view in a 10 November article by Sengupta in the *Independent*: 'The American attack on our people in Fallujah has led and will lead to more killings and genocide without mercy from the Americans' (cited in Sengupta 2004b: 4). On 10 November, in a news item in the *New York Times*, Wong (2004a: 14) mentioned the Iraqi Islamic Party's 'withdrawing from the interim Iraqi government' (*ibid*). Wong cited various critical voices suggesting that the Fallujah assault could lead to a political fallout. Wong referred to US historian Juan Cole who considered 'whether a mass Sunni Arab boycott of the elections is in the offing, thus fatally weakening the legitimacy of any new government' (cited in *ibid*). In a further paragraph, the article highlighted an indignant statement by Moktada al-Sadr, the popular Shiite Muslim cleric, whose spokesperson said that the attack on Falluja was '"an attack on all the Iraqi people", and that Iraqis must not help the American forces' (*ibid*). In the 11 November *Independent*, Kim Sengupta (2004c: 4) cited Dr Sami al-Jumaili, who had witnessed an US air strike that hit a clinic in Fallujah killing 20 Iraqi doctors and dozens of civilians, with the words: 'I really don't know if they want to tackle the insurgents or the innocent civilians from the city.' In the *Frankfurter Rundschau*, Erwin Decker (2004: 2) cited an Iraqi civilian saying the Americans would '[...] proceed against a large population of the city'. The Association of Muslim Scholar's chairman, al-Dhari, was quoted in a 14 November *New York Times* article by Wong claiming what Fallujah was going through was '[...] genocide at the hands of the occupiers' (cited in Wong 2004b: 13). Such statements were representative of a broader and highly indignant Iraqi discourse about the Fallujah 2 incident. Yet, there were hardly any statements of Outrage by Western government officials whose indignation appears to be reserved for 'enemy' countries.

A range of comment and editorial writings in the UK newspapers provided indignant statements in the Outrage category. For instance, Zangana's (2004a: 26) comment in the *Guardian* depicted Fallujah as 'collective punishment' and 'civilian carnage' (*ibid*). Zangana (*ibid*) argued that since

> the nominal handover of sovereignty on June 30, we have witnessed an escalation of Israeli-style collective punishment of Iraqi cities. Civilian carnage, coupled with enormous damage to homes and infrastructure, has became our daily reality.

Similarly, the editorial in the *Guardian*, on 9 November, argued that critics of the US had already written the assault off as 'a war crime' (2004a: 21). But this framework was not frequently found in the *Guardian*'s news and editorial coverage, which adopted the official perspective. Thus, the ideological bias of the *Guardian* is apparent in its conclusion of the editorial, where the newspaper acknowledged the basic legitimacy of the Fallujah 2 operation: 'The most we can probably hope for is that this Iraqi battle will be fought with care, restraint and speed.' (*ibid*) Moreover, the *Guardian*'s editorial (*ibid*) effectively swallowed the official discourse on Iraq when suggesting that the US/Coalition operation could '"pacify" Falluja before January's elections, the centrepiece of the US-British exit strategy and of hopes that post-Saddam Iraq can progress towards democracy and stability despite the current mayhem'.

The *Guardian* editorial is indicative of the ideological alignment of the Western press during its reporting of the Fallujah 2 incident. Thus, together with the quantitative evidence, this contextual study clearly demonstrates that indignation was muted during news coverage of Fallujah. While the press included a range of indignant voices ranging from mild calls for Investigations to sentiments of Outrage largely voiced by Iraqi actors as well as human rights organisations, statements demanding the implementation of specific Military and Sanctions policies that could have impacted on the US/Coalition's ability to use force were virtually absent from reporting. Moreover, it was hardly evident from US, UK and German news reporting that carnage in Fallujah and Iraq was on the same level – in fact exceeded – the levels found in Kosovo, Libya and Syria. Thus, the news media's moderate utilisation of indignation suggested an extreme double standard in reporting.

Cairo

In July 2013, 51 civilians were killed in Cairo, where Egyptian security forces dispersed protest meetings by the Muslim Brotherhood. The so-called Cairo incident constituted the first in a series of crackdown against the Muslim Brotherhood and its supporters. Furthermore, the incident unfolded shortly after the military had overthrown Mohamed Morsi, the first democratically elected President of Egypt. The Cairo incident led to intensive news media reporting and indignation. Yet, news media coverage largely resembled the campaigns identified with reference to the other 'allied' cases studies. The frequency of indignation and its quality were restrained if compared with 'enemy' countries. In spite of the violence of the Cairo incident, the Egyptian military, led by General Abdel Fattah el-Sisi, could proceed with its suppression of the Brotherhood and wider societal dissent – without serious challenge in the Western news media. In the upcoming period, the military regime should firstly install an interim government headed by Adly Mansour, and later take political power in Egypt, when el-Sisi was sworn in as President after dubious elections in June 2014.

Since the start of the 2011 Egyptian Revolution, the military and security forces had killed more than 1,200 protestors in Egypt (see sources in Chapter 4). This number excludes casualties from the insurgency in Sinai and is broadly comparable with the toll in Kosovo and Libya, although gathered over a longer time period.

In a report published in October 2012, Amnesty International (2012b) provided a summary of the 16 months that the Supreme Council of the Armed Forces (SCAF) had ruled the country in the time frame between the overthrow of President Hosni Mubarak and the election of President Morsi. According to the report, the SCAF 'unleashed violent repression against peaceful protesters and took steps to retain as much power as possible and remain beyond the reach of the law' (Amnesty International 2012b: 5). The army had 'repeatedly used unnecessary and excessive force, including lethal force, to disperse peaceful demonstrations and sit-ins that escalated into clashes, killing dozens of protesters, assaulting bystanders in the process, and intimidating people simply for daring to protest' (*ibid*).

Between June 2012, when Morsi became President of Egypt, and July 2013, when the Cairo incident took place, reports by human rights organisations similarly suggested that the Egyptian military and security forces used 'excessive force against protesters' on several occasions (Amnesty International 2013: 87; see also Amnesty International 2014/2015; Human Rights Watch 2013, 2014a). Thus, commenting on the 8 July Cairo incident, Joe Stork, acting Middle East Director of Human Rights Watch, said the military had 'a track record of resorting quickly and excessively with lethal force to break up protests' (cited in Human Rights Watch 2013). In its report on the incident, Human Rights Watch suggested that some of the protestors might have been armed and shooting indicating they might have been killed lawfully in such instances (*ibid*). Yet significantly, the organisation also found that it was 'clear from the death toll and witness evidence' that 'the army responded with lethal force that far exceeded any apparent threat to the lives of military personnel' (*ibid*).

In the two weeks after the coup against Morsi, the violence would sharply accelerate because the Egyptian military faced various protests. As the *Guardian* (2013: 28) editorial of 9 July stated: 'According to our body count, more Egyptians have been killed and injured in two weeks of protests than in one year under Morsi.'

Considering the evidence discussed above, particularly the amount of civilian deaths, conflict patterns in Egypt broadly resemble those found in Libya and Kosovo. Furthermore, the military crackdown in Egypt unfolded shortly after the Western community had deliberated on 'humanitarian intervention' and R2P in Libya and Syria. It is, thus, of interest to assess how the news media handled the violence in Cairo.

News media coverage

As Table 1 shows, the relative amount of indignant news items is higher than in other 'allied' countries. Moreover, the news media included a range of items in the Sanctions category. The Sanctions discourse will be further elaborated below. One explanation for the larger amount of indignation in this case is that the political distance between Egypt and Western power centres in the US, UK and Germany is relatively large. In the Fallujah cases, on the other hand, the US and to a lesser extent the UK were the perpetrators of human rights violations and this muted the intensity of coverage. Furthermore, Egypt has been an important ally of the US, UK and Germany and that further explains why the news media would cover the Cairo incident in some detail. Yet, because of this predicament, the news media would not incorporate indignant items demanding Military policy. Furthermore, the Sanctions discourse undertook a benign course. In fact, 'R2P' and 'humanitarian intervention' were not on the agenda.

Table 1 shows that Cairo received a significant amount of news items in the Sanctions category. Firstly, and as was the cases when 'enemy' countries conducted human rights violations, we find the victims of violence had called for help in the international community. Thus, on 9 July, Spencer, Tait and Samaan (2013: 13), of the *Daily Telegraph*, cited a statement from the Muslim Brotherhood's Freedom and Justice Party: 'The party calls on the international community and international organisations and bodies, and all the free world, to intervene to stop further massacres and end military rule, so as not to create a new Syria in the Arab world' (cited in *ibid*). Yet, intervention on a scale comparable to the Sanctions agenda we have seen applied towards 'enemy' countries should not be realised. Overall, the following issues were discussed in relation to Sanctions:

- Suspension of US and/or EU aid and/or arms shipments to Egypt.
- Military to show more restraint and/or stop retributive actions and/or protect human rights.
- Protect demonstrators.
- Regime to work in dialogue with other parties, including Muslim Brotherhood, and return to democratic process.
- Demands that other states recognize coup against Muslim Brotherhood and/or influence Muslim Brotherhood and/or do something to support democracy in Egypt and/or recognize Morsi as legitimate president.

- Demands that other states condemn the Egyptian military in stronger terms.
- Military to release Morsi and/or Muslim Brotherhood supporters from prison.
- Exclude Egypt from African Union until further democratic elections.

Discussions about Sanctions measures were significant and pointed to a different quality of indignation in comparison to Fallujah 1 and 2. Notwithstanding, the Sanctions discussions still exempted the Egyptian regime from serious repercussions. In fact, Egypt has been a long-term ally of the West and the second largest recipient of Western military aid outside of NATO. The funding was an easy entry point for Sanctions. Hence, the news media incorporated a range of statements discussing the potential suspension of aid to Egypt. Nevertheless, Western powers would not withdraw support from the military dictatorship. This demonstrated a closer examination of the Sanctions discourse about the distribution of financial aid.

All newspapers under review highlighted discussions in the US, where political actors reportedly considered as to whether US aid to Egypt should be suspended either in response to the military coup or the Cairo incident. For instance, an item by Londoño in the *Washington Post* of 9 July highlighted the fact that, according to US law, financial aid cannot be provided to a government whose elected leader has been toppled by the military (see Londoño 2013: A 08). Londoño mentioned how Senator Patrick J. Leahy (D-Vt.), who was chair of a panel overseeing the State Department's foreign aid budget, 'said immediately after the military deposed Morsi on Wednesday that as a matter of law, financial assistance would need to be cut' (Londoño 2013: A 08). According to Londoño, this view was shared by several lawmakers and experts in the US including Senator John McCain (see *ibid*). Londoño (*ibid*) provided further information about the importance of US aid to Egypt:

> The Egyptian military has received the bulk of U.S. aid, about $1.3 billion each year since Cairo signed a peace treaty with Israel in 1979. The aid has been rendered in the form of tanks, fighter planes and other materiel, which have made Egypt a regional military power.

The quote above suggested a longstanding US-Egyptian military alliance. By implication, the close US-Egyptian relationship also explained why Egypt's crackdown would not lead to more substantive repercussions. Incidentally, as the article by Londoño mentioned, the Obama administration's reaction to the Cairo event was to call 'on the military to exercise "maximum restraint responding to protestors" but' also to announce that 'it was disinclined to suspend military aid to the Arab world's most populous country' (*ibid*). On 10 July, the *Washington Post's* Dana Milbank (2013: A15) poignantly summarised why the US even denied the existence of a coup:

> Section 508 of the Foreign Assistance Act says unequivocally that there can be no aid 'to any country whose duly elected head of government is deposed by military coup or decree.' Morsi was duly elected, so his ouster pretty much requires the United States to cut off $1.5 billion in foreign aid. But Morsi governed as an Islamist thug—and the administration doesn't want to punish the Egyptian military for doing the good deed of removing him from power.

Note how US law reportedly was unambiguous about the requirement to freeze US aid to Egypt. Moreover, such policy was supported by several senators in Washington. The Egyptian military had been engaged in what reportedly constituted a major crackdown on protestors. Yet significantly, Obama had announced he would not change US aid policies towards Egypt and this fact was not met with much opposition in the news media. Consequently, the episode about US aid demonstrates how indignant discourses were mitigated in the case of Egypt.

Similarly, on 10 July, the German *Frankfurter Allgemeine Zeitung* reported the discussion about US aid. A news item by Hans-Christian Rößler (2013: 5) added an important detail, namely that 'according to information provided by the Israeli newspaper "Haaretz", the Israeli government campaigned in the previous week in Washington that US military aid continued'. According to Rößler (*ibid*), Israel feared that an aid freeze could have a negative impact on Israel's security and also lead the Egyptian generals to reconsider the peace treaty with Israel. Hence, as Rößler (*ibid*) further wrote, Israel was relieved after Obama's spokesperson proclaimed that 'it would not be in the best interest of the United States to immediately change our aid programmes for Egypt' (cited in *ibid*). This perspective was also confirmed in a 14 July op-ed by Carol Giacomo (2013: 10) in the *New York Times*, saying that many lawmakers and analysts 'say the surest way to protect American interests in the Egypt-Israel peace treaty, the Suez Canal and Egypt's cooperation in countering terrorism is to work with the army, Egypt's most powerful institution'. Such statements indirectly affirmed that US interests are more important than human rights. This priority is also reflected in news coverage since the media's emphasis of human rights violations is, as highlighted in this case study, a function of Western interests.

Several news items further discussed how the European Union should handle its foreign aid to Egypt. On 11 July, Michael Borgstede and Silke Mülherr (2013: 7) wrote in *Die Welt* how 'calls about the suspension of economic aid, which currently amounts to 500 million Euro, are increasing'. Borgstede and Mülherr (*ibid*) further cited the EU High Representative saying: 'At this point in time, there are no plans to change EU aid'. EU policy towards Egypt thus appeared to resemble the US approach.

Overall, statements of US and EU policy-makers, which were coded in the Sanction category, suggested a relatively mild response to the Egyptian military regime's crackdown. On 18 July, Borgstede (2013: 9) of *Die Welt* quoted William Burns, US Assistant Secretary of State, and Catherine Ashton, EU Foreign Affairs Commissioner, to that effect. Burns demanded 'a "sincere and fundamental dialogue" between all sides' and envisioned '"a second chance for democracy" in Egypt' (cited in *ibid*). Similarly, Ashton reportedly indicated that the '[…] EU is determined to support the Egyptian people on their journey towards a better future with real freedom and economic growth' (cited in *ibid*). Such indignant statements suggested that the US and EU approach towards Egypt was mildly supportive. Consider the pressure that US and EU spokespersons signalled towards FRY/Serbia, Libya and Syria. The Egyptian military's crackdown, by comparison, received relatively benign treatment and this reflected also how the press handled regime.

The articles above further indicated that the parameters of debate were set by Western officialdom. The official discourse appeared to define the scope of deliberations about Sanctions. Hence, while the aid issue would be discussed extensively in the press, there was no campaign to enforce harsher Sanctions policies in terms of a suspension of aid and other measures. The press rather reported the official deliberations in neutral terms, without critically exploring the US-Egyptian relationship or why Israel was keen to lend its support to the military. The most serious measure to be actually implemented against Egypt was a British export embargo on equipment-components that could be of value for military use. Thus, on 20 July, the *Guardian*'s Patrick Kingsley (2013a: 19) reported how the British government had 'revoked five export licences for equipment destined for Egypt in response to reports that security forces have used excessive force in dealing with protests since the fall of ex-president Mohamed Morsi'.

On the other hand, the Egyptian military coup regime reportedly received significant backing from the US and their regional allies. On 12 July, a news item by the *Guardian*'s Kingsley and Black (2013: 21) suggested US support for the Egyptian army: 'The US has agreed to donate four fighter jets to Egypt's army, in the latest indication of international support for the country's interim government despite growing international unease at the new regime's management of the power transition.' Moreover, Egypt should be granted significant monetary subsidies. As the article further noted:

> The aircraft donation follows a telephone conversation between the European Union's foreign affairs representative, Lady Catherine Ashton, and Egypt's new interim president, Adly Mansour. It follows the issuing of $12bn in grants and loans from Saudi Arabia, the United Arab Emirates and Kuwait, all conservative Gulf states known for their opposition to Morsi and his Muslim Brotherhood. (*ibid*)

The financial injection delivered by the Gulf States, all allies of the West and proponents for military intervention in Libya and Syria, was widely reported in the news media.

On 8 July, an op-ed published in the *New York Times* (2013) by television journalist Tim Sebastian even went so far to argue the events in Egypt were orchestrated: 'In early May a trusted source in Cairo told me: "The military will be back in power by the autumn and the West has already signed off. The one condition is that the army is fronted by a civilian face."' (*ibid*) Stephan Roll (2013: 2) of the *Süddeutsche Zeitung* of 15 July, similarly wrote that the twelve billion dollar emergency aid from the Gulf States within several days 'evidenced special arrangements that were initiated before the coup'. As Roll further argued, Saudi-Arabia, Kuwait and the United Arab Emirates feared that the success of the Muslim Brotherhood could stimulate domestic opposition (*ibid*). Furthermore, Gulf State support for Egypt was in alignment with US and EU policies: As Roll (*ibid*) observed, the Egyptian 'generals can count on their traditional allies, the USA and EU'. Hence, while the news media transported indignant statements in the Sanctions category, this discourse was skewed towards US- and EU-interests. Effectively, the Egyptian military was off the hook and could proceed with its serial crackdown.

The newspapers would also include items coded in the Investigations category. For instance, on 9 July an article by Kirkpatrick and Fahim (2013: 1), in the *New York Times*, referred to Mohamed ElBaradei, the former diplomat and liberal leader, stating on Twitter that an 'independent investigation is a must' (cited in *ibid*). On the same day, Black and Kingsley (2013a: 6), of the *Guardian*, pointed out that 'Egypt's interim presidency announced a judicial investigation into the killings'. A news item by the *Independent's* Cornwell (2013: 4, 5) discussed the approach by Western countries, which appeared to be hesitant in their reactions although they demanded investigations. According to the article by Cornwell (*ibid*) which was published on 9 July:

> The cautious reaction of the US, the one Western country seen to have the leverage with the Egyptian military, was broadly followed by its Western allies yesterday. The word 'coup' was generally conspicuous by its absence as Britain urged [...] an investigation by the Egyptian authorities into the circumstances of the killings, and steps towards free and fair elections. Similarly, Germany [...] demanded 'speedy clarification' by an independent body of what had happened.

Accordingly, the Investigation issue appeared to be used as a token: Western powers showed some concern in public while at the same time providing crucial financial and diplomatic support to the military dictatorship.

On 13 July, Bickel (2013: 5) of the *Frankfurter Allgemeine Zeitung*, mentioned that 'interim president Mansur had announced the formation of a committee to investigate the clashes'. Yet, Bickel (*ibid*) suggested that since the fall of Mubarak two and a half years ago such bodies only rarely complete their mandates. According to Bickel (*ibid*): 'A culture of impunity runs through the interim period since Mubarak's disempowerment by the military command, which is led by army chief Abd al Fattah Sisi since last August.'

On 19 July, an extensive article by Kingsley (2013b: 1) was published in the *Guardian*, based on 'a week-long investigation – including interviews with 31 witnesses, local people and medics, as well as video analysis' into the Cairo incident. According to Kingsley (*ibid*), the exploration revealed a narrative 'in which the security forces launched a co-ordinated assault on a group of largely peaceful and unarmed civilians'. Kingsley further commented how the Egyptian regime handled the incident:

> Adly Mansour, Egypt's interim president, announced a judicial investigation into the killings, though previous inquiries have shown that the army is unwilling to submit itself to outside scrutiny. The military has been reluctant to give a full account of the incident. (*ibid*)

In deed, a range of investigations were conducted by human rights groups and news media organisations. But there appeared to be no serious repercussions for the Egyptian regime. The ICC in The Hague was apparently not called in. The developments in Egypt demonstrate how human rights shaming and enforcement is linked to political power. Political actors in Western states may demand investigations and inquiries. Yet, without further pressure, such policies peter out. Similarly, calls for Investigations ebbed away in news media reporting and the Egyptian military could proceed without fundamental challenge.

Finally, the newspapers would also feature indignant statements of Outrage, voiced by Arab actors, human rights organisations, Western politicians and journalists. Such statements were frequently voiced as shown in Table 1. Thus, the *New York Times's* Kirkpatrick and Fahim (2013: 1) mentioned Essam el-Erian, a senior leader of the Muslim Brotherhood, calling 'the killings "an outright massacre" by "a fascist coup government"'. Black and Kingsley (2013a: 6) of the *Guardian* referred to the US, which 'said it was "deeply concerned" and called on Egypt's military to "exercise maximum restraint"'. Moreover, the article cited an indignant tweet by Heba Morayef of Human Rights Watch urging the military and police to '[...] exercise restraint and not use excessive and lethal force' (cited in *ibid*). Additionally, Black and Kingsley (*ibid*) reported an immediate 'political fallout' of the incident as 'the conservative Salafi Noor party withdrew from already faltering talks on a transitional government'. Bickel (2013: 5) of the *Frankfurter Allgemeine Zeitung* quoted a report by Amnesty International, which referred to 'excessive and unnecessary violence by the security services' (cited in *ibid*). Cornwell (2013: 4, 5) of the *Independent* wrote that the UK demanded 'calm and restrained' (cited in *ibid*) while Germany 'expressed "dismay" over what had happened'. An editorial of the *Guardian* (2013: 28) demanded from the Egyptian army to 'back down'. In his investigative report, Kingsley (2013b: 1) cited a range of indignant Iraqis including Dr Alaa Mohamed Abu Zeid, the doctor responsible for recording the numbers of injuries at one of the hospitals that received casualties from the Cairo incident, saying he wanted '[...] to emphasise that this is a massacre' (cited in *ibid*).

In sum, indignant news reporting on Egypt was muted if compared with indignation on Račak and Benghazi. Initially, the Cairo incident generated a broader discourse about Sanctions and other measures. Yet, there was no political will on behalf of the 'international community' to implement such policies because Egypt's military regime constituted an important strategic asset. This was reflected in news reporting in so far as the discourse of indignation faded away during the days following the incident. On 16 July, the *Independent's* Beach (2013: 26, 27) reported from US Deputy Secretary of State William Burns' first official visit since the day of the coup. As Beach (*ibid*) wrote, Burns had 'said America will not take sides in Egypt's political turmoil'. The news media took a similar position. This was striking since, as Cockburn (2013: 34, 35) commented sarcastically on the same day for the same newspaper: '[…] the tainted functionaries of the Mubarak era are confidently back in business' in Egypt while those 'great proponents of democracy and human rights – Saudi Arabia, the United Arab Emirates and Kuwait – have shovelled in cash and credits worth $12 billion to keep the good ship Mubarak II afloat'.

This episode demonstrates the crucial difference about how violence by 'allied' and 'enemy' states is met in the international arena of governance and media reporting: while 'allied' states receive diplomatic rapprochement and cash, 'enemy' states face sanctions and military intervention.

$$\cdot \; 6 \; \cdot$$

THE POLITICS OF ATROCITIES MANAGEMENT

The framing of atrocity vs. war: nefarious, benign and constructive bloodbaths in the propaganda system

The previous chapter has demonstrated how the international news media engages in a highly dichotomised process of shaming in response to human rights breaches. It was shown that indignant campaigns against 'enemy' countries are pronounced. The news media provides a platform for the discussion of various interventionist policies. In contrast, indignation in response to violence conducted by powerful 'allied' states is muted and does largely not include calls for interventionist measures. This double standard is linked to the news media's reporting of atrocious facets of events and the culpability of actors. In fact, indignant discourses are underpinned by extensive displays of carnage and self-righteous finger-pointing even if evidence is contested or hard to verify. These facets of news reporting will be further explored in the following chapter.

An important aspect of campaigns of shaming constitutes the framing of incidents in terms of their atrocious dimensions and the responsibility for crimes. Framing relates to how the news media highlights certain facets of events and relegates responsibility to actors, amongst other issues (for framing see also Entman 2004). This process is dichotomised in news media reporting of human rights violations: high casualty incidents involving 'enemy' countries are explored in great detail and responsibility for nefarious behaviour is relegated to the highest levels of governance. High casualty incidents involving 'allied' countries, on the other hand, are investigated with journalistic distance and responsibility for nefarious behaviour is confined to lower ranks, if at all. Furthermore, the ways in which incidents are classified is remarkably different. Human rights violations by 'enemy' countries are classified as atrocities and massacres. Human rights violations by 'allied' countries are classified as military operations or reciprocal clashes.

There are two models proposed here which the press may apply in its framing of human rights issues during conflict: (1) Coverage can operate in an 'atrocity' framework referring to one party and its actions as nefarious. In such instances, the news media focuses on indiscriminate military tactics, massacres or crackdowns. (2) Coverage can operate in a 'war' framework assuming a reciprocal conflict with two parties fighting each other in battles. In such cases, humanitarian issues are ascribed to the tragedies of 'war' or to individual soldiers ('bad apples') but not to a nefarious party or a systematic rationale.

Generally, coverage can operate in a combination of these models. Moreover, no clear-cut performance is to be expected. Even if coverage is identified as operating in a 'war' framework there might be aspects which fit another model. Yet, the general distinction is useful in order to broadly compare coverage of different theatres.

In the reporting of 'enemy' countries, the press has largely resorted to reporting model 1. Actions of 'enemy' states are closely monitored and tend to be framed as nefarious. In such instances, the so-called 'journalism of attachment' (model 1) is operative. This means that atrocious dimensions of incidents will be highlighted and reported in detail (*cf.* Hammond and Herman 2000; Herman and Chomsky 2008; Herman and Peterson 2007, 2010).

In the reporting of 'allied' countries, on the other hand, the press has largely resorted to reporting model (2) focusing on 'war' and its undesirable albeit inevitable outcomes as well as the benevolent aims of the state. This means that martial dimensions of incidents are highlighted whereas atrocious dimensions are mentioned in passing or in the back pages (Herman and Chomsky 2008).

In sum, human rights incidents involving 'enemy' countries are largely framed in atrocious terms whereas similar incidents involving 'allied' countries are more or less framed in martial terms. Such dichotomisation of relatively similar incidents constitutes a programme of 'atrocities management' because the highlighting of atrocious and martial dimensions depends on political convenience rather than fact (Chomsky and Herman 1979a: 18). According to Chomsky and Herman (*ibid*: 96):

> Some bloodbaths seem to be looked upon as benign or even positive and constructive; only particular ones have been given publicity and regarded as heinous and deserving of indignation.

Accordingly, Chomsky and Herman classify bloodbaths as nefarious, benign or constructive. Nefarious bloodbaths are 'publicized and condemned' because they are executed by 'enemy' states, 'whose victims are deserving of serious concern' (*ibid*: 97). Nefarious bloodbaths serve 'an extremely important public relations function in mobilizing support for U.S. military intervention' (*ibid*). Hence, nefarious bloodbaths are reported in terms of their atrocious dimensions, which are highlighted and scrutinised (reporting model 1). In contrast, benign bloodbaths are covered with 'sheer indifference' because there is a 'lack of significant community or interest group identification with the victims' and the violence is 'carried out by a power whose goodwill and prosperity weigh more heavily in policymaking than mere human suffering, however large its scale' (*ibid*: 105). Hence, benign bloodbaths are reported in terms of war and fighting (reporting model 2). Finally, constructive bloodbaths make 'a direct contribution to' Western 'ends and interests, as in the case of counterrevolutionary bloodbaths that destroy radical and reformist political movements' (*ibid*). Here, the reporting model is more open (mix of 1 + 2) as violence is not conducted by the power centre or its closest allies, yet it is useful for their interests such as when reformist movements are crushed.

This chapter looks at dichotomised reporting of atrocious and martial dimensions of similar human rights incidents and how the news media relegates responsibility for nefarious actions. It will be demonstrated that the news media's designation of incidents as nefarious, benign or constructive bloodbaths is based on political ideology rather than fact. I will firstly look at quantitative aspects of the framing of incidents in terms of the use of atrocious as opposed to martial terminology. Afterwards, I will assess the context of the chosen events in a case-by-case fashion.

Atrocities management: quantitative evidence

Table 3 below displays the keywords that the news media used to classify or describe each incident. Each case study heading depicts the name of the incident and theatre as well as the casualty estimates for the incident and theatre as derived from mainstream sources.[1] Row 1 under each case study headline shows the amount of martial classifications in per cent. Row 2 under each case study heading shows the amount of atrocious classifications in per cent.

All incidents under review entailed atrocious as well as martial dimensions (see evidence in Chapter 5 and below). Yet, as Table 3 shows, the framing of relatively similar 'enemy' and 'allied' human rights violations differed remarkably. The Western press quite unanimously framed 'enemy' incidents in atrocious terms: at least 70 per cent of the descriptions used to classify these incidents were coded as such. This means that the Račak, Benghazi and Houla incidents were mainly described with terms such as massacre, atrocity, crime, violation, crackdown, carnage, etc. Hence, the Western propaganda system treated these incidents as *nefarious* bloodbaths.

In contrast, 'allied' incidents were quite unanimously framed in martial terms, particularly the Fallujah 1 + 2 incidents. Accordingly, at least 76 per cent of descriptions used to classify Fallujah 1 and 92 per cent of descriptions to classify Fallujah 2 were coded as martial (for an explanation about why there were quantitative differences between Fallujah 1 and 2 see Zollmann 2012). This means that the Fallujah 1 and 2 incidents were mainly described with terms such as siege, battle, operation, assault, fighting etc. Thus, these incidents were treated as *benign* bloodbaths in the propaganda system.

The Cairo incident was a rather ambiguous case: atrocious and martial terms were relatively evenly distributed across newspapers. However, the Cairo incident also received special treatment in the news media: firstly, as explored in Chapter 5, the violence by security forces was not met with severe indignation if compared with the 'enemy' cases under review. Secondly, the counterrevolutionary Egyptian military regime was quickly rewarded with substantive financial aid and this policy was neutrally reported, virtually without challenge (see Chapter 5 and below). Thus, this incident was treated as a *constructive* bloodbath in the propaganda system.

Atrocities management: further findings

This chapter assesses the news media's framing of human rights incidents in relation to the publication of details of slaughter and the relegation of responsibility for nefarious behaviour. The study uses qualitative content analysis in conjunction with external evidence.

Table 3: Martial and atrocious descriptions for various incidents in per cent.

Newspaper	NYT	WP	G	I	T	DT	FR	SZ	TAZ	FAZ	W
1. Račak/Kosovo (01/1999): Civilian deaths: 45/nationwide deaths: 2,000											
Martial	21.1	25.5	19.6	23.8	20.5	27.3	15.5	13.3	22.9	29.5	24.7
Atrocious	78.9	74.5	80.4	76.2	79.5	72.7	84.5	86.7	77.1	70.5	75.3
2. Benghazi/Libya (02–03/2011): Civilian deaths: 228/nationwide deaths: 500–700											
Martial	29.6	29	16.8	26.1	24.3	27.2	14.8	22	21.7	25.3	26.9
Atrocious	70.4	71	83.2	73.9	75.7	72.8	85.2	78	78.3	74.7	73.1
3. Houla/Syria (05–06/2012): Civilian deaths: 116/nationwide deaths: 6,000–15,000											
Martial	18.1	28	21	26.6	20.6	25.9	10.7	7	19.4	14.4	9.2
Atrocious	81.9	72	79	73.4	79.4	74.1	89.3	93	80.6	85.6	90.8
4. Fallujah 1/Iraq (04/2004): Civilian deaths: 600/nationwide deaths: 6,990–55,000											
Martial	90.4	93.3	85.2	81.8	89.3	88.5	76.5	93	87.5	85.2	95.2
Atrocious	9.6	6.7	14.8	18.2	10.7	11.5	23.5	7	12.5	14.8	4.8
5. Fallujah 2/Iraq (08/2004): Civilian deaths: 800–6,000/nationwide deaths: 13,644–98,000											
Martial	99.1	100	94.2	92.3	95.1	98.6	92.9	96.5	95.7	98.5	98.8
Atrocious	0.9	0	5.8	7.7	4.9	1.4	7.1	3.5	4.3	1.5	1.2
6. Cairo/Egypt (07/2013): Civilian deaths: 51/nationwide deaths: +1,000											
Martial	52.2	41.2	50.4	37.3	49.4	35.3	46.2	59.1	52.9	41	55.8
Atrocious	47.8	58.5	49.6	62.7	50.6	64.7	53.8	40.9	47.1	59	44.2

'Enemy' countries

Račak

The press's framing of Račak as a nefarious bloodbath was underpinned by detailed depictions of slaughter. This is typical for the news media's reporting of human rights violations involving 'enemy' countries. In the Račak case, the news media focused on forensic aspects and gruesome facets of the incident. Reporting was approached with investigatory zeal and attention to culpability. This handling was firstly indicated by how the press reported on details.

In the *Sunday Telegraph*, Strauss (1999: 29) described an 'orgy of death' in Račak where 'most of the man had gaping bullet holes in their faces, some in their chests or other parts of the body'. Strauss (*ibid*) depicted one man who 'had been shot in the head at close range' while another man's 'eye had been shot away, a bullet passing through his brain'. Note the detailed portrayal of entry wounds and their bodily locations. The *Independent*'s Wood (1999: 2) included the following descriptions in a news item:

> AROUND every corner in the village of Racak, there seems to be a body. One ethnic Albanian man lay in the courtyard at the centre of his family compound, his face completely obliterated. The villagers said he had been shot at close range. 'We could not even find his teeth,' one said. [...]
>
> Further on were yet more bodies. I counted 30; monitors later said the total was 45. Several had their eyes gouged out or their heads smashed in, and one had been decapitated.

The article provided a close look at the victims emphasising shocking details of trauma, decay and death. Similarly, Perlez (1999d: 1), of the *New York Times*, quoted from a report by the monitors of the Kosovo Verification Mission:

> 'One adult male killed outside his house. The top of his head had been removed and was found approximately 15 feet away from his place of death. The wound appeared to have been caused by an ax, but may have been from a bullet.' [Excerpts, page A 10.]

Such details of slaughter were underlined by all newspapers under review and contributed towards framing the incident as a nefarious bloodbath. Of course, from an ethical point of view, such depictions are warranted if the press reports on atrocities. However, the newspapers' focusing on wounds and forensic details was politicised. As I will discuss in the sections further below, the press rather zoomed out and depicted violence from a wide-angle perspective when reporting on 'allied' countries.

News coverage of the details of slaughter is linked to how an incident is labelled in the framing process. Thus, many actors who were referenced by the press would describe Račak using atrocious terminology. For example, the *Independent*'s, Sarah Schaefer (1999: 8) quoted then British Foreign Secretary Robin Cook saying it was 'simply not credible that those who were killed were the casualties of a military conflict. The eye-witness accounts of international observers make it only too clear that they were murdered' (cited in *ibid*).

This example illustrated the negligence of the 'war' at the expense of an 'atrocity' framework, which was congruent with the press's overall handling of the Račak incident. This means that atrocious dimensions of the incident were highlighted and it was then quasi established as a matter of fact that the incident constituted a nefarious bloodbath. Hence, the press de-emphasised a possible 'war' context in Račak. I will later demonstrate that the 'war' context was stringently evoked in reporting of Fallujah 1 and 2 – both incidents were framed as benign bloodbaths, even by critical writers such as Patrick Cockburn. It is significant that the usage of a 'war' or 'atrocity' framework is based on subjective decisions to use martial or atrocious words to classify an event. In both instances, the description is an ideological construct because at the time of reporting it is often not possible to come to conclusive insights about the nature of incidents. Hence, dichotomised framing of comparable incidents suggests a double standard of the Western press evident in its usage of different reporting models for relatively similar occurrences. In their coverage on the second Fallujah incident, for example, each newspaper used between one and eleven atrocious words (e.g. massacre, atrocity, etc.) to label the incident in all of their items during the two-week period. In the case of Račak, newspapers included atrocious words in virtually every news story and sometimes such notions amounted to nine mentions in one item. From the outset, the incident had been defined as a nefarious bloodbath and it seems that the press did not consider the presumption of innocence when covering Račak and the Kosovo conflict.

Next to the reporting of details and the use of descriptions to classify the incident, responsibility for nefarious behaviour was assigned to the FRY/Serbs.

The following examples are representative for the handling of Račak: On 17 January, two days after the operation by FRY/Serbian forces had been conducted, a report by Chris Bird (1999a: 1) in the *Observer* was titled: 'The butchers came at dawn to slay village.' Bird (*ibid*) referred to 'one of the biggest massacres to date in Kosovo, where Serb security forces have tried for over a year to stamp out ethnic Albanian support for the separatist guerrillas in the province'. The *New York Times*'s Perlez (1999c: 6) reported also on 17 January that the 'top international official in Kosovo, William Walker, a seasoned American diplomat who heads the monitoring mission there, said at the massacre site that he had no hesitation in accusing Serbian Government forces of the killings'. A report in the *Frankfurter Rundschau* referred to the OSCE and the Council of Europe, which were holding the Yugoslavian Security Services to account for the 'massacre' (RTR/AFP/DPA/AP 1999: 1). Wood (1999: 2), of the *Independent*, referred to Bill Clinton who 'condemned "the massacre of civilians by the Serb security forces" in the "strongest possible terms"'. In the *Frankfurter Rundschau* of 18 January, Stephan Israel (1999: 2) described the event as a 'massacre' and 'murders' writing that 'Serbian police' had 'executed Albanian civilians'.

The press's frequent usage of strong notions without quotation marks constituted a further difference to coverage of 'allied' incidents like the Fallujah operations during which atrocious notions were not only marginalised but often quoted as statements by Iraqi actors. Note also how responsibility was assigned to FRY/Serbian actors as well as higher levels of planning (Serb security forces, Serbian Government forces) although, at the time of reporting, independent evidence was hardly conclusive. Thus, Perlez (1999d: 1), of the *New York Times*, referred to the report by the monitors of the Kosovo Verification Mission, who were at the scene before and after the incident, saying that international monitors 'who discovered the bodies of 45 ethnic Albanians shot execution-style concluded in their official report that the attack in a Kosovo village was an act of revenge by Serbian forces for the killing of four of their men'. Yet, it was also reported in the text that the monitors arrived at the scene only after the Serbs had left (see *ibid*). How could the observers, led by Walker who hardly constituted an independent actor (see Herman and Peterson 2010: 96), have verified what had happened before an forensic investigation? Similarly, when journalists referred to Serbian forces as the perpetrators, recriminations seemed to be based on hearsay evidence because Western reporters were not present during the incident and only later arrived at the site. In sum, the process of shaming was related to the labelling of the incident and the depiction of details: if the event visibly constituted an atrocity, then someone must have been responsible.

In many news items, higher ranks were implicated: For instance, a *Washington Post* (1999: A 22) editorial was titled 'Mr. Milosevic's Massacre' arguing that the Serbian President 'has been waging war against the people of Kosovo'. Similarly, the *New York Times*' Perlez (1999d: 1) wrote the Clinton administration 'has blamed the Yugoslav leader, Slobodan Milosevic, for allowing his troops to use disproportionate force against people the Administration maintains are civilians'. In another item, Perlez (1999a: 6) wrote about 'the massacre of 45 ethnic Albanian civilians by Serbian forces under the control of Mr. Milosevic' then President of the FRY/Serbia. In an op-ed for the *New York Times*, historian Misha Glenny (1999: 31) argued that there is little doubt that Milosevic 'approved the police action in Racak'. Furthermore, Glenny (*ibid*) added that 'certainly, the decision to allow Serbian security forces to return to the village after the massacre for "cleanup" operations must have had his specific approval'. The argument that high-level planners were responsible for the bloodbath was further aligned with the publication of Western intelligence. Towards the end of January, many of the newspapers under review reported the content of 'intercepts of telephone conversations' leaked by the US government which would show 'that Belgrade ordered the assault and then tried to cover up the massacre' (Bird 1999c: 1). Similarly, the *Post's* Smith (1999: A 01) wrote:

> The calls show that the assault on Racak was monitored closely at the highest lev-
> els of the Yugoslav government and controlled by the senior Serbian military com-
> mander in Kosovo – a province of Serbia, Yugoslavia's dominant republic.

The intercepts were treated as 'smoking gun' evidence that implicated the Serbian high command. More specifically, the intercepts incriminated Nikola Sainovic, a Deputy Prime Minister, and General Sreten Lukic of the Serbian Interior Ministry (Whitaker and Marshall 1999: 1) as well as other officials. Yet, it appeared that the authenticity of the intercepts had not been veri-fied by the journalists. For example, Smith (1999: A 1) referred 'to Western sources familiar with the intercepts' saying that details of the conversations were 'made available by Western sources'. It is not clear from reading the news items as to whether the journalists had actually been in the possession of the intercepts. Bird (1999c: 1) provided the following explanation about the con-tent of the intercepts as well as the evidence at the scene, which was regarded as further proof for FRY/Serbian responsibility:

> They [the intercepts] said the two [Nikola Sainovic, and General Sreten Lukic] were
> worried about international reaction to the attack and talked about ways to make it
> look as if the deaths were from combat.
>
> The aim, the Western officials said, was to muddy the claims by ethnic Albanian
> survivors of the assault and international monitors who saw its results that Serbian
> forces were responsible.
>
> 'The 35 bodies I saw were all in civilian clothes and had no weapons,' said an expe-
> rienced Western investigator, one of the first international monitors to arrive on
> the scene. 'We found (Serbian military) bullet casings around the bodies, it was not
> indicative of a struggle.'

The quote suggested that the conversation detailed in the intercepts had been reported to Bird (*ibid*) by 'Western officials'. The allegations about FRY/Serbian responsibility reportedly provided by Western officials were largely taken at face value. Yet, even the monitor quoted in the statement above did not strictly disprove the FRY/Serbian argument that the incident might have been staged (see further context below).

Incidentally, the intercepts were reported at around the same time when 'Tony Blair and President Jacques Chirac announced jointly that France and Britain were ready to send troops to Kosovo' (Bird 1999c: 1). The intercepts had strategic value: Whitaker and Marshall (1999: 1) argued in the *Independent* that 'the leaked US revelations will add pressure on Europe to take action against Serbia'. Hence, it could be argued that the relegation of responsibility to higher levels of planning, in this case based on intercepts leaked by an interested party, was helpful for those who aimed at intervening in Kosovo. In fact, the newspapers could have highlighted the coincidence that the intercepts were leaked by the US at a crucial time when NATO opted for intervention in Kosovo. Was the leak part of a strategic communication campaign during preparations for intervention? This question was not asked by the press under study.

Notwithstanding, the press also covered the official FRY/Serbian narrative about the Račak incident. The FRY/Serbia argued it had the right to pursue military operations in Kosovo since an Albanian insurgency was trying to separate the province from the country (see Perlez 1999b: 3; also quote by Wood 1999 in Chapter 5). For instance, the FRY/Serbs reportedly had claimed they have killed '"terrorists" in battle' as Julius Strauss (1999: 29) wrote in the *Sunday Telegraph*. While this 'war' angle was featured in virtually all newspapers under review, it was marginalised or placed in negative contexts. For instance, Strauss (*ibid*) contextualised his statement arguing: 'There was not a sign of a uniform or weapon' which suggested that the Serbs 'have murdered more than 50 civilians in cold blood'. It is also noteworthy that the FRY/Serbian narrative basically proclaimed that Račak constituted a 'battle' incident. Yet, this context was de-emphasised by the press, which had framed Račak as a nefarious bloodbath.

There was a further narrative about the actual facts of the incident. The French newspapers *Le Figaro* and *Le Monde* published reports indicating that 'the Racak massacre of ethnic Albanians was a set-up' as Walker in *The Times* reported (Walker 1999: 15). In the French newspapers it was highlighted how 'a television team from Associated Press filmed part of the police operation and little of the evidence from its footage tallied with Albanian accounts of the killings' (*ibid*). Furthermore, the French newspapers suggested that 'when the international furore over Racak began, the Kosovo Liberation Army could have fabricated evidence and even mutilated some of the bodies' in order to 'transform a military defeat into a political victory' (*ibid*). This view was shared by the state-controlled press in Serbia asserting 'that the massacre was a fake, staged by the ethnic Albanian rebels' (Perlez 1999d: 1). Like the official FRY/Serbian account about the incident most newspapers under study referred to this second narrative, albeit in a negative context.

In conclusion, while the news media was not monolithic in their coverage, they over-emphasised the Western narrative framing Račak as a nefarious bloodbath and depicting the FRY/Serbs as the responsible actor. The news media failed to provide a balanced picture. Moreover, this was inaccurate reporting because, as discussed in Chapter 5, the KLA had killed as much people in Kosovo as the FRY/Serbs. Additionally, it turned out that forensic examinations did not find conclusive evidence to prove the Western version of the incident. In fact, forensic evidence could not rule out the conclusion that the dead in Račak were killed in battle (see Herman and Peterson 2010: 98–99; Mandel 2005: 121–125).

Benghazi

Newspaper reporting on the Benghazi incident featured detailed depictions of slaughter. However, in contrast to the Račak incident, news items on Benghazi did focus on such details to a lesser extent. Because Benghazi was reported in conjunction with a range of events that unfolded in other parts of Libya at the same time, the press did not always confine the full news item to Benghazi. Moreover, due to access restrictions, journalists were reportedly not able to investigate the incidents from the ground. Thus, depictions of slaughter drew from observations made by other sources and were less frequently included, if we compare the reporting of Benghazi with Račak and Houla. Notwithstanding, depictions of civilian carnage were regular featured in the news which had framed Benghazi as a nefarious bloodbath.

Hence, in the *New York Times*, Shadid (2011: 1) provided the following account:

> Citing doctors' reports in Benghazi, Samira Boussalma, a member of Amnesty International's North Africa team, said a majority of those killed were shot in the head and the chest. An opposition figure, citing a source at the Jalaa Hospital there, said that most of the dead were 13 to 36 years old and that as many as 50 people had been wounded.

It is noteworthy how the quote accentuated humanising aspects like the precise location of bullet impact spots as well as the age of those who were killed. Highlighting similar details of slaughter, Black (2011b: 1) of the *Guardian* referred to 'shocked witnesses' who 'talked of "massacres" and described corpses shot in the head, chest or neck piling up in hospitals running short of blood and medicines'. Black (*ibid*) added further context on military tactics when arguing that there were 'multiple claims of the army firing into crowds and the targeting of mourners at the funerals of those killed on Saturday'.

The London *Times'* Fletcher (2011c: 6, 7) provided details by quoting human rights groups who 'accused the regime of opening fire on funeral processions with machine guns, operating a shoot-to-kill policy against unarmed protesters, and deploying snipers and foreign mercenaries'. Stewart, of the *Independent* (2011: 4, 5), reported a witness from Benghazi, who had seen a gruesome discovery at a military compound: "'I went to the camp [...] and I saw big drains with people inside them. We only found them because of the smell," he said, adding that he saw "many, many" bodies'. According to the article, the witness stated further that the victims 'had been killed by government forces' (*ibid*). In the German *Frankfurter Rundschau*, Gehlen (2011: 8) wrote it was reported from Libyan cities 'that the police apparently had instantly used live ammunition' and 'security forces allegedly were to have shot from helicopters into the crowd and – as previously in Egypt – used snipers positioned on roof tops'.

Note how next to highlighting atrocious dimensions of the incident, the referenced statements implicated several Libyan actors including the regime and army as well as government, police and security forces. The reported statements also had in common that they were based on reports by sources and not on journalistic 'first-hand' inquiries. The newspapers even acknowledged the limitations of their journalistic approach. Hence, Gehlen (*ibid*) added a sentence in his article stating 'there has yet not been an independent confirmation' of the facts. Black (2011b: 1) similarly pointed out how facts were 'hard to pin down in the face of a news blackout that included jamming of the signal of the al-Jazeera satellite TV network and interference with telephone and internet connections'. The *Post's* Raghavan (2011b: A 01) summarised the news flow from Libya as follows:

> With the Internet and other communications limited and outside journalists and observers denied access, information came mostly through secondhand reports from residents reached by phone or from people leaving Libya across its eastern border with Egypt.

Did such a two-staged process of fact gathering allow for professional journalistic quality controls? Depictions of slaughter indeed often rested on hearsay. Circumstantial evidence was largely derived from local actors embedded with the rebels or from human rights organisations whose inquiries equally relied on testimony by local sources who were more likely to have ties with the opposition than with the Gaddafi regime. Largely based on such 'second hand' source-evidence, Benghazi was framed as a nefarious bloodbath.

On a second level and in comparison with newspaper reporting on Račak, responsibility was often assigned to higher levels of governance. Hence, the *Washington Post's* (2011: A 12) editorial argued: '[...] Gaddafi was waging war against its own people and committed atrocities [...].' Moreover, the editorial said that what was occurring in Tripoli and other cities was 'not only lethal repression but also crimes against humanity' (*ibid*). In another item, the *Post's* Fadel and Raghavan (2011: A 01) gave space to President Obama demanding that the Libyan government 'must be held accountable for its failure [...] and face the cost of continued violations of human rights' (cited in *ibid*). The *Independent's* Stewart (2011: 4, 5) referred to 'a brutal crackdown by the Libyan leader, Colonel Muammar Gaddafi'. Spencer (2011: 14), of the *Telegraph*, quoted elders of one of the country's most important tribal groups, the Warfalah, who had denounced 'the hideous crimes of Gaddafi and his regime' (cited in *ibid*). Fletcher (2011c: 6, 7), of *The Times*, published the following quote by Tom Porteous, London Director of Human Rights Watch:

> 'It looks like the most ferocious effort by any regime so far to stamp out the demonstrations with brute force. The Libyan government has shown no sign of compromise. Instead we are seeing an escalation of the crackdown.'

In the *Observer*, Sharrock (2011: 7) quoted Libyan diplomats who had resigned from the Washington DC mission, saying Gaddafi 'bears responsibility for genocide against the Libyan people' (cited in *ibid*). Black (2011b: 1) of the *Guardian* referred to 'Gaddafi's sons, Khamis and Saadi, and intelligence chief Abdullah Sanussi' who 'were reportedly commanding efforts to crush the protests in Benghazi'. Black (*ibid*) further framed the incidents in Libya as 'a bloody crackdown that saw troops and mercenaries firing at unarmed protestors as the death toll rose to more than 200'. German legal scholar Ambos quoted from UN Resolution 1970, which described the events as 'an incitement of violence by the highest level of the Libyan government' (cited in 2011: 2). Ambos also discussed as to whether actions could amount to 'crimes against humanity', 'genocide' or 'war crimes' (*ibid*). Ambos further wrote that 'from the point of view of the US American human rights organisation Human Rights Watch, there is no authority in Libya which could have ordered such acts independent of Gaddafi' (*ibid*). Even Navi Pillay, the UN human rights chief, appeared to have formed an opinion on the incident prior to any investigation. As Black (2011a: 1), of the *Guardian*, wrote:

> [...] Navi Pillay [...] called for the 'immediate cessation of grave human rights vio-
> lations committed by Libyan authorities'. [...] 'The callousness with which Libyan
> authorities and their hired guns are reportedly shooting live rounds of ammunition at
> peaceful protesters is unconscionable,' Pillay said.

The Western based human rights sector, including spokespersons of the UN, human rights bodies, Western politicians and academics, disseminated opinions in the news media which classified the actions of the Libyan regime and its forces as nefarious. Yet, this narrative drew from 'second hand' allegations rather than substantive evidence. Those who condemned the Gaddafi regime often relied on sources associated with the Libyan opposition or on the problematic evidence reviewed in Chapter 5. On that basis, Benghazi was framed as a nefarious bloodbath. At this stage, it might thus be worth to further quote Kuperman (2013: 111), whose research found 'that Qaddafi did not use force indiscriminately, but rather targeted the rebels narrowly'. Kuperman (*ibid*: 133–134) summarised his findings as follows:

> Libya's initial uprising was not peaceful, nationwide, and democratic – as reported
> and perceived in the West – but violent, regional, and riven with tribalism and
> Islamist extremism. Qaddafi's response was not to slaughter peaceful protesters or
> bombard civilian areas indiscriminately, as reported in the West, but rather to target
> rebels and violent protesters relatively narrowly, reducing collateral harm to non-
> combatants. By no means does this excuse the Libyan government's response, which
> likely included criminal acts. The statistics, testimony, and documentary evidence,
> however, indicate that the Qaddafi regime committed no bloodbaths during the war,
> and had no intention of doing so.

Hence, if Kuperman's view is accurate, then the Benghazi 'bloodbath' was manufactured in the news media.

A second, reoccurring responsibility theme in news items concerned the issue of mercenaries. Many newspapers assigned responsibility for crimes to mercenaries from African nations who had allegedly been brought into Libya by the Gaddafi regime in order to clamp down on the rebellion. Take the following examples: Stewart, of the *Independent* (2011: 4, 5), reported of 'foreign mercenaries' many of which 'shipped in from countries such as Chad and Zimbabwe' who 'have been reviled for their indiscriminate killing of Libyans' and were 'accused of firing wildly at anyone in the streets, even children'. The *Telegraph's* Spencer (2011: 14) said residents in Tripoli 'insisted that many of the attackers were the African mercenaries Col Gaddafi is said to have hired to defend his regime to the end'. Fadel (2011: A01) of the *Post* reported statements by young men at the northeastern Libyan border who

> eagerly displayed cellphone videos that they said depicted government mercenaries shooting down women, children and men. They told of rapes, looting and killings over the past week, as demonstrators have risen up in open revolt and the government of Moammar Gaddafi has cracked down hard.

In the *Independent*, Johnson and Mesure (2011: 6, 7) wrote that several reports said government-recruited mercenaries 'were behind the worst violence including sniper attacks and the use of heavy machine guns'. Accordingly, a

> British-based IT consultant, Ahmed Swelim, 26, originally from Benghazi, said relatives told him the situation had reached a 'critical point'. 'People are living in fear since he [Mr Gaddafi] brought in African mercenaries. They are dressing as normal people but doing random killings. They will shoot or cut people's hands off. [...]'
> (*ibid*)

In the *Süddeutsche Zeitung*, Arne Perras (2011: 6, 7) reported of 'killers' who Libyan demonstrators described as 'blacks' or 'foreigners' (cited in *ibid*) and who possibly stemmed from different African countries like Chad, Niger or Sudan (*ibid*). Perras reflected on the reputation of the fighters: 'They are regarded as ruthless killers who even hunt women and children.' The report, as Perras acknowledged, drew from eyewitness material publicised by al-Jazeera, blogs and online videos, which lacked 'independent verification' (*ibid*). So Perras' story alleged Gaddafi's use of African mercenaries without actually providing substantive evidence for their existence, nor the scope of the issue. In fact, this was not the only news story on mercenaries that relied on secondary source evidence, which was either provided by partisan sources or could hardly be verified (e.g. online or cellphone videos). Moreover, the black mercenary story had racist connotations. For example, the news item by Perras (*ibid*) was titled 'Gaddafi's sinister helpers'. In the German language, the term 'sinister' (German: 'finster') has two meanings: 1) Sinister, in the sense of having an evil mindset and 2) dark, in the sense of brown or black colour or of darkness at night. Hence, the headline was ambiguous. In the context of the negative content of the news story, the headline could be understood as carrying a twofold meaning which conflated being evil with being of dark colour.

It turned out that the mercenary theme had virtually no basis in fact. Thus, Amnesty International wrote in a report published in September 2011: 'Amnesty International found that widespread rumours that al-Gaddafi forces used large numbers of sub-Saharan African mercenaries in February had been significantly exaggerated.' (2011b, see also Forte 2012: 232) Forte (2012: 232), who reviewed the documentary record, further remarked that 'no evidence was ever found of any foreign African fighters being employed by the government to fight the insurgents, not even as much as an interview with a "mercenary"'. Yet, Forte also documented the 'racist targeting and killing of black Libyans and migrant Africans workers' by the insurgents which 'continued through the entirety of NATO's military campaign' (*ibid*: 227). Thus, the report by Amnesty (2011b, see also Forte 2012: 232 for further evidence) commented on rebel advances after the NATO air war had begun:

> When Al-Bayda, Benghazi, Derna, Misratah and other cities first fell under the control of the NTC [National Transitional Council] in February, anti-Gaddafi forces carried out house raids, killings and other violent attacks against suspected mercenaries, either sub-Saharan Africans or black Libyans.

These human rights violations were widespread and largely ignored by the 'humanitarian interventionists' who advocated R2P in Libya (see Forte 2012: 234). In reality, the Libyan rebels had engaged in similar actions for which the Gaddafi regime had previously been accused of. Thus, 'humanitarian intervention' and 'R2P' were initially evoked on false pretexts. In contrast, when the Libyan rebels later engaged in real bloodbaths and ethnic cleansing the 'international community' and the news media remained silent. As Forte (*ibid*: 234–235) further commented:

> It has now become impossible for advocates of the 'responsibility to protect' (R2P) and closely related liberal imperialist ideals to be taken seriously. Throughout the war in Libya, they diligently ignored the reports of atrocities against black civilians in Libya, even as they laboured at characterizing the government's actions as 'genocide' and that only its violence needed to be stopped. Thus of the 24 'human rights groups' that jointly invoked R2P and called for foreign military intervention [...], not one had mentioned, even once, the plight of black Libyans and African migrant workers targeted and killed by the Libyan opposition because of the colour of their skin and/ or their national origin.

Houla

Houla was consistently framed as a nefarious bloodbath and newspaper reporting entailed extensive depictions of slaughter. The press focused on forensic aspects and meticulously explored atrocious details of the incident. In their writing, the news media also highlighted photographic material displaying civilian carnage. Take the following examples: MacFarquhar and Saad (2012: 1), of the *New York Times*, wrote on 27 May, just after the incident had occurred:

> Amateur videos said to be taken in the aftermath showed row after row of victims, many of them small children with what appeared to be bullet holes in their temples. Other videos showed gruesome shrapnel wounds caused by what activists said was a barrage of shelling that started Friday in response to demonstrations […].

On the same day, Chulov (2012a: 1), of the *Observer*, wrote:

> Videos uploaded to the internet and purporting to be from Houla show many dead and badly mutilated infants. Residents say some victims were killed with knives, while many more died from relentless shelling that left buildings wrecked and homes destroyed in a large residential area near the centre of town.

In the London *Times*, Jaber and Macleod (2012: 27) wrote:

> Videos posted on YouTube showed horrifying images of children's bodies lined up on the floor of a Mosque, some badly mangled. At least one child had part of his head blown away.

Such depictions were representative of reports appearing shortly after the Houla incident had taken place. Note the attention given to atrocious details and shocking images of slaughter. As is also apparent, many of the descriptions were derived from video clips uploaded to the Internet. Later, further photo footage of the incident was publicised in the press. For example, *The Times'* Fletcher (2012: 1, 6, 7) included distressing material displaying some 'of the 49 children killed in the Houla massacre':

> One photograph shows a cherubic baby girl, no older than 2, with a tiny gold ear-stud. She is wrapped in a white shroud. Half her skull has been hacked or blown away. A saucer of bone juts from a bloody gash in what remains of her head.

> Another shows what appears to be a boy of perhaps 6 or 7. The blanket in which he is wrapped has fallen away to expose a bare white shoulder. He looks as if he is sleeping, but the back of his head has been lopped off like the top of a boiled egg. His brain lies on the blanket behind him.

> A third shows a pretty young girl staring upwards, her mouth slightly open as if smiling. Above her right eye there is a large, bloody bullet hole surrounded by a mess of flesh and bone. The pictures go on, some mercifully out of focus, most far too shocking to print in The Times though failure to do so spares the Assad regime. (*ibid*)

The pictures were reported with sensitivity to detail and pointed to extremely troubling events. Note also how the newspapers appeared to mainly assign responsibility to the Syrian regime. In their reporting, newspapers would often embed gruesome details of the incident with quotes that relegated responsibility to the Syrian government and its forces. This cemented the dominant narrative about who was responsible for the incident. Houla was indeed largely framed in atrocious terms and responsibility for the violence was often relegated to the Syrian government side of the conflict.

For example, in the first paragraph of his news story, Chulov of the *Observer* (2012a: 1), wrote about a 'regime-backed massacre' that 'left 32 children among more than 90 dead'. In the already featured item of the *Times*, Fletcher (2012: 1, 6, 7) further assigned responsibility for the 'Houla massacre' to 'President Assad's Shabiha thugs'. An item published in the *Guardian* by Jonathan Miller (2012: 15), a foreign affairs correspondent with Channel 4, opened his story saying that new evidence has emerged that members of Bashar al-Assad's family and inner circle were 'directly ordering the commission of crimes against humanity in Syria'. The evidence presented appeared to be based on testimony by defectors from Syrian intelligence and security agencies alleging government culpability (see *ibid*). The news reports were underpinned by eyewitness testimony from civilians and local activists from Houla and this lent further credibility to the narrative. For instance, the article by Fletcher (2012: 1, 6, 7) in the *Times* quoted Maysara Hilaoui, a local activist saying

> that Shabiha militia 'broke into houses and farms and killed everyone they saw'. He added: 'It's painful to describe what I saw. Some bodies had their eyes ripped from them, and others had their heads cut off. There were also bodies covered with knife wounds. We have reports that five women were raped before they were killed.'

But it is of significance that during the period that my study covered and beyond, responsibility for Houla was contested as the Syrian regime and Russia had blamed the Syrian opposition for the carnage. Hence, during the days after the incident had taken place, several scenarios about who actually had executed the massacre would be conveyed in the press (see discussion below). While the newspapers would report these different scenarios, the narrative of Syrian government responsibility was emphasised whereas the narrative of Syrian opposition responsibility was de-emphasised.

In the following discussion I will look in more detail at the investigations by the *Independent's* Patrick Cockburn who has a long-standing record as a reporter on Syria and the Middle East. Cockburn provided extensive detail on the Houla incident. Cockburn also discussed the different scenarios of responsibility for the incident. Cockburn's reporting can also be regarded as a benchmark for newspaper coverage because the journalist is considered to be one of the most critical and respected writers on the region.

On 27 May, Cockburn (2012b: 2, 3) wrote at the beginning of an article that anti-government militants were blaming pro-regime gunmen for carrying out 'the butchery in which children and their parents were hacked and shot to deaths'. Cockburn added that militants were saying that the perpetrators were 'pro-regime gunmen, known as the shabiya, who had captured Houla'. The Shabiha, Cockburn argued, may have belonged to the Alawi sect of which the Syrian regime 'is largely drawn' (*ibid*). This scenario of proxy responsibility was updated in another report on 28 May. In this article, Cockburn (2012c: 4, 5) suggested that the killings in Houla could have been done by rogue Alawi militia-men and this would indicate 'a leadership not quite in control of its own forces'. In a third article, also published on 28 May, Cockburn (2012d: 4, 5) shed further light on the Syrian leadership issue:

> The government in Damascus yesterday appeared to be somewhat leaderless and seemed slow to take on board the impact of an outrage in which people across the world are blaming the Syrian authorities for the murder and mutilation of children. 'I get the impression that there is nobody in firm control of Syrian policy and the Syrian armed forces,' said a diplomat yesterday.

The source evidence pointed to the possibility that the Syrian regime had not instructed the Houla massacre. Thus, in a fourth news item, published on 30 May, Cockburn (2012f: 4, 5) argued it was indeed in Syria's 'interest to avoid any atrocity that would draw international attention' and Houla would demonstrate 'a lack of effective decision-making within the regime that they could not restrain their own forces'.

In sum, the facts collated in these items by Cockburn pointed to two scenarios of Syrian regime responsibility: 1) Houla might have constituted a deliberate action overseen by the Syrian government. 2) Houla might have constituted a spontaneous action by militias that were associated with the Syrian regime but had acted independently of it.

The first scenario was widely reported in the news media and constituted the narrative largely put forward by the opposition and also by Western government spokespersons. Of course, the first scenario was plausible if the evidence provided by opposition forces and civilians from opposition held territory was accurate. Nonetheless, the second scenario was similarly plausible: as already discussed in Chapter 5, the Syrian government had no rational incentive to carry out an atrocity because it was expectable that such an incident could incite foreign intervention as recently witnessed in Libya. Moreover, and as further discussed in the previous chapter, during the period of the Annan peace plan, the Syrian army had reduced violence probably in order to cement the status quo. Thus, the contextual evidence did not necessarily point to Syrian regime responsibility. Yet, the second scenario was de-emphasised by the news media or reported in a fashion that co-assigned responsibility to the Syrian regime. Furthermore, the news media neglected to thoroughly investigate the factual basis of this second scenario.

Finally, there was a third scenario that would point to opposition responsibility for the massacre. Indeed, the Syrian government had denied any responsibility for the Houla incident. Thus, in the third article discussed above, Cockburn (2012d: 4, 5) discussed the Syrian regime's position, which claimed

> that the massacre happened after 100 heavily armed men attacked government checkpoints around Houla early on Saturday morning and then butchered the inhabitants of Houla over a nine-hour period. Blaming 'terrorists' for the massacre, Foreign Ministry spokesman Jihad Makdissi told reporters in Damascus that 'women, children and old men were shot dead. This is not the hallmark of the heroic Syrian army.'

This narrative was often mentioned in press reporting, albeit balanced with statements suggesting Syrian regime culpability. Hence, Cockburn (*ibid*) further added in his item that the Houla incident comprised of 'claims and counterclaims' (*ibid*). Other newspapers would report the official Syrian government narrative often only in passing or embedded in negative contexts. The newspapers would thus elevate the opposition narrative pointing to Syrian government responsibility although the scenario purported by the Syrian regime was mentioned as a means of formal journalistic balance.

An article by MacFarquhar and Saad (2012: 1), in the *New York Times* on 27 May, provided an indicative example of how the press 'balanced' the different scenarios of responsibility. In their news story, MacFarquhar and Saad (*ibid*) published multiple statements implicating the Syrian regime. Firstly, at the start of the text, the journalists wrote that international officials 'largely blamed the government' (*ibid*) for what happened in Houla. Syrian regime responsibility was then alleged with reference to several statements made by powerful sources and opposition actors including UN Secretary General Ban Ki-moon and his predecessor Kofi Annan ('[...] flagrant violation of international law and commitments of the Syrian government to cease the use of heavy weapons in population centres [...]'), the White House ('a vile testament to an illegitimate regime that responds to peaceful protest with unspeakable and inhuman brutality'), activists ('much of the slaughter had been carried out by pro-government thugs, or "shabiha," from the area'), a man with a mask on a YouTube video (it is time 'to prepare for vengeance against this awful sectarian regime'), and the Free Syrian Army (the peace plan is 'buying time for the government to kill civilians') (*ibid*). After these actors were quoted, the text included the counter-narrative (scenario 3) provided by the Syrian regime (the 'Syrian government blamed "terrorists," its catchall phrase for the opposition, for killing the civilians'), state television ('calling the deaths "part of the ugly crimes that the terrorists are committing against the Syrians with the financial support of some Arab states and others"') and a statement of the SANA news agency, which 'said that "armed terrorist groups attacked law-enforcement forces and civilians" in the nearby town of Teldo, which prompted security forces to "intervene and engage the terrorists"' (*ibid*). These counter-statements were then further balanced with reference to the UN, which 'rebutted the government's standard claims that outsiders or their domestic dupes are to blame for the violence' (*ibid*). The article then also claimed that the UN had not 'suggested that the opposition was involved in the deaths of civilians in Houla' (*ibid*). Yet, MacFarquhar and Saad (*ibid*) admitted that 'the United Nations statements called for stopping violence on both sides'. Furthermore, the article acknowledged that the UN's 'statement stopped short of accusing the government of responsibility for the entire toll' (*ibid*). Moreover, General Robert Mood, Head of the United Nations Supervision Mission in Syria (UNSMIS), was referenced in the text stating 'that the circumstances behind all the deaths remained "unclear"' (*ibid*). After this quote, the authors provided several official statements further alleging Syrian regime responsibility: by Clinton ('vicious assault that involved a regime artillery and tank barrage on a residential neighbourhood', 'And the United States will work with the international community to intensify our pressure on Assad and his cronies, whose rule by murder and fear must come to an end'), by Fabius (who 'issued a statement accusing Syria's government of committing "new massacres"'), and by an activist ('government forces had shelled Houla heavily', 'government soldiers moved in, along with volunteers from surrounding hamlets, to kill civilians') (*ibid*).

Hence, the news item clearly advantaged the narrative of Syrian government culpability, if the amount of quotes purveying this line was considered (scenarios 1 and 2). In contrast, the counter-perspective was marginalised and refuted (scenario 3).

It should be noted, however, that the main independent source cited in the article, the Head of the United Nations Supervision Mission in Syria General Robert Mood, did not confirm Syrian government responsibility. Rather, the opposition, 'activists' on the side of the opposition, Western spokespersons, as well as two high level UN officials acted as the sources of such claims. Note also that MacFarquhar and Saad (2012: 1) mentioned in their article that details of what happened were murky because 'Syria sharply limits access to the country for foreign correspondents, making independent verification of events there difficult'. Hence, a careful reading of the news item allowed for the conclusion that Syrian government responsibility was largely alleged on the basis of statements by interested-party sources whose claims could not independently be verified. Overall, many news items appeared to allege Syrian government responsibility on similar grounds.

Yet significantly, facts pointed to further facets of the third scenario that largely remained unexplored by the press. The Houla incident comprised of two dimensions: indiscriminate killings as well as close range executions. Thus, the Russians, who generally supported the narrative provided by the Syrian government, reportedly backed 'a UN Security Council statement condemning the deaths' (Walker and Cockburn 2012: 8, 9). According to Walker and Cockburn (*ibid*), of the *Independent*, 'Mr Lavrov conceded that government forces bore the main responsibility for the massacre, but insisted the presence of knife and bullet wounds on some corpses meant the opposition was also involved'. Following from this rationale, responsibility of the shelling was assigned to the Syrian regime whereas responsibility for close range killings implicated elements within the opposition who had largely controlled the Houla area. This narrative was consistent with scenario 3. Furthermore, if this line of reasoning was accurate, then opposition members were seriously implicated: as Cockburn wrote in one of his texts: 'Most of the 108 victims of the Houla massacre were executed at point-blank range in their homes and fewer than 20 were killed by shellfire, the UN human rights office said' (Cockburn 2012e: 4, 5).

However, the third scenario was not emphasised by the press. When reporting on the close range killings, most news items blamed the Shabiha militia for the massacre assuming that the militia had received orders from or was closely connected to the Syrian regime. Accordingly, on 28 May, the *Daily Telegraph* published an item by Alex Thomson (2012a: 16, 17), chief correspondent for Channel 4 News, who was the first journalist entering Houla after the incident had occurred. Thomson (*ibid*) referred to Martin Griffiths, Deputy Commander of the UN observer mission, who had attempted to lead a small team into the Houla area. According to Thomson (*ibid*) 'Mr Griffiths said both the Free Syrian Army (FSA) command in Rastan and civilian eye-witnesses in Houla itself had said the same thing' that after shelling 'groups of armed civilian militias – known as the Shabiha – began moving house to house and the killings, using knives and firearms, began'. Furthermore, according to Thomson (*ibid*), 'all around you in Houla, there is compelling evidence to suggest it is Syria's government and Syria's army who are telling the lies about the massacre on Friday'. On 31 May, in another article for the *Telegraph*, Thomson (2012b: 21) reported how he had 'scarcely witnessed such extraordinary scenes of people desperate to tell the world what they have been through' when the journalist was 'passed from family to family, house to house, by people, sometimes literally fighting to get their story to the wider world'. Furthermore, Thomson (*ibid*) described how everybody 'points to a group of Shia and Alawite villages to the west and east of town' saying 'the killers came from these villages to attack the Sunni people of Houla'.

Thomson's news items thus broadly confirmed the Syrian opposition narrative, which was backed by Western spokespersons and implicated paramilitary forces under order of or connected to the Syrian regime for the close range executions (scenarios 1 and 2). The eyewitness testimony, based on local inquiries, lent further credibility to the reports.

Newspapers would rarely investigate scenario 3, which pointed to the Syrian opposition as mainly responsible for the Houla incident. Only on 8 June, Rainer Hermann (2012: 1) of the German *Frankfurter Allgemeine Zeitung* published more detailed evidence in support of this scenario. Hermann's news story was based on sources stemming from selected Syrian opposition fractions, namely elements which had rejected to use violence (see *ibid*). It should be noted that there was a Syrian opposition strand that acted independently of the armed opposition. This non-violent opposition movement was largely neglected in news reporting. The article by Herrmann constituted a rare exception, which featured spokespersons of the non-violent Syrian opposition (*ibid*). According to Hermann, these non-violent opposition actors were treated as anonymous sources in his article because they feared reprisals from the militant opposition (see *ibid*). From what these sources had told him, Hermann (*ibid*) reported the following progression of events, which 'contradicted the allegations of the rebels': Sunni rebels had attacked three Syrian army checkpoints surrounding Houla. The checkpoints had been established in order to protect Alawite villages surrounding Houla. The fighting lasted for about 90 minutes and dozens of soldiers and rebels were killed (see *ibid*). During these clashes, civilians might have been killed in Houla due to indiscriminate shelling by the Syrian army. Hermann (*ibid*) then stated the following chain of events about how the close range killings in Houla had unfolded:

> According to eyewitnesses, the massacre had occurred during that time. Almost only families belonging to the Alawite and Shiite minorities were killed in Houla, whose inhabitants to more than ninety per cent were Sunni. Several dozens of members of a family, which had converted from Sunni to Shia Islam were slaughtered. Moreover, members of the Alawite Shomaliya family were killed and the family of a Sunni member of parliament who was regarded as a collaborator. Immediately after the massacre, the perpetrators had filmed their victims, disguised them as Sunni victims and distributed the videos over the Internet. Representatives of the Syrian government had confirmed this version, but stressed the government was obliged to not speak of Alawites and Sunnis in public.

While the newspapers in the sample would provide statements by Syrian, Russian and Iranian actors in support of this narrative (scenario 3), Hermann's news story appeared to be the only item providing substantive context about the circumstances surrounding the close range killings. Of course, Hermann's story is based on anonymous sources and has to be further explored. Yet, it is still striking that the angle in support of scenario 3 was seemingly not further pursued by the press under study.

Yet, several other news organisations had found sources whose testimonies were in broad agreement with the statements provided by Hermann (for an overview of this set of evidence see Anderson 2016: 74–77). For instance, Alfred Hackensberger (2012), of the German *Berliner Morgenpost*, went to Syria and interviewed a refugee from Houla, whose story was consistent with the testimony sourced by Hermann. According to the eyewitness statement given to Hackensberger (*ibid*), the rebels and not the Shabiha had killed the civilians in Houla because the residents did not support the revolution against the government and/or defied orders of the FSA. Hackensberger (*ibid*) cited the witness (whose name was changed) saying that many people in Houla knew what really happened but 'whoever speaks today can only repeat the rebel version' adding that everything else meant 'certain death'. In his study on Syria, Anderson collected reports by Syrian, German, Dutch and Russian sources providing further witness testimony in support of scenario 3 (see 2016: 77).

In summary, despite the existence of a range of scenarios, the news media would largely relegate responsibility to the Syrian regime and its associated forces (scenarios 1 and 2). An objective approach would have been to inquire the claims and counter claims more thoroughly before assigning responsibility. There was, indeed, a range of civilian and independent sources who had claimed that the bloodbath was executed by opposition forces. This narrative was largely ignored by the news media. Moreover, it was largely not investigated that the Houla massacre served the militant Syrian opposition rather well: it could be used to invite foreign intervention and reject the Annan plan cease-fire (see also discussion in Chapter 5).

Finally, under due impartiality criteria, the news media's treatment of Houla was questionable. General Robert Mood, Head of the United Nations Supervision Mission in Syria, who had visited Houla with his monitoring team shortly after the incident had happened, actually found it difficult to assign culpability. Three weeks after Houla took place, on 16 June 2012, Mood made the following statement:

> We have interviewed locals with one story and we have interviewed locals that have another story. The circumstances and [...] the facts related to the incident itself still remain unclear to us [...] we have sent [statements and witness interviews] as a report to UN headquarters New York [...] if we are asked [to assist] obviously we are on the ground and could help. (cited in Anderson 2016: 72–73)

Mood's statement indicated the prevalence of two different narratives of the event. Hence, three weeks after the incident had taken place, the factual context was far from clear. In fact, Mood's statement supported the journalists who had found civilians arguing that the opposition shared responsibility for the Houla incident (scenario 3). Yet, the newspapers in my sample hardly reported the views of these actors. It is important that two, albeit competing, narratives emerged from Houla during the time of reporting. Moreover, the newspapers lent more credibility to the opposition narrative that was also supported by Western government officials (scenarios 1 and 2). The newspapers would report the narrative provided by the Syrian regime, yet in a less developed and rather de-contextualised fashion (scenario 3). It was further problematic that many of the facts and testimonies provided by the news media were derived from so-called activist and opposition sources. Even civilian testimonies were largely collected from areas under control and management of opposition forces. This set of eyewitness material was not sufficiently balanced with independent evidence. In their reporting on Iraq, the newspapers neither based their stories on eyewitness testimony provided by activists and opposition sources nor on Sunni civilians stemming from resistance-controlled areas in Fallujah. In Syria, reliance on such sources appeared to be the norm. Hence, the newspapers provided a similarly selective perspective when assigning responsibility for and framing the incident in Houla as a nefarious bloodbath.

'Allied' countries

Fallujah 1

In the reporting of the Fallujah 1 incident, the press would apply different reporting standards. Fallujah was largely framed as a military endeavour with benevolent intent. Details of slaughter were presented as humanitarian disaster stories. Responsibility for crimes was rarely designated to US/Coalition actors. The press explained civilian deaths as tragic casualties of war. Newspapers would only rarely regard US/Coalition policies as a cause for civilian deaths. Evidence for potential war crimes was mentioned in passing and without investigatory zeal. News media attention to atrocious dimensions of the incident was scarce. For instance, al-Jazeera, relief organisations and other news media had broadcasted shocking images from Fallujah (see discussion below). Unlike in the reporting on Houla this set of factual material was not prominently featured in news coverage. When the news media highlighted details of the civilian plight, they did largely not assign causal responsibility. Furthermore, the framing of Fallujah as a martial incident shielded the occurrence of atrocious dimensions. Fallujah 1 was thus contextualised in benign terms.

For example, when reporting on the Fallujah 1 incident on 9 April, Cockburn (2004d: 5) discussed the impact of US military tactics in the context of 'fighting':

AMERICAN MARINES besieging Fallujah, west of Baghdad, have killed 280 Iraqis and wounded more than 400 in fighting this week, the doctor at the city's hospital said yesterday. The city of 300,000 people on the Euphrates has been under attack from ground and air since the beginning of the week, during which it has been sealed off from the outside world.

The figure for the number of dead and wounded is likely to be even higher said Dr Taher al-Issawi at the small local hospital. 'We also know of dead and wounded in various places buried under the rubble but we cannot reach them because of the fighting,' he said.

Cockburn was among the most critical journalists reporting on Fallujah. The article highlighted the humanitarian situation in Fallujah and referenced a range of Iraqi actors depicting the incident as a humanitarian catastrophe. But the reference to 'fighting' indirectly denied responsibility for nefarious behaviour. Additionally, the writing did not focus on forensic details. Perhaps because Cockburn did not report directly from the theatre, such a focus was impossible. On the other hand, when reporting on 'enemy' countries, the press would easily rely on video and picture material provided by local sources. This was less so in the reporting of Fallujah 1, where journalists operated in a more 'objective' and detached modus in regard to the coverage of the atrocious facets of the incident. Hence, violence was reported in the same fashion as natural disasters when casualties resulted from tragic events rather than from nefarious actions. Hence, Fallujah 1 was framed as a benign bloodbath.

Similarly, in a news item published on 9 April, the *New York Times*' Eric Schmitt (2004b: 9) referred to civilian casualties of the fighting:

> But the cost in civilian lives, shattered buildings and fractured good will – whatever was left after months of combative relations with United States troops – have already taken a toll, and wire services have reported as many as 300 Iraqi civilian casualties from the fighting.

In this case, the journalist reported in the fashion of a detached and neutral observer. Fatalities and destruction resulted from 'fighting'. The US/Coalition military rationale thus remained de-contextualised. There was no focus on the details, such as wounds and forensic aspects of the killing. Similarly, Hider (2004e: 5), of the London *Times*, reported of the 'constant fighting' that

> has prompted tens of thousands of Fallujah's women, children and elderly men to take up an offer by coalition forces to leave the city, although men of fighting age are not allowed to go. Nevertheless, there are many civilians still trapped in their homes, too afraid to go outside.

Again, the journalist depicted humanitarian suffering with reference to 'fighting'. There was no reflection on the role and nature of US/Coalition violence. Moreover, it was mentioned in passing that men of fighting age were not allowed to leave the city. This detail indicated that the US/Coalition could have acted in violation of the Geneva Conventions, where such practices prohibited. Yet, this rather sensitive issue was disregarded and not further explored. Together with the quantitative evidence displayed further above, these examples of reporting demonstrated that Fallujah 1 was largely framed in terms of fighting and war. While a diligent reader could potentially sense that a major humanitarian crisis had unfolded in Fallujah for which the US/Coalition bore significant responsibility, the news media largely reported in a detached modus operandi.

Only on some occasions did newspapers publish more explicit material. To that effect, the *Guardian* provided space for an eyewitness report by British human rights activist Jo Wilding (2004: 13). Wilding (*ibid*) travelled to Fallujah as an aid worker and reported of indiscriminate military tactics. In her dispatch, Wilding (*ibid*) linked human suffering to the military conduct of the US/Coalition:

> People have been under bombardment for the last eight days. A lot of people are trapped in their houses still – despite the ceasefire – without food, without water and terrified to leave. Food and medical aid is now arriving but the problem is getting the aid around the city. A lot of it is delivered to the mosque, but then getting it to the hospitals, past the American snipers, is proving to be impossible. The main hospital apparently has been destroyed by bombing and the second largest is covered by US snipers – the Iraqis call it sniper alley. So Iraqi people are not able to get to and from the hospitals. [...]

> We saw two kids arriving with their grandmother, they had all been wounded by gunfire, they said by American snipers, while they were trying to leave their house to flee to Baghdad.

> An elderly woman with a wound to the head was still carrying the white flag she had been holding when she was shot. They were all saying it was American snipers shooting [...]. [...]

> We saw mainly bullet wounds for the majority of civilians. Families are getting injured when they try to leave the house, trying to escape for Baghdad. A bullet goes astray or it gets them in their house. Then a lot of people are injured from shelling. They get hit by shrapnel that gets into the house.

Wilding's observations stood out for being zealous, highlighting gruesome aspects and nefarious behaviour by the US/Coalition. Yet, such reports would not generate more sustained investigations into the atrocious dimensions of the Fallujah incident. The extent to which US/Coalition snipers might have killed civilians in Fallujah was hardly investigated. Fallujah was not depicted as a nefarious bloodbath. Yet, independent and foreign journalists as well as relief workers and civilians had reported of numerous atrocities during April 2004 (see e.g. Holmes 2007; Jamail 2007). Examples included the indiscriminate targeting of civilians by US snipers leading to the shooting of women, men and children as well as ambulances. Other dispatches reported the blocking of the main Fallujah hospital by US troops and the prevention of civilians from leaving the city (see Zollmann 2008: 8). The independent journalist Dahr Jamail (2007: 137), who wrote dispatches from Fallujah in April 2004, reported from a clinic where he witnessed 'an endless stream of women and children who had been shot by the U.S. soldiers':

> Another small child lay on a blood-spattered bed, also shot by a sniper. The boy's grandmother lay nearby, shot as she was attempting to carry children from their home and flee the city. She lay on a bed dying, still clutching a bloodied white surrender flag. Hundreds of families were trapped in their homes, terrorized by U.S. snipers shooting from rooftops and the minarets of mosques whenever they saw someone move past a window. (*ibid*: 138)

In a book about Fallujah, Al-Jazeera host Ahmed Mansour (2009: 162) documented his experience when broadcasting from the city in April. Mansour (*ibid*) described how the people of Fallujah had turned a 'sports field in the city into a cemetery'. Like Wilding and Jamail, Mansour witnessed 'the constant threat of snipers' and 'Marines who routinely fired at' people in the city when 'they buried their dead' (*ibid*). Mansour (*ibid*: 163) recounted the following episode:

> On the eve of Saturday, April 10, I passed by a field hospital just after midnight. I found dead bodies belonging to one family in a pile in front of the hospital-a family of three generations represented by its dead. There was the grandfather, a man names Muhammad Jassim al-Matloub. Next to him, on one side, lay the body of his son-in-law. Next to Muhammad, on the other side, lay the body of his young grandson. [...]

> The three dead had stayed in the house for some reason, and a fighter jet had bombed the house, killing them all. The bodies were badly mutilated and their skin was ripped off in some places, exposing muscles and organs. I tried to maintain my composure, but I got weak. It was too painful a sight to keep looking at. I left the cameraman to film the bodies and ran out. We aired these gruesome images on al-Jazeera Saturday morning.

Such dispatches were reported by Al-Jazeera on a regular basis and infuriated the US/Coalition. The depictions resembled the pictures and videos that the Western press would feature on their front pages when reporting on Houla and Benghazi. In fact, R2P and 'humanitarian intervention' had been evoked in Libya because Gaddafi had allegedly used his air force indiscriminately. When reporting on Fallujah, the US/Coalition's indiscriminate use of air power was hardly questioned in the same fashion by the press. Al-Jazeera source material, detailing gruesome images and stories of civilian carnage (see *ibid*), was not prominently covered in the Western news. The press did, at times, touch on the civilian plight. Yet, the Fallujah 1 incident was rarely depicted as an atrocity although the newspapers cited a range of Iraqi actors who described the Fallujah incident in such terms. Examples of such voices include members of the Iraqi Governing Council (IGC) who said the siege amounted to 'collective punishment' (cited in Cockburn 2004b: 10). In the context of coverage, however, such quotes remained scattered. In fact, the newspapers neglected evidence of US/Coalition responsibility for major carnage. While cursorily referring to atrocious details and possible crimes, the press appeared far less willing to assign responsibility. Hence, multiple story-queues for critical reporting remained unexplored. Such performance was in striking contrast to the newspapers handling of actions by 'enemy' countries, which were investigated with scrutiny. In conclusion, the reporting on Fallujah evoked a 'war' context. Fallujah was framed as a benign bloodbath.

Fallujah 2

In their reporting on Fallujah 2, the newspapers viewed humanitarian issues even more stringently from an 'objective' distance. The overwhelming use of martial terminology to classify the Fallujah 2 incident is evidence of this (see Table 3 above). Civilian casualties were reported as the tragic outcomes of war and the press hardly assigned responsibility for war crimes. Yet, similar as in their reporting on Fallujah 1, the newspapers provided factual evidence that pointed to high levels of destruction and casualties in Fallujah. Such material was treated as background facts and did not lead to sustained coverage. The press adopted the position of a neutral observer and humanitarian issues were reported from a wide-angle perspective. There was no focus on details of slaughter and nefarious actions.

A critical assessment of the US/Coalition's military rationale could have suggested that the military operation during the Fallujah 2 incident was hardly reconcilable with the Geneva Conventions. This would have explained the high amount of civilian deaths during the operation (see Chapter 5 and below). It seemed obvious from a common sense and also journalistic perspective that there was a connection between a reported humanitarian crisis, US/Coalition military strategy and responsibility for civilian deaths. Yet, as will be demonstrated below, this connection largely remained unexplored. Because the Fallujah 2 incident did not generate much attention in terms of its atrocious dimensions, it makes sense to review this case in more detail. In the following section, I will therefore investigate a range of issues. They include assessments of how the press handled information on (1) civilians who stayed in Fallujah during the incident, (2) US/Coalition military strategy and tactics, (3) civilian deaths and (4) potential war crimes. It will be demonstrated that the factual record and the newspapers own reporting indicated that Fallujah had the properties of a massacre for which the US/Coalition and its leaders shared responsibility. Yet, the incident was largely framed as a benign bloodbath (reporting model 2). This means that atrocious details of the operation were marginalised in reporting and virtually no responsibility for potential war crimes was assigned.

(1) 60,000–100,000 civilians in Fallujah, but many were 'believed to have left'

When General George Casey, Commander of the Multinational Forces in Iraq, announced the beginning of the operation in Fallujah at the official US Department of Defense teleconference on 8 November 2004, he said:

> Our estimates are that, again, 50 (per cent) to 70 per cent of the population [which is just over 200,000] has departed. That is borne out by heat signatures and generator signatures that we observe there during darkness. That's about as good an estimate as I can give you on what's there inside of Fallujah. (US Department of Defense 2004)

Hence, by implication, US military planners must have expected that between 60,000–100,000 civilians were inside Fallujah. In their reporting, newspapers would virtually not assign responsibility to top US/Coalition planners although the occurrence of extensive civilian casualties could have been linked with the US Department of Defense's knowledge about the amount of civilians in the city.

Reports by relief organisations published on the eve of the operation similarly indicated a high number of civilians in Fallujah. The Emergency Working Group (EWG), which comprised of the UN, the Red Cross/Crescent and various ministries of the IIG, published several reports based on 'preliminary estimates' of internally displaced persons (IDP) (see EWG 2004a, b, c: 1). On 7 November, the EWG expected approximately '50,000 persons, probably men' remaining in Fallujah (EWG 2004a). The same figure was provided in EWG updates on 9 and 11 November (see EWG 2004b, c).[2] An 8 November report by IRIN (2004a), the news service of the UN Office for the Coordination of Humanitarian Affairs, cited Fadhel Youssef, a spokesman for the local governorate, saying 30,000 people had stayed in Fallujah.[3] On 16 November, a Red Cross official assumed 'at least 50,000 residents' to be trapped in the city (Jamail 2004b).

The newspapers in my study similarly published estimates pointing to a substantial amount of civilians to be present in the city – roughly between 30,000 and 100,000. Yet significantly, numerical estimates were cursory included and presented as background facts without contextualisation or investigatory zeal. There were no inquiries into the accuracy of the varying figures and what it actually meant if a dense city populated by 30,000–100,000 people was under heavy air and ground fire (for the US/Coalition military strategy see the next section below). For instance, the *New York Times'* Richard A. Oppel (2004b: 1) quoted an assessment by Dr. Rasheed al-Janabi, a surgeon at the hospital, that 30 per cent of the population had remained. Similarly, Filkins and Glanz (2004a: 1) provided an estimate by American military officials that 'of a usual population of 300,000, 70 percent to 90 percent of civilians had fled'. Yet, further context was not provided.

The *Washington Post* and the *Guardian* would publish reports indicating that 100,000 civilians might have stayed in Fallujah (see Bunting 2004: 17; Graham 2004: A 24; McCarthy and Borger 2004: 1). In the *Post*, which was the single newspaper in the sample directly referring to the estimate provided by Casey in relation to the number, the news item appeared on page 24 and the estimate was balanced by Donald Rumsfeld saying 'the discipline of U.S. troops would prevent "large numbers of civilians killed"' (Graham 2004: A 24). News coverage in the *Guardian* mentioned the number in passing and in the next to last paragraph of the article (see McCarthy and Borger 2004: 1). Only an 8 November *Guardian* comment by Bunting (2004: 17), who argued 'there could be 100,000 or more still in their homes', further developed the issue. According to Bunting (*ibid*), 'as in any war, those who don't get out of the way are a mixture of the most vulnerable - the elderly, the poor, the sick; the unlucky, who left it too late to get away; and the insanely brave, such as medical staff'.

Generally, no newspaper gave weight to the fact that Casey, the most senior US military commander in Iraq, and the EWG, comprised of a range of authoritative organisations, had provided assessments of large numbers of civilians to be present in Fallujah. This was indicated by the absence of the Casey and EWG figures. Considering the official importance of these actors, it appears to be striking that their statements did not generate more prominent and sustained coverage.[4]

In all newspapers under review, but particularly in the US press and the *Guardian*, there were also statements similar to the following printed in the *New York Times* suggesting that most/many civilians 'were believed to have left' (Oppel and Worth 2004: 1). Such depictions were literally in accord with the Casey and EWG estimates discussed above signifying the absence of more than 50 per cent (i.e. the majority) of Fallujah's population. But the emphasis on those who had left and the missing context about the density of Fallujah suggested a largely uninhabited city. Yet, considering its geographic shape, Fallujah was still packed with civilians even if only a 'minority' of 50,000 people remained. This reality was virtually absent in the newspapers under review. Furthermore, these issues hardly generated international outrage. Consider Benghazi, where the news media carried highly indignant statements about the alleged indiscriminate use of air forces in population centres. Not so in Fallujah, where such military tactics were widely reported (see discussion below) albeit without similar levels of indignation.

(2) Fallujah 'shooting gallery'

The newspapers featured statements about the US/Coalition's use of extreme force.[5] On 10 November, the *Süddeutsche Zeitung* published a report by *Reuters* which cited Lt Col. John Morris saying US troops would slog through Fallujah 'like a fist' (Reuters 2004a: 1). The *Observer's* Lindsey Hilsum, who was embedded with the 1st Marine Expeditionary Force, wrote on 14 November about US tactics: 'The attitude is that overwhelming force is necessary.' (Hilsum 2004: 20) The *New York Times* (2004b: 20) editorial on 15 November argued how from the start 'the military advance has been relentless'. *The Times's* defence editor Michael Evans (2004c: 34) spoke of the use of 'mass firepower' on the same day. The *Independent's* (2004b: 30) editorial compared Fallujah 'with the application of overwhelming military power' at the start of the Iraq War. Indeed, two authors in my sample claimed the Fallujah campaign was 'based on shock and awe' (Evans 2004a: 8; see also Sampson 2004: 41). Mainstream military history accounts also classified US tactics in Fallujah as 'overwhelming force' (West 2005: 257; *cf.* Camp 2009: 123–131; O'Donnell 2006: 53–54).

To implement this strategy of overwhelming fire power, the US/Coalition reportedly used a large range of military equipment: Air force (F-18s, AC-130 gunships, Cobra helicopter gunships, drones, variously sized bombs), tanks

(Abrams tanks, Bradley armoured vehicles, Buffalo mine protected vehicles, variously sized cannons), motor vehicles (humvees with mounted gatling guns), infantry weapons (assault rifles, 50. calibre machine guns, long-range sniper rifles, rocket propelled grenades), artillery weapons (Paladin howitzers, mortars, miclic explosive coils to clear minefields, phosphorous rounds), psychological weapons ('psyops' trucks), and special equipment (bulletproof vests, head mounted displays, thermal imagine, night vision, GPS navigation, Meerkat mine detectors, PakBot detection devices, Warlock bomb jammers) (see Evans 2004b: 9; Filkins 2004a, b: 1; Filkins and Glanz 2004a: 1; Filkins and Worth 2004c; Oppel 2004a: 10; Sengupta 2004i; Spinner 2004a: A 33; Stürmer 2004: 7).[6]

The resistance had a narrow range of light weaponry: infantry weapons (AK-47 Kalashnikov rifles, long-range sniper rifles, rocket propelled grenades, grenade launchers, booby traps, roadside bombs, car bombs, remote controlled explosives), and special equipment (flares, mobile telephones) (see Evans 2004b: 9; Filkins 2004a: 1; Oppel 2004a: 10; Stürmer 2004: 7).

A range of news items discussed how the military had prepared the assault and advanced into the city: According to an AP report published in *Die Welt*, during August and September, Fallujah was repeatedly bombed by airstrikes and US sources say more than 100 people died as a result in September (AP 2004a: 10; see also Filkins and Glanz 2004a: 1 who write of 'weeks of bombings by American airplanes'). On 7 November 2004, US battalions had formed an 'impenetrable chain around the city' (Filkins and Glanz 2004a: 1). US strategy was to then enter Fallujah from the north and rapidly move southwards, thereby capturing or killing the dispersing resistance comprised of small groups of fighters. Adjacent units would engage in house-to-house searches in order to clear the taken areas (see Filkins and Worth 2004a: 1; Harnden and Russell 2004: 1).[7] These strategic issues were accurately reported in the newspapers under review.

A major tactic of US/Coalition forces was to use artillery and air power (see Filkins 2004a). An 11 November report by Jackie Spinner in the *Washington Post* highlighted how these devices were used at the start of the operation:

> Before ground troops entered Fallujah on Monday night, warplanes pounded insurgent targets with bombs; mobile artillery batteries followed with cannon and mortar fire. The effect was significant, according to military commanders and soldiers inside the city. (Spinner 2004a: A 33)

In the *Independent*, Sengupta and Huggler (2004: 1, 4) also reflected on early operational tactics:

An AC-130 gunship raked the city all night long with cannon fire as heavy explosions from US artillery continued well into the morning.

The city was pounded all day with air strikes, artillery and mortar fire. War planes carried out some two dozen sorties against the city, and four 500-pound bombs were dropped over Fallujah before dawn.

Spinner (2004a: A 33) provides the further context on the firepower which was applied:

[...] two artillery pieces have fired more than 300 rounds in the first three days of the battle. The Marines' Mike Battery 414, which has six big guns at the same military outpost, has launched more than 500 rounds. [...]

The shells typically strike within about five yards of their target and are likely to kill anyone within 55 yards of the point of impact.

It seems noteworthy that Spinner and Sengupta and Huggler again contextualised the intensive long-range shelling of Fallujah within the commonly applied 'war' framework as indicated by in-text references to the 'battle'. Yet, the resistance had no military means to counter US/Coalition air force or artillery. Hence, there was no air or artillery battle. Significantly, in contrast to the Benghazi case study, the newspapers showed extensive evidence about US/Coalition use of air forces and artillery in populated areas. Yet, no statements demanding the establishment of no-fly zones or humanitarian corridors were featured in the press.

The US/Coalition also applied other heavy explosives like mine clearing-systems that had firstly been used on D Day to sweep the beaches of the Normandy (Evans 2004b: 9). The *New York Times'* Dexter Filkins (2004a: 1), who was embedded with the US military in Fallujah, depicted the soldiers 'firing a 200-yard cord containing 1,800 pounds of explosive southward from the berm, toward downtown Falluja'. *The Times's* defence editor Michael Evans (2004b: 9) commented:

The Miclic is normally designed for open spaces because it generates tremendous pressure, setting off mines over a large area. [...] It is highly effective but also indiscriminate, and not normally considered suitable for an urban environment.

Despite such descriptions of one-sided, indiscriminate warfare the newspapers often inferred an equal battle: For instance, the *New York Times'* Richard A. Oppel (2004a: 10) wrote: 'The Americans had tanks and bombs.

The insurgents had the shadows' – as if the resistance's alleged territorial advantage would balance the disparities in military technology and fire-power. Filkins and Glanz (2004a: 1) highlight how 'hundreds or thousands of insurgents met the American attack, sometimes contesting every inch of the advance and sometimes melting back into the darkened houses of the city'. Such depictions suggest heavy fighting. But the authors also describe how fire from buildings was attacking the US military only 'until heavy return fire destroyed them one by one, leaving only smoking ruins' (*ibid*). Similarly, the *Independent's* Michael Georgy and Kim Sengupta (2004: 4–5) wrote: 'The reaction of US troops to attacks, say residents, have been out of all proportion; shots by snipers have been answered by rounds from Abrams tanks, dev-astating buildings [...].' *The Sunday Times's* Hala Jaber (2004a: 16) depicts a resistance sniper who repeatedly attacked US forces during one day. Accord-ing to Jaber (*ibid*):

> The Americans fired at least 35 155 mm artillery shells at the buildings where the sniper was believed to be hidden. Tanks fired another 10 rounds, marines opened up with 30,000 rounds of automatic rifle fire, and two airstrikes were called in.

As one Iraqi sergeant told the *Washington Post*: 'The U.S. artillery shaved them all [...]. We took care of the insurgents hiding inside the houses' (cited in Fekeiki 2004a: A 18). According to Oppel (2004a: 10), the US military capitalised on its long-range advantage: 'The Americans were 500 meters to 600 meters away – close enough for the insurgents to strike, but only with a high trajectory, and luck.' And when the Marines got shelled 'spotters tried to locate pockets of insurgents and wipe them out with the big guns' (Filkins 2004a: 1). Toby Harnden (2004b: 16), of the *Daily Telegraph*, reports a sol-dier explaining how one imperishable fighter was targeted: '"We fired Bradley [25 mm] rounds, tank rounds, incendiary grenades and everything at him and he still kept going," said Sgt. Laser.'

Next to the one-sidedness of the 'battle', there were indeed episodic fire fights particularly after surprise attacks when resistance fighters used the cover of buildings and there were incidents involving heavy US casualties (see O'Donnell 2006: 196). But the general picture was different: whenever enemy combatants were spotted, the US replied with overwhelming force leaving virtually no space for fighting in the sense of traditional warfare. Indeed, parts of the newspapers' reporting further suggest extreme imbalances in fighting. This was indicated by coverage whose information content was inconsistent: the press applied a framework of war emphasising fights and battles while at the same time including descriptions which actually displayed how US-military power was applied without defence. For instance, Hilsum (2004: 20) saw the unit she was accompanying 'on its way to war'. Yet, in the final paragraph of her article she writes: 'Despite reports of "heavy fighting", the overwhelming majority of the firing has been one way.' (*ibid*) Similarly, Jaber (2004a: 16) starts her article with reference to 'fierce street fighting for the rebel-held city'. But 38 paragraphs further down, she identified 'a pattern of combat' (*ibid*): the Americans were taking the city 'as their vastly superior firepower and training took a heavy toll of insurgents.' (*ibid*) In the German *Die Welt* Kalnoky (2004c: 6) used notions such as 'battlefield', 'street fighting' and 'combat' to describe the operation. Yet, he explained that already on the second day it seemed 'as if the rebels were outmanoeuvred, surprised and overwhelmed on all fronts' (*ibid*).

A careful reading of the newspapers further reveals a one-sided pattern: On 9 November, *The Times'* James Hider (2004b: 8), who was embedded with US forces, observed how 'one rebel gunman dared to loose off a few rounds at the iron beasts' and then 'was quickly shot dead, just like a fly swatted aside as the observers returned to their mission'. The next day, Hider (2004c: 1) made the following observation when watching the movement of 'guerrillas' on an LED screen inside a Bradley fighting vehicle: 'They emerged from gates, alleyways and rooftops, alone or in small groups. Wherever they faced an armoured vehicle, they died where they stood.' (*ibid*) Hider followed with a quote by Lieutenant Colonel Rainey: 'I think there are committed fighters out there who want to die in Fallujah. We are in the process of allowing them to self-actualise' (cited in *ibid*). Another soldier, Captain Ed Twaddell, was cited by Hider (2004d: 60) on 13 November saying: 'It's like a shooting gallery. They pop up and pop down'. Jaber (2004a: 16) described the usage of a Long Range Acquisition System (LRAS) which could spot enemy fighters one mile off. According to Jaber (*ibid*): 'Each time men with weapons were seen, the co-ordinates were passed to a mortar team and within seconds shells rained down on them. A marine officer thought it was "like a video game".' Harnden (2004a: 4) cited Lt Jack Farley, a US Marines, commenting on the LRAS: 'You guys get to do all the fun stuff [...]. We've taken small arms fire here all day. It just sounds like popcorn going off.' There was virtually no enemy threat. Indeed, US forces were more concerned about friendly than enemy fire: As Harnden (*ibid*) further writes: 'Lt Col Newell, the force's commander, told his troops before the battle. "The biggest threat out there is not them, but us."'

This picture of a physical inviolability is supported by numerical evidence. According to US military accounts from 19 and 21 November 2004, there were 59 US/Coalition (51 US and 8 Iraqi) and 1,200 resistance casualties during the whole operation – a casualty attrition exchange rate of about 1: 20 (see Filkins 2004c; Shadid 2004a; Spinner 2004b). According to Camp (2009: 299), who provides a slightly higher figure of 63 US casualties, two out of the seven active US battalions suffered 38 of all US casualties (*ibid*).[8] Imbalances in kill ratios thus likely depended on the operational tasks suggesting that some units were engaged in intense fighting while others, probably the majority, merely applied their weaponry.

The military historian Patrick K. O'Donnell (2006: 81) emphasised how 'urban fighting is extremely personnel-intensive and, in terms of casualties, one of the most expensive military operations'. Hence, if the Fallujah operation had actually been regular urban warfare, casualty rates would have been higher and more evenly distributed.[9] Accordingly, the military strategist Lt. Col. Ralph Peters regards the kill ratio in Fallujah as 'revolutionary' because 'the rule has been that the attackers would take about a quarter to a third of its force in casualties' (cited in Kelly 2004). And in Fallujah, about 60 out of an attacking force of 10,000 US soldiers were killed, which means that the attackers took about 1/150 of its force in casualties.[10]

Generally, casualty attrition exchange rates and kill ratios support the assumption of a one sided 'battle'. This is not to say that there was no fighting in Fallujah. There were indeed battles during house-to-house searches and initial encounters of the adversaries. But press coverage largely suggested that these partial elements were representative for the whole operation (this is also evidenced by my keyword analysis displayed in Table 3). And this was inaccurate even in light of the actual facts provided by the newspapers.

The configuration of force levels and weaponry already suggested limited capacities for fighting because one side had far superior means at its disposal. This context was virtually ignored by the news media although the facts provided were indicative. Moreover, despite referring to facts and tactics that suggested a one-sided 'battle', the newspapers under review contextualised the US/Coalition engagement in the sense of 'fighting'. This was an inaccurate depiction as my following analysis of civilian deaths during the 'battle' further reveals. In fact, the framing of 'war' had shielded the occurrence of a massacre. Moreover, the collated evidence on military tactics could have encouraged the press to investigate US/Coalition responsibility for indiscriminate shelling.

(3) 800 civilians killed in Fallujah but the US 'did not know of any civilian deaths'

Numerical evidence on civilian deaths emerged relatively late. On 16 November 2004, an Inter Press Service (IPS) report by independent journalist Dahr Jamail (2004b) cited 'a high-ranking official with the Red Cross in Baghdad' saying that '"at least 800 civilians" have been killed in Fallujah'. According to the official, the estimate was based on reports by aid workers stationed around Fallujah, residents in the city and refugees (*ibid*). The Red Cross estimate undermined the US/Coalition claim of precise warfare. Consider how the press would have reported if the Red Cross had found 800 civilians killed after an intensive military assault conducted by the FRY/Serbs in Kosovo, the Syrian army in Houla or Gaddafi's forces in Benghazi. Wouldn't such a figure be repeatedly reported in front page and headline news? Not so in coverage on Fallujah. The Red Cross estimate of 800 civilian dead was mentioned only once in the *New York Times*, the *Guardian* and the *Independent*.

On 20 November, Edward Wong (2004c: 9), of the *New York Times*, suggested 'while no neutral group has been able to enter the city to count casualties, officials of the International Red Cross in Baghdad estimate that as many as 800 civilians may have died'. The statement was balanced with Genereal John F. Sattler, commander of the First Marine Expeditionary Force, who argued 'he did not know of any civilian deaths' (*ibid*). Neither Wong's nor any other item in the *New York Times* sample under review did further investigate the Red Cross figure.

In the *Guardian*, a critical comment by Zangana (2004a: 26), published on 17 November, pointed to 'the Red Crescent' according to which 'as many as 800 civilians had died during the bombardment'. This appeared to be the only news item in the *Guardian* in which the figure of 800 civilian deaths was mentioned.

The *Independent* was the only newspaper in which the Red Cross estimate was headline news albeit in an item published on page 6. On 17 November, Buncombe (2004a: 6) explained that 'the number of civilians killed during the eight-day battle for the city remains unclear' although 'one report yesterday quoted an unnamed Red Cross official in Baghdad as saying up to 800 civilians were feared dead'. Buncombe also referred to 'Anatonella Notari, the chief spokeswoman for the International Committee of the Red Cross (ICRC)' who 'said that the agency had been unable to make an independent examination of most of the city [...] "because the information we're getting is only partial"' (*ibid*). This was likely related to the fact that, as Buncombe further wrote, US troops had prevented Red Crescent officials 'from crossing the Euphrates river into the centre of Fallujah' (*ibid*). Buncombe then again cited the 'unnamed official with the Red Cross who' further assumed 'up to 50,000 civilians had remained in the city' (*ibid*). But, as Buncombe concluded, 'most estimates have put the figure much lower than this but there is no way of accurately telling how many may remain' (*ibid*). Finally, the author referred to 'reporters inside the city' who 'have described streets strewn with charred bodies' and collections of bodies 'in line with Muslim burial rites' (*ibid*).

The *Independent* was among the newspapers most frequently highlighting civilian victims. Buncombe's text focused in great detail on civilian deaths and the civilian situation in Fallujah. This was an example of coverage seemingly independent of the administration in terms of the sources and perspectives provided. Still, on the basis of how Buncombe handled evidence, the *Independent*'s limitations become evident: according to the information provided by Buncombe, the Red Cross and reporters in Fallujah had consistently found evidence for large amounts of civilian deaths. Furthermore, the article depicted how the military had prevented the Red Cross from making a comprehensive assessment of the situation. Additionally, the article described how civilian bodies were quickly buried in accord with Muslim customs. Access restrictions as well as quick burials indicated that not all civilian deaths could have been observed. Consequently, the Red Cross official, who had originally been cited in the IPS article mentioned above, said his estimate was 'likely to be too low' (cited in Jamail 2004b). While Buncombe drew on the IPS text, he did not utilise this information (see Buncombe 2004a: 6). Buncombe did also not discuss if the access restrictions could have impacted on the visibility of dead civilians. Indeed, the justification for and rationale of the access restrictions were not scrutinised. Instead, Buncombe played down the significance of civilians in Fallujah by arguing that 'most estimates' put the population much lower than 50,000 (*ibid*). But, as discussed in the previous section, authoritative assessments reckoned similar or higher numbers as likely to be present.

Such evidence further supported a high casualty hypothesis particularly in consideration of the US/Coalition military strategy. Yet, neglecting this evidence, Buncombe treated the Red Cross estimate cautiously assuming that 'the number of civilians killed during the eight-day battle for the city remains unclear' (*ibid*). This final statement was unreasonable because the contextual evidence available to Buncombe suggested that a high number of civilians could likely have been killed. At the very least, further inquiries appeared to be warranted in order to establish the accuracy of the Red Cross estimate. Yet, as my data suggests, the *Independent* (like the *New York Times* and the *Guardian*) dropped the 800 civilian deaths story.

Aside from the Red Cross estimate, virtually no numerical assessments on the overall magnitude of civilian deaths were featured in coverage during the two-week period. The US military did not count civilian bodies (Süddeutsche Zeitung 2004b: 4) and the absence of official figures likely contributed to the underreporting of numerical statements because journalists followed official proclamations. This was particularly evident in US newspapers, which overwhelmingly relied on military announcements in regard to civilian deaths.

Yet, high estimates of civilian deaths were consistent with US/Coalition military tactics and official estimates of civilians in Fallujah. The press did not connect these dots: the numbers on civilian deaths presented above were almost entirely ignored by the Western news media. And after November 2004, no further investigations were conducted (see also the discussion of the news media's reporting on casualty figures in Chapter 5). That is why Fallujah was not framed as a nefarious bloodbath. The newspapers would critically depict some details of the slaughter. Yet, the handling of humanitarian issues happened largely without labelling the incident in atrocious terms or assigning responsibility. To illustrate this further, news reporting of civilians will be elaborated in more detail below.

The US American newspapers were among those providing the lowest amount of information on civilian details. Yet, there were instances when the US press actually included details on killed and wounded civilians. The *New York Times* mentioned the humanitarian crisis in Fallujah. In this context, Filkins and Worth (2004a: 1) reported on 14 November:

> Hospitals in Baghdad began receiving civilian casualties from the fighting in Falluja. In Numaan General Hospital, a taxi driver, Farhan Khalaf, 45, stared at two bedridden sons who had been wounded by shrapnel. Alaa, 11, was hit in the chest, and Nafe, 7, lost one of his legs.

This paragraph virtually stood for itself without further elaboration. Moreover, the reference to 'casualties from the fighting' (*ibid*) implied that civilian deaths were an accidental outcome of war. It could generally be argued that when the *New York Times* reported civilians as being 'wounded or killed during the week-long Falluja offensive' (Wong 2004c: 9) such incidents were depicted as isolated events for which no one shared responsibility. Thus, on 13 November, Filkins described the story of an Iraqi family that had been shot: 'But for whatever reason, the Americans held off, and the man produced his wife, mother and two children, all struck by gunfire. His daughter had been shot in the back and his mother in the head' (Filkins 2004d: 1). Again, the scene was reported as an episode of civilian suffering without naming any perpetrator. On 15 November Eric Schmitt (2004a: 1) proclaimed a military success in the *New York Times* and pointed, in consistency with his newspaper's reporting, to 'lower than expected [...] Iraqi civilian casualties'.

The *Washington Post* also covered civilian details as singular incidences and without investigatory zeal albeit on more occasions than the *New York Times*. On 10 November, Spinner, Vick and Fekeiki (2004a: A 1) mentioned how 'civilians caught in the crossfire were gathered in a hospital'. In the next paragraph, the news article went on as follows:

> The Jolan and Askali neighborhoods seemed particularly hard hit, with more than half of the houses destroyed. Dead bodies were scattered on the streets and narrow alleys of Jolan, one of Fallujah's oldest neighborhoods. Blood and flesh were splattered on the walls of some of the houses, witnesses said, and the streets were full of holes. (*ibid*)

Strikingly, the *Post* did not question what had happened to the population of the Jolan and Askali districts and whether the observed bodies were civilians. Yet, the *Post* article indicated that the responsibility for large-scale destruction rested at the US/Coalition because, as Spinner, Vick and Fekeiki (*ibid*) went on, 'some of the heaviest damage apparently was incurred Monday night from air and artillery attacks that coincided with the entry of ground troops in the city'. The *Post* authors (*ibid*) described this strategy as 'ripping open entire neighbourhoods'. Without further inquiry, they then cited Iraqi General Abdul-Qadir Muhammed Jasim, whose unit was part of the new Iraqi army participating in Fallujah, as saying: 'The operation is going very precise and with a very small number of casualties' (cited in *ibid*).

Generally, the *Washington Post* largely operated under the assumption put forward by the military that there were no significant numbers of civilians in Fallujah. That may explain why the newspaper's 11 November editorial (The Washington Post 2004a: A 36) argued that 'reported casualties so far have been relatively light, though there appears to be extensive destruction of buildings in Fallujah'. If the 50,000 or more civilians present in Fallujah had been factored in the equation, a different assessment would have emerged.

On 12 November, another news item by Spinner, Vick and Fekeiki (2004b: A 1) emphasised that 'those who had survived the fighting found leaflets dropped by U.S. aircraft offering safe passage out of the city'. For the press, it was not an issue to raise the question as to whether leaflets were an appropriate measure to prevent civilian killings. The authors cited a hospital doctor who 'counted 32 civilian wounded by Wednesday, including nine women and four children' (*ibid*). Yet, further assessments were not conducted. In the text it was only stated that the numbers of 'civilian casualties could not be independently determined' (*ibid*). And again, the references to fighting and casualties suggested civilian deaths as a side effect of war.

The *Washington Post* also reflected on the humanitarian crisis: On 17 November, Anthony Shadid (2004b: A 1) balanced the perspective by 'Allawi and other Iraqi officials' who 'have dismissed suggestions of a humanitarian crisis in Fallujah' with Amnesty International saying 'the city still lacked water, electricity and organised means for evacuating the wounded'. This was one among many examples that demonstrated the journalistic commitment to the professional convention of objectivity. Nonetheless, the humanitarian crisis angle was short and placed further down in the news item.

On 18 November, Spinner (2004c: A 1), who accompanied US troops in Fallujah, presented interviews with remaining residents explaining how they had coped with the situation. According to Spinner (*ibid*), one civilian was 'stunned by the sight of crumbled concrete, damaged mosques and shops blistered by bullets and artillery shells during fighting between U.S. forces and insurgents'. A man described how 'he hid in his house until it was damaged by an artillery round' (*ibid*). Here, we see another example of a news item which presented independent perspectives. Yet again, Spinner's text included various assumptions which were questionable: US Major Jim Orbock's claim that 'fewer than 1,000' (*ibid*) residents had remained in Fallujah was presented as a fact suggesting a largely uninhabited city. Moreover, claims by US and Iraqi officials that 'the fight for Fallujah [...] was over and that the city had been liberated from insurgents' (*ibid*) were presented without balance. This seemed to imply a justified operation with a relatively light impact on civilians. Hence, the news item was skewed towards the official perspective although a substantial amount of independent sources were included.

A 19 November article by Fekeiki (2004b: A 20) highlighted the suffering of an Iraqi family which 'had hidden in their home in central Fallujah for four days last week while U.S. artillery and aircraft pounded the buildings around them'. The article then described the troubled journey of the family to a refugee camp in Baghdad (*ibid*). In conclusion, Fekeiki found much of the city 'in ruins' emphasising that 'civilians will not be able to return until the damage is cleaned up and the U.S. military deems it safe' (*ibid*). In the same fashion as the previous items, Fekeiki's article underplayed the civilian presence by highlighting the return of civilians and portraying the US military as a credible force.

A 20 November news item by Spinner (2004d: A 12) focused on the perspective of Iraqi civilians 'Abdul-Karim Shahin Shaiti and his crew' who 'began burying the dead on Friday, the bloated corpses that had been rotting in the streets'. Spinner (*ibid*) framed the cleanup as a task 'that will prepare the city for the eventual return of its 250,000 citizens, most of whom fled before the Nov. 8 ground assault'. Again, the impression of an empty city was created. Moreover, it remained unexplored whether the bodily remains were of civilians or fighters. However, Spinner (*ibid*) referred to US troops who indicated 'anyone who remained was a suspect'. In consistency with this statement, Spinner (*ibid*) pointed to civilians in Fallujah arguing 'they had simply been caught up in a sweep for insurgents that unfairly targeted all military-age males'. Yet, this evidence for high casualties and indiscriminate massacres was not further investigated.

The British press focused more closely on civilian details than the US American. The *Guardian's* 9 November editorial (2004a: 21) highlighted 'reports' referring 'to victims being buried in graves in Falluja's municipal soccer stadium, in a grim echo of the siege of Sarajevo'. This analogy could have suggested civilian carnage in Fallujah. Nonetheless, the *Guardian* still hoped 'that this Iraqi battle will be fought with care, restraint and speed' (*ibid*).

The *Guardian* and the other British newspapers based their news and editorial output on the official US/Coalition perspective. Accordingly, coverage on the civilian plight was largely framed within the assumption of Western benevolence, suggesting that civilian deaths resulted from wrong military tactics or were natural albeit tragic outcomes of war. A massacre angle was not developed in the British press.

A 10 November news report by al-Badrani (2004a: 4), who stayed in Fallujah and reported on civilians, wrote: 'Residents say scores of civilians have been killed or wounded in 24 hours of fighting'. Al-Badrani (*ibid*) also depicted 'Mohammed Abboud' who 'said he watched his nine-year-old son bleed to death' when 'fighting raged in the streets'. According to al-Badrani (*ibid*), the child was wounded 'in the midst of a US onslaught' because of which his father could not reach medical help. The article was framed in the context of 'fighting' suggesting that civilian deaths were the by-product of war. Generally, al-Badrani took a position as a seemingly neutral observer. Thereby, al-Badrani (*ibid*) mentioned in passing, without further contextualisation, how, according to witnesses, 'air raids destroyed a clinic funded by an Islamic relief organisation in the centre of Falluja'.

On 10 November, Rory McCarthy's (2004a: 4) news report centred on 'tens of thousands of civilians' who were 'thought to have stayed behind' because 'under the terms of a curfew imposed on Monday they cannot leave their homes'. Thus, in effect, civilians were trapped in Fallujah because the US/Coalition had sealed off the town – this again suggested responsibility for civilian deaths. But as in the case of the clinic mentioned above, this episode was neutrally reported and did not illicit further comment although a man was cited as saying he saw 'a lot of people dead' (*ibid*).

On 11 and 12 November, news reports by McCarthy (2004c, e) presented the concerns of relief officials who painted a grim picture of the situation. According to McCarthy (2004e: 19):

> Iraqi aid officials said they were increasingly concerned about the families still in Falluja and the thousands camped in villages nearby. [...]

> 'It is a disaster inside Falluja,' said Firdoos al-Abadi, head of the Red Crescent's emergency committee.

> 'There is no water, no electricity, no food. They are forbidding doctors from helping the people. [sic]'

Like the previous items, this article presented a perspective of civilian suffering which was independent of the official discourse. The report also pointed to a third significant incident (after the bombing of a clinic and the prevention of citizens from leaving the city) namely the banning of doctors from doing their work. Again, this incident was mentioned in passing without further investigation.

A 14 November report in the *Observer* by McCarthy and Beaumont (2004: 2) pointed to 'the full cost of the battle of Fallujah' which 'emerged last night as large numbers of wounded civilians were evacuated to hospitals in Baghdad'. This was a rare news item that connected US military strategy with details about the civilian plight. The authors observed:

> The horrific conditions for those who remained in the city have begun to emerge [...] as it became clear that US military claims of 'precision' targeting of insurgent positions were false.

> According to one Iraqi journalist who left Fallujah on Friday, some of the civilian injuries were caused by the massive firepower directed on to city neighbourhoods during the battle. (*ibid*)

McCarthy and Beaumont debunked the myth of precision warfare and seemingly provided a perspective in disagreement with US/Coalition authorities. Yet, concerns about civilian deaths remained tactical as the authors (*ibid*) feared 'the suffering in Falluja will be used to rally insurgents across northern Iraq'. Additionally, the concept of 'civilian injured' (*ibid*), which was consistently used in the text, appeared to be inaccurate in the context of indiscriminate warfare because it suggested the absence of civilian deaths.

In a further news article on 17 November, McCarthy and Mansour (2004: 17) also focused on wounded civilians: 'Evidence began to emerge yesterday of civilians, including children, who were seriously injured in the US assault on the Iraqi city of Fallujah.' (*ibid*) While this article discussed the plight of children in detail, and also found evidence for a few civilian deaths in Fallujah, a comprehensive figure, such as the Red Cross estimate claiming 800 civilian deaths, which was published a day earlier, on 16 November, was missing. The focus on injured civilians was thus misleading because a large number of civilians had evidentiary been killed. Yet, the emphasis on injured and not civilian deaths was in accord with the *Guardian's* overall reporting. The journalists even explained their careful use of evidence by pointing to the 'limited independent information' available 'from inside Falluja because of the intense fighting and the security cordon around the city' (*ibid*). The journalists' handling of information could be regarded as appropriate. However, as discussed above, there were many examples when *Guardian* journalists seemed to have brushed aside evidence of possible war crimes. Similarly, the US/Coalition strategy of sealing off the city, which was likely implemented in order to prevent information from getting out of Fallujah, was not further scrutinised. Also note the reference to fighting which was often used in the *Guardian's* news pages. Finally, consider that in their reporting on Libya and Syria, journalists also acknowledged that it was difficult to verify information due to government restrictions. In the latter cases, it was unproblematic for the press to rely on hearsay evidence provided by opposition and online sources. In fact, such material was used to frame the Benghazi and Houla incidents in atrocious terms and relegate responsibility for the bloodbaths to higher levels of planning.

Another news article in the *Observer* (Beaumont 2004: 15) provided a summary of the situation. Beaumont argued 'the fate of those who have remained – perhaps between 30,000 and 50,000' was 'largely unknown'. As a reason, the author (*ibid*) identified another facet of the official propaganda strategy: the seizing of Fallujah's 'general hospital to prevent what one US officer described as "insurgent propaganda" over casualty figures'. This *flak* operation, which can be described as the fourth significant incident mentioned in *Guardian* news reports, did not generate further discussion either, for instance over whether the Geneva Conventions were violated when the US military stormed the hospital. Rather, Beaumont assessed Fallujah in the context of 'bitter urban war' (*ibid*).

The *Independent* published more statements on civilian details than the *Guardian*. On 10 November, the *Independent* featured al-Badrani's (2004b: 1, 5) eyewitness report, which had similarly been printed in the *Guardian*. On 14 November, a detailed news analysis by Sengupta and Whitaker (2004: 20–21) emphasised how aid agencies had warned of a 'humanitarian catastrophe' in Fallujah. The article was riddled with statements by civilians, relief organisations and doctors. According to Sengupta and Whitaker (*ibid*), 'escaping residents described incidents in which non-combatants, including women and children, were killed by shrapnel or hit by bombs'. Furthermore:

> Sami al-Jumaili, a doctor at the main Fallujah hospital who escaped arrest when it was taken, said the city was running out of medical supplies, and only a few clinics remained open. 'There is not a single surgeon in Fallujah,' he said. 'We had one ambulance hit by US fire and a doctor wounded. There are scores of injured civilians in their homes whom we can't move. A 13-year-old child just died in my hands.' (*ibid*)

Such coverage transgressed the perspective of the US/Coalition administration. At the same time civilian deaths were framed within the sphere of tactical criticism: Sengupta and Whitaker (*ibid*) identified a 'military strategy' that was 'driven by a White House obsessed with "smoking terrorists out of their holes"' making Fallujah a 'victim of this misconception'. It seems further noteworthy that Sengupta and Whitaker (*ibid*) also mentioned – in passing – the taking of Fallujah hospital as well as indiscriminate shootings of civilians and ambulances. Yet, as in the case of the *Guardian*, it was inconsistent with the *Independent's* reporting to suggest nefarious behaviour such as violations of the Geneva Conventions.

On 15 November, a range of articles in the *Independent* depicted civilian deaths and suffering. For example, Sengupta (2004d: 1, 5) found bodies 'scattered in the streets, where rows of buildings lay in ruins'. A news report by Georgy and Sengupta (2004: 4–5) included voices of civilians who 'described rotting corpses being piled up and thousands still trapped inside their homes, many of them wounded and without access to food, water or medical aid'. A short news item by Buncombe (2004b: 5) focused on 'the death toll' presenting 'a report collated by the UN' according to which '20 doctors had died during a US air strike on a clinic'. Moreover, it was pointed to 'numerous reports of the US dropping huge bombs' (*ibid*). These news items included perspectives that balanced US/Coalition claims such as Rumsfeld's who argued 'there aren't going to be large numbers of civilians killed and certainly not by US forces' (cited in *ibid*). On the other hand, the *Independent's* news and editorial reports regarded civilian deaths as 'civilian casualties' (Buncombe 2004b: 5; Georgy and Sengupta 2004: 4–5; The Independent 2004a: 30) who had been 'killed or wounded in the fighting' (Sengupta 2004d: 1, 5). As the *Independent* (2004a: 30) even acknowledged in its 15 November lead article: '[...] we have only the most blurred and partial picture of the assault.' How could the newspaper then distinguish between accidental or indiscriminate killings? Additionally, like the *Guardian*, the *Independent* neglected evidence of indiscriminate killings and other possible war crimes (e.g. the bombing of a hospital, the dropping of huge bombs), which were described in its own reports but not contextualised.

The *Independent's* editorial (2004a: 30) also found 'a blank where figures for civilian casualties – "collateral damage", so-called – should be'. Buncombe (2004b: 5) could only identify the existence of a 'few reports on civilians killed'. Similarly, Sengupta (2004g: 23) argued on 16 November that 'the fate of the city's civilians is still unclear [...] a convoy of the Iraqi Red Crescent was unable to gain access'. Thus, it seems also striking that the Red Cross figure, once it appeared on 16 November (see Buncombe 2004a), was not further reported and Sengupta as well as the *Independent's* editorial did not mention the figure when consecutively writing on Fallujah (see Sengupta 2004e, h; The Independent 2004b).

An editorial in *The Times*, whose headline pointed to 'a difficult but absolutely essential military operation' argued the US army had considered 'the danger of civilian deaths' by encouraging 'ordinary people to leave Fallujah' (2004a: 19). Despite an editorial stance supportive to US/Coalition operations, *The Times* highlighted details about civilian deaths on several occasions. For example, on 11 November, Parry and Hamdani (2004: 9) reported claims by refugees of 'civilian casualties left to die' in Fallujah where 'women and children' were 'killed by the US bombardment or' died 'for lack of medical treatment, medicines and sanitation'. Furthermore, as the authors pointed out, the US military had 'not responded to appeals by the Iraqi Red Crescent to send medical teams into the city' (*ibid*). Firdoos al-Ubaidi, of the Red Crescent, stressed the situation was '[...] a disaster [...]' (cited in *ibid*). Parry and Hamdani included arguments contradicting US/Coalition claims of precise warfare suggesting responsibility for civilian deaths. Yet, in the same fashion as the other newspapers so far reviewed, the authors did not contextualise evidence of indiscriminate warfare (i.e. US bombardment) and possible war crimes (i.e. the US/Coalition not responding to a Red Cross appeal) – perhaps because the issue of civilian deaths was framed in the context of 'battle' (*ibid*).

On 14 November, *The Sunday Times* published one news item and two news features by correspondent Hala Jaber (2004a, b, d). Each item included sections on civilian details or suffering, albeit at the end. Generally, all reports were framed in the context of 'battle' (*ibid*). Jaber (2004d: 16) cited one civilian as saying: 'Bodies are everywhere on the streets and pavements and are beginning to decompose.' Such detailed eyewitness evidence, it seemed, warranted further inquiries. Yet, on 21 November, another report by Jaber (2004c: 22) found 'no official figures on estimated civilian deaths'.

Of the Anglo-American newspapers, the *Daily Telegraph* arguably produced the least amount of information on civilian deaths. On 14 November, Hussein and Harnden (2004: 26) had found 'no independent confirmation of the number of insurgent or civilian fatalities' although 'witnesses speak of the stench from piles of bodies lying in the street'. Hussein and Harnden (*ibid*) also cited one civilian who had 'seen "hundreds of bodies" thrown in the streets'. Anwar (2004: 13), who covered the humanitarian crisis story on 15 November, stated: 'There are no statistics on the number of civilians killed or wounded in the fighting, only personal accounts of pain, hunger and fear from those trapped in the city.' Again, there were no further inquiries into the actual magnitude of civilian deaths.

The German newspapers featured information on civilian details, often provided by civilians, doctors, relief organisations or officials, albeit on a lower quantity as the Anglo-American press. For example, on 16 November, the *Frankfurter Rundschau* referred to 'a member of an Iraqi relief organisation' who saw '22 bodies spread under the rubble including two children' (DPA/AP/ RTR 2004a: 6). Writing on the same day in the *Süddeutsche Zeitung*, Georgy and Harris (2004: 6), who accompanied the US army in Fallujah, observed 'bodies laying on the streets' some of which 'so torn that it was impossible to say whether they were rebels or civilians'. On 15 November, a news item in the *tageszeitung* (AFP/AP/TAZ 2004: 1) paraphrased 'reports from eye witnesses' that described 'dozens of bodies on streets and squares'. A brief news item in the *Frankfurter Allgemeine Sonntagszeitung* (AP/Reuters 2004: 2) from 14 November pointed to 'residents and relief organisations who described the situation in Fallujah as disastrous'.

The coverage on civilian details and suffering appeared largely cursory. Moreover, each of the four news items quoted above also featured statements indicating that the number of civilian deaths was 'unclear' (DPA/AP/RTR 2004a: 6) or 'unknown' (AFP/AP/TAZ 2004: 1; AP/Reuters 2004: 2; Georgy and Harris 2004: 6). It was characteristic for all German newspapers to include such statements, which mostly appeared in news items based on agency material. Moreover, the issue was framed in the context of 'battles' (DPA/AP/RTR 2004a: 6), 'urban warfare' (Georgy and Harris 2004: 6), 'ferocious fighting' (AFP/AP/TAZ 2004: 1), or 'clashes' (AP/Reuters 2004: 2). Consequently, the main drift in coverage was to suggest an unknown number of civilian casualties of war.

The German news media did also not identify the total number of civilian deaths. Notwithstanding, a single news article in the *tageszeitung*, from 15 November, indicated the possibility of large scale civilian deaths. The news item paraphrased Iraqi National Security Minister, Kasim Daud, saying 'more than 1,000 insurgents were killed' (AFP/DPA/TAZ 2004: 9). In the following paragraph, Abu Aad al-Dlimi, the spokesperson of the Fallujah Mujahedeen Council, challenged 'Daud's account and declared there were no more than 100 "martyrs"' further claiming 'all others who were killed were unarmed civilians' (*ibid*). While both statements needed to be verified, the *tageszeitung* did not investigate whether the civilian count could be higher. Indeed, Daud's claim of large numbers of civilian deaths was supported by the Red Cross estimate of 800 civilian deaths published by IPS on 16 November (see Jamail 2004b). But this estimate was not reported in the *tageszeitung* or any other German newspaper. Consequently, on 20 November, it was consistent with the *tageszeitung*'s coverage to point to a high ranking US officer who 'did not know of any killed civilians' (AP/DPA/TAZ 2004: 9).

Die Welt, together with the *Frankfurter Allgemeine*, incorporated the least amount of statements on civilian details and largely mentioned the issue in passing.

One item in *Die Welt* by Kalnoky (2004e: 7) stood out for balancing the US/Coalition, who claimed 'no civilians had died in Fallujah', with contradicting statements by other actors. Kalnoky (*ibid*) paraphrased 'a doctor who told how about 20 paramedics and physicians died, as their clinic in Fallujah was destroyed on 9 November'. Moreover, Kalnoky (*ibid*) reported that Bilal Hussein, an AP photographer who stayed in Fallujah, had described how US troops had killed 'guerrillas and civilians' and 'a family of five' when they tried to cross the Euphrates river. The author (*ibid*) also referred to Amnesty

International reporting 'on a woman and three girls, who died in an air raid of their house'. Similar events 'were described during the battle by families who could still be reached by phone' Kalnoky (*ibid*) finally wrote. This testimony was consistent with the evidence on the civilian presence in Fallujah and on US/Coalition military strategy. But like the rest of the Western news media, *Die Welt* did not attach much weight to indiscriminate bombings and killings, which were reported cursorily and framed in the context of battle rather than indiscriminate military force or nefarious behaviour.

In conclusion, there were similarities and differences in how the Western news media covered civilians in Fallujah. In all countries under review, news correspondingly operated within a 'war' framework (model 2). Hence, civilian deaths and the humanitarian crisis story were reported in the context of 'battle' implying that civilians were casualties of war. This was in striking discordance to its reporting on 'enemy' countries, where the news media would use an atrocious framework to depict details about the civilian plight. Yet, in reporting on Fallujah 2, evidence of nefarious behaviour was mentioned in passing and not contextualised. Consequently, coverage was restrained in that responsibility for civilian deaths remained unexplored. This performance was consistent with the news media's overall handling of 'allied' countries – evoking benevolent aims. On 17 November, *The Times'* Jenkins (2004: 16) had observed in a critical commentary how 'we blank out the use of cluster shells against villages and thousand pounders on residential districts because the resulting horror is beyond our ken'. Jenkins was right in the sense that the Western news media would largely not depict Fallujah as a nefarious bloodbath.

Considering the factual use of numerical and verbal statements, civilian deaths tended to be reported as a sequence of incidents and virtually no overall figure was provided. The civilian presence was also not contextualised in relation to the geographic shape of Fallujah and US military strategy. Furthermore, the issue appeared a few days into the operation and was not sustained. As a consequence, an episodic and incoherent picture emerged. While the news media reported the humanitarian disaster in Fallujah, it did not focus on forensic aspects of the slaughter in the same fashion as when reporting on 'enemy' countries.

The British newspapers provided a more comprehensive picture of civilian details than the American, particularly information on the humanitarian situation and on civilian deaths in Fallujah was frequently included. The US press rather emphasised the absence of civilians in Fallujah and reported casualties as isolated incidents. The German press included the least amount of information and this was likely related to the low quantity of baseline coverage as well as the reliance on agency material.

The US/Coalition propaganda strategy could be one explanation for the episodic nature of coverage and the low amount of numerical information featured in coverage. The US/Coalition had prevented relief organisations, hospitals and doctors from assessing the situation and handing out information. Access restrictions had also made it virtually impossible for journalists to report from Fallujah if they were not embedded with US/Coalition forces. The few remaining journalists in Fallujah could hardly move in a city under heavy fire. Moreover, journalists working in Iraq were jeopardised by criminal gangs that targeted Westerners for kidnappings and assassinations (for information reporting restrictions in Iraq see Carroll 2004; CPJ 2004, 2005; Gourevitch 2003; Jamail 2004a; Kiss 2004; Paterson 2011). Accordingly, on 21 November, a comment by Michael Getler (2004: 6) in the *Post* pointed out how 'news organisations have had many stories about the impact of the fighting on Iraqi civilians, but not recently' because 'journalists face the risk of being killed or kidnapped' (*ibid*). This was quite similar to access restrictions witnessed in Syria and Libya. However, in the latter cases, the news media made use of second-hand source material and video clips.

As my study on Fallujah 2 further found out, newspapers used a range of evidence and sources, which were independent of the US/Coalition in their coverage of civilians. However, this set of information was weighted and classified in a selective fashion. Additionally, evidence for nefarious US/Coalition actions was displayed without further inquiries. As a consequence, the net outcome of coverage did not represent the actual magnitude of civilian deaths and carnage in Fallujah. Coverage on civilians thus included independent perspectives that refuted US/Coalition claims of precise warfare while being inaccurate at the same time. This evidences propaganda. The dynamic of coverage becomes further evident when assessing how the press handled some of the US/Coalition actions and their outcomes in more detail.

(4) War crimes in Fallujah: 'Weapons-free means the Marines can shoot whatever they see – it's all considered hostile'

There were multiple references in the press providing *prima facie* evidence about atrocities and war crimes during the Fallujah 2 incident. This evidence was mentioned in passing and in a factual, descriptive matter. Paradoxically, the evidence indicated US/Coalition war crimes on the one hand but was not used to assign responsibility on the other. In the following discussion I will review examples of such evidence.

Aggression

As mentioned in the introduction, the occupation of Iraq followed a military invasion of a sovereign state and it could thus have been questioned whether it constituted aggression as defined by the United Nations General Assembly (1974).[11] The media sample did not contain any reference suggesting that the US/Coalition occupation could have constituted such a case of aggression. This resonates with the 'war' framework used by the press, which contradicts an aggression thesis. Thus, the press's emphasis on 'war' provided a cover for actions, which, under the terms of the UN General Assembly definition, might have been part of 'the most serious and dangerous form of the illegal use of force' (United Nations General Assembly 1974: 143).

The Geneva Conventions

If the matter of fact of aggression is left aside, then the laws of armed conflict may apply. According to the Nuremberg Tribunal and the Rome Statute, which established the International Criminal Court (ICC), grave breaches of the laws of armed conflict constitute war crimes (see Rehman 2010: 718–739). The following contextual study analyses press coverage of the Geneva Conventions. The focus of my analysis is to identify occurrences where the press framed incidents which literally resembled violations of the Geneva Conventions without actually labelling them as such, or instances where the press mentioned or discussed such violations. Of course, the matter of fact of what constitutes a war crime eventually needs to be investigated by a legal body. For this study, nonetheless, it is of interest how the press handled evidence and information indicating possible war crimes. Such an assessment also sheds further light on the context of the incident. It is also interesting to compare the press's handling of such information with its framing of actions by 'enemy' countries.

The military option

As already discussed, according to official figures, up to 100,000 civilians were expected to be present in Fallujah.

The Geneva Conventions demand that civilians 'shall in all circumstances be treated humanely' (Article 3, Convention IV, 1949) and that 'indiscriminate attacks are prohibited' (Article 51, *Protocol I*, 1977).[12] A military rationale aimed at driving through a city 'like a fist' (Lieutenant Colonel John Morris cited in Reuters 2004a: 1) could hardly be justified under these circumstances. Yet, legal treatises were not evoked by any newspaper in regard to whether the whole operation was justified on grounds embedded in the laws of armed conflict such as proportionality and necessity. Yet all newspapers carried statements suggesting that the US/Coalition used overwhelming force to attack a city in which a large segment of the populace was evidently present.

Indiscriminate military tactics

Apart from whether the military rationale of the entire operation was justified, the legitimacy of individual military actions as well as their outcomes could have been questioned. Even if the operation was regarded as necessary, it also needed to be assessed whether the force employed was not excessive in relation to the anticipated military advantage (this can be described as proportionality) and whether the means employed were generally not in violation of the Geneva Conventions. Accordingly, at the 8 November DoD meeting already mentioned, General Casey (US Department of Defence 2004) had claimed the US/Coalition would use 'a very disciplined targeting process that's designed to strike valid military targets and to avoid collateral damage and unnecessary loss of life, and we take this responsibility very carefully'. If these standards had been met, the military means employed could have been regarded as lawful under the Geneva Conventions. The newspapers virtual absence of a discussion on legal matters implied that this was the case. Yet significantly, each newspaper carried multiple statements literally describing violations of the Geneva Conventions without discussing whether this could actually have been the case.

In news items the use of heavy weaponry and ordnance (such as AC-130 gunships with automatic cannons, Cobra gunships firing anti-tank missiles, F-18s, Abrams tanks firing 120 mm rounds, Bradley tanks firing 25 mm rounds, explosive coils to clear minefields containing 1,800 pounds of explosives, 500 and 2,000 pound bombs, rocket assisted shells with a 55 yard killing range, 155-millimeter artillery shells, howitzer shells, mortar rounds, heavy cannons, or high velocity machine guns) in residential areas was regularly described and many of such examples have already been presented in the section on military strategy. For instance, every newspaper reported statements similar to the following indicating that 'extensive airstrikes and artillery fire pummeled [...] sections of Falluja' (Oppel and Worth 2004: 1). Also, on many occasions, the Anglo-American press depicted the indiscriminate use of force by infantry units. It was displayed how 'rebels opened up with sporadic small-arms fire or mortars launched from rooftops, only to meet with a hail of high-explosives from the massed cavalry and Marine battalions spread out in the rugged desert less than a mile away' (Hider 2004b: 8). As Hider summed up the early phase of the operation:

> The assault had begun with a day of intense bombardment of the rebels' positions on Monday -a vast display of artillery, tanks and war planes hitting the buildings where guerrillas were believed to be lurking, ready to detonate huge buried mines as the US Army advanced. (Hider 2004c: 1)

Variations in coverage occurred mainly in regard to the amount and details. In the US and UK press, more information was provided about the appliance of specific assault strategies and weaponry. But the intensity of military actions was consistently described as 'extensive' (Oppel and Worth 2004: 1), 'overwhelming' (McCarthy and Borger 2004: 1), or 'massive' (Süddeutsche Zeitung 2004c: 1). The *Guardian's* McCarthy (2004b: 3) anticipated the operation to be 'unrivalled in its ferocity'.

General Casey (US Department of Defence 2004) had also argued the US/ Coalition would prompt people to 'stay at home, stay away from the windows and we will do everything we can to ensure that you're not caught in the line of fire here'. While civilians could thus technically avoid being shot by gunfire this hardly mattered in consideration of the heavy explosives used. Moreover, the US/Coalition reportedly applied indiscriminate tactics during house-to-house 'battles'. As Filkins and Glanz wrote in the *New York Times*: 'Fearing booby traps, the troops generally entered the houses only after tanks rammed through walls or specialists put explosive charges on doors' (Filkins and Glanz 2004b: 1). In the *Guardian* Hilsum reported: 'Every day, the marines open up with mortars, mini grenade launchers, machine guns and tank rounds, aiming to kill anyone hiding behind a wall or in a house.' (Hilsum 2004: 20) And in the German *tageszeitung*, El-Gawhary (2004: 14) cited the following orders given by Captain Jil Juarez to his men: 'Don't send a Marine inside if you can fire a volley first' (see also Spinner 2004f). Whether these strategies could have led to indiscriminate killings of civilians was not explored. Coverage was largely void of legal or moral challenges to official US/Coalition claims of precise warfare.

The US/Coalition had also placed Fallujah under a curfew and several newspaper items suggested that the city was marked as a free-fire zone. In the *Daily Telegraph*, Harnden (2004c: 11) reported an official meeting as follows:

> Briefing his squad, Sgt Jamal Alexander could sense the apprehension. 'You all know what you're getting into,' he said. 'Stay alert and stay alive. There aren't any friendlies [sic] in there. Anybody walks up, you kill them.' (Harnden 2004c: 11)

The Times's Hider (2004f: 42) quoted Staff Sergeant Coy Embry, 24, from Oklahoma, saying: 'By now anybody who's left, you know they're bad, they gotta be.' Worth, of the *New York Times* (2004: 15), cited a website journal by NBC journalist Kevin Sites, who was embedded with Marines in Fallujah, writing the military had operated 'with liberal rules of engagement'. According to Worth (*ibid*), the writing went

> on to quote a marine saying everything to the west of his position in Falluja was 'weapons free.' It continues, 'Weapons free means the marines can shoot whatever they see – it's all considered hostile.' (Worth 2004: 15)

Hence, a few news items cited statements similar to the following in which remaining civilians said 'they had simply been caught up in a sweep for insurgents that unfairly targeted all military-age males' (Spinner 2004d: A 12). Such information, however, was presented as a background fact and not related to the free-fire zones. Similarly, the general issue of 'weapons free' areas was neutrally presented as a tactical facet and not further evaluated. Imagine how the news media would have reported evidence of 'weapons free' zones in relation to Kosovo, Libya or Syria. In these cases, it was difficult to find such evidence. Yet, the press was vitriolic about how these countries' forces engaged in military/police operations.

All newspapers in my sample also reported that the US/Coalition had formed a tight cordon around the city allegedly to prevent enemy fighters from leaving the territory (see McCarthy 2004f: 1). In the *New York Times*, Worth and Wong (2004a: 1) described one incident when 'about 300 people, most of them men,' tried to escape Fallujah:

> All of them were detained by American military patrols, who allowed the women and children to continue but tested the men for explosive residue. All tested negative, and were sent back to Falluja in accordance with procedures established by the American military to maintain the city's isolation. (*ibid*)

Similarly, the *Guardian* (see Klein 2004a: 23; Zangana 2004a: 26), the *Independent* (Sengupta 2004a: 26), *The Times* (Jaber 2004a: 16), the *Süddeutsche Zeitung* (AP 2004c: 11), the *Frankfurter Allgemeine Zeitung* (Busse 2004: 5), and *Die Welt* (Kalnoky 2004b: 6) mentioned incidents when 'troops guarding exits from the city were allowing only women and children to pass' (Jaber 2004a: 16). Only the *New York Times* discussed in two items that 'human rights experts said American soldiers might have committed a war crime [...] when they sent fleeing civilians back into Falluja' (The New York Times 2004d: 2; see also Janofsky 2004: 8). The *New York Times's* Janofsky (2004: 8) quoted Jordan Paust, a law professor at the University of Houston and a former army prosecutor, saying: 'This is highly problematical conduct in terms of exposing people to grave danger by returning them to an area where fighting is going on'. Even in the *Times's* case, the issue was not further examined. It was also not questioned whether male civilians had actually been forced to return into a 'weapons free' zone.

Considering these descriptions of military tactics together with the information about civilians in Fallujah, it seems very likely that clauses of Article 51 of Protocol I of the Geneva Conventions regulating the protection of civilian populations had been violated. Yet, similar as in the case of civilians, the military rationale, if at all, elicited tactical concerns about 'casualties' particularly in the UK press. For instance, in the *Guardian* McCarthy and Beaumont (2004: 2) wrote that 'the horrific conditions for those who remained in the city have begun to emerge in the last 24 hours as it became clear that US military claims of "precision" targeting of insurgent positions were false'. Such critical assessments, of course, contradicted the official perspective. But only on few occasions did the US, UK and German press discuss if these incidents could have actually amounted to war crimes. Moreover, the newspapers failed to relate the high civilian death rates (which were ignored) to the indiscriminate targeting process and 'weapons free' zones. Indeed, factual details were framed in the context of reciprocal 'war' rather than 'atrocity'. And this was inaccurate.

Similarly, towards the end of the operation, isolated statements described how 'almost all of the city has been heavily damaged [...] the landscape is now dotted by broken minarets, many destroyed by airstrikes' (Worth and Wong 2004b: 14; see also Spinner 2004e). Such depictions did not elicit concern because as Worth and Wong (2004b: 14) argued in the *New York Times* 'the biggest question is how residents will react to seeing the vast swaths of destruction' – as if the citizens would return to Fallujah after the operation.

In the *Süddeutsche Zeitung* 'the immense destruction of the city' was regarded as the outcome of 'persistent combat between US-forces and Iraqi rebels' (Matern 2004: 1).

Thus generally, the absence of references to legal and moral contexts suggested that the wholesale destruction of Fallujah, although visible in the reporting, was rationalised by references to an empty city or the tragic outcomes of war.

The targeting of hospitals

One of the first military actions of the operation was the raid of Fallujah general hospital by US/Coalition forces (see The Washington Post 2004b). All newspapers neutrally reported how the military had crushed the facility's doors, forced patients and staff out of their rooms and tied their hands in order to evaluate whether there were enemy fighters in the building (see e.g. Oppel 2004b: 1). To justify the action, US officials had described the hospital as 'a haven for insurgents' (*ibid*). Moreover, officials had claimed that 'propaganda' in the form of 'inflated civilian casualty figures' had regularly flown 'from the hospital' (*ibid*).

The newspapers did not entirely present the official picture of the event. For example, the *New York Times's* Oppel (2004b: 1) cited Dr. Rasheed al-Janabi, a general surgeon at the hospital, saying he did not know about any fighters in the facility. Similarly, the *Independent* Sengupta and Huggler (2004: 1, 4) reported:

> He [Dr Salih al-Issawi, the director of Fallujah Hospital] said: 'The American troops' attempt to take over the hospital was not right because they thought that they would halt medical assistance to the resistance. But they did not realise that the hospital does not belong to anybody, especially the resistance.'

While these examples appear to be evidence for coverage independent of US/Coalition claims, such reporting still failed to investigate other possible reasons for the hospital takeover as well as implications under the Geneva Conventions.

Regarding the first issue, it could be argued that it was part of the US/Coalition propaganda strategy to attack hospitals in order to prevent the publication of civilian body counts. This was indirectly acknowledged by reporters of some the newspapers under review: The *New York Times's* Filkins and Glanz (2004a: 1) assumed that the April operation in Fallujah had to be abandoned because of 'unconfirmed reports of heavy civilian casualties' that 'sparked out-rage among both Sunni and Shiite Iraqis'. In the German *Die Welt*, Kalnoky (2004d: 10) even argued the April operation had 'failed because of the hospi-tal's doctors who diurnally presented increasing death tolls to the global pub-lic' thus causing 'dismay'. The *New York Times's* Oppel and Worth similarly argued Fallujah general hospital was initially targeted 'because the American military believed that it was the source of rumors about heavy casualties' (2004: 1).

There were also reports suggesting that other hospitals were bombed. Sev-eral news items in the US, UK and German press described an incident when 'up to 20 Iraqi medical staff and patients were killed when a missile destroyed a health clinic in the centre of town' (McCarthy and Mansour 2004: 17). This event, which I have already discussed in the section on civilian deaths, was mentioned in passing and from the various accounts presented in the newspa-pers it may well be the case that actually two different clinics were destroyed by US raids (see Kalnoky 2004c: 6).

Considering the effect of the hospital attacks, one rare news item in the German *Die Welt* suggested that 'there was no information about the fate of civilians or the losses of the rebels particularly because the American troops had seized the largest hospital at the start and destroyed two of the remaining four smaller infirmaries with bombs' (Kalnoky 2004c: 6). A similar argument was provided by Sheikh Younis al-Hamdani, spokesman for the Association of Muslim Scholars (see Hamdani and Parry 2004: 8). Yet, the press did not investigate whether the US/Coalition had actually targeted hospitals deliber-ately and the implications thereof if this had been the case. For example, in a rare instance, *Die Welts'* Kalnoky (2004c: 6) paraphrased Iraqis who actually saw the purpose of the hospital takeover as to 'deny medical assistance to the rebels as well as to prevent casualty figures from getting out to public'. Kalnoky also cited one of the remaining doctors in Fallujah who said there '[...] was not a single surgeon and hardly any medicine left in the city' (*ibid*). But as in other cases when the press included deviant statements that could be classified as substantial criticism together with evidence on the humani-tarian crisis such information appeared garbled and de-contextualised. News stories did not pursue an angle, which suggested nefarious intent. Indeed, even Kalnoky was hardly concerned about the hospital takeover, which he elsewhere regarded as a 'clever move' (2004d: 10).

Considering the second issue, it was striking that although 36 articles in my newspaper sample mentioned one of the hospital incidents, *The Times's*

Hamdani and Parry (2004: 8) were the only journalists who pointed out that hospitals 'are protected under the Geneva Convention, unless they are being used by combatants'.[13] And in consideration of the cases described by the newspapers, violations of different clauses were possible concerning the treatment and maintenance of hospital services in general, the treatment of hospital staff and patients as well as the US/Coalition's obligation to maintain medical supplies for civilians and wounded enemy combatants. None of these issues was raised.

Supply and relief

As already discussed, the UK and German press highlighted details about the deteriorating humanitarian situation in Fallujah with reference to voices by civilians, doctors and humanitarian organisations. For instance, in the *Independent*, Sengupta (2004f: 34–35) quoted Rasoul Ibrahim who 'said families left inside Fallujah were in desperate need. "There's no water," he said. "People are drinking dirty water. Children are dying. People are eating flour because there's no food."' Furthermore, local doctors referred to 'an increase in typhoid cases' (Beaumont 2004: 15) and a general lack in surgeons (Reuters 2004a: 1). On 15 November, a news article in the German *tageszeitung* summarised the situation in Fallujah as follows: 'There is no water, no electricity and no medical supplies' (AFP/DPA/TAZ 2004: 9).

At the start of the operation water and electric support systems had been cut off – facts which were reported by all newspapers under review. In conjunction with the disabling of hospitals and large scale destruction of Fallujah these actions contributed to the humanitarian crisis.

My analysis suggests that while the press provided a picture of the situation in Fallujah it was not able to connect cause and effect of the crisis. Furthermore, in no item did the press provide information on whether the US/Coalition was prohibited to 'render useless objects indispensable to the survival of the civilian population' (Article 54, Geneva Conventions, Protocol I, 1977). Indeed, as in the previous cases, the press framed the humanitarian crisis in the context of heavy 'fighting' and the US/Coalition's use of overwhelming military force. While such coverage could include procedural critiques of military tactics, it avoided substantial challenges. For instance, a goal of the operation could have been to starve the population as this was the result of the electricity and power cuts. Such an argument was supported by the US military's refusal to allow a Red Crescent convoy to deliver supplies in Fallujah (see e.g. McCarthy 2004g: 17) – a fact which was reported by all newspapers under review. As Sengupta wrote in the *Independent*, 'the US military has barred aid convoys from Fallujah, insisting they have enough resources to look after the remaining civilians' (Sengupta 2004e: 7). There were also scattered references by 'doctors in Fallujah' who 'complained that U.S. troops were preventing them [and ambulances] from moving in the city to treat wounded' (Shadid 2004b: A 1; see also Sengupta and Huggler 2004: 1, 4). Again, these issues were not further investigated although the newspapers' own reports described the starving civilian population, which visibly lacked supplies. Furthermore, the press did not inquire whether specific clauses of the Geneva Conventions – involving the protection of objects important for the populace, the duty of an occupying power to maintain food, medical supplies and public hygiene as well as to allow relief organisations and doctors to pursue their work – were disregarded.

In conclusion, the newspapers provided facts suggesting the occurrence of major war crimes under the Geneva Conventions. Yet, when reporting on the responsibility for possible crimes, the news media focused on individual soldiers rather than officers in higher ranks. Most items including critiques about responsibility focused on the mosque shooting (see Chapter 5). It was further discussed as to whether individual soldiers might have conducted a war crime. Only in rare instances did writers suggest responsibility for officials in higher ranks and this was often conducted in an indirect fashion. For instance, the press cited humanitarian actors who demanded that all sides comply with the laws of armed conflicts (see McCarthy 2004h: 17). Or it was argued that 'American soldiers might have committed a war crime' (Janofsky 2004: 8). Like in coverage of the mosque shooting, such depictions focused on individual soldiers. In rare instances comment writers alleged that 'Western governments' were committing a 'crime' (Zangana 2004a: 26; see also Klein 2004b), thus directly referring to the higher levels of planning.

Overall, the press covered a diverse range of views and facts, thus highlighting the US/Coalition military strategy, civilian suffering and punctual violations of the laws of war particularly in the UK press but also in newspapers of other countries under review. On closer examination, however, it becomes apparent that although coverage on civilians tended to be relatively independent from the US/administration, it was still inaccurate. An analysis of the dynamics of coverage suggested that the inclusion and exclusion of factual detail as well as their placement lead to an incongruent picture about humanitarian issues in Fallujah. To uphold this picture, authoritative data about civilians in Fallujah, civilian deaths, and war crimes were ignored or relegated to marginal spaces. Moreover, the press used a selective framework emphasising war, fighting and battle at the expense of other notions such as massacre, atrocity or crime. Fallujah 2 was reported in terms of a benign blood-bath. Civilian deaths were thus framed as 'casualties' – the tragic outcomes of war. This framing was contradicted by the factual evidence provided by the newspapers under review, as well as legal documents that codify the properties of war crimes. It also did not match with the factual record established in the previous chapter. Considering the range of newspapers under review, it is striking that their ideological alignment was similar. Differences in coverage were related to the factual detail and in this regard the *Guardian*, the *Independent* and the *Post* published the most comprehensive accounts.

Cairo

The Cairo incident was reported in an ambiguous fashion, if compared with the other cases under review. The newspapers would provide space for the narrative put forward by the military regime as well as the Muslim Brotherhood and its supporters. However, in contrast to the two other 'allied' cases, the newspapers would more often assign responsibility for crimes and label the incident in atrocious terms. On balance, however, the newspapers would not campaign on these issues and rather convey the differing narratives in a neutral fashion. While it was evident from reporting that the Egyptian regime had conducted a major crackdown, this did not lead to serious discussions about intervention in Cairo. Moreover, after several days of reporting, the press would shift its focus away from the incident. Unlike when reporting on Račak, Benghazi and Houla, the military leadership was treated in constructive terms. In fact, the Cairo incident constituted a constructive bloodbath in accord with Western interests. I will further review the handling of the incident in the following section.

An analysis of news media reporting evidences reports that focused on the details of the incident. For instance, the 9 July report by Kirkpatrick and Fahim's (2013: 1) in the *New York Times* stated about the event:

> It was by far the deadliest day of violence since the revolt that overthrew former President Hosni Mubarak in early 2011. Within a few hours around dawn, advancing soldiers and police officers killed at least 51 civilians and wounded more than 400, almost all hit by gunfire, health officials said.

Similar facts about the slaughter were arguably reported in most of the newspapers (see also below). Furthermore, Kirkpatrick and Fahim's (2013: 1) article illustrated how the press conveyed the issue of responsibility: 'Some who vehemently denounced Mr. Mubarak's use of brute force to silence critics were far more tepid about criticizing the killings of Mr. Morsi's supporters,' the journalists wrote. Moreover, the 'United States, which has conspicuously not condemned Mr. Morsi's ouster, was also mild, calling on security forces to exercise restraint' (*ibid*). Only a few lines after this statement did the article refer to the Muslim Brotherhood, who assigned responsibility for the incident to the military government (*ibid*). Thus, the article (*ibid*) referred to Essam el-Erian, a senior Brotherhood leader who 'called the killings "an outright massacre" by "a fascist coup government"'. Several lines further below, Kirkpatrick and Fahim's (2013: 1) provided space for Ahmed Ali, a military spokesman who said 'the security forces had responded with rubber bullets and gas bombs after coming under attack by heavy gunfire'. Furthermore, other voices were mentioned which 'also suggested that Mr. Morsi's supporters might be to blame for the fighting'. These statements were then balanced with announcements by 'both supporters and opponents of Mr. Morsi' who 'said the military and the police had fired with little or no provocation, unloading tear gas, birdshot and bullets'. Hence, if this news item is seen as an indicator for coverage, it seemed that the Cairo incident was treated in a rather objective and balanced fashion. Claims about responsibility by both sides were reported and responsibility was not immediately assigned to one side in the conflict. This was a middle-of-the-road approach when compared with reporting on 'enemy' countries as well as Fallujah, where one narrative dominated the news agenda. In fact, many news items should follow this 'balancing' approach.

An 8 July, op-ed (2013) by Tim Sebastian in the *New York Times* is perhaps further representative for how the press treated the Cairo incident. Sebastian critically pointed to the human rights record of the Egyptian military: 'Over the last two years human rights reports have been littered with accusations of unlawful killings by Egypt's security forces, torture in military jails and thousands of unfair trials of civilians in military courts.' Here was an acknowledgement that Egyptian forces might have been responsible for serious human rights violations. Reflecting on the coup against Morsi, Sebastian (*ibid*) then described how people he respected in Egypt told him there was 'no choice' as Egypt 'was collapsing around Morsi; the entire machine was faltering, his closest allies jumped ship'. Sebastian basically argued that Morsi's political faults, including abuses of power, the Islamisation of society and an economic downturn, had encouraged many Egyptians and the military 'to bring a swift end to the country's first free democratic experiment' (*ibid*). Hence, while being critical of the military, this narrative still appeared to lend mild support to the coup and the policies that followed it including the Cairo incident.

Let's examine further examples of reporting to illustrate the news media's approach to the Cairo incident. Kingsley (2013c: 1), of the *Guardian*, reported details of slaughter in an eye-witness account from an Egyptian hospital:

> On several floors of Cairo's Health Insurance hospital, room after room was filled with bloodied, moaning protesters, many of them waiting to be treated. Supporters queued up to donate blood as doctors rushed more wounded past them on stretchers. Security officials screamed at journalists to leave; families of victims implored them to stay.

The report also gave space to display testimony by the protestors who argued that the army had started firing at them (see *ibid*). Kingsley provided the following accounts:

> 'It was like pouring rain,' said Mohamed Atia, one of the hundreds injured in the subsequent bloodbath, speaking in hospital. A pool of dried blood darkened his once-grey trousers, the gunshot wound to his shoulder still awaiting medical attention. 'They started shooting teargas and then live ammunition. We were shouting 'peaceful, peaceful', but the shooting continued.'

These statements indicated regime responsibility and also evidenced that Cairo was to some extent reported in atrocious terms (see reference to the bloodbath). Yet, comparable to the approach by the *New York Times* discussed above, Kingsley (*ibid*) also stressed that 'the narrative of history is rarely straightforward' and 'the city was awash with claims and counterclaims about whether the bloody events had been provoked'. According to the army, the article went on, Morsi supporters had attacked its compound and it 'had no choice but to return fire'. Hence, this article also employed a rather objective journalistic approach that balanced the competing narrative provided by the Muslim Brotherhood and the Egyptian army Similarly, on 10 July, Black and Kingsley (2013b: 12), of the *Guardian*, referred to the different narratives: 'Morsi supporters were still gathering near the scene of Monday's killings, described as a massacre by the brotherhood, but defended by the army and a uniformly uncritical state media as a response to a "terrorist" attack.'

Sengupta and Beach (2013: 1, 4, 5), of the *Independent*, also started their article on 9 July with eyewitness depictions of slaughter:

> The bodies lay on the grey floor smeared with streaks of blood. Three were covered with a purple and green blanket; two more lay under an Egyptian flag. Alongside the dead, a steady stream of victims was carried in to the hospital near the Rabaa Adiwiya mosque. Many of them looked unlikely to survive, such was the severity of the injuries.

After these detailed descriptions of slaughter, the article referred to the different narratives, highlighting that 'Pro- and anti-Morsi fractions accused each other of starting the killing spree'. Yet, the journalists (*ibid*) added that 'there is evidence that some of the dead and wounded were hit while they were saying their dawn prayers, kneeling with their backs to the direction from which the shots had come'. This description was followed by references to the army, which 'claimed that it had shot back in self-defence' (*ibid*). Several paragraphs below, Sengupta and Beach (2013: 1, 4, 5) stressed that even if the military had faced shots and petrol bombs, 'an objective inquiry will need to look at whether the scale and ferocity of the response was justified'.

A similar journalistic approach was also applied by the German press. For instance, an article in the *Frankfurter Rundschau* included a range of statements indicating different narratives about who was responsibility for the incident then arguing that 'both versions could have a true core' (DPA/AFP 2013: 10).

In conclusion, these examples of reporting demonstrated that while the newspapers focused on the details of slaughter, they remained cautious in their assignment of responsibility. Additionally, the Cairo incident was not consistently framed as a massacre or crackdown but also with reference to military terminology. Moreover, it is significant that in their reporting on Račak, Benghazi and Houla, the newspapers would not follow a similarly balanced approach. In these latter cases, the press stressed 'enemy' state culpability from the beginning and generously highlighted atrocious dimensions of the incidents. The press engaged in this kind of reporting even before any comprehensive investigation into the incidents had been conducted.

In Cairo, on the other hand, the press had better access to the scene of the incident and comprehensive inquiries were conducted. Thus, on 19 July, the *Guardian's* Kingsley (2013b: 1) found after 'a week-long investigation' based on 'interviews with 31 witnesses, local people and medics, as well as video analysis' that the Cairo incident was, in fact, 'a co-ordinated assault on a group of largely peaceful and unarmed civilians' by the Egyptian security forces. The detailed investigation also stressed that the army was 'using excessive force against [...] a largely unarmed group of protestors' during the course of which military snipers were 'picking off unarmed civilians'. These findings were broadly consistent with a report by Human Rights Watch published on 14 July 2013 (see Human Rights Watch 2013).

Hence, it was quite quickly established that the Cairo incident actually constituted a massacre for which the Egyptian security forces were mainly responsible. Yet, the newspaper's reporting of these issues appeared to be far more objective and impartial as in reporting of incidents involving 'enemy' states. In the case of Cairo, responsibility was not regularly assigned to the highest levels of military planning and, as already discussed in the previous chapter, the incident should not lead the news media to advocate more serious policy measures to constrain the violence of the Egyptian military regime. Hence, Egyptian General el-Sisi could remain in power and continue to lead the military's serial crackdowns against the Muslim Brotherhood and other opposition groups. Thus, the Cairo incident constituted a constructive bloodbath because the Egyptian military regime had positive value for Western powers.

Significantly, it was well established that the military coup, which preceded the Cairo incident, was organised by the Egyptian security apparatus together with elements of the traditional establishment. This was even argued in an item published on 11 July in the *New York Times*. According to Hubbard and Kirkpatrick (2013: 4):

> Working behind the scenes, members of the old establishment, some of them close to Mr. Mubarak and the country's top generals, also helped finance, advise and organize those determined to topple the Islamist leadership, including Naguib Sawiris, a billionaire and an outspoken foe of the Brotherhood; Tahani el-Gebali, a former judge on the Supreme Constitutional Court who is close to the ruling generals; and Shawki al-Sayed, a legal adviser to Ahmed Shafik, Mr. Mubarak's last prime minister, who lost the presidential race to Mr. Morsi.

Hence, it could be argued that the Egyptian military had engineered a coup and then engaged in major crackdowns. The Egyptian military's policies were underwritten by special domestic interests and received significant support by outside powers including Saudi-Arabia and the US (see also Chapter 5). Considering these contexts, the Egyptian military was hardly engaged in legitimate activities. Yet, this was not emphasised in the press. Note, on the other hand, how the FRY/Serbia as well as the Libyan and Syrian governments had acted against militant uprisings within their own territories of governance. Yet, in these latter cases, the news media emphasised the narratives of the opposition.

Because the Egyptian regime received support by Western powers and their allies, it could arguably proceed clamping down on the wider Egyptian opposition that had gained momentum after the Arab uprisings of 2011. It is thus of further interest how the news media reported on potential future crackdowns. In the aftermath of the Cairo incident, members of the Muslim Brotherhood feared further retribution. On 10 July, the *Guardian's* Chulov (2013: 12) reported the statement of a man near a Mosque in Port Said, a base of the Muslim Brotherhood: 'What has happened there is just the beginning for us [...]. They will come for us wherever we are and they will find any pretext to do it' (cited in *ibid*).

In fact, the first Egyptian raid incident was followed by a series of crackdowns that culminated in the Rab'a incident, a mass killing of almost unprecedented scale. Several weeks after the Cairo incident took place, police and army forces killed 817 people when dispersing the Rab'a al-Adawiya sit-in on 14 August 2013 (Human Rights Watch 2014b). In its 2014 report, Human Rights Watch commented on the event as follows (*ibid*): 'The indiscriminate and deliberate use of lethal force resulted in one of the world's largest killings of demonstrators in a single day in recent history.' Furthermore, according to Human Rights Watch (*ibid*):

> Following its year-long investigation, Human Rights Watch has further concluded that the government used disproportionate force, failed to take measures to minimize loss of life, and knowingly opened fire on unarmed protesters with live ammunition, therein committing serious violations of international human rights laws. The systematic and widespread nature of the deliberate and indiscriminate killings, coupled with evidence indicating that the government anticipated and planned to engage in mass unlawful killings, i.e. murder, and that they fit into a consistent pattern of protester killings, indicate that the violations likely amount to crimes against humanity. One year later, authorities have made no effort to investigate or otherwise hold police and army officers and other officials accountable for their actions.

We should remember that in the case of Libya, commentators had argued that a 'humanitarian intervention' was necessary in order to protect the people in Benghazi from future massacres by Gaddafi's forces. This was a powerful discourse that resonated on the 'right' and 'left' of the political spectrum in the West and was used to justify NATO intervention. It turned out, however, that in every single city that Gaddafi's forces retook before the NATO onslaught, no massacre had occurred (see Kuperman 2013). It is thus plausible to assume that the 'Benghazi massacre threat' was manufactured to incite intervention. The Rab'a incident in Cairo, on the other hand, constituted a real 'Benghazi' event in the sense that it was a pre-mediated 'massacre' (see Human Rights Watch 2014b). Yet significantly, when Egyptian forces engaged in serial crackdowns during the preceding weeks of the Rab'a incident, one of which constituted the first Egyptian raid incident which is under study, virtually no concerns about an impending massacre were voiced across the Western political and news media spectrum. Similarly, the 'liberal interventionists' largely remained silent. The Rab'a incident might have been prevented if Western powers had used their diplomatic leverage in Egypt. But unlike in the case of Benghazi, the press was hardly transporting strong concerns about a coming massacre in Egypt during the weeks preceding the incident.

This case comparison thus further demonstrates the propaganda aspect of dichotomised media campaigns. Western intervention will only be on the public agenda when victimisation meets elite utility. In the case of Cairo, the crackdowns against the Egyptian opposition had constructive value. Western powers relied on the Egyptian military as the best broker for their interests in the region. That is why news media reporting on Cairo was muted.

$$\cdot\ 7\ \cdot$$

CONCLUSION

Media, Propaganda and Intervention

General findings

My study contributes to the findings of major content analytical treatises which found that during international conflicts and wars 'as institutions, the media have generally served the military [and the state-corporate elites] rather well' (Carruthers 2000: 271–272; see also Bennett 1990; Bennett, Lawrence and Livingston 2007; Entman 2004; Hallin 1989; Mermin 1999).

The international scope of my work, which goes beyond the usually applied single country studies, contributes an important and original finding to knowledge about international press news coverage. Firstly, it could be shown that the international press displayed comparable ideological alignment. This is clearly demonstrated by the relative similarity in terms of the quantitative provision of indignation and the use of similar keywords to frame the studied incidents.

Secondly, the political distance of the countries in which the press is situated manifested in some variations in coverage, which appear to reflect specific national elite interests. These findings are congruent with an international propaganda model. While it has been assumed by scholars that the international press could display such pattern in coverage (see Nacos *et al.*

2000: 41) this has yet not been empirically demonstrated in regard to US, UK and German press news coverage of conflict. My study closes this gap.

Thirdly, my international findings mitigate the scholarly perspective that European press systems are more adversarial than the US press due to differing reporting practices and institutionalised norms (see Hallin and Mancini 2005; Sparks 2007). While the variations identified in coverage might point to influences of professional norms, the ideological similarities across US, UK and German press news coverage appear to be more decisive pointing to the press's reflection of a trans-Atlantic elite consensus.

Finally, the study supports a large body of scholarly work that may be classified within the so-called elite-driven paradigm (see Robinson *et al.* 2010). More specifically, my study confirms the applicability of Herman and Chomsky's propaganda model (2008), which is a significant component of the elite-driven model, in am US, UK and German context.

In the following section, I will thus further validate the propaganda model's predictions. The chapter closes with a brief reflection on the politics of intervention.

Confirming the predictions of the propaganda model

On a general level, the propaganda model predicts the news media to be highly critical of 'enemy' states and uncritical in the 'acceptance of certain premises in dealing with self and friends' (Herman and Chomsky 2008: 32).

According to my findings, the Western press framed incidents involving human rights violations by 'allied' countries as military and/or police endeavours. The international newspapers did not tend to classify the Fallujah and Cairo incidents as major atrocities, if the quantity of atrocious descriptions is compared with news reporting on 'enemy' states. The general assumption adopted by the corporate press is that Western states and their 'allies' act in accord with beneficial intent. The main thrust of coverage is to regard these countries as benevolent forces that engage in warfare/policing as part of democracy and/or state building. As a consequence of this ideological outlook, the amount of items including indignation in reporting on Fallujah and Cairo was moderate and no pronounced campaigns to stop human rights violations could be observed. It was particularly striking that indignation in terms of Military policy and Sanctions was virtually absent from reporting despite high levels of violence.

The press is, of course, no monolith and there were variations in coverage. In some instances did the news media featured atrocious statements depicting the Fallujah and Cairo incidents as massacres or crackdowns. Yet, such information was placed in an ideological context, which still assumed that 'allied' countries constitute legitimate and positive forces. In particular, the Fallujah incidents were framed in terms of reciprocal war and fighting. Accordingly, the Fallujah incidents were treated as benign bloodbaths in the propaganda system. This politicised discourse served to obscure the well-documented fact that both incidents also shared the properties of massacres and war crimes.

There were some further nuances in reporting on 'allied' states: the Cairo incident received more critical scrutiny and was more frequently labelled in atrocious terms than the Fallujah incidents. Also, a more pronounced Sanctions discourse could be observed after the Cairo incident took place. This resulted from the fact that Cairo involved the actions of an ally of the main Western powers rather than the actions of these powers themselves. Hence, news media reporting on Cairo was more open. Aside from that, the actions of the Egyptian military regime were still viewed in relatively positive terms and the press's indignation discourse did not include voices demanding significant repercussions. In fact, because the military regime was useful for geo-strategic reasons, it continued to receive major financial aid from Western states and their Arab allies (see Chapters 5 and 6). The Cairo incident was thus handled as a constructive bloodbath in the propaganda system.

In stark contrast, incidents involving human rights violations conducted by 'enemy' countries were largely framed as atrocities. The keyword analysis demonstrated the overwhelming use of atrocious at the expense of martial terms in relation to the Račak, Benghazi and Houla cases. This framing was underpinned by extensive and detailed depictions of slaughter. The various incidents were further explained as an outcome of systematic policies with nefarious intent. Thus, in the framing process, the news media largely assumed government culpability. 'Enemy' states and their forces were designated to be illegitimate actors. Furthermore, there was a pronounced campaign of indignation featuring extensive demands for various Military policy and Sanctions measures. In fact, military and other interventions were undertaken in relation to the actions of all 'enemy' countries under review. Hence, Račak, Benghazi and Houla constituted nefarious bloodbaths in the prisms of the propaganda system. And this handling was consistent among the international newspapers under review. There were only a few exceptions in the comment pages. Moreover, moderate differences across countries could be observed: a country's political distance to a conflict allowed for more nuanced media coverage (see also Zollmann 2012, 2015a).

In conclusion, the quantitative and qualitative data suggests that similarities in reporting across newspapers and countries were more striking than differences. Hence, it could be shown that reporting patterns in the international press were similar in terms of indignation, framing, details and responsibility. Thus, 'enemy' states were consistently shamed although their human rights abuses were comparable with those conducted by 'allied' states. This treatment suggests the news media's application of different standards and premises when dealing with 'enemy' as opposed to 'allied' states.

Secondly, a propaganda model predicts that in the case of 'enemy' states, 'propaganda themes' are facilitated by Western government 'authority figures' and can thus easily become 'established as true even without real evidence' (Herman and Chomsky 2008: 32).

Accordingly, my study found that the baseless claim that the Libyan air force was targeting protestors was highlighted by the news media without substantive challenge. In fact, even when high-level authority figures later acknowledged that there were no confirmed reports that the Libyan air-force had targeted protestors, this did not alter the dominant discourse about government culpability and the need for intervention.

In the case study on Kosovo, the press had framed high-level FRY/Serbian officials as responsible for the Račak incident. These depictions were facilitated by officials and were based on hearsay evidence provided by local actors or official sources. Furthermore, the news media highlighted FRY/Serbian responsibility on the basis of leaked phone intercepts whose authenticity was questionable. The FRY/Serbia had long been designated as a villain and this made it easy to push such information in the news media (see Herman and Peterson 2007). In fact, the long-time and consistent handling of FRY/Serbian actors as aggressors in the propaganda system might have closed out 'dissenting views even more comprehensively' (Herman and Chomsky 2008: 32). Thus, when it came to Račak, the incident was overwhelmingly regarded as an atrocity perpetrated by the Serbian regime. And this narrative obtained prominence in the news, even before any independent legal investigation had been conducted. Furthermore, while counter evidence to the contrary was available and at times even featured in the press, this did not significantly alter the discourse on FRY/Serbian culpability. This is not to say that critical voices were ignored in news media reporting. However, counter narratives were often less developed and placed in negative contexts. The quantitative and qualitative disadvantage of alternative facts and perspectives hardly made such narratives to appear credible.

A similar process could be observed in the case of Houla. Already a short time after the incident had occurred were the Syrian government and its forces designated to be the culprits. The framing of Syrian regime responsibility was rooted in statements provided by Western government, Syrian opposition as well as local civilian sources. Yet, a close reading of the news media and alternative evidence suggested that the official scenario about the incident was contested. Thus, even several weeks after Houla had taken place, independent sources like General Robert Mood, Head of the United Nations Supervision Mission in Syria, pointed to conflicting statements by local Syrian civilians as well as factual ambiguity surrounding the Houla evidence (see Anderson 2016: 72–73). Alternative evidence, which was available at the time of reporting, even suggested a plausible scenario of Syrian opposition culpability for the Houla incident (see *ibid*). Yet, this set of evidence was virtually excluded from coverage or mentioned in passing.

Thirdly, the propaganda model predicts 'different criteria of evaluation to be employed, so that what is villainy in enemy states will be presented as an incidental background fact in the case of oneself and friends' (Herman and Chomsky 2008: 32).

As documented in this study, the numbers of civilian deaths during the Fallujah incidents more specifically and the occupation of Iraq more generally exceeded those in Račak/Kosovo, Benghazi/Libya and Houla/Syria. Yet, indignant campaigns in Fallujah did generate less outrage and virtually no calls for action. Moreover, in their reporting on the Fallujah incidents, the press described multiple events, which could have amounted to war crimes. Still, such facets of the Fallujah incidents were neutrally reported and largely remained de-contextualised and scattered. There was no investigatory zeal in regard to whether reported incidents like the targeting of civilians in free-fire zones, the blocking of aid and hospitals, the destruction of hospitals, or the extensive use of heavy weaponry in population centres could have constituted human rights violations or war crimes. In reporting on 'enemy' countries, on the other hand, an atrocious context was initially established without seriously factoring contradicting facts and opinions. Hence, in coverage on Benghazi and Houla, reports about the government army's use of heavy weapons in populated areas were met with great indignation and self-righteous zeal. In the case of 'enemy' countries, the news media would focus precisely on those atrocious details, which it ignored or mentioned in passing when reporting on incidents involving 'allied' countries. Thus, as Herman and Chomsky (2008: 32) write: 'What is on the agenda in treating one case will be off the agenda in discussing the other.'

Moreover, when reporting on 'enemy' countries, the press carried multiple articles including calls for specific actions voiced by Western politicians, domestic actors and journalists. Significantly, such calls for intervention were extensively featured in news coverage on 'enemy' countries without fundamental challenge. In news media reporting on 'allied' countries, specific calls for action were muted and there were virtually no calls for any form of direct intervention. It is also interesting that the villainy of 'enemy' countries was further established with reference to evidence provided by a broad set of sources including local civilian actors, opposition groups, expats, domestic voices and public officials. In contrast, an evaluation of the conduct of 'allied' countries largely followed from statements provided by high-level officials and the military while local civilian and other society sources appeared to be muted or carefully balanced with the official perspective. This further confirms Herman and Chomsky (2008: 32) who 'would expect official sources of the United States and its client regimes to be used heavily – and uncritically – in connection with one's own abuses and those of friendly governments, while refugees and other dissident sources will be used in dealing with enemies'.

The propaganda model fourthly predicts 'the [search for] responsibility of high officials for abuses in enemy states, but diminished enterprise in examining such matters in connection with one's own and friendly states' (*ibid*).

Accordingly, this study suggests the press only acknowledged that low-level military personnel might have been responsible for violations by 'allied' countries. The opposite was the case in reporting on 'enemy' countries where it was easy to frame high-level officials as perpetrators although no proper legal investigation had been conducted.

In the final conclusion it can be confirmed on the basis of this study that press coverage on 'allied' and 'enemy' incidents was dichotomised and this treatment could not be related to event specifics as evidence about quite similar human rights violations was available at the time of reporting. In sum, the study broadly finds, in agreement with Herman and Chomsky (2008: 32–33),

> that worthy victims will be featured prominently and dramatically, that they will be humanized, and that their victimization will receive the detail and context in story construction that will generate reader interest and sympathetic emotion. In contrast, unworthy victims will merit only slight detail, minimal humanization, and little context that will excite and enrage.

The politics of intervention

It is well documented in the declassified governmental record that economic interests constitute the driving force behind Western foreign policy (see Blum 2004, 2006; Curtis 1995, 1998, 2003, 2004). As the US Defense Intelligence Agency declared in an US Senate hearing before the Select Committee on Intelligence in 1996:

> We must have fair market access to the resources and markets of the world. In some cases, such as the need for oil, the denial of such access carries with it unacceptable consequences. (cited in Curtis 1998: 38)

Western powers' greatest concern has consequently been the threat of independent nationalist states because they share the desire to block foreign access to their resources and prevent the establishment of corporation friendly investment climates. That is why such states are marked for intervention. As John Pilger (2016) has argued:

> The attack on Iraq, the attack on Libya, the attack on Syria happened because the leader in each of these countries was not a puppet of the West. The human rights record of a Saddam or a Gaddafi was irrelevant. They did not obey orders and surrender control of their country.

> The same fate awaited Slobodan Milosevic once he had refused to sign an 'agreement' that demanded the occupation of Serbia and its conversion to a market economy. His people were bombed, and he was prosecuted in The Hague. Independence of this kind is intolerable.

The overt NATO interventions in Kosovo and Libya were clearly conducted in alignment with such concerns. The separation of Kosovo from the FRY/Serbia was the outcome of NATO intervention and sealed the fragmentation of Yugoslavia. During the 'Balkanisation' of the former Yugoslavian territories, the state-controlled economy was dismantled and integrated into the 'Washington Consensus'. Similarly, Libya's support for an African Union and its drive toward political and economic independence was halted by NATO intervention (see Forte 2012). Consequently, Libya was turned from one of the most developed African nations into a failed state. Similarly, Kosovo has been disintegrating into a failed state. Crucially, news media shaming in response to Benghazi and Račak paved the way for these interventions and outcomes.

In Egypt, on the other hand, the counterrevolutionary forces have well served Western strategic interests. The military dictatorship keeps Arab nationalism in line and co-operates with the US and Israel. That is why the Cairo incident did not generate much indignation. In fact, the regime was quickly rewarded with aid and news media shaming was muted. The regime could basically proceed with its crackdown that aimed at rolling back the achievements of the so-called 2011 Arab Uprising. Significantly, several weeks after the Cairo incident took place, the military executed one of the worst atrocities in recent history, the August 2013 Rab'a Massacre. Rab'a was the real 'Benghazi event' in that it was devastating and foreseeable. But unlike the manufactured Libyan Benghazi incident, Rab'a was not decried in the same way by the Western news media and intellectual human rights sector.

Iraq and Syria have long been in the focus of Western intervention due to their geostrategic and economic outlook. A unified Iraq – with its massive oil resources – could be at the heart of an independent Arab nationalism in the Middle East. Furthermore, it is of high priority for corporate interests to remain a foothold in Iraq and privatise its economy. This would incidentally allow to strengthening US control of (rather than access to) the flow of oil, which gives the US power over other countries. That is why the US/Coalition occupation of Iraq was a priority after 2003. In this context, the slaughter in Fallujah in April and November 2004 was hardly depicted as such. Fallujah was consequently reported in military terms without much reference to the carnage or the fact that the Iraqi resistance was mainly consisting of local rather than foreign actors. The US/Coalition consequently remained in Iraq for years to come, in spite of the extremely high levels of violence that the occupation generated and which exceeded the levels of violence found in Syria, Libya and Kosovo.

Syria, on the other hand, has been a main ally of Russia and Iran and thus served as a buffer between those countries and the major Western powers including Israel. Consequently, it has been a goal of the West to remove the Syrian obstacle. It has to be seen in this context that the Syrian government has been heavily scrutinised for the Houla incident. In fact, Syrian actions in the Houla area resemble US 'counter-insurgency' operations in Iraq. Furthermore, Syrian cities were clearly attacked by foreign fighters. Yet, when the Syrian army responded with massive force, news media shaming would encourage even further proxy intervention.

As a consequence of overt and secret intervention, both Iraq and Syria are currently fragmenting along sectarian lines. This disintegration is in accord with the long-standing Western policy objective of establishing a set of obedient and weak Arab client states in the Middle East (see Curtis 2010).

In order to destroy the Syrian regime, Western powers have operated in tandem with allied states such as Saudi-Arabia and Qatar. Moreover, Western powers have made use of radical Islamist currents as this served their policy aim of destabilising the independent nationalist outlook of Syria (see Anderson 2016; see also Curtis 2010 for an assessment of the long-term Western support for Islamist proxies).

In conclusion, the politics of intervention manifest as selective human rights shaming. This entails highly dichotomised propaganda campaigns during which 'enemy' countries are marked for 'humanitarian intervention'. Yet significantly, the actual interventions are not humanitarian. Interventionist policies have led to the dismantlement of independent states and the 'reconstruction' of failed client states. The shaming of and intervention in countries such as the FRY/Serbia, Kosovo, Iraq, Libya, and Syria have proceeded along those lines. Atrocities have mainly been highlighted in the news media and intellectual discourse, if responsibility could be assigned to 'enemy' states of the West. Once state villainy was engraved in the public consciousness, military intervention followed. 'Humanitarian intervention' has thus served a hyper militarist agenda that has destabilised the provisions of non-intervention as enshrined in the UN Charter. Far from bringing peace and human rights to distant countries, Western imperial strategy has been wreaking havoc in the Balkans, Middle East and elsewhere.

NOTES

Foreword

1. See, for instance, http://www.bbc.co.uk/news/world-middle-east-37734173, http://www.telegraph.co.uk/news/2016/10/11/we-must-find-a-way-to-end-the-bloodshed-in-yemen-the-forgotten-w/, https://www.theguardian.com/commentisfree/2016/jan/28/britain-war-yemen-saudi-arabia-military-advisers

Chapter 1

1. For the Preamble of the UN Charter see http://www.un.org/en/sections/un-charter/preamble/ (accessed 18 November 2016).
2. All subsequent citations from primary or secondary literature printed in German language were translated by the author. Generally, there are different English spellings for Fallujah. I used the term Fallujah. Other sources are at times quoted referring to Falluja without [h]. This book is a substantially revised and updated version of my PhD thesis, which assesses US, UK and German news reporting of the Fallujah incidents, amongst other issues (see Zollmann 2012). Some of the background materials discussed in the PhD thesis were published in academic journals before the dissertation hand-in (see appendix of Zollmann 2012). Some material on the Fallujah 1 and 2 incidents was published in the *Occasional Working Paper Series* of the University of Lincoln and *Ethical Space: the International Journal of Communication Ethics*. Material on US/Coalition propaganda was published in the

Westminster Papers in Communication and Culture. Discussions on coverage of the Iraq War and legal issues were published in *Peace Journalism, War and Conflict Resolution.* Discussions of elite media theories and the occupation of Iraq were published in *Global Media and Communication.* For the complete references of the texts see Zollmann (2012, appendix). Some of the quotations used in this book in the discussion of indignation on the Fallujah 1 and 2 incidents, the data on newspapers in the methodology section as well as the data on the Iraq/Fallujah background were also used in Zollmann (2008) and/or Zollmann (2015a). Some aspects on the foundations of the propaganda model were published in Zollmann (2015b). The factual research on Libya and Syria drew from Forte (2012), Anderson (2016) and Cartalucci and Bowie (2012). The propaganda model framework drew from Herman and Chomsky (2008), Chomsky and Herman (1979a, b), Herman and Peterson (2010), Keeble (1997), Edwards and Cromwell (2006, 2009), Mullen (2010), Klaehn (2002) and DiMaggio (2009). The case study comparisons drew from the work by Herman and Chomsky (2008) as well as the work published by David Edwards and David Cromwell on their Media Lens website (see www.medialens.org). Some aspects of the research method such as the factoring of civilian deaths in coverage as well as the assessment of the properties of 'fighting' in Fallujah drew from the approach by Finkelstein (2011), Chomsky (1989) and Keeble (1997).

Chapter 2

1. *Four Theories of the Press* has been highly prominent in the Anglo-American media and communications studies. As Hallin and Mancini (2005: 215) write: '*Four Theories of the Press* is still widely used as a framework for comparison worldwide [emphasis in the original].' According to McQuail (2010: 175): 'The book has been widely sold, translated, used in education and debated ever since.' And Curran (2002: 167) writes: 'This analysis was viewed as a landmark study for the next forty years. It was summarised, and gravely discussed, in key international textbooks.'

2. Social responsibility theory was taken from recommendations formulated by the reports of the Commission on Freedom of the Press, particularly the report *A Free and Responsible Press* (Siebert, Peterson and Schramm 1984 [1956]: 75), which was published in 1947 under the chairmanship of Robert M. Hutchins, then Chancellor of the University of Chicago (Commission on Freedom of the Press 1947: II). Because of societal concerns, the Commission proposed a set of norms and policies for press and broadcasting freedom. They range from external government measures (such as regulation of concentration, support for new ventures, introduction of new legislations, and establishment of new media channels in areas where private media is insufficient) to self-regulatory guidelines and initiatives (such as that the press should publish a range of views including dissent and mutual criticism, provide a truthful and meaningful account of events, represent all groups in society, finance niche activities, and enhance professional education) (Siebert, Peterson and Schramm 1984 [1956]: 79–105).

3. Accordingly, Humphreys (1996: 10) argues social responsibility theory 'was elaborated with the US situation very much in mind' although 'the West European press has [also] functioned largely in a free market context with certain "social responsibility" features'.

Social responsibility theory gained prominence in the UK in 1949, when a Royal Commission of the Press, under Sir David Ross, retiring head of an Oxford college, reported on public concerns over concentration and monopoly tendencies in the press (Whale 1977: 13–17). The Commission recommended the establishment of the Press Council (which started operating in 1953) 'to encourage the growth of the sense of public responsibility and public service among all engaged in the profession of journalism' (cited in *ibid*: 17).

4. It should be noted that a mediatised model of intermediary systems in political communication research expects the media to hold this position indicating the importance of liberal theories in other research areas (see Jarren and Donges 2002: 143).

5. A prominent liberal treatise was formulated by Alexander who takes an abstract perspective derived from Parsonian system theory developed through historical and comparative study (1981: 18, 23). According to Alexander (*ibid*: 24), the media's development is a 'process parallel to the "classic" cases of differentiation [...], the emergence of the autonomous economic market, independent state, and independent religious and cultural activities'. This perspective assumes that society comprises different sub-systems with special societal functions. The media has the function to be a 'substitute for concrete group contact, for the now impossible meeting-of-the-whole' (*ibid*: 18). Moreover, the media is further differentiated into news and entertainment media both of which also comprise of specific functions (*ibid*).

6. Thus, Alexander (1981: 21) writes: 'By daily exposing and reformulating itself *vis-à-vis* changing values, group formations, and objective economic and political conditions, the media allows "public opinion" to be organised responsively on a mass basis.' For a substantial discussion of the liberal democratic position see Meiklejohn (1960: 8–28).

7. They include researchers who discuss the need for or applicability of different societal modes of media regulation (e.g. Albarran 2002: 190–191; Doyle 2002a: 163–174; Frost 2000; Lichtenberg 1990b: 127, 1990c; McQuail and Siune 2001; O'Neill 1990: 176–181; Stepp 1990; Trettenbein 1994; Tunstall 1996: 377–417), enforcement of self-regulatory or compulsory mechanisms, such as codes of practice and charters to enhance journalistic autonomy (e.g. Bromley 2000; Frost 2000; Lichtenberg 1990c: 13; Sparrow 1999: 188–204; Stepp 1990; Tunstall 1996: 391–407), or guidelines for entire personnel of news operations including owners, managers and journalists (Kovach and Rosenstiel 2003: 63–68).

8. This viewpoint arguably traces back to Marx's (1904 [1859]: 11) assertion that 'forms of state' are 'rooted in the material conditions of life' and the consequent dictum that an understanding of civil society 'is to be sought in political economy' (*ibid*: 11). Marx explains this as follows:

> In the social production which men carry on they enter into definite relations that are indispensable and independent of their will; these relations of production correspond to a definite stage of development of their material powers of production. The sum total of these relations of production constitutes the economic structure of society–the real foundation, on which rise legal and political superstructures and to which correspond definite forms of social conscious [sic]. (*ibid*)

Thus, classical Marxist theory would expect the capitalist structure (base) of society to manifest in media structures (super structure) that produce culture which is consonant with capitalism.

9. In Marx's (1904 [1859]: 11) words: 'The mode of production in material life determines the general character of the social, political and spiritual processes of life.' Thus, this discourse includes a structural-functional component which can also be transferred to the media. In *The German Ideology*, Marx and Engels (1977 [1932]: 64) declared:

> The ideas of the ruling class are in every epoch the ruling ideas [...]. The class which has the means of material production at its disposal, has control at the same time over the means of mental production, so that thereby, generally speaking, the ideas of those that lack the means of production are subject to it.

Marx and Engels suggested that because the news media was controlled, owned and funded by the ruling class they reproduced their ideology thus maintaining ruling class domination and exploitation. And it was claimed by later political economy theorists that the ruling class maintained its leeway over media content production despite the formal autonomy the media had obtained (Curran, Gurevitch and Woollacott 1982: 20–22, 28; Mullen and Klaehn 2010: 216).

10. In Hall's conceptualisation, ideology constitutes of the practices, values and meanings of a set of people who constitute a class (1977: 331–332). The ideological effect refers to the news media's overrepresentation of one class's ideology at the expense of others via systematic inclusions and exclusions (*ibid*: 346). According to Hall, the media shapes a 'structured consensus, constructed in the unequal exchange between the unequal masses and the great organising centres of power and opinion' (*ibid*: 342). Hall defines the process of assigning meaning to events as '*encoding*' claiming that journalists choose 'strikingly selective' configurations 'drawn from an extremely limited [and naturalised] *repertoire* [emphasis in the original]' (*ibid*: 342).

11. Louis Althusser takes a similar perspective, arguing that ideological state apparatuses which operate outside of the economic sphere (in the super structure) – the religious, educational, family, legal, political, trade-union, communications and cultural – subject individuals to ideology and guarantee the reproduction of 'capitalist relations of exploitation' (Althusser 1971: 154; see also Hall 1977: 335–336).

12. According to Miller and Dinan (2008: 5–6):

> It is not that the public or decision makers actively agree and support the policy ideas promulgated by business lobbies and the corporations. What is critical is that they do not actively and aggressively oppose them. This is what makes the melding of ideology and action so powerful. In other words the aim and effect of much corporate propaganda is the manufacture of compliance.

13. The propaganda model combines economic ('filters' 1–4) and ideological elements ('filter' 5), which had been identified in previous research and in the discussion described above (see Herman and Chomsky 2008: 1–29). Miliband (1987 [1973]: 203) suggests comparable 'influences' on the news media: (1) ownership, control and concentration, (2) advertising, (3) public relation, (4) pressure from the state system and, (5) ideological tendencies (*ibid*: 203–210). The propaganda model differs from Marxist approaches in that it is based on industrial organisation and functional analyses. Hence, the model puts strong emphasis on assessing how corporate control and market forces shape the

respective behaviour of owners, managers, journalists and external actors/institutions that provide information to or put pressure on the media (Herman 1981, 1986, 2000; Herman and Chomsky 1988a, b, 2008). Merton (1968: 104) identified the following elements, among others, to which functional analysis relates: institutional pattern, social structures and devices for social control. Functional analysis aims at attributing functions and dysfunctions (consequences) to the societal elements described above (*ibid*: 104–105). Similarly, the model emphasises dysfunctions (production of propaganda) and relates them to the structures of the media and their environment. Herman and Chomsky do not make references to Merton's work. Elsewhere, however, Herman (1999: 57) emphasises that the propaganda model 'is in the tradition of the Breed approach' particularly his study 'Social Control in the Newsroom: A Functional Analysis' (Breed 1955). Breed, in turn, acknowledges that his study is based on Merton's functional analysis (*ibid*: 328). Thus, it should be noted that PM is rooted in functional analysis and political economy.

14. Although media effects are sometimes inferred (see Herman and Chomsky 2008: 286; Lazarsfeld and Merton 1957 [1948]: 457–458).

15. The earliest gatekeeper study in the communication field was conducted by White (1950) who derived the concept from Kurt Lewin (see White 1950).

16. Gatekeeper studies apply one or more of the following five levels of analysis, each of which may represent a gate through which news material must pass before it gets published: (1) the individual communication worker (e.g. attitudes), (2) the routines or practices of communication work (such as deadlines or the inverted pyramid), (3) the organisational level (ownership pattern or other variables), (4) the social and institutional level (advertising, interest groups or the news media), and/or (5) the social system level (ideology and culture) (Shoemaker 1991: 32).

17. There were also dissimilarities: for instance, in the later study Mr. Gates picked different types of stories which were 'better balanced' than in 1949 (Snider 1967: 427).

18. Breed (1955) and White's (1950) studies are regarded as early classics in the field (see Reese and Ballinger 2001: 641–642).

19. Herman (1999: 58) stresses that professional journalism has often only been able to meet the 'objectivity' criteria in form but not in substance. Journalists tend to cite 'two sides of a story' but give 'a preferred side prominence and space for a full argument and allowing the other side only a feeble and empty response'. Journalists also quote officials without providing the context necessary for a recipient to 'evaluate the truthfulness of the statement' (*ibid*). Such 'objectivity', Herman (*ibid*) concludes, 'facilitates news management by the government and other powerful sources'.

20. It should be noted that Gans seems generally not to agree with radical critiques which he sees as 'unrealistic' because they assume journalists could 'stand outside nation and society, free to report news, raise issues, and present ideas without limit' (Gans 1980: 278). According to Gans, such independence is impossible because journalists 'cannot ignore [...] the existence of pressure and of the power behind it. Were they able to do so, they would be all-powerful themselves and unaccountable to anyone' (*ibid*). Gans also stressed that news performance was related to large audience interests (*ibid*). However, Gans failed to acknowledge that the news media is not equally accountable to anyone in society and

that they do not necessarily relate to majority audience interests (see my discussion in the next two sections). For a critique of the gatekeeper studies see Herman (1986).

21. Bennett's work particularly build's on Sigal's (1973) foundational study (see Livingston and Bennett 2003: 365).

22. Scholars have used three main applications of the 'indexing' concept:
    (1) To identify if the parameters (i.e. the breadth) of debate is less or equal to official debate.
    (2) To identify if the proportion of pro- and anti-administration voices in the news reflects similar proportions among public officials.
    (3) A combination of (1) and (2) (Althaus *et al.* 1996: 408).

23. Hallin writes that government and other officials became the 'primary source of information' (1989: 69) making it 'easy for officials to manipulate day-today-news content' (*ibid*: 25). Hallin identified 'the ideology of the Cold War' (*ibid*: 110) as the second cause for deferential media performance. According to Hallin, Cold War ideology fostered a 'tight consensus on the nature of world politics and the American role in it' which could assimilate new 'political phenomena' (*ibid*: 48–49). Thus, news coverage was framed in accordance with American interests which were officially defended elsewhere against so called Communist expansions, while crucial facts about the nature of conflicts, 'that might have provoked deeper doubts' (*ibid*: 58) about such rationales, remained uncovered. As a result, Hallin (*ibid*: 110) notes, this kind of framing made deviance or 'fundamental questioning of American policy essentially unthinkable'. Consequently, Hallin (*ibid*: 116–117) conceptualised three 'journalistic standards': the *Sphere of Consensus* representing consensus values, the *Sphere of Legitimate Controversy* representing objectivity or legislative elite debates, and the *Sphere of Deviance* representing values which the establishment and journalists reject. This model defines the range of political debate. Since deviance is under constraint, challenges to the political consensus or the sphere of legitimate debate are rare. The effect is that criticism is mostly about tactics and not principles whereas media is reflecting elite opinions. Furthermore, American (Western) motives are characterised as benign and honourable while motives of the enemy are stigmatised and essentially evil (*ibid*: 28, 52–53, 208).

24. A general problem of the 'indexing' studies has been that the identified relationship between elite and media discourses is based on a 'qualitative observation, the dependence of reporters on sources' and it has not been able to establish causal relationships (Zaller and Chiu 1996: 392). Thus, more research into 'indexing' processes is needed to establish the relation between media and elite discourses. There are also exceptions: 'indexing' applies to major elite media whereas smaller, special interest media might deviate from this norm. Media also tend to choose rather influential officials at the expense of others who are not 'indexed'. Outside voices are occasionally allowed access to the media, thus disproving the norm, although often in negative interpretative contexts. Furthermore, 'indexing' might not apply to special events such as elections and there are instances when it is completely irrelevant (Bennett 1990: 106–107; see Gitlin 1980 for outside voices).

25. The *Mobro* garbage barge left from Islip, New York, in March 1987 for cargo disposal after the Islip, New York Town Board disallowed waste disposal in local facilities whose capacities were exhausted. The *Mobro* became a symbol of a garbage crisis when it returned three months later after a 5,000-miles journey during which it was refused permission to

dispose its garbage in five states and two foreign countries (see Bennett and Lawrence 1995: 28–29).

26. Rodney King was beaten by police officers after a car chase. The incident was filmed by a bystander. The pictures were broadcasted by a range of media inciting outrage and social tensions.

27. According to a Pew survey, in 2010, 80 per cent of online traffic to news and information sites was concentrated on 7 per cent of sites. 67 per cent of these top sites were under control of traditional news organisations, 13 per cent were content gathering sites, and only 14 per cent were online only operations (see Curran 2012: 19). A study on German online news providers found that 77.1 per cent of all journalistic online suppliers were offshoots from traditional media organisations (Neuberger, Nuernbergk and Rischke 2009: 222). Only 8 per cent constituted journalistic online-only operations (*ibid*). If online visits are considered, in 2010/11 the world's top ten sites included only one online only operation (Curran 2012: 19). Similarly, in the US, there was only one online operation in the top ten whereas in Britain the top ten included only television and newspaper offshoots as well as content aggregators (*ibid*). A study by Hindman (2009: 17) concludes that 'online audience concentration equals or exceeds that found in most traditional media'.

28. James Winter (2007: 45–46) extracted extensive evidence for direct management influences in newsrooms from the sociology of news literature. Examples of direct management control are: 'veto over' stories that 'journalists themselves initiate', dropping of reports or framing of stories 'within a particular angle or perspective', suggesting of 'sources or contacts to interview', proofreading and major editing 'which may mean significant additional changes', deciding headlines as well as assigning journalists to rewrite their stories or removing the journalist's by-line if they object to changes and then printing a version of the story that fits with the management's agenda.

29. There are two forms of commercial news-penetration by advertisers: first, the direct penetration of adverts into media content because of collusion and, second, the media's positive reporting on their own ventures and investments. Besides, businesses might threaten to cancel advertising if a newspaper's political line is violating their interests (Franklin 1997: 94; McChesney 2003: 310–311).

30. Merit goods are goods desired by society, for example diverse political news. Ideally, in a market system, price and competition should adapt the products on offer to consumer preferences. Because of the novelty of news, consumers lack the necessary information and/or knowledge to evaluate the quality of news before consumption. That is why, in theory, the market system cannot enable a sufficient production and consumption of merit goods (see Kiefer 2001: 136–139).

31. Perfect competition refers to a market situation in which many sellers offer a good or service which is homogeneous (i.e. exactly the same) without any firm dominating the market. Furthermore, no barriers (i.e. restricted spectrum or high start-up costs) to enter the market exist (Albarran 2002: 34–35; Doyle 2002a: 8).

32. The dismantlement of trade restrictions (i.e. deregulation), the privatisation of formerly public news media (i.e. commercialisation), and the digital integration of communication technologies (i.e. convergence) encouraged internationalisation of media products

and global concentration (see Doyle 2002b: 2–3). Losses of advertising revenue to online based non-media firms have increased oligopolistic competition leading to mergers and acquisitions (i.e. ownership concentration) (see Röper 2002: 478–479; also Doyle 2002a: 150–152). This process has been accompanied by a decline in press circulation in the US and most European countries. Resulting economic pressures have been countered by severe cost cutting and the downsizing of news rooms (i.e. journalistic concentration) (Franklin 1997; Röper 2010: 218–220). Such concentration processes have always been characteristic of the modern capitalist system and the media operating in it (see Habermas 1989: 186–187). For instance, concentration in the global capitalist system has constantly increased in the 20th century, particularly since the 1970s when neoliberal policies were instituted (see Foster, McChesney and Jonna 2011).

33. Scholars have discussed the effects of horizontal (e.g. Heinrich 2002; Kruse 1996; Leidinger 2003), vertical (e.g. Heinrich 2001, 2002; Leidinger 2003), diagonal (or cross-media) (e.g. Bender 1997; Heinrich 2001; Kruse 1996; Leidinger 2003; Trettenbein 1994), and multi-sectoral (Leidinger 2003) concentration.

34. In a study summarising 17 content analyses of Canadian newspapers by the Canadian media monitoring project NewsWatch, Robert A. Hackett and Scott Uzelman came to 'broadly compatible findings' (2003: 342) suggesting the press's tendency to favour corporate interests. The researchers concluded that newspapers': '[…] editorial stance (ultimately determined by ownership) influence their news coverage; and that double standards or patterns of omission related to politics and class tend broadly to be consistent with what one would expect from corporate and commercial pressures' (*ibid*).

35. 'Indexing' can be associated with the work of Hallin, Entman, Wolfsfeld, Mermin, Zaller and Chiu and various other authors (for an overview see Herring and Robinson 2003; Zollmann 2009).

36. Resources include monetary funds for election campaigns, systems to acquire and analyse information, policy planning networks, committees for legal and other consultations (e.g. public relations, political advisors) and management tools to optimise diverse sets of interests and store important information (Ferguson 1995: 29–30, 381–384).

37. The Washington Consensus includes the implementation of neo-liberal policies under auspices of the International Monetary Fund (IMF) and the World Bank. The peace dividend refers to a transfer of public spending from the 'defense' to other societal sectors. Debate on this rose suddenly following the collapse of the Berlin Wall in 1989.

38. This is supported by opinion studies: For example, polls in the US and UK show that public opinion on many domestic policy issues is 'far to the left of the mainstream pro-corporate parties' (Miller and Dinan 2010: 3). Page (1996: 118–119) argues on US foreign policy issues Americans significantly disagree with political officials, experts and media personnel on a 'wide range of issues'. Page (*ibid*) further writes US citizens disagree with 'foreign-policy elites about the use of force abroad, about economic or (especially) military aid or arms sales, and about free-trade agreements'. Moreover, Page (*ibid*: 119) suggests that if there are bipartisan agreements on foreign policy issues 'public deliberation in the mass media tends to be severely restricted'. Finally, Page (*ibid*) sees similar elite-mass gaps in regard to domestic issues in the US.

39. Wolfsfeld provides the Palestinian Intifada as an exemplary case in which the news media became advocates for the weak (1997: 203). Wolfsfeld (*ibid*) explains the media's 'higher level of independence' as follows:

> The Israeli attempts at official control were largely unsuccessful; the press' need for official information was low; and almost all of the national and international news media had sufficient organisation and resources to cover the conflict. (*ibid*)

Wolfsfeld thereby neglects Western elite disagreements with Israeli policies. McNair (1991: 143) identified 'changing attitudes towards Israeli policy amongst primary definers in the west [sic]'. 'As the Intifada heightened', McNair (*ibid*) further argues, 'many western [sic] governments […] made public statements highly critical of Israel'. Could it have been the case that critical coverage was not a result of media independence but of changes in Western elite attitudes which were, as usually, 'indexed' by the media? Wolfsfeld seemingly neglected this issue.

40. Entman's chapter on independent framing and the increase of media power since the Cold War almost exclusively cites tactical/procedural government criticism as evidence for media independence (see 2004: 95–104). But it has been well established that procedural criticism can be an element of hegemonic coverage (see Althaus 2003: 383; Herman and Chomsky 2008: 159–160; Hertog 2000; Mermin 1999). I believe that an increase in procedural criticism does not constitute convincing evidence for an increase in media openness and independency. After all, it can also be argued that the end of the Cold War increased policy options for the West thus making procedural criticism an important necessity in elite decision-making processes.

Chapter 3

1. For a description see Herman and Chomsky (2008: 2–29). The propaganda model relates a set of five interacting 'filters' (independent variables) to the properties of media content (dependent variables) (see Thompson 2009: 76). It is well established in the literature that these 'filters' are constraining elements during journalistic news selection and production processes (see e.g. Herman and Chomsky 2008; Sparks 2007; Thompson 2009). As a result, the model postulates a propaganda function of the media and predicts media content to be aligned with state-corporate elite interests (Herman and Chomsky 2008). Yet, it is contested whether the five 'filters' are always determining (see e.g. Hallin 1994; Robinson *et al.* 2010; Sparks 2007) and the model does not consider intervening variables. To compensate for this shortfall, it has also to be tested whether intervening variables such as societal interests, journalistic professionalism, uncontrolled events/technology, and country specifics are co-determinants of media performance.

2. Herman and Chomsky also point to the media's use of experts who could provide 'dissident views' but, for various reasons, 'regularly echo the official' line (2008: 22–23).

3. The following elaboration discusses the propaganda model's 'first-order predictions about how the media function' (Chomsky 1989: 153). The model also makes 'second-order

predictions about how media performance will be discussed and evaluated' and 'third-order predictions about the reactions to studies of media performance' (*ibid*: 153). The latter two sets of predictions are not relevant for this study and will thus not be discussed.

4. Herman and Chomsky stress that their model does not suggest total closure and that the quantity and quality of coverage on human rights violations by a given country have to be balanced with the country's (1) baseline coverage, (2) magnitude of violations (i.e. quantity and quality of human rights abuses as well as violations of international norms and treaties etc.), and (3) level of favourable reporting. Israel's human rights violations, for example, have been covered by the media and contenders might see this as evidence for media openness. But after including the above-mentioned factors, it becomes clear that, for several reasons, coverage of Israel was biased: (1) Israel receives a substantial amount of coverage in the media of which only a fraction focuses on its human rights abuses. (2) The extent to which Israeli abuses were reported does not reflect their actual magnitude and Israel's human rights violations far exceed those by the Palestinians. (3) Israel receives more positive coverage than its Palestinian counterparts. Thus, it could be argued that Israeli abuses have been downplayed and that the Palestinians have been the unworthy victims in media coverage of this conflict (for a methodical overview see Chomsky 1989: 151–152; for coverage on the Israel-Palestine conflict see Friel and Falk 2007b; Philo and Berry 2011; for an assessment of the amount of Israeli and Palestinian human rights violations as reported by mainstream human rights organisations see Finkelstein 2005).

5. Sampson cites Lord Browne, BP chief executive, saying in October 2002: 'We would like to make sure, if Iraq changes its regime, that there should be a level playing-field for the selection of oil companies to go in there.' (cited in Sampson 2002: 17)

6. Herman and Chomsky (2008: 281) refer of course to US coverage of the Watergate scandal. Nonetheless, I believe the analogy with the Suez Crisis and Iraq to be accurate.

7. Aside from the Suez Crisis of which I have not obtained a study of US coverage.

8. Aside from rhetoric, the German government has tacitly approved the Iraq War and subsequent occupation: Germany provided significant logistic support to US troops, 80 per cent of all military transports during the Iraq War came from German airports and bases which were secured by German personnel. Furthermore, German intelligence cooperated with the US military and the DIA in Iraq (Högemann 2004; Leyendecker and Krach 2010). After the Iraq War, the German military trained Iraqi police and military forces (see *ibid*). Hence, a decision of the federal administration court in Leipzig in 2005 concluded the German government was not 'neutral' during the Iraq War (Triebe 2005).

Chapter 4

1. Generally, the use of 'paired examples' rests on analogies and constitutes a 'classic method of analysis' (Herman and Chomsky 2009: 16).

2. Many content studies rely on face validity which encapsulates 'the correspondence between investigators' definitions of concepts and their definitions of the categories that

measured them' (Weber 1990: 18; see also Neuendorf 2002: 113–115). The problem with this is that an invalid concept might be proven right because a content analysis is reliable in terms of replicability. More solid validity is obtained when applying an external criterion such as construct validity (Weber 1990: 19). According to Weber (*ibid*) 'a measure has *construct validity* [emphasis in the original] to the extent that it is correlated with some other measure of the same construct'. One way of assessing construct validity is to test 'whether the measures relate as they theoretically should with other variables' (Neuendorf 2002: 117).

3. 10 per cent of the items from the Fallujah 1, Fallujah 2 and Račak data sets were coded by second raters and reliability figures were acceptable. I coded the data together with two further raters, one English coder for the US and UK newspapers and one German coder for the German newspapers. 10 per cent of the articles published on the Fallujah 1, Fallujah 2 and Račak incidents were selected with a random generator. The following formula, derived from Holsti (1969: 140), was used: CR = 2M/(N1 + N2). M is the amount of coding decisions on which two coders are in agreement, and N1 and N2 describe the number of coding decisions administered by raters 1 and 2 (*ibid*). For the US/UK newspapers the aggregated rating was as follows: indignation [.81]. For the German newspapers the rating was: indignation [.97] (for reliability testing see Neuendorf 2002: 143, 158–159).

4. For applications in media studies see e.g. Entman (2004); Gitlin (1980); Hammond (2007); Iyengar and Simon (1994); Norris (1995).

5. The OSCE had placed international monitors in Kosovo the so called Kosovo Verification Mission (KVM).

6. Kuperman writes that 'in all of eastern Libya, including Benghazi, medics estimated that at least 400 people had been killed by March 9, though the basis of this estimate is unknown' (2013: 119).

7. The first Fallujah incident differed from the one in November in that it was smaller in scope with less impact on the city. It also had the properties of an uncontrolled event: it featured a range of sudden incidents and coincided with a Shiite uprising. Moreover, an Al-Jazeera camera team stationed in Fallujah daily broadcast pictures from the city enabling technologically driven coverage potentially shaping news icons. More generally, press coverage was less restricted than during November in regard to official propaganda activities such as access regulations, the use of embedded reporters and news management. There was also an element of policy uncertainty as the uprisings took the US/Coalition administration by surprise.

8. US/Coalition forces taking part in the assault on Fallujah consisted of various contingents: US army, US Marines, and Iraqi army (Lange 2006: 12).

9. This is important because a critical approach to press analysis is not so much interested in differences within the spectrum of debate (for example between 'left-' and 'right-wing' extremes) but rather in assessing the nature of the most comprehensive and critical coverage in the mainstream (the 'left-liberal' extreme or margin).

10. According to a 1998 Pew Research Center survey: '96 per cent of executive branch officials and 67 per cent of members of Congress read the *Washington Post* regularly' and 'large majorities also read the [...] the *New York Times*' (see Pew Research Center for the People & the Press (1998) 'Public Appetite For Government Misjudged', 17 April, p. 10).

Chapter 5

1. I use the term Western loosely to describe the US dominated trans-Atlantic bloc comprising the hegemonic states US, UK, and Germany at its core but also featuring other European powers like France, Italy, Belgium and the Netherlands (*cf.* Carroll 2010).

2. For the sources of the respective casualty figures see the sections under each case study heading in Chapter 5 further below as well as the section outlining the case selection in Chapter 4.

3. For the sources of the respective casualty figures see the sections under each case study heading in Chapter 5 further below as well as the section outlining the case selection in Chapter 4.

4. For further evidence in this regard see also Chomsky (2003: 72–74).

5. On 18 January 1999, the then-Secretary of State for Foreign and Commonwealth Affairs, Robin Cook, said in the House of Commons that the KLA had even killed more people than Serbian forces: 'On its part, the Kosovo Liberation Army has committed more breaches of the ceasefire, and until this weekend was responsible for more deaths than the security forces' (Parliament 1999).

6. An exception was the *Frankfurter Rundschau* which only carried one item that was classified as Military policy. This had partly to do with the search term (Bengasi) that was used. If the search term Libya was applied, other news items could be identified that carried statements classified as Military policy.

7. The Website Examiner.com has seemingly closed down. The articel can still be found on the Wikileaks Supporters Forum, see: http://www.wikileaks-forum.com/global-intelligence-files/161/us-helping-to-train-and-arm-islamic-mercenaries-to-fight-in-syria/10595/

8. It is often stated that the city is about 3×3.5 kilometres in square. For comparable estimates on the size of Fallujah, see Camp (2009: 13), GlobalSecurity.org (n.d.b) and Taheri (2004).

9. The CPA came into power under the implementation of UN Resolution 1483 on 22 May 2003 and was effectively run by the US Department of Defense (see Allawi 2007: 105–106). On 28 June 2004, the Iraqi Interim Government (IIG) and its head, Prime Minister Ayad Allawi, were instituted as an Iraqi transitional government. The IIG formally inherited the government powers from the US-run occupation administration, the CPA, and was tasked with the mandate to pave the way for nationwide elections scheduled for January 2005 (Filkins 2004e: 1). The IGC was dissolved. Furthermore, Iraq's new status had already been established by UN-Resolution 1546, codified on 8 June 2004. The resolution reaffirmed the sovereignty of Iraq. Furthermore, its annex included letters by Ayad Allawi and the US Secretary of State, Colin L. Powell. In the writing of the letters, Allawi requested and Powell approved the maintenance of Multi-National Forces (MNF) in Iraq (United Nations Security Council 2004).

10. According to Anthony Cordesman (2004: 2), the resistance movement was 'largely domestic in character' and 'had significant popular support'. In 2003 and 2004, reports pointed to the near absence of al-Qaida or foreign-Arab fighters in Iraq. Furthermore, the terrorist element of the resistance was clearly in the minority. This was indicated by the chosen targets: about 75 per cent of resistance attacks between September 2003 and

October 2004 were directed against Coalition forces, only 4 per cent targeted civilians (numbers derived from Cordesman 2004: 4). In July 2004, Brig. Gen. John Custer, the director of intelligence for Central Command, was cited by ABC News saying it was a 'big myth' that thousands of foreign fighters were in Iraq and he did not 'see a lot of evidence in Iraq of al Qaeda' (cited in ABC News 2004). Already in June 2004, Ahmed Hashim (2004) identified the following composition of the rebels:

> The insurgency does not have the support of all Sunni Arabs, but its range encompasses all classes, both urban and rural. Its ranks include students, intellectuals, former soldiers, tribal youths, farmers, and Islamists. It also has the tacit support of many within the Sunni Arab community. While many Sunni Arabs may not actively support the insurgents, they are not reticent about expressing their admiration for insurgents' activities. [...]

> While this analysis has detailed much of the Sunni components of the insurgency, it is important to keep in mind the rise of the Shi'a resistance as well. By the end of March 2004 – and to everyone's surprise – significant elements of the Shi'a community rose in open rebellion against the coalition, when the firebrand cleric Muqtada al-Sadr unleashed his so-called Mahdi's Army against the coalition.

11. US/Coalition forces taking part in the assault on Fallujah consisted of various contingents: US army, US Marines, and Iraqi army (Lange 2006: 12).

12. A study on deaths from war injuries in 13 countries over 50 years compared deaths from databases of passive reports such as those using surveillance (mostly media reports but also health service statistics and partial civil registration reports) with nationally representative surveys and found that passive reports covered on average 30 per cent of the number of deaths estimated by surveys (Obermeyer, Murray and Gakidou 2008). Particularly during periods of intense conflict, passive reports are faulty. For instance, between 1960–1990 passive reports were only able to report 5 per cent of the deaths occurring in Guatemala during times of high violence. In years of low violence, passive reports detected about 50 per cent of deaths in Guatemala (see Burnham *et al.* 2006: 1426). 2004 constituted a period of relatively high violence in Iraq suggesting that passive reports likely detected lower than 50 per cent of violent deaths (see *ibid*: 1426–1427). That is why the IBC database, which is certainly useful, undercounts deaths by comparable margins.

13. For the UK press a LexisNexis search was conducted with the search terms [Fallujah or Falluja and 550, or 700 or 800 or 6,000 or 6000] during the period [08/11/2004-31/12/2005]. For the US and German press similar searches were conducted with the Factiva database. Data from the *Frankfurter Allgemeine Zeitung* was obtained through the FAZ Archive.

14. Mike Marqusee (2005: 32), co-founder of Iraq Occupation Focus, published a comment in the *Guardian* on 10 November 2005 (*ibid*). According to Marqusee (*ibid*) 'Iraqi NGOs and medical workers estimate between 4,000 and 6,000 dead [in Fallujah], mostly civilians'. This was, as Marqusee further highlighted, 'a proportionately higher death rate than in Coventry and London during the blitz'. On 18 December 2005, *The Times*'s Jaber (2005: 22) reported the same estimate with reference to the SCHRD. Already on 8 November

2005, the *Guardian* had published a letter by peace activists Milan Rai and Emma Sangster (2005: 35) who called attention to the 'more than 700 bodies' which 'would later be recovered from the rubble [in Fallujah], including more than 550 women and children'.

15. There were articles discussing the Geneva Conventions albeit only in relation to the mosque shooting (see e.g. Bellamy 2004) and there were articles featuring further indignant statements for example by Louise Arbour (see e.g. Buncombe 2004a).

Chapter 6

1. For the sources of the respective casualty figures see the sections under each case study heading in Chapter 5 as well as the section outlining the case selection in Chapter 4.

2. The EWG, which estimated the whole population at 300,000, additionally identified about 250,000 IDPs from Fallujah in various Iraqi cities (see EWG 2004a: 1).

3. Consecutive IRIN reports suggested a possible higher figure: On 10 November, IRIN claimed that 'more than two-thirds' of the population had left (IRIN 2004b). On 12 November, the organisation referred to reports which 'indicate that at least 50 percent of the local population of nearly 300,000 people have fled the city' (IRIN 2004c).

4. It seems also noteworthy that news items in the *New York Times* and *Frankfurter Allgemeine* referred to Casey's telecast conference without mentioning his statements on civilians (see Filkins and Glanz 2004a: 1; Hermann 2004a: 1; Jehl and Shanker 2004: 11; Schmitt and Worth 2004: 1).

5. This section drew from the approach of Finkelstein (2011: 55–86) when assessing Israel's military strategy during Israel's Gaza invasion in December 2008.

6. This is an inconclusive list based on the facts provided by the newspapers under review. The US/Coalition used a broader range of weaponry, ordnance and technology (for a detailed overview see Camp 2009).

7. Military historians have described a similar 'battle' plan: a frontal attack with six battalions entering Fallujah from the north then pushing southwards on a three mile line accompanied by tank platoons as well as heavy artillery and air support (see Camp 2009: 128; West 2005: 268).

8. West provides a figure of 70 US casualties in November (2005: 316).

9. The First Battle of Grozny, in January 1995, might be used as a comparison to Fallujah (see Kelly 2004). 800 soldiers of the 131st brigade of the Russian army were killed in three days of fighting with the Chechens. The total toll of the battle was relatively even with 2,805 Russians and 3,500 Chechen combatants dead (see Vautravers 2010: 446).

10. Jonathan F. Keiler (2005) claims the US casualty ratio in Fallujah does not significantly differ from other battles if wounded casualties are included. Keiler provides an extrapolated number of 1,200 wounded US soldiers in Fallujah. Furthermore, Keiler argues the active US element in Fallujah consisted of 6,000 soldiers (*ibid*). According to this estimate, about 1/5th of the attacking force were casualties which would indeed evidence a rather usual pattern. But most estimates put the number of wounded soldiers in Fallujah much lower: West (2005: 316) provides a figure of 609, Lange (2006: 13) suggests 450, and Camp (2009: 299) gives an estimate of 535 wounded, of which 309 returned to duty.

This evidence suggests a ratio of about 1/10. And if soldiers who returned to duty were not included, the ratio would be about 1/20. Moreover, the active element among US troops was likely higher, between 10,000 and 15,000, thus further increasing the ratio (for the numbers see Evans 2004a: 8; Hider 2004a: 30). It should also be noted that the resistance casualty figure could have been deflated because it was based on incomplete casualty estimates by the US/Coalition (see Elworthy 2007: 21 and sources cited above). For instance, the *Daily Telegraph's* Harnden (2004c: 11) quoted Specialist Nick Price of Legion platoon as saying: 'It's weird how we killed so many people last night but haven't seen any bodies today' [...]. 'Where are they?' The resistance might have attempted to quickly bury its fighters according to Muslim customs. Casualties could also have been submerged under the rubble. This would suggest a higher figure and further increase the evidence for imbalances in fighting. On the other hand, the 1,200 count could also have been inflated because it might have included civilians. There has not yet been an independent investigation in Fallujah and resistance casualty figures thus remain contested (see Zollmann 2010a).

11. Article 3 (a) annexed to UN General Assembly Resolution 3314 states that 'the invasion or attack by the armed forces of a State against the territory of another State, or any military occupation, however temporary, resulting from such invasion or attack [...]' qualifies as an act of aggression (United Nations General Assembly 1974: 143). It might be worth mentioning that according to a considerable amount of legal scholars the Iraq War constituted a violation of international law (see Mandel 2005: 33; also Ambos and Arnold 2003).

12. For all the relevant texts of the Geneva Conventions referred here and subsequently see International Committee of the Red Cross (2005).

13. In the *Guardian*, McCarthy argued that 'although Fallujah general hospital' was 'protected under the Geneva Conventions, it was deemed legitimate by US commanders because they said it had been taken over by insurgents' (McCarthy 2004b: 3).

BIBLIOGRAPHY

Primary References

AFP/AP/TAZ (2004) Erbitterte Kämpfe im Irak. *die tageszeitung*, 15 November, p. 1.

AFP/DPA/TAZ (2004) Ein Erster Hilfskonvoi für Falludscha. *die tageszeitung*, 15 November, p. 9.

al-Badrani, Fadel (2004a) Hidden Tragedies of Helpless City. *The Guardian*, 10 November, p. 4.

al-Badrani, Fadel (2004b) The Day the Americans Came to Town. *The Independent*, 10 November, pp. 1, 5.

Alexander, Dietrich and Hackensberger, Alfred (2011) Gaddafis Makabrer Totentanz in Tripolis. *Die Welt*, 23 February, p. 7.

Ambos, Kai (2011) Gaddafis Verbrechen – Ein Fall für Den Haag. *Süddeutsche Zeitung*, 28 February, p. 2.

Anwar, Omar (2004) Civilians Suffering Amid Ruins of Battle. *The Daily Telegraph*, 15 November, p. 13.

AP (2004a) Falludscha und die Chronik Einer Krise. *Die Welt*, 9 November, p. 10.

AP (2004b) TV Report Says Marine Shot Prisoner. *New York Times*, 16 November, p. 12.

AP (2004c) Al-Sarkawi Ruft Angeblich zum Durchhalten auf. *Süddeutsche Zeitung*, 13 November, p. 11.

AP/DPA/TAZ (2004) Moschee Gestürmt. *die tageszeitung*, 20 November, p. 9.

AP/Reuters (2004) Noch vor Ende aller Kämpfe. *Frankfurter Allgemeine Sonntagszeitung*, 14 November, p. 2.

Ashdown, Paddy (1999) We Cannot Allow the Serbs to Attempt a 'Final Solution'. *The Independent*, 20 January, p. 4.

Bahrampour, Tara (2011) Libyan Americans Turn Worries into Protests. *Washington Post*, 23 February, p. A 9.

Beach, Alastair (2013) US 'Refuses to Take Sides' in Egyptian Political Turmoil. *The Independent*, 16 July, pp. 26, 27.

Beaumont, Peter (2004) Iraqi Leaders Say the Operation to Clear Falluja of Insurgents is Almost Complete. *The Observer*, 14 November, p. 15.

Beeston, Richard (2004) Marines Storm Fallujah as Street Fighting Begins. *The Times*, 9 November, p. 1.

Bellamy, Chris (2004) The Americans are Sowing Dragons' Teeth in Iraq. *The Independent*, 17 November, p. 31.

Bickel, Markus (2013) Aussöhnung in Weiter Ferne. *Frankfurter Allgemeine Zeitung*, 13 July, p. 5.

Bird, Chris (1999a) The Butchers Came at Dawn to Slay Village. *The Observer*, 17 January, p. 1.

Bird, Chris (1999b) Cook Call for War Crimes Inquiry. *The Guardian*, 18 January, p. 1.

Bird, Chris (1999c) Kosovo Massacre 'Was Ordered'. *The Guardian*, 29 January, p. 1.

Black, Ian (2011a) Gaddafi Urges Violent Showdown. *The Guardian*, 23 February, p. 1.

Black, Ian (2011b) Libya Defiant as Hundreds Feared Dead. *The Guardian*, 21 February, p. 1.

Black, Ian (2012a) As Annan Plan Falters, Russia Remains Key. *The Guardian*, 8 June, p. 21.

Black, Ian (2012b) Assad Knows that He Can Kill Civilians with Virtual Impunity. *The Guardian*, 29 May, p. 16.

Black, Ian (2012c) Syrian Regime Accused of Killing 100 Villagers in New Massacre. *The Guardian*, 7 June, p. 2.

Black, Ian and Borger, Julian (2011) What Next for a Divided Land Riven by Bloodshed? *The Guardian*, 1 March, p. 16.

Black, Ian and Elder, Miriam (2012) Syria: Annan Arrives for Talks as Russia Blames Both Sides for the Killings. *The Guardian*, 29 May, p. 16.

Black, Ian and Kingsley, Patrick (2013a) Country Braced for More Violence after 'Massacre' of Morsi Faithful. *The Guardian*, 9 July, p. 6.

Black, Ian and Kingsley, Patrick (2013b) Tension High as Egypt Gets a New PM. *The Guardian*, 10 July, p. 12.

Blair, David (2012a) Despite the Houla Atrocity, President Assad's Position Remains Firm and Regime Change a Vain Hope. *The Daily Telegraph*, 29 May, p. 21.

Blair, David (2012b) Envoys Expelled As World Shuns Syria. *The Daily Telegraph*, 30 May, p. 17.

Borger, Julian (2004a) Violent US Gamble on Election Success. *The Guardian*, 9 November, p. 2.

Borger, Julian (2004b) Bush in Talks as Deaths and Criticism Mount. *The Guardian*, 8 April, p. 4.

Borger, Julian (2012) Assad Compares Syria Crackdown to Surgeons Saving Patients' Lives. *The Guardian*, 4 June, p. 12.

Borger, Julian, Wintour, Patrick and Chulov, Martin (2011) West Tightens Military Grip on Gaddafi. *The Guardian*, 1 March, p. 1.

Borgstede, Michael (2013) Ägypten Sucht Neuanfang. *Die Welt*, 18 July, p. 9.

Borgstede, Michael and Mülherr, Silke (2013) Ägypten in der Sackgasse. *Die Welt*, 11 July, p. 7.

Bremner, Charles (1999) Nato Threatens Belgrade over Kosovo Massacre. *The Times*, 18 January.

Brössler, Daniel (2012) Bundesregierung Weist Syrischen Botschafter Aus. *Süddeutsche Zeitung*, 30 May, p. 1.

Buncombe, Andrew (2004a) Red Cross: 900 [sic] Civilians Killed in Fallujah. *The Independent*, 17 November, p. 6.

Buncombe, Andrew (2004b) The Death Toll. *The Independent*, 15 November, p. 5.

Buncombe, Andrew (2004c) "This One's Faking He's Dead". *The Independent*, 16 November, p. 1.

Bunting, Madeleine (2004) Screams Will not be Heard. *The Guardian*, 8 November, p. 17.

Busse, Nikolas (2004) Berichte über 600 Getötete Aufständische in Falludscha. *Frankfurter Allgemeine Zeitung*, 12 November, p. 5.

Butler, Katherine (1999) Nato Forces Mobilise Against Serbs. *The Independent*, 21 January, p. 1.

Chulov, Martin (2012a) Massacre of the Children as Syrian Forces Hit Rebels. *The Observer*, 27 May, p. 1.

Chulov, Martin (2012b) Russia Votes against UN Call for Houla Inquiry. *The Guardian*, 2 June, p. 35.

Chulov, Martin (2013) Letter From the Streets: 'Everything Has Been Undone'. *The Guardian*, 10 July, p. 12.

Coates, Sam, Asthana, Anushka and Savage, Michael (2011) We Are Extremely Sorry Cameron Tells Britons Stranded in Libyan Hell. *The Times*, 25 February, pp. 10, 11.

Cockburn, Patrick (2004a) A Guided Missile, a Misguided War. *The Independent*, 8 April, p. 1.

Cockburn, Patrick (2004b) Bush's 'Vietnam': Apocalypse Now? *The Independent*, 11 April, p. 10.

Cockburn, Patrick (2004c) Guerrillas Gun Down US Helicopter But Ceasefire Takes Hold in Besieged Fallujah. *The Independent*, 12 April, p. 4.

Cockburn, Patrick (2004d) US Has Killed 280 in Fallujah this Week Says Hospital doctor. *The Independent*, 9 April, p. 5.

Cockburn, Patrick (2012a) I Fear this Terrible Massacre Will be the Beginning of a Long Civil War. *The Independent*, 27 May, pp. 36, 37.

Cockburn, Patrick (2012b) Assad Blamed for Massacre of the Innocents. *The Independent*, 27 May, pp. 2, 3.

Cockburn, Patrick (2012c) As the Bodies Continue to Mount Up, a People on Edge Prepare for Civil War. *The Independent*, 28 May, pp. 4, 5.

Cockburn, Patrick (2012d) Assad Regime Blames Murderous Onslaught on Houla's Rebel Army. *The Independent*, 28 May, pp. 4, 5.

Cockburn, Patrick (2012e) Most of Houla Victims Shot at Close Range. *The Independent*, 30 May, pp. 4, 5.

Cockburn, Patrick (2012f) Move Pushes Syria – and Russia – Further Out Into the Cold. *The Independent*, 30 May, pp. 4, 5.

Cockburn, Patrick (2013) Hidden Hand of Old Regime Did not Go Away. *The Independent*, 14 July, pp. 34, 35.

Cooper, Helene and Landler, Mark (2011) U.S. Announces Sanctions in Bid to Deter Libya. *New York Times*, 26 February, p. 1.

Cornwell, Rupert (1999) This Repellent War Crime. *The Independent*, 19 January, p. 1.

Cornwell, Rupert (2013) US Is Concerned – But Not Enough to Cut Aid. *The Independent*, 9 July, pp. 4, 5.

Decker, Erwin (2004) Störrisch in Falludscha. *Frankfurter Rundschau*, 10 November, p. 2.

DeYoung, Karen and Sly, Liz (2012) U.S. and Allies Expel Top Syrian Diplomats. *Washington Post*, 30 May, p. A 01.

DeYoung, Karen and Whitlock, Craig (2011) U.S. Defense Leaders Warn of Risks in Enforcing No-Fly Zone. *Washington Post*, 2 March, p. A 08.

Die Welt (2011) Gaddafi Will als Märtyrer Sterben. *Die Welt*, 23 February, p. 1.

DPA/AFP (2013) Gefährliche Spannung in Ägypten. *Frankfurter Rundschau*, 9 July, p. 10.

DPA/AP/RTR (2004a) Kein Ende der Gefechte in Falludscha. *Frankfurter Rundschau*, 16 November, p. 6.

DPA/AP/RTR (2004b) Irakhilfe "Fast Unmöglich". *Frankfurter Rundschau*, 18 November, p. 1.

DPA/Reuters/AP (2004) Angriff auf Sitz des Gouverneurs in Mossul. *Frankfurter Allgemeine Zeitung*, 19 November, p. 1.

Drozdiak, William (1999) Top NATO Generals to Warn Milosevic. *Washington Post*, 18 January, p. A 17.

El-Gawhary, Karim (2004) Der Sturmangriff auf Falludscha Beginnt. *die tageszeitung*, 9 November, p. 14.

Erlanger, Steven (1999) Force Possible If Milosevic Stays Defiant, West Warns. *New York Times*, 23 January, p. 4.

Evans, Michael (2004a) Attack is based on Shock and Awe but the City Must Be Left Standing. *The Times*, 9 November, p. 8.

Evans, Michael (2004b) Deadly Rockets Blast Way Through. *The Times*, 10 November, p. 9.

Evans, Michael (2004c) Deception and Mass Firepower Were Key to Success. *The Times*, 15 November, p. 34.

Evans, Michael (2004d) Task Needs 'Overwhelming Force'. *The Times*, 2 November, p. 36.

Evans, Michael and Webster, Philip (1999) Kosovo envoy ejected. *The Times*, 19 January.

Fadel, Leila (2011) Amid Lingering Support for Status Quo, a Burgeoning Call for Revolution. *Washington Post*, 23 February, p. A 01.

Fadel, Leila and Faiola, Anthony (2011) In Libya, Struggle to Gain Control of West Intensifies. *Washington Post*, 28 February, p. A 07.

Fadel, Leila and Raghavan, Sudarsan (2011) Gaddafi Loyalists Inundate Tripoli. *Washington Post*, 24 February, p. A 01.

Fahim, Kareem and Kirkpatrick, David D. (2011a) Libyan Rebels Said to Debate Seeking U.N. Airstrikes Against Qaddafi. *New York Times*, 2 March, p. 11.

Fahim, Kareem and Kirkpatrick, David D. (2011b) Qaddafi Orders Brutal Crackdown as Revolt Grows. *New York Times*, 23 February, p. 1.

Farrell, Stephen (2004) Anger and Anguish after 'One Lost Year'. *The Times*, 10 April, p. 16.

FAZ (2011) EU Kündigt Sanktionen Gegen Libyen an. *Frankfurter Allgemeine Zeitung*, 26 February, p. 1.

Fekeiki, Omar (2004a) For an Iraqi Soldier, the Battle in Fallujah is Personal. *Washington Post*, 15 November, p. A 18.

Fekeiki, Omar (2004b) For Fallujah Family, a Daring Escape. *Washington Post*, 19 November, p. A 20.

Festerling, Arnd (2004) Tödliche Logik. *Frankfurter Rundschau*, 17 November, p. 3.

Filkins, Dexter (2004a) Urban Warfare Deals Harsh Challenge to Troops. *New York Times*, 9 November, p. 1.

Filkins, Dexter (2004b) In Taking Falluja Mosque, Victory by the Inch. *New York Times*, 10 November, p. 1.

Filkins, Dexter (2004c) In Falluja, Young Marines Saw the Savagery of an Urban War. *New York Times*, 21 November, p. 1.

Filkins, Dexter (2004d) Disguised in Iraqi Uniforms, Rebels Kill a Marine. *New York Times*, 13 November, p. 1.

Filkins, Dexter and Glanz, James (2004a) U.S. Begins Main Assault in Falluja, Setting off Street Fighting. *New York Times*, 9 November, p. 1.

Filkins, Dexter and Glanz, James (2004b) Rebels Routed in Falluja. *New York Times*, 15 November, p. 1.

Filkins, Dexter and Worth, Robert F. (2004a) U.S.-Led Assault Marks Advances against Falluja. *New York Times*, 10 November, p. 1.

Filkins, Dexter and Worth, Robert F. (2004b) Armored Forces Blast their Way Into Rebel Nest. *New York Times*, 14 November, p. 1.

Filkins, Dexter and Worth, Robert F. (2004c) Will Meets Resistance in Deadly Logic of War. *New York Times*, 14 November, p. 1.

Fletcher, Martin (2011a) Libya – the Brutal Truth. *The Times*, 23 February, pp. 1, 8.

Fletcher, Martin (2011b) Opposition to Gaddafi Is Suicide, Activists Warned. *The Times*, 19 February, p. 9.

Fletcher, Martin (2011c) Gaddafi's Grip on Power Slips Amid Reports that Second City Is Falling. *The Times*, 21 February, pp. 6, 7.

Fletcher, Martin (2012) The Tipping Point. *The Times*, 30 May, pp. 1, 6, 7.

Fletcher, Martin and Haynes, Deborah (2011) It's Time for Gaddafi to Leave, West Tells Libya. *The Times*, 25 February, p. 1.

Fras, Damir (2011) Sanktionen gegen Gaddafi. *Frankfurter Rundschau*, 1 March, p. 7.

Fried, Nico and Ulrich, Stefan (2012) Neue Berichte Über Massaker. *Süddeutsche Zeitung*, 31 May, p. 1.

GB (2004) Falludscha in Geiselhaft. *die tageszeitung*, 14 April, p. 1.

Gehlen, Martin (2011) Tag des Zorns in Libyen. *Frankfurter Rundschau*, 18 February, p. 8.

Georgy, Michael and Harris, Edward (2004) Nur Ein Toter Mudschahedin ist ein Guter Mudschahedin. *Süddeutsche Zeitung*, 16 November, p. 6.

Georgy, Michael and Sengupta, Kim (2004) A City Lies in Ruins, Along with the Lives of the Wretched Survivors. *The Independent*, 15 November, pp. 4–5.

Getler, Michael (2004) Drawing Complaints, Online and Off. *Washington Post*, 21 November, p. B 6.

Giacomo, Carol (2013) Is Democracy Possible in Egypt? *New York Times*, 14 July, p. 10.

Gladstone, Rick and Lowrey, Annie (2012) Amid Reports of a New Massacre, Nations Seek to Step Up Pressure on Syria. *New York Times*, 7 June, p. 8.

Glenny, Misha (1999) Motives for a Massacre. *New York Times*, 20 January, p. 31.

Goldenberg, Suzanne (2004) Inquiry into Shooting of Wounded Iraqi Shown in Television Footage. *The Guardian*, 16 November, p. 2.

Graham, Bradley (2004) Rumsfeld Says Fallujah Attack Won't Go Halfway. *Washington Post*, 9 November, p. A 24.

Graw, Ansgar (2012) Neue Amerikanische Zögerlichkeit. *Die Welt*, 31 May, p. 7.

GUZ (2004) Protest Gegen US-Offensive. *Frankfurter Rundschau*, 11 November, p. 33.

Hamdani, Ali and Parry, Richard Lloyd (2004) Militants Unleash Wave of Attacks Across Iraq. *The Times*, 10 November, p. 8.

Harnden, Toby (2004a) I Got My Kills … I Just Love My Job. *The Daily Telegraph*, 9 November, p. 4.

Harnden, Toby (2004b) Commanders Learn to Respect Organised Hit-and-Run Guerrilla Tactics. *The Daily Telegraph*, 12 November, p. 16.

Harnden, Toby (2004c) This is Where the Foreign Fighters Hang Out. *The Daily Telegraph*, 10 November, p. 11.

Harnden, Toby and Russell, Alec (2004) All-Out Assault on Fallujah. *The Daily Telegraph*, 9 November, p. 1.

Hermann, Rainer (2004a) Der Kampf um Falludscha hat Begonnen. *Frankfurter Allgemeine Zeitung*, 9 November, pp. 1–2.

Hermann, Rainer (2004b) Heftige Kämpfe im Irak. *Frankfurter Allgemeine Zeitung*, 8 April, pp. 1, 2.

Hermann, Rainer (2012) Abermals Massaker in Syrien. *Frankfurter Allgemeine Zeitung*, 8 June, p. 1.

Hider, James (2004a) Battle for Fallujah Begins as US and Iraqi Troops Launch Attack. *The Times*, 8 November, p. 30.

Hider, James (2004b) Marines Launch High-Risk Assault to Break the Back of Insurgency. *The Times*, 9 November, p. 8.

Hider, James (2004c) A Savage Dance of Death in the Alleys of Fallujah. *The Times*, 10 November, p. 1.

Hider, James (2004d) US Forces Hunt Down Guerrillas in Fallujah's Shooting Gallery. *The Times*, 13 November, p. 60.

Hider, James (2004e) Claims of Ceasefire Fail to Stop Fighting in Fallujah. *The Times*, 12 April, p. 5.

Hider, James (2004f) US Soldiers Set to Move in on Martyrs' Land. *The Times*, 12 November, p. 42.

Hider, James and Bennett, Rosemary (2004) Iraqi Leaders Revolt over US Action to Quell Rebel Uprising. *The Times*, 10 April, p. 1.

Hilsum, Lindsey (2004) A City in Ruins, Sky Thick with Smoke. *The Observer*, 14 November, p. 20.

Hubbard, Ben and Kirkpatrick, David D. (2013) Sudden Improvements in Egypt Suggest a Campaign to Undermine Morsi. *New York Times*, 11 July, p. 4.

Hussein, Aqeel and Harnden, Toby (2004) Iraqi Rebels Slip Away to Fight Another Day Families Leaving Fallujah Talk of the Stench of Corpses and Fighters Escaping in Mercedes Cars. *The Daily Telegraph*, 14 November, p. 26.

Israel, Stephan (1999) Massaker Sorgen für Zulauf bei der UCK. *Frankfurter Rundschau*, 18 January, p. 2.

Jaber, Hala (2004a) Showdown in the City of Snipers. *The Sunday Times*, 14 November, p. 16.

Jaber, Hala (2004b) Falluja Suicide Bombers Escape Back to Baghdad. *The Sunday Times*, 14 November, p. 1.

Jaber, Hala (2004c) Falluja: Last Words of the Living Dead. *The Sunday Times*, 21 November, p. 22.

Jaber, Hala (2004d) Zealot Tells of Last Stand. *The Sunday Times*, 14 November, p. 16.

Jaber, Hala (2005) Terror Reborn in Fallujah Ruins. *The Sunday Times*, 18 December, p. 22.

Jaber, Hala and Macleod, Hugh (2012) Stop Them Killing Our Children. *The Times*, 27 May, p. 27.

Jagger, Suzy (2012) As Mortar Fire Hit the Town, Families Began to Flee in Their Thousands. *The Times*, 28 May, pp. 6, 7.

Jagger, Suzy and Boyes, Roger (2012) Annan Battles to Save His Peace Mission as West expels Syrian Diplomats and Ratches Up Pressure. *The Times*, 30 May, p. 6.

Janofsky, Michael (2004) Rights Experts See Possibility of a War Crime. *New York Times*, 13 November, p. 8.

Jehl, Douglas and Shanker, Thom (2004) Falluja Offensive is Seen as a Test of U.S. Pledge to Pacify Iraq in Time for January Elections. *New York Times*, 9 November, p. 11.

Jenkins, Simon (2004) A Wrecked Nation, a Desert, a Ghost Town. *The Times*, 17 November, p. 16.

Johnson, Andrew and Mesure, Susie (2011) Gaddafi Fights for His Future as Up to 200 Die in Benghazi. *The Independent*, 20 February, pp. 6, 7.

Jordans, Frank (2012) U.N. Body Condemns Syria Over Massacre. *Washington Post*, 2 June, p. A 06.

Kalnoky, Boris (2004a) Falludscha. *Die Welt*, 9 November, p. 8.

Kalnoky, Boris (2004b) US-Truppen Kontrollieren Falludscha. *Die Welt*, 13 November, p. 6.

Kalnoky, Boris (2004c) US-Truppen Erobern Zentrum von Falludscha. *Die Welt*, 10 November, p. 6.

Kalnoky, Boris (2004d) Der Sturm auf die Irakische Stadt Falludscha hat Begonnen. *Die Welt*, 9 November, p. 10.

Kalnoky, Boris (2004e) Falludscha Ist Frei, aber Zerstört. *Die Welt*, 16 November, p. 7.

Keller, Gabriela (2012) Mörderischer Wahnsinn. *Die Welt*, 30 May, p. 8.

Keller, Gabriela and Smirnova, Julia (2012) Wir Können Nicht Einmal Weinen. *Die Welt*, 29 May, p. 6.

Kingsley, Patrick (2013a) Britain Halts Exports of Arms Parts to Egypt. *The Guardian*, 20 July, p. 19.

Kingsley, Patrick (2013b) Gunfire in Cairo: The Anatomy of a Massacre. *The Guardian*, 19 July, p. 1.

Kingsley, Patrick (2013c) At Least 51 Killed in Egypt as Army Opens Fire 'Like Pouring Rain'. *The Guardian*, 9 July, p. 1.

Kingsley, Patrick and Black, Ian (2013) Jet Donations Signal US's Backing for Egyptian Army. *The Guardian*, 12 July, p. 21.

Kinsley, Michael (2004) It Hurts, but Don't Stop. *Washington Post*, 21 November, p. B7.

Kirkpatrick, David D. and Fahim, Kareem (2013) Killing of Islamists Deepens Crisis in Egypt. *New York Times*, 9 July, p. 1.

Klein, Naomi (2004a) Die, then Vote. This is Falluja. *The Guardian*, 13 November, p. 23.

Klein, Naomi (2004b) Die Doppelmoral der Kriegsgegner. *Die Welt*, 18 April, n.p.

Knuf, Thorsten (2011) Europäische Union Richtet Lagezentrum Ein. *Frankfurter Rundschau*, 25 February, p. 4.

Knuf, Thorsten (2012) Syriens Botschafter Müssen Nach Hause. *Frankfurter Rundschau*, 30 May, p. 7.

Kornelius, Stefan (2011) Virtuelle Lufthoheit. *Süddeutsche Zeitung*, 1 March, p. 4.

Kristof, Nicholas D. (2011) On the Line with Libya. *New York Times*, 24 February, p. 27.

Kulish, Nicholas, and MacFarquhar, Neil (2012) Putin Rejects Intervention but Fears Civila War in Syria. *New York Times*, 2 June, p. 8.

Landler, Mark (2012) Romney Calls for Action, But His Party Is Divided. *New York Times*, 30 May, p. 6.

Londoño, Ernesto (2013) Obama Administration Calls on the Military to Show Restraint. *Washington Post*, 9 July, p. A 08.

MacAskill, Ewen, Wintour, Patrick and Watt, Nicholas (2011) Obama Warns of Sanctions as Pressure Grows for No-Fly Zone. *The Guardian*, 24 February, p. 6.

MacFarquhar, Neil (2004) Arabs Worry over Extremism While Evoking Vindication. *New York Times*, 9 April, p. 10.

MacFarquhar, Neil (2012a) Security Council Condemns Syria Over Massacre. *New York Times*, 28 May, p. 1.

MacFarquhar, Neil (2012b) 10 Allies Join U.S. in Move to Expel Syrian Diplomats. *New York Times*, 30 May, p. 2.

MacFarquhar, Neil and Saad, Hwaida (2012) Many Children Among Victims in Syria Attack. *New York Times*, 27 May, p. 1.

Malek, Mohamed Abdul (2011) We Can No Longer Live Under Gaddafi's Evil Subjugation. *The Guardian*, 22 February, p. 30.

Marqusee, Mike (2005) A Name That Lives in Infamy. *The Guardian*, 10 November, p. 32.

Matern, Tobias (2004) In Treue zu den Truppen. *Süddeutsche Zeitung*, 18 November, p. 1.

McCarthy, Rory (2004a) Medicines and Food Scarce for Trapped Civilians. *The Guardian*, 10 November, p. 4.

McCarthy, Rory (2004b) Go Kick Some Butt and Make History, Vietnam-Style, US Troops Urged. *The Guardian*, 9 November, p. 3.

McCarthy, Rory (2004c) Falluja Forces Find Hostage Killing Houses. *The Guardian*, 11 November, p. 1.

McCarthy, Rory (2004d) Nine Killed in US Convoy as Shia Militias Fight On. *The Guardian*, 10 April, p. 4.

McCarthy, Rory (2004e) American Injury Toll Grows Amid Fierce Resistance. *The Guardian*, 12 November p. 19.

McCarthy, Rory (2004f) House by House, Falluja Falls. *The Guardian*, 10 November, p. 1.

McCarthy, Rory (2004g) Curfews as Iraq Rebellion Spreads. *The Guardian*, 13 November, p. 17.

McCarthy, Rory (2004h) Four Die in US Raid on Mosque. *The Guardian*, 20 November, p. 17.

McCarthy, Rory and Beaumont, Peter (2004) Civilian Cost of Battle for Falluja Emerges. *The Observer*, 14 November, p. 2.

McCarthy, Rory and Borger, Julian (2004) US Troops Enter Falluja as Jets Pound Rebel-Held City. *The Guardian*, 9 November, p. 1.

McCarthy, Rory and Mansour, Osama (2004) Children Pay a Price for Assault on Falluja. *The Guardian*, 17 November, p. 17.

McGreal, Chris (2012) US Threatens Use of Force in Syria after Massacre. *The Guardian*, 29 May, p. 1.

Michaels, Jim (2007) Thousands of Enemy Fighters Reported Killed [online], 27 September. Available at: http://usatoday30.usatoday.com/news/world/iraq/2007-09-26-insurgents_N.htm [accessed 29 June 2016].

Milbank, Dana (2013) The Non-Coup in Cairo. *Washington Post*, 10 July, p. A 15.

Miller, Jonathan (2012) Syrian Defectors Accuse Assad's Relatives of Ordering Crimes Against Humanity. *The Guardian*, 28 May, p. 15.

Milne, Seumas (2012) Foreign Intervention Will Only Shed More Syrian Blood. *The Guardian*, 6 June, p. 30.

Moniac, Rüdiger (1999) Klaus Naumann, ein Strikter Soldat mit Mut zur Zivilcourage. *Die Welt*, 19 January, p. 11.

Münch, Peter (1999) Nato in Fesseln. *Süddeutsche Zeitung*, 19 January, p. 4.

Oppel Jr., Richard A. (2004a) Machines of War Grope in the Dust and Shadows. *New York Times*, 9 November, p. 10.

Oppel Jr., Richard A. (2004b) Early Target of Offensive Is a Hospital. *New York Times*, 8 November, p. 1.

Oppel Jr., Richard A. and Worth, Robert F. (2004) G.I.'s Open Attack to Take Falluja from Iraq Rebels. *New York Times*, 8 November, p. 1.

Parry, Richard Lloyd and Hamdani, Ali (2004) Refugees Claim that Civilian Casualties Left to Die. *The Times*, 11 November, p. 9.

Perlez, Jane (1999a) NATO Presses Milosevic After Massacre but Doesn't Plan Raids. *New York Times*, 18 January, p. 6.

Perlez, Jane (1999b) NATO Fails in Belgrade. *New York Times*, 20 January, p. 3.

Perlez, Jane (1999c) U.S. Weighs Its Reaction to Massacre in Kosovo. *New York Times*, 17 January, p. 6.

Perlez, Jane (1999d) Kosovo Massacre Is Called Revenge. *New York Times*, 22 January, p. 1.

Perras, Arne (2011) Gaddafis Finstere Helfer. *Süddeutsche Zeitung*, 25 February, p. 7.

Pincus, Walter (2012) Big Risks, and No Easy Solutions, in Syrian Intervention. *Washington Post*, 31 May, p. A 13.

Pitel, Laura (2011) The Angry Tribesmen Who Hold the Key ... and the Oil. *The Times*, 22 February, pp. 6, 7.

Pletka, Danielle (2011) Helping Syria Would Help Obama. *Washington Post*, 3 June, p. B 02.

Raghavan, Sudarsan (2011a) Libyan Regime Under Threat. *Washington Post*, 21 February, p. A 01.

Raghavan, Sudarsan (2011b) Gaddafi Vows to Fight Until 'the End'. *Washington Post*, 23 February, p. A 01.

Rai, Milan and Sangster, Emma (2005) Letters and Emails: Fallujah Victims Deserve Justice. *The Guardian*, 8 November, p. 35.

Rathfelder, Erich (1999) Ich Wäre Bereit, Zurückzutreten. *die tageszeitung*, 19 January.

Reuters (2004a) US-Truppen Erreichen Zentrum Falludschas. *Süddeutsche Zeitung*, 10 November, p. 1.

Reuters (2004b) Annan: Zorn Nicht Schüren. *Frankfurter Allgemeine Sonntagszeitung*, 7 November, p. 1.

Reuters Beirut (2012) Syrian Rebels 'Kill 80 Soldiers' in Clashes. *The Guardian*, 5 June, p. 18.

Rößler, Hans-Christian (2013) Das Geld und die Generäle in Kairo. *Frankfurter Allgemeine Zeitung*, 10 July, p. 5.

Roll, Stephan (2013) Putsch mit Plan. *Süddeutsche Zeitung*, 15 July, p. 2.

Roser, Thomas (1999) UN-Chefanklägerin Baut Belgrad eine Brücke. *Frankfurter Rundschau*, 22 January, p. 2.

Rovera, Donatella (2012) Who Will Document Syria's Atrocities. *Washington Post*, 31 May, p. A 15.

RTR/AFP/DPA/AP (1999) Belgrad Brüskiert UN und OSZE. *Frankfurter Rundschau*, 19 January, p. 1.

RTR/DPA/AP/TAZ (2011) Letzte Schläge für Gaddafi. *die tageszeitung*, 28 February, p. 1.

Sampson, Anthony (2004) After the Brutality of Fallujah, the Americans Need to Change Their Image. *The Independent*, 13 November, p. 41.

Schaefer, Sarah (1999) Kosovo Massacre: Send Troops to Kosovo, Say Labour MPs. *The Independent*, 19 January, p. 8.

Schmitt, Eric (2004a) A Goal Is Met. *New York Times*. 15 November, p. 1.

Schmitt, Eric (2004b) Marines Battle Guerrillas in Streets of Fallujah. *New York Times*, 9 April, p. 9.

Schmitt, Eric and Worth, Robert F. (2004) Marine Officers See Risk in Cuts in Falluja Force. *New York Times*, 18 November, p. 1.

Seale, Patrick (2012) This is no Plan for Peace. *The Guardian*, 28 May, p. 27.

Sebastian, Tim (2013) The Generals or the Brothers. *New York Times*, 8 July.

Sharrock, David (2011) Former Pillars of Regime Around the World Desert a Dictator Whose Time Has Run Out. *The Observer*, 27 February, p. 7.

Sengupta, Kim (2004a) US Begins Its Biggest Urban Offensive since Vietnam With Long-Awaited Fallujah Assault. *The Independent*, 8 November, p. 26.

Sengupta, Kim (2004b) US "Pacifies" City but Rebels Take Violence to Rest of Country. *The Independent*, 10 November, p. 4.

Sengupta, Kim (2004c) Black Watch Under Fire While Assault on Fallujah Continues. *The Independent*, 11 November, p. 4.

Sengupta, Kim (2004d) A Hollow Victory. *The Independent*, 15 November, pp. 1, 5.

Sengupta, Kim (2004e) Escape from Fallujah: Refugees Flood Nearby Towns. *The Independent*, 18 November, p. 7.

Sengupta, Kim (2004f) Black Watch in Running Battles with Militants. *The Independent*, 13 November, pp. 34–35.

Sengupta, Kim (2004g) Black Watch Is Needed in South, Say Military Chiefs. *The Independent*, 16 November, p. 23.

Sengupta, Kim (2004h) The Soldiers' Story: The War the Video Cameras Do not See. *The Independent on Sunday*, 21 November, pp. 20–21.

Sengupta, Kim (2004i) Allawi Declares Martial Law as 21 Policemen Shot Dead. *The Independent*, 8 November, p. 26.

Sengupta, Kim and Beach, Alastair (2013) Dozens Dead. *The Independent*, 9 July, pp. 1, 4, 5.

Sengupta, Kim and Huggler, Justin (2004) Battle for Fallujah Rages. *The Independent*, 9 November, pp. 1, 4.

Sengupta, Kim and Whitaker, Raymond (2004) When the Smoke Has Cleared, what Horrors Will Be Revealed? *The Independent*, 14 November, pp. 20–21.

Shadid, Anthony (2004a) Baghdad Suffers a Day of Attacks, Assassinations. *Washington Post*, 21 November, p. A 30.

Shadid, Anthony (2004b) Troops Move to Quell Insurgency in Mosul. *Washington Post*, 17 November, p. A 1.

Shadid, Anthony (2004c) U.S. Commander in Iraq Calls Shooting 'Tragic'. *Washington Post*, 17 November, p. A 15.

Shadid, Anthony (2011) Clashes in Libya Worsen as Army Crushes Dissent. *New York Times*, 19 February, p. 1.

Sly, Liz (2012a) Annan in Syria to Try to Rescue U.N. Peace Plan. *Washington Post*, 29 May, p. A 06.

Sly, Liz (2012b) Houla Massacre Raises the Stakes on Syria. *Washington Post*, 4 June, p. A 01.

Smith, Jeffrey (1999) Serbs Tried To Cover Up Massacre. *Washington Post*, 28 January, p. A 01.

Sparrow, Andrew (2004) Blair Does Not Exert Enough Influence, Says Howard. *The Daily Telegraph*, 12 April, p. 5.

Spencer, Richard (2011) Gaddafi Warns His People of Swift, Violent Retribution. *The Daily Telegraph*, 23 February, p. 14.

Spencer, Richard, Tait, Robert and Samaan, Magdy (2013) Islamists Call for Uprising After 50 Are Shot Dead on Streets of Cairo. *The Daily Telegraph*, 9 July, p. 13.

Spinner, Jacki (2004a) Artillerymen Clear Path for the Infantry. *Washington Post*, 11 November, p. A 33.

Spinner, Jacki (2004b) Insurgent Base Discovered in Fallujah. *Washington Post*, 19 November, p. A 18.

Spinner, Jacki (2004c) Fallujah Residents Emerge, Find 'City of Mosques' in Ruins. *Washington Post*, 18 November, p. A 1.

Spinner, Jacki (2004d) Fallujans Staying at Mosque Get Grim Task: Grave Digging. *Washington Post*, 20 November, p. A 12.

Spinner, Jacki (2004e) In Fallujah, Marines Feel Shock of War. *Washington Post*, 14 November, p. A 31.

Spinner, Jacki (2004f) Ammo Crews Give Troops Shots at Success. *Washington Post*, 15 November, p. A 16.

Spinner, Jacki and Vick, Karl (2004) U.S. and Iraqi Troops Push Into Fallujah. *Washington Post*, 9 November, p. A1.

Spinner, Jacki, Vick, Karl and Fekeiki, Omar (2004a) U.S. Forces Battle into Heart of Fallujah. *Washington Post*, 10 November, p. A 1.

Spinner, Jacki, Vick, Karl and Fekeiki, Omar (2004b) U.S. Tries to Corner Fallujah Insurgents. *Washington Post*, 12 November, p. A 1.

Steele, Jonathan (2004a) Annan Adviser Attacks US Occupation. *The Guardian*, 15 April, p. 14.

Steele, Jonathan (2004b) While Our Troops Remain on Iraq's Streets There Is No Hope. *The Guardian*, 12 April, p. 16.

Stewart, Catrina (2011) Refugees from Libya Tell of Descent into Chaso. *The Independent*, 24 February, pp. 4, 5.

Stewart, Catrina and Sengupta, Kim (2011) Gaddafi Regime: We Will Fight to the End. *The Independent*, 21 February, pp. 1, 2.

Strauss, Julius (1999) Serbian Police Massacre Albanians. *The Sunday Telegraph*, 17 January, p. 29.

Stürmer, Michael (2004) Der Sieg der Amerikaner Könnte Schnell Verspielt Sein. *Die Welt*, 15 November, p. 7.

Süddeutsche Zeitung (1999) NATO Berät Über Konsequenzen für Belgrad. *Süddeutsche Zeitung*, 18 January, p. 7.

Süddeutsche Zeitung (2004a) Aufstand im Irak. *Süddeutsche Zeitung*, 8 April, p. 2.

Süddeutsche Zeitung (2004b) Falludscha und der Böse Geist. *Süddeutsche Zeitung*, 15 November, p. 4.

Süddeutsche Zeitung (2004c) Luftangriffe auf Falludscha Dauern an. *Süddeutsche Zeitung*, 16 November, p. 1.

TAZ/RTR/AFP (2011) Massen Verlassen Gaddafi. *die tageszeitung*, 24 February, p. 1.

The Guardian (1999a) Kosovo massacre 'was ordered'. *The Guardian*, 29 January, p. 1.

The Guardian (1999b) Kosovo in Crisis. *The Guardian*, 21 January, p. 17.

The Guardian (2004a) Fearful in Falluja. *The Guardian*, 9 November, p. 21.

The Guardian (2004b) US Tactics: Losing Falluja. *The Guardian*, 15 April, p. 25.

The Guardian (2012) Syria: No Peace, No Plan. *The Guardian*, 8 June, p. 36.

The Guardian (2013) Disorder, Death and the Generals. *The Guardian*, 9 July, p. 28.

The Independent (1999) We Must Intervene in Kosovo to Secure Justice for the Slain. *The Independent*, 20 January, p. 3.

The Independent (2004a) The Resistance in Fallujah May Have Been Crushed, But the Cost Has Yet to Be Counted. *The Independent*, 15 November, p. 30.

The Independent (2004b) In Cold Blood. *The Independent*, 17 November, p. 30.

The New York Times (1999) Crisis in Kosovo. *New York Times*, 20 January, p. 30.

The New York Times (2004a) 'I'm Ready for the Job,' Bush Says in News Conference After Election. *New York Times*, 5 November 2004, p. 20.

The New York Times (2004b) The Larger Battle in Iraq. *New York Times*, 15 November, p. 20.

The New York Times (2004c) News Summary. *New York Times*, 10 November, p. 2.

The New York Times (2004d) News Summary. *New York Times*, 13 November, p. 2.

The Times (2004a) Taking Fallujah. *The Times*, 10 November, p. 19.

The Times (2012a) Massacre at Houla. *The Times*, 28 May, p. 2.

The Times (2012b) Charles Taylor Receives a Just Sentence. Assad Should also Account for Terrible Acts. *The Times*, 31 May, p. 2.

The Washington Post (1999) Mr. Milosevic's Massacre. *Washington Post*, 18 January, p. A 22.

The Washington Post (2004a) The Battle in Fallujah. *Washington Post*, 11 November, p. A 36.

The Washington Post (2004b) Today's News. *Washington Post*, 9 November, p. C 14.

The Washington Post (2011) Atrocities in Libya. *Washington Post*, 22 February, p. A 12.

Thomson, Alex (2012a) They Moved From Family to Family Killing Them One by One. *The Daily Telegraph*, 28 May, pp. 16, 17.

Thomson, Alex (2012b) Fear and Hate in the Killing Zone of Houla. *The Daily Telegraph*, 31 May, p. 21.

Usborne, David (2011) Anger Over UN 'Waffle' Delaying Action to Combat Dictator's Brutal Crackdown. *The Independent*, 24 February, pp. 4, 5.

Walker, Martin (1999) Observers Deny Racak Massacre was Fabricated. *The Times*, 21 January, p. 15.

Walker, Martin, Bird, Chris and Black, Ian (1999) Nato's Generals Warn Serbia. *The Guardian*, 20 January, p. 3.

Walker, Shaun and Cockburn, Patrick (2012) Hague Sent Packing by Russia as Annan Peace Plan Crumbles. *The Independent*, 29 May, pp. 8, 9.

Watt, Nicholas and Norton-Taylor, Richard (2004) Blair Heads for Crucial US Talks – as Frustrations Grow. *The Guardian*, 15 April, p. 1.

Whitaker, Raymond and Marshall, Andrew (1999) Massacre Ordered at Top Level in Belgrade, Says US. *The Independent*, 29 January, p. 1.

Wilding, Jo (2004) Getting Aid Past US Snipers Is Impossible. *The Guardian*, 17 April, p. 13.

Wong, Edward (2004a) Sunni Party Leaves Iraqi Government Over Falluja Attack. *New York Times*, 10 November, p. 14.

Wong, Edward (2004b) For Iraqi Leader, Political Risks of Attack on Falluja Grow. *New York Times*, 14 November, p. 13.

Wong, Edward (2004c) For One Family in Falluja, a Simple Drive Turns Deadly. *New York Times*, 20 November, p. 9.

Wood, Paul (1999) I Counted 24 Dead in the Hills Above Kosovo. *The Independent*, 17 January, p. 2.

Worth, Robert F. (2004) Newsman Who Taped Marine Shooting Captive Keeps Silent. *New York Times*, 18 November, p. 15.

Worth, Robert F. and Wong, Edward (2004a) Assault Slows, But G.I.'s Take Half of Falluja. *New York Times*, 11 November, p. 1.

Worth, Robert F. and Wong, Edward (2004b) House in Falluja Seems to Have Been Base for Top Jordanian Terrorist. *New York Times*, 19 November, p. 14.

Younge, Gary and Whitaker, Brian (2004) Marines Defend Soldier's Killing of Iraqi. *The Guardian*, 17 November, p. 15.

Zangana, Haifa (2004a) We Salute the Fighters in Flip-Flops. *The Guardian*, 17 November, p. 26.

Zangana, Haifa (2004b) Iraq's Enemy Within. *The Guardian*, 10 April, p. 19.

Secondary References

ABC News (2004) Official: Some Iraqis Forced to Be Bombers. *ABC News* [online], 23 July. Available at: http://abcnews.go.com/WNT/story?id=129061&page=1#.Tr1RalZSnqE [accessed 10 November 2011].

Achcar, Gilbert (2013) *The People Want: A Radical Exploration of the Arab Uprisings*. London: Saqi Books.

Adorno, Theodor W. (1991) *The Culture Industry: Selected Essays on Mass Culture*. London: Routledge.

Adorno, Theodor W. and Horkheimer, Max (1997 [1944]) *Dialectic of Enlightenment*. London: Verso.

Albarran, Alan B. (2002) *Media Economics: Understanding Markets, Industries and Concepts*. 2nd edn. Ames: Iowa State Press.

Albarran, Alan B. and Chan-Olmsted, Sylvia M. (1998) Global Patterns and Issues. In: Albarran, Alan B. and Chan-Olmsted, Sylvia M., eds. *Global Media Economics: Commercialisation, Concentration and Integration of World Media Markets*. Ames: Iowa State University Press, pp. 99–118.

Alexander, Jeffrey C. (1981) The Mass News Media in Systemic, Historical, and Comparative Perspective. In: Katz, Elihu and Szecskö, Tamás, eds. *Mass Media and Social Change*. London: Sage, pp. 17–51.

Alexseev, Mikhail A. and Bennett, W. Lance (1995) For Whom the Gates Open: News Reporting and Government Source Patterns in the United States, Great Britain and Russia. *Political Communication*, 12, pp. 395–412.

Allawi, Ali A. (2007) *The Occupation of Iraq: Winning the War, Losing the Peace*. New Haven and London: Yale University Press.

Althaus, Scott L. (2003) When News Norms Collide, Follow the Lead: New Evidence for Press Independence. *Political Communication*, 20(3), pp. 381–414.

Althaus, Scott L., Edy, Jill A., Entman, Robert M., and Phalen, Patricia (1996) Revising the Indexing Hypothesis: Officials, Media, and the Libya Crisis. *Political Communication*, 13(4), pp. 407–421.

Altheide, David L. (1996) *Qualitative Media Analysis*. London: Sage.

Althusser, Louis (1971) *Lenin and Philosophy and other Essays*. New York: Monthly Review Press.

Ambos, Kai and Arnold, Jörg (2003) *Der Irak-Krieg und das Völkerrecht*. Berlin: Berliner Wissenschafts Verlag.

Amnesty International (2004) *Iraq: One Year on the Human Rights Situation Remains Dire* [online], 18 March. London: Amnesty International. Available at: https://www.amnesty.org/en/documents/MDE14/006/2004/en/ [accessed 4 May 2017].

Amnesty International (2011a) *The Battle for Libya: Killings, Disappearances and Torture.* London: Amnesty International.

Amnesty International (2011b) *Libya: NTC Must Take Control to Prevent Spiral of Abuses* [online], 13 September. Available at: https://www.amnesty.org/en/press-releases/2011/09/libya-ntc-must-take-control-prevent-spiral-abuses/ [accessed 12 July 2016].

Amnesty International (2012a) *Amnesty International Report 2012: The State of the World's Human Rights.* London: Amnesty International.

Amnesty International (2012b) *Brutality Unpunished and Unchecked: Egypt's Military Kill and Torture Protesters with Impunity.* London: Amnesty International.

Amnesty International (2013) *Amnesty International Report 2013: The State of the World's Human Rights.* London: Amnesty International.

Amnesty International (2014/2015) *Amnesty International Report 2014/15: The State of the World's Human Rights.* London: Amnesty International.

Anderson, Tim (2016) *The Dirty War on Syria: Washington, Regime Change and Resistance.* Montréal: Global Research Publishers.

AP (2013) Gaddafi Forces Retake Town Near Capital. *The Sydney Morning Herald* [online], 2 March. Available at: http://www.smh.com.au/world/gaddafi-forces-retake-towns-near-capital-20110302-1bejx.html [accessed 11 May 2015].

Bagdikian, Ben (2004) *The New Media Monopoly.* Boston: Beacon Press.

Bakan, Joel (2005) *The Corporation: The Pathological Pursuit of Profit and Power.* London: Constable.

Baker, Raymond W., Ismael, Shereen, T. and Ismael, Tareq Y. (2010) Ending the Iraqi State. In: Baker, Raymond W., Ismael, Shereen, T. and Ismael, Tareq Y., eds. *Cultural Cleansing in Iraq: Why Museums Were Looted, Libraries Burned and Academics Murdered.* London: Pluto Press, pp. 3–48.

Balanyá, Belén, Doherty, Ann, Hoedeman, Olivier, Ma'anit, Adam and Wesselius, Erik (2000) *Europe Inc.: Regional & Global Restructuring & the Rise of Corporate Power.* London: Pluto Press.

Barnouw, Erik (2006 [1978]) *The Sponsor: Notes on Modern Potentates.* 3rd edn. New Brunswick: Transaction Publishers.

BBC News (2003) Breakfast with Frost. *BBC News* [online], 29 June. Available at: http://news.bbc.co.uk/1/hi/programmes/breakfast_with_frost/3029526.stm [accessed 30 January 2012].

BBC News (2004) Aid Reaches Falluja's Citizens. *BBC News* [online], 27 November. Available at: http://news.bbc.co.uk/2/hi/middle_east/4047469.stm [accessed 20 May 2012].

BBC News (2011) *Egypt Unrest: 846 Killed in Protests – Official Toll* [online], 19 April. Available at: http://www.bbc.co.uk/news/world-middle-east-13134956 [accessed 15 November 2016].

BBC News (2013) *Egypt Protestors Clash with Police at Presidential Palace* [online], 1 February. Available at: http://www.bbc.co.uk/news/world-middle-east-21289729 [accessed 11 May 2015].

Bellamy, Alex J. (2008) The Responsibility to Protect and the Problem of Military Intervention. *International Affairs*, 84(4), pp. 615–639.

Bender, Gunnar (1997) *Cross-Media-Ownership. Eine Rechtsvergleichende Untersuchung der Kontrolle Multimedialer Unternehmenskonzentration in der Bundesrepublik Deutschland und den Vereinigten Staaten*. PhD Westfälische Wilhelms-Universität zu Münster.

Bennett, W. Lance (1990) Toward a Theory of Press-State Relations in the United States. *Journal of Communication*, 40(2), pp. 103–125.

Bennett, W. Lance (1994) The News about Foreign Policy. In: Bennett, W. Lance and Paletz, David L., eds. *Taken by Storm: The Media, Public Opinion, and U.S. Foreign Policy in the Gulf War*. Chicago: University of Chicago Press, pp. 12–40.

Bennett, W. Lance (1996) An Introduction to Journalism Norms and Representations of Politics. *Political Communication*, 13(4), pp. 373–384.

Bennett, W. Lance and Lawrence, Regina G. (1995) News Icons and the Mainstreaming of Social Change. *Journal of Communication*, 45(3), pp. 20–39.

Bennett, W. Lance, Lawrence, Regina G. and Livingston, Steven (2007) *When the Press Fails: Political Power and the News Media from Iraq to Katrina*. Chicago: University of Chicago Press.

Bennett, W. Lance and Paletz, David L., eds. (1994) *Taken by Storm: The Media, Public Opinion, and U.S. Foreign Policy in the Gulf War*. Chicago: University of Chicago Press.

Bennett, W. Lance and Serrin, William (2005) The Watchdog Role. In: Overholser, Geneva and Jamieson, Kathleen Hall, eds. *The Press*. New York: Oxford University Press, pp. 169–188.

Blum, William (2004) *Killing Hope: US Military & CIA Interventions since World War II*. 2nd edn. London: Zed Books.

Blum, William (2006) *Rogue State: A Guide to the World's Only Superpower*. 3rd edn. London: Zed Books Ltd.

Borjesson, Kristina (2002) *Into the Buzzsaw: Leading Journalists Expose the Myth of a Free Press*. New York: Prometheus Books.

Boyd-Barrett, Oliver (2004) Judith Miller, *The New York Times* and the Propaganda Model. *Journalism Studies*, 5(4), pp. 435–449.

Breed, Warren (1955) Social Control in the Newsroom: A Functional Analysis. *Social Forces*, 33(4), pp. 326–335.

Bremer III, L. Paul (2006) *My Year in Iraq: The Struggle to Build a Future of Hope*. New York: Threshold Editions.

Bromley, Michael (2000) The Manufacture of News – Fast Moving Consumer Goods Production, or Public Service? In: Berry, David, ed. *Ethics and Media Culture: Practices and Representations*. Oxford: Focal Press.

Brzezinski, Zbigniew (2003/2004) Hegemonic Quicksand. *National Interest*, 74, pp. 5–16.

Burnham, Gilbert, Lafta, Riyadh, Doocy, Shannon and Roberts, Les (2006) Mortality after the 2003 Invasion of Iraq: A Cross-Sectional Cluster Sample Survey. *The Lancet*, 368 (October), pp. 1421–1428.

Bussemer, Thymian (2005) *Propaganda: Konzepte und Theorien*. Wiesbaden: VS Verlag für Sozialwissenschaften.

Camp, Dick (2009) *Operation Phantom Fury: The Assault and Capture of Fallujah, Iraq*. Minneapolis, MN: Zenith Press.

Carcano, Andrea (2006) End of the Occupation in 2004? The Status of the Multinational Force in Iraq After the Transfer of Sovereignty to the Interim Iraqi Government. *Journal of Conflict & Security Law*, 11(1), pp. 41–66.

Carroll, Jill (2004) Letter from Baghdad: Not that Independent. *American Journalism Review* [online], June/July. Available at: http://www.ajr.org/Article.asp?id=3687 [accessed 2 December 2011].

Carroll, William K. (2010) *The Making of a Transnational Capitalist Class: Corporate Power in the 21st Century*. London: Zed Books.

Carruthers, Susan L. (2000) *The Media at War*. New York: Palgrave Macmillan.

Cartalucci, Tony and Bowie, Nile (2012) *Subverting Syria: How CIA Contra Gangs and NGOs Manufacture, Mislabel and Market Murder*. San Diego, CA: Progressive Press.

Castells, Manuel (2010) Communication Power: Mass Communication, Mass Self-Communication, and Power Relationships in the Network Society. In: Curran, James, ed. *Media and Society*. 5th edn. London: Bloomsbury Academic, pp. 3–17.

CBS/AP (2012) UN: Syrian Uprising Death Toll Passes 8,000. *CBS News* [online], 15 March. Available at: http://www.cbsnews.com/news/un-syrian-uprising-death-toll-passes-8000/ [accessed 11 May 2015].

Chalabi, Mona (2013) Egypt's Dead and Injured: The Toll so Far. *The Guardian* [online], 8 July. Available at: http://www.theguardian.com/news/datablog/2013/jul/08/egypt-dead-injured-toll-so-far [accessed 11 May 2015].

Chomsky, Noam (1989) *Necessary Illusion*. London: Pluto Press.

Chomsky, Noam (1997) What Makes Mainstream Media Mainstream. *Z Magazine*, October.

Chomsky, Noam (2003) *Hybris: Die Endgültige Sicherung der Globalen Vormachtstellung der USA*. Hamburg: Europa Verlag.

Chomsky, Noam (2012) *A New Generation Draws the Line: Humanitarian Intervention and the "Responsibility to Protect" Today*. Boulder: Paradigm Publishers.

Chomsky, Noam and Herman, Edward S. (1979a) *The Washington Connection and Third World Fascism: The Political Economy of Human Rights: Volume I*. Nottingham: Spokesman.

Chomsky, Noam and Herman, Edward S. (1979b) *After the Cataclysm: Postwar Indochina and the Reconstruction of Imperial Ideology: The Political Economy of Human Rights: Volume II*. Nottingham: Spokesman.

Chossudovsky, Michel (2002) *Global Brutal: Der Entfesselte Welthandel, die Armut, der Krieg*. Frankfurt am Main: Zweitausendeins.

Christensen, Beau (2016) Propaganda Spin Cycle: 'Syrian Observatory for Human Rights' Is Funded by US and UK Governments. *Friends of Syria* [online], 24 September. Available at: https://friendsofsyria.wordpress.com/2016/09/24/propaganda-spin-cycle-syrian-observatory-for-human-rights-is-funded-by-us-and-uk-governments/ [accessed 11 November 2016].

Cohen, Bernard C. (1963) *The Press and Foreign Policy*. Princeton, NJ: Princeton University Press.

Commission on Freedom of the Press (1947) *A Free and Responsible Press*. Chicago: University of Chicago Press.

Cordesman, Anthony H. (2004) *The Developing Iraqi Insurgency: Status at End-2004*. Washington: Center for Strategic and International Studies.

Cottle, Simon (2006) *Mediatized Conflict*. New York: Open University Press.

Couldry, Nick and Downey, John (2004) War or Peace? Legitimation, Dissent, and Rhetorical Closure in Press Coverage of the Iraq War Build-Up. In: Allan, Stuart and Zelizer, Barbie, eds. *Reporting War: Journalism in Wartime*. London: Routledge, pp. 266–282.

CNN (2003) Bush Makes Historic Speech Aboard Warship. *CNN U.S.* [online], 1 May. Available at: http://edition.cnn.com/2003/US/05/01/bush.transcript/ [accessed 4 May 2017].

CNN (n.d.) *Casualties* [online]. Available at: http://edition.cnn.com/SPECIALS/war.casualties/index.html?country=iraq [accessed 29 June 2016].

CPJ (2004) Attacks on the Press 2003: Iraq. *Committee to Protect Journalists* [online], 11 March. Available at: http://cpj.org/2004/03/attacks-on-the-press-2003-iraq.php [accessed 2 December 2011].

CPJ (2005) Attacks on the Press 2004: Iraq. *Committee to Protect Journalists* [online], 14 March. Available at: http://cpj.org/2005/03/attacks-on-the-press-2004-iraq.php [accessed 2 December 2011].

Cunliffe, Philip, ed. (2011) *Critical Perspectives on the Responsibility to Protect: Interrogating Theory and Practice.* London: Routledge.

Curran, James (1977) Capitalism and Control of the Press, 1800–1975. In: Curran, James, Gurevitch, Michael and Woollacott, Jane, eds. *Mass Communication and Society.* London: Edward Arnold, pp. 195–230.

Curran, James (2002) *Media and Power.* London: Routledge.

Curran, James (2012) Reinterpreting the Internet. In: Curran, James, Fenton, Natalie and Freedman, Des, eds. *Misunderstanding the Internet.* London: Routledge, pp. 3–33.

Curran, James, Gurevitch, Michael and Woollacott, Janet (1982) The Study of the Media: Theoretical Approaches. In: Gurevitch, Michael, Bennett, Tony, Curran, James and Woollacott, Janet, eds. *Culture, Society and the Media.* London: Routledge, pp. 11–29.

Curran, James and Seaton, Jean (2003) *Power Without Responsibility: The Press, Broadcasting, and New Media in Britain.* 6th edn. London and New York: Routledge.

Curran, James and Seaton, Jean (2010) *Power Without Responsibility: Press, Broadcasting and the Internet in Britain.* 7th edn. London and New York: Routledge.

Curtis, Mark (1995) *The Ambiguities of Power: British Foreign Policy since 1945.* London: Zed Books.

Curtis, Mark (1998) *The Great Deception: Anglo-American Power and World Order.* London: Pluto Press.

Curtis, Mark (2003) *Web of Deceit: Britain's Real Role in the World.* London: Vintage.

Curtis, Mark (2004) *Unpeople: Britain's Secret Human Rights Abuses.* London: Vintage.

Curtis, Mark (2010) *Secret Affairs: Britain's Collusion with Radical Islam.* London: Serpent's Tail.

DiMaggio, Anthony (2009) *When Media Goes to War: Hegemonic Discourse, Public Opinion and the Limits of Dissent.* New York: Monthly Review Press.

Dinan, William and Miller, David, eds. (2007) *Thinker, Faker, Spinner, Spy: Corporate PR and the Assault on Democracy.* London: Pluto Press.

Domhoff, William G. (2002) *Who Rules America: Power and Politics.* Boston: McGraw-Hill.

Domhoff, William G. and Dye, Thomas R., eds. (1987) *Power Elites and Organizations.* Newbury Park: Sage.

Dorman, William A. and Livingston, Steven (1994) News and Historical Content: The Establishing Phase of the Persian Gulf Policy Debate. In: Bennett, W. Lance and Paletz, David L., eds. *Taken by Storm: The Media, Public Opinion, and U.S. Foreign Policy in the Gulf War.* Chicago: University of Chicago Press, pp. 63–81.

Doyle, Gillian (2002a) *Understanding Media Economics*. London: Sage.

Doyle, Gillian (2002b) *Media Ownership*. London: Sage.

Edwards, David (2016) 'Death Is Everywhere': Gaddafi Lashes Out as Power Slips Away. *Media Lens* [online], 3 October. Available at: http://www.medialens.org/index.php/alerts/alert-archive/2016/827-the-great-libya.html [accessed 10 November 2016].

Edwards, David and Cromwell, David (2006) *Guardians of Power: The Myth of the Liberal Media*. London: Pluto Press.

Edwards, David and Cromwell, David (2009) *Newspeak in the 21st Century*. London: Pluto Press.

Edwards, David and Cromwell, David (2011) To Avert a Bloodbath – Libya and the Press Parts 1 & 2. *Media Lens* [online], 1 and 5 September. Available at: http://www.medialens.org/index.php?option=com_content&view=category&id=24&Itemid=68 [accessed 10 November 2011].

Eilders, Christiane (1999) Synchronization of Issue Agendas in News and Editorials of the Prestige Press in Germany. *Communications*, 24(3), pp. 301–328.

Eilders, Christiane (2002) Conflict and Consonance in Media Opinion: Political Positions of Five German Quality Newspapers. *European Journal of Communication*, 17(1), pp. 25–63.

Eilders, Christiane (2005) Media Under Fire: Fact and Fiction in Conditions of War. *International Review of the Red Cross*, 87(860), pp. 639–648.

Eilders, Christiane and Hagen, Lutz M. (2005) Kriegsberichterstattung als Thema Kommunikationswissenschaftlicher Forschung: Ein Überblick zum Forschungsstand und den Beiträgen in diesem Themenheft. *Medien & Kommunikationswissenschaft*, 53(2–3), pp. 205–221.

Eilders, Christiane and Lüter, Albrecht (2000) Germany at War: Competing Framing Strategies in German Public Discourse. *European Journal of Communication*, 15(3), pp. 415–428.

Ellul, Jacques (1973) *Propaganda: The Formation of Men's Attitudes*. New York: Vintage Books.

Elworthy, Scilla (2007) Background: The Situation in Fallujah. In: Holmes, Jonathan, ed. *Fallujah: Eyewittness Testimony from Iraq's Besieged City*. London: Constable.

Entman, Robert M. (1993) Framing: Toward Clarification of a Fractured Paradigm. *Journal of Communication*, 43(4), pp. 51–58.

Entman, Robert M. (2000) Declarations of Independence: The Growth of Media Power after the Cold War. In: Nacos, Brigitte L., Shapiro, Robert Y., and Isernia, Pierangelo, eds. *Decision Making in a Glass House: Mass Media, Public Opinion, and American and European Foreign Policy in the 21st Century*. Lanham, Maryland: Rowman & Littlefield Publishers, pp. 11–27.

Entman, Robert M. (2004) *Projections of Power: Framing News, Public Opinion, and U.S. Foreign Policy*. Chicago: University of Chicago Press.

Entman, Robert M. and Page, Benjamin I. (1994) The News Before the Storm: The Iraq War Debate and the Limits to Media Independency. In: Bennett, W. Lance and Paletz, David L., eds. *Taken by Storm: The Media, Public Opinion, and U.S. Foreign Policy in the Gulf War*. Chicago: University of Chicago Press, pp. 82–101.

Epstein, Edward Jay (2000 [1973]) *News from Nowhere: Television and the News*. Chicago: Ivan R. Dee.

Esser, Frank, Schwabe, Christine, and Wilke, Jürgen (2005) Metaberichterstattung im Krieg. Wie Tageszeitungen die Rolle der Nachrichtenmedien und der Militär-PR in den

Irakkonflikten 1991 und 2003 framen. *Medien & Kommunikationswissenschaft*, 53(2–3), pp. 314–332.

Evans, Gareth (2006) From Humanitarian Intervention to the Responsibility to Protect. *Wisconsin International Law Journal*, 24(4), pp. 703–722.

EWG (2004a) Emergency Working Group Update Note. 7 November.

EWG (2004b) Emergency Working Group Update Note. 9 November.

EWG (2004c) Emergency Working Group – Falluja Crisis Update Note. 11 November.

EWG (2004d) Emergency Working Group – Falluja Crisis Bulletin Update. 30 November.

Felter, Joseph and Fishman, Brian (2007) *Al-Qa'ida's Foreign Fighters in Iraq: A First Look at the Sinjar Records*. Westpoint: Combating Terrorism Centre.

Ferguson, Thomas (1995) *Golden Rule: The Investment Theory of Party Competition and the Logic of Money-Driven Political Systems*. Chicago and London: University of Chicago Press.

Filkins, Dexter (2004e) U.S. Transfers Power to Iraq 2 Days Early. *New York Times*, 29 June, p. 1.

Finkelstein, Norman G. (2005) *Antisemitismus als Politische Waffe: Israel, Amerika und der Mißbrauch der Geschichte*. München: Piper.

Finkelstein, Norman G. (2011) *'This Time We Went too Far': Truth and Consequences of the Gaza Invasion*. Revised and expanded edn, New York: O/R Books.

Finkelstein, Norman G. (2014) *Method and Madness: The Hidden Story of Israel's Assault on Gaza*. New York: O/R Books.

Fones-Wolf, Elizabeth A. (1994) *Selling Free Enterprise: The Business Assault on Labor and Liberalism*. Urbana and Chicago: University of Illinois Press.

Foreign Affairs Committee (2016) *Libya: Examination of Intervention and Collapse and the UK's Future Policy Options* [online], 9 September. London: Commons Select Committee. Available at: http://www.publications.parliament.uk/pa/cm201617/cmselect/cmfaff/119/11905. htm#_idTextAnchor015 [accessed 10 November 2016].

Forgacs, David, ed. (1988) *The Antonio Gramsci Reader: Selected Writings 1916–1935*. London: Lawrence and Wishart.

Forte, Maximilian (2012) *Slouching Towards Sirte: NATO's War on Libya and Africa*. Montréal: Baraka Books.

Foster, John Bellamy, McChesney, Robert W. and Jonna, Jamil R. (2011) Monopoly and Competition in Twenty-First Century Capitalism. *Monthly Review* [online], 62(11). Available at: http://monthlyreview.org/2011/04/01/monopoly-and-competition-in-twenty-first-century-capitalism [accessed 6 April 2011].

Franklin, Bob (1997) *Newszak & News Media*. London: Arnold.

Friel, Howard and Falk, Richard (2007a) *The Record of the Paper: How the New York Times Misreports US Foreign Policy*. Paperback edn. London: Verso.

Friel, Howard and Falk, Richard (2007b) *Israel-Palestine on Record: How the New York Times Misreports Conflict in the Middle East*. London: Verso.

Frost, Chris (2000) *Media Ethics and Self-Regulation*. Harlow: Pearson.

Gans, Herbert J. (1980) *Deciding What's News: A Study of CBS Evening News, NBC Nightly News, Newsweek and Time*. London: Constable.

Gerhart, Eugene C. (1998) *World Reference Guide to More than 5,500 Memorable Quotations from Law and Literature*. New York: William S. Hein and Co.

Gieber, Walter (1956) Across the Desk: A Study of 16 Telegraph Editors. *Journalism Quarterly*, 33, pp. 423–433.

Gitlin, Todd (1980) *The Whole World is Watching: Mass Media in the Making & Unmaking of the New Left*. Berkeley and Los Angeles, CA: University of California Press.

Glasgow University Media Group (1976) *Bad News*. London: Routledge & Kegan Paul.

Glasgow University Media Group (1980) *More Bad News*. London: Routledge & Kegan Paul.

Glasgow University Media Group (1985) *War and Peace News*. London: Milton Keynes: Open University Press.

GlobalSecurity.org (n.d.a) *Iraq Pacification Operations* [online]. Available at: http://www.globalsecurity.org/military/ops/iraq_ongoing_mil_ops.htm [accessed 22 January 2012].

GlobalSecurity.org (n.d.b) *Fallujah* [online]. Available at: http://www.globalsecurity.org/military/world/iraq/fallujah.htm [accessed 12 April 2011].

Gourevitch, Alex (2003) Exporting Censorship to Iraq. *The American Prospect*, 14(9), October, pp. 34–36.

Gramsci, Antonio (1971) *Selections from the Prison Notebooks of Antonio Gramsci*. London: Lawrence and Wishart.

Habermas, Jürgen (1989) *The Structural Transformation of the Public Sphere*. Cambridge: Polity Press.

Habermas, Jürgen (1992) Further Reflections on the Public Sphere. In: Calhoun, Craig, ed. *Habermas and the Public Sphere*. Cambridge: MIT Press, pp. 421–461.

Hackensberger, Alfred (2012) In Syrien Gibt es mehr als eine Wahrheit. *Berliner Morgenpost* [online], 23 June. Available at: http://www.morgenpost.de/politik/ausland/article107255456/In-Syrien-gibt-es-mehr-als-nur-eine-Wahrheit.html [accessed 18 July 2016].

Hackett, Robert A. and Uzelman, Scott (2003) Tracing Corporate Influences on Press Content: A Summary of Recent NewsWatch Canada Research. *Journalism Studies*, 4(3), pp. 331–346.

Hall, Stuart (1977) Culture, the Media and the 'Ideological Effect'. In: Curran, James, Gurevitch, Michael and Woollacott, Jane, eds. *Mass Communication and Society*. London: Edward Arnold, pp. 315–348.

Hall, Stuart (1982) The Rediscovery of 'ideology': Return of the Repressed in Media Studies. In: Gurevitch, Michael, Bennett, Tony, Curran, James and Woollacott, Janet, eds. *Culture, Society and the Media*. London: Routledge, pp. 56–90.

Hall, Stuart, Critcher, Chas, Jefferson, Tony, Clarke, John and Roberts, Brian (1978) *Policing the Crisis: Mugging, the State, and Law and Order*. Houndmills: Macmillan.

Hallin, Daniel C. (1989) *The "Uncensored War": The Media and Vietnam*. Berkeley and Los Angeles, CA: University of California Press.

Hallin, Daniel C. (1994) *We Keep America on Top of the World: Television Journalism and the Public Sphere*. London: Routledge.

Hallin, Daniel C. and Gitlin, Todd (1994) The Gulf War as Popular Culture and Television Drama. In: Bennett, W. Lance and Paletz, David L., eds. *Taken by Storm: The Media, Public*

Opinion, and U.S. Foreign Policy in the Gulf War. Chicago: University of Chicago Press, pp. 149–163.

Hallin, Daniel C. and Mancini, Paolo (2005) Comparing Media Systems. In: Curran, James and Gurevitch, Michael, eds. *Mass Media and Society.* 4th edn. London: Hodder Arnold, pp. 215–233.

Hallin, Daniel C. and Mancini, Paolo (2010) Western Media Systems in Comparative Perspective. In: Curran, James, ed. *Media and Society.* 5th edn. London: Bloomsbury Academic, pp. 103–121.

Hallin, Daniel C., Manoff, Robert Karl and Weddle, Judy K. (1993) Sourcing Patterns of National Security Reporters. *Journalism Quarterly,* 70(4), pp. 753–766.

Hammond, Philip (2007) *Framing Post-Cold War Conflicts: The Media and International Intervention.* Manchester: Manchester University Press.

Hammond, Philip and Herman, Edward S. (2000) *Degraded Capability: The Media and the Kosovo Crisis.* London: Pluto Press.

Hardy, Jonathan (2010) The Contribution of Critical Political Economy. In: Curran, James, ed. *Media and Society.* 5th edn. London: Bloomsbury Academic, pp. 186–209.

Harnisch, Sebastian (2004) German Non-Proliferation Policy and the Iraq Conflict. *German Politics,* 13(1), pp. 1–34.

Hart, Peter (2011) 'Humanitarian War' in Libya or the Regular Kind? *Extra!* [online], August. Available at: http://www.fair.org/index.php?page=4361 [accessed 10 November].

Hashim, Ahmed (2004) Terrorism and Complex Warfare in Iraq. *Terrorism Monitor* [online], 2(12). Available at: http://www.jamestown.org/programs/gta/single/?tx_ttnews[tt_news]=29972&tx_ttnews[backPid]=179&no_cache=1 [accessed 10 November 2011].

Hedges, Chris and Al-Arian, Laila (2007) The Other War: Iraq Vets Bear Witness. *The Nation* [online], 30 July. Available at: http://www.thenation.com/article/other-war-iraq-vets-bear-witness-0 [accessed 20 January 2012].

Heinrich, Jürgen (2001) *Medienökonomie. Band 1: Mediensystem, Zeitung, Zeitschrift, Anzeigenblatt.* 2nd edn. Wiesbaden: Westdeutscher Verlag.

Heinrich, Jürgen (2002) *Medienökonomie. Band 2: Hörfunk und Fernsehen.* 2nd edn. Wiesbaden: Westdeutscher Verlag.

Herman, Edward S. (1981) *Corporate Control, Corporate Power.* Cambridge: Cambridge University Press.

Herman, Edward S. (1982) *The Real Terror Network: Terrorism in Fact and Propaganda.* Boston: South End Press.

Herman, Edward S. (1986) Gatekeeper Versus Propaganda Models: A Critical American Perspective. In: Golding, Peter, Murdock, Graham and Schlesinger, Philip, eds. *Communicating Politics: Mass Communications and the Political Process.* New York: Holmes & Meier, pp. 171–196.

Herman, Edward S. (1995) *Triumph of the Market: Essays on Economics, Politics and the Media.* Boston, MA: South End Press.

Herman, Edward S. (1999) *The Myth of the Liberal Media: An Edward Herman Reader.* New York: Peter Lang.

Herman, Edward S. (2000) The Propaganda Model: A Retrospective. *Journalism Studies*, 1(1), pp. 101–112.

Herman, Edward S. and Chomsky, Noam (1988a) *Manufacturing Consent: The Political Economy of the Mass Media*. New York: Pantheon Books.

Herman, Edward S. and Chomsky, Noam (1988b) Propaganda Mill: The Media Churn out the Official Line. *The Progressive*, 52(6), pp. 14–17.

Herman, Edward S. and Chomsky, Noam (2008) *Manufacturing Consent: The Political Economy of the Mass Media*. 3rd edn. London: The Bodley Head.

Herman, Edward S. and Chomsky, Noam (2009) *The Propaganda Model after 20 Years*. Interviewed by Mullen, Andrew. *Westminster Papers in Communication and Culture*, 6(2), pp. 12–22.

Herman, Edward S. and McChesney, Robert W. (1997) *The Global Media: The New Missionaries of Corporate Capitalism*. London: Cassell.

Herman, Edwars S. and Peterson, David (2000) CNN: Selling Nato's War Globally. In: Hammond, Philip and Herman, Edward S., eds. *Degraded Capability: The Media and the Kosovo Crisis*. London: Pluto Press, pp. 111–122.

Herman, Edward S. and Peterson, David (2007) The Dismantling of Yugoslavia. *Monthly Review* [online], 59(5). Available at http://monthlyreview.org/2007/10/01/the-dismantling-of-yugoslavia [accessed 6 March 2012].

Herman, Edward S. and Peterson, David (2010) *The Politics of Genocide*. New York: Monthly Review Press.

Herring, Eric and Rangwala, Glen (2006) *Iraq in Fragments: The Occupation and Its Legacy*. London: Hurst & Company.

Herring, Eric and Robinson, Piers (2003) Too Polemical or too Critical? Chomsky on the Study of the News Media and US Foreign Policy. *Review of International Studies*, 29, pp. 553–568.

Hersh, Seymour M. (2005) Up in the Air. *The New Yorker* [online], 5 December. Available at: http://www.newyorker.com/archive/2005/12/05/051205fa_fact?currentPage=1 [accessed 20 January 2012].

Hertog, James K. (2000) Elite Press Coverage of the 1986 U.S.-Libya Conflict: A Case Study of Tactical and Strategic Critique. *Journalism & Mass Communication Quarterly*, 77(3), pp. 612–627.

Hesmondhalgh, David (2010) Media Industry Studies, Media Production Studies. In: Curran, James, ed. *Media and Society*. 5th edn. London: Bloomsbury Academic, pp. 145–163.

Hindman, Matthew (2009) *The Myth of Digital Democracy*. Princeton: Princeton University Press.

Högemann, Elvira (2004) Musterknabe Macht mit. *Junge Welt*, 9 November, p. 5.

Holmes, Jonathan, ed. (2007) *Fallujah: Eyewitness Testimony from Iraq's Besieged City*. London: Constable.

Holsti, Ole R. (1969) *Content Analysis for the Social Sciences and Humanities*. Menlo Park, CA: Addison-Wesley Publishing Company.

Hoskins, Andrew and O'Loughlin, Ben (2010) *War and Media: The Emergence of Diffused War*. Cambridge: Polity Press.

Human Rights Watch (2003a) *Off Target: The Conduct of the War and Civilian Casualties in Iraq*. New York: Human Rights Watch.

Human Rights Watch (2003b) *Violent Response: The U.S. Army in al-Falluja* [online], 17 June. New York: Human Rights Watch. Available at: http://www.hrw.org/reports/2003/iraqfalluja/ [accessed 22 September 2007].

Human Rights Watch (2003c) *Hearts and Minds: Post-war Civilian Deaths in Baghdad Caused by U.S. Forces*. New York: Human Rights Watch.

Human Rights Watch (2012) *Syria: Armed Opposition Groups Committing Abuses* [online], 20 March. Available at: https://www.hrw.org/news/2012/03/20/syria-armed-opposition-groups-committing-abuses [accessed 22 June 2016].

Human Rights Watch (2013) *Egypt: Investigate Police, Military Killings of 51. Accountability Essential to Break Cycle of Impunity* [online], 14 July. New York: Human Rights Watch. Available at: https://www.hrw.org/news/2013/07/14/egypt-investigate-police-military-killings-51 [accessed 16 May 2016].

Human Rights Watch (2014a) *Egypt: New Leader Faces Rights Crisis* [online], 9 June. New York: Human Rights Watch. Available at: https://www.hrw.org/news/2014/06/09/egypt-new-leader-faces-rights-crisis [accessed 16 May 2016].

Human Rights Watch (2014b) *All According to Plan: The Rab'a Massacre and Mass Killings of Protestors in Egypt* [online], 12 August. New York: Human Rights Watch. Available at: https://www.hrw.org/report/2014/08/12/all-according-plan/raba-massacre-and-mass-killings-protesters-egypt [accessed 16 May 2016].

Humphreys, Peter J. (1996) *Mass Media and Media Policy in Western Europe*. Manchester: Manchester University Press.

IBC (2004a) Civilian Deaths in "Noble" Iraq Mission Pass 10,000. *Iraq Body Count* [online], 7 February. Available at: http://www.iraqbodycount.org/analysis/beyond/ten-thousand/ [accessed 22 January 2012].

IBC (2004b) No Longer Unknowable: Falluja's April Civilian Toll is 600. *Iraq Body Count* [online], 26 October. Available at: http://www.iraqbodycount.org/analysis/reference/press-releases/9/ [accessed 10 September 2012].

IBC (2013) The War in Iraq: 10 Years and Counting. *Iraq Body Count* [online], 19 March. Available at: https://www.iraqbodycount.org/analysis/numbers/ten-years/ [accessed 12 May 2016].

IBC (n.d.) Documented Civilian Deaths from Violence. *Iraq Body Count* [online]. Available at: https://www.iraqbodycount.org/database// [accessed 12 May 2016].

ICC (2011) *First Report of the Prosecutor of the International Criminal Court to the UN Security Council Pursuant to UNSCR 1970 (2011)* [online], 4 May. The Hague: The Office of the Prosecutor. Available at: https://www.icc-cpi.int/NR/rdonlyres/A077E5F8-29B6-4A78-9EAB-A179A105738E/0/UNSCLibyaReportEng04052011.pdf [accessed 4 May 2017].

International Committee of the Red Cross (2005) *1949 Conventions and Additional Protocols* [online]. Available at: http://www.icrc.org/ihl.nsf/CONVPRES?OpenView [accessed 10 August 2012].

IRIN (2004a) IRAQ: Thousands of Residents Have Fled Fallujah. *IRIN* [online], 8 November. Available at: http://www.irinnews.org/Report/24274/IRAQ-Thousands-of-residents-have-fled-Fallujah [accessed 10 March 2012].

IRIN (2004b) IRAQ: Medical Needs Massive in Fallujah – Red Crescent. *IRIN* [online], 10 November. Available at: http://www.irinnews.org/Report/24277/IRAQ-Medical-needs-massive-in-Fallujah-Red-Crescent [accessed 10 March 2012].

IRIN (2004c) IRAQ: IRCS Delivers Aid to Displaced Around Fallujah. *IRIN* [online], 12 November. Available at: http://www.irinnews.org/Report/24281/IRAQ-IRCS-delivers-aid-to-displaced-around-Fallujah [accessed 10 March 2012].

IRIN (2004d) IRAQ: IRCS Delivered Aid to Fallujah. *IRIN* [online], 26 November. Available at: http://www.irinnews.org/fr/Report/24297/IRAQ-IRCS-delivered-aid-to-Fallujah [accessed 10 May 2012].

IRIN (2005) IRAQ: Death Toll in Fallujah Rising, Doctors Say. *IRIN* [online], 4 January. Available at: http://www.irinnews.org/report.aspx?reportid=24527 [accessed 10 May 2011].

Iyengar, Shanto and Simon, Adam (1994) News Coverage of the Gulf War and Public Opinion: A Study of Agenda Setting, Priming, and Framing. In: Bennett, W. Lance and Paletz, David L., eds. *Taken by Storm: The Media, Public Opinion, and U.S. Foreign Policy in the Gulf War*. Chicago: University of Chicago Press, pp. 167–185.

Jamail, Dahr (2004a) Media Repression in 'Liberated' Land. *Inter Press Service* [online], 18 November. Available at: http://www.ipsnews.net/2004/11/iraq-media-repression-in-liberated-land/ [accessed 4 May 2017].

Jamail, Dahr (2004b) 800 Civilians Feared Dead in Fallujah. *Inter Press Service* [online], 16 November. Available at: http://www.ipsnews.net/2004/11/iraq-800-civilians-feared-dead-in-fallujah/ [accessed 4 May 2017].

Jamail, Dahr (2005) Life Goes On in Fallujah's Rubble. *Antiwar.com* [online], 24 November. Available at: http://www.antiwar.com/jamail/?articleid=8147 [accessed 10 July 2012].

Jamail, Dahr (2007) *Beyond the Green Zone: Dispatches from an Unembedded Journalist in Occupied Iraq*. Chicago, IL: Haymarket Books.

Jarren, Otfried and Donges, Patrick (2002) *Politische Kommunikation in der Mediengesellschaft. Eine Einführung Band 1: Verständnis, Rahmen und Strukturen*, Wiesbaden: Westdeutscher Verlag.

Jowett, Garth S. and O'Donnell, Victoria (1992) *Propaganda and Persuasion*. 2nd edn. London: Sage.

Karmasin, Matthias (1998) *Medienökonomie als Theorie (Massen-)Medialer Kommunikation. Kommunikationsökonomie und Stakeholder Theorie*. Graz-Wien: Nausner & Nausner.

Keane, John (1991) *The Media and Democracy*. Cambridge: Polity Press.

Keeble, Richard (1997) *Secret State, Silent Press: New Militarism, the Gulf and the Modern Image of Warfare*. Luton: John Libbey Media.

Keeble, Richard (2000) New Militarism and the Manufacture of Warfare. In: Hammond, Philip and Herman, Edward S., eds. *Degraded Capability: The Media and the Kosovo Crisis*. London: Pluto Press, pp. 59–69.

Keeble, Richard (2004) Information Warfare in an Age of Hyper-Militarism. In: Allan, Stuart and Zelizer, Barbie, eds. *Reporting War: Journalism in Wartime*. London: Routledge, pp. 43–58.

Keeble, Richard (2006) *The Newspapers Handbook*. 4th edn. London: Routledge.

Keeble, Richard (2009) *Ethics for Journalists*. 2nd edn. London: Routledge.

Keeble, Richard (2011) *Operation Moshtarak* and the Manufacture of Credible, 'Heroic' Warfare. *Global Media and Communication*, 7(3), pp. 187–191.

Kegel, Sandra (2003) Im Krieg findet jeder zu seiner Wahrheit. *Frankfurter Allgemeine Zeitung*, 14 April, p. 42.

Keiler, Jonathan F. (2005) Who Won the Battle of Fallujah? *Proceedings* [online], January. Available at: http://www.military.com/NewContent/1,13190,NI_0105_Fallujah-P1,00. html [accessed 23 March 2012].

Kelley, David and Donway, Roger (1990) Liberalism and Free Speech. In: Lichtenberg, Judith, ed. *Democracy and the Mass Media*. Cambridge: Cambridge University Press, pp. 66–101.

Kelly, Jack (2004) U.S. Tactics, Training Kept Casualties down in Fallujah. *Pittsburgh Post-Gazette* [online], 21 November. Available at: http://old.post-gazette.com/pg/04326/414662. stm [accessed 23 March 2012].

Khera, Jastinder (2012) Syria Crisis: Counting the Victims. *BBC News* [online], 29 May. Available at: http://www.bbc.co.uk/news/world-middle-east-18093967 [accessed 11 May 2015].

Kiefer, Marie Luise (2001) *Medienökonomik: Einführung in eine ökonomische Theorie der Medien*. München: R. Oldenbourg Verlag.

Kiss, Jemima (2004) Undercover in Iraq: Safety Slowly Improving for Iraq's Home-Grown Reporters. *Journalism co.uk* [online], 29 July. Available at: http://www.journalism.co.uk/ news/undercover-in-iraq/s2/a51009/ [accessed 2 December 2011].

Klaehn, Jeffery (2002) A Critical Review and Assessment of Herman and Chomsky's "Propaganda Model". *European Journal of Communication*, 17(2), pp. 147–182.

Klaehn, Jeffery (2005) *Filtering the News: Essays on Herman and Chomsky's Propaganda Model*. Montreal: Black Rose Books.

Klaehn, Jeffery (2009) The Propaganda Model: Theoretical and Methodological Considerations. *Westminster Papers in Communication and Culture*, 6(2): 43–58.

Klare, Michael T. (2005) More blood, less oil. The failed U.S. mission to capture Iraqi petroleum. *TomDispatch.com* [online], 20 September. Available at: http://www.tomdispatch. com/post/22859/ [accessed 1 May 2011].

Klein, Naomi (2007) *Die Schock Strategie: Der Aufstieg des Katastrophen-Kapitalismus*. Frankfurt am Main: S. Fischer Verlag.

Kolko, Gabriel (1976) *Main Currents in Modern American History*. New York: Harper & Row.

Kovach, Bill and Rosenstiel, Tom (2003) *The Elements of Journalism*. London: Atlantic Books.

Krippendorff, Klaus (1980) *Content Analysis: An Introduction to Its Methodology*. London: Sage.

Krüger, Udo M. (2003) Der Irak-Krieg im Deutschen Fernsehen: Analyse der Berichterstattung in ARD/Das Erste, ZDF, RTL und SAT.1. *Media Perspektiven*, 34(9), pp. 398–413.

Krüger, Uwe (2013) *Meinungsmacht: Der Einfluss von Eliten auf Leitmedien und Alpha-Journalisten – Eine Kritische Netzwerkanalyse*. Köln: Herbert von Halem Verlag.

Kruse, Jörn (1996) Publizistische Vielfalt und Medienkonzentration – Zwischen Marktkräften und Politischen Entscheidungen. In: Altmeppen, Klaus-Dieter, ed. Ökonomie der Medien und des Mediensystems. *Grundlagen, Ergebnisse und Perspektiven medienökonomischer Forschung*. Opladen: Westdeutscher Verlag, pp. 25–52.

Kuperman, Alan, J. (2013) A Model Humanitarian Intervention? Reassessing NATO's Libya Campaign. *International Security*, 38(1), pp. 105–136.

Lang, Kurt and Lang, Gladys Engel (1953) The Unique Perspective of Television and Its Effect: A Pilot Study. *American Sociological Review*, 18(1), pp. 3–12.

Lange, Sascha (2006) Falludscha und die Transformation der Streitkräfte. *Europäische Sicherheit*, 6, pp. 12–16.

Lanine, Nikolai, Edwards, David and Cromwell, David (2007) Invasion – A Comparison of Soviet and Western Media Performance. *Media Lens* [online], 20 November. Available at: http://www.medialens.org/index.php?option=com_content&view=article&id=526:invasion-a-comparison-of-soviet-and-western-media-performance&catid=21:alerts-2007&Itemid=38 [accessed 10 November 2011].

Lawrence, Regina G. (1996) Accidents, Icons, and Indexing: The Dynamics of News Coverage of Police Use of Force. *Political Communication*, 13(4), pp. 437–454.

Lawrence, Regina G. (2000) *The Politics of Force: Media and the Construction of Police Brutality*. Berkeley, CA: University of California Press.

Lazarsfeld, Paul F. and Merton, Robert K. (1957 [1948]) Mass Communication, Popular Taste and Organised Social Action. In: Rosenberg, Bernard and White, David Manning, eds. *Mass Culture: The Popular Arts in America*. New York: The Free Press, pp. 457–473.

Leidinger, Christiane (2003) *Medien – Herrschaft – Globalisierung. Folgenabschätzung zu Medieninhalten im Zuge transnationaler Konzentrationsprozesse*. Münster: Westfälisches Dampfboot.

Lewis, Justin, Brookes, Rod, Mosdell, Nick and Threadgold, Terry (2006) *Shoot First and Ask Questions Later: Media Coverage of the 2003 Iraq War*. New York: Peter Lang.

Lewis, Justin, Williams, Andrew and Franklin, Bob (2008) A Compromised Fourth Estate? UK News Journalism, Public Relations and News Sources. *Journalism Studies*, 9(1), pp. 1–20.

Leyendecker, Hans and Krach, Wolfgang (2010) BND Half Amerikanern im Irak-Krieg. *Süddeutsche Zeitung* [online], 17 May. Available at: http://www.sueddeutsche.de/politik/geheime-kooperation-bnd-half-amerikanern-im-irak-krieg-1.783196 [accessed 8 November 2016].

Lichtenberg, Judith, ed. (1990a) *Democracy and the Mass Media*. Cambridge: Cambridge University Press.

Lichtenberg, Judith (1990b) Foundation and Limits of Freedom of the Press. In: Lichtenberg, Judith, ed. *Democracy and the Mass Media*. Cambridge: Cambridge University Press, pp. 102–135.

Lichtenberg, Judith (1990c) Introduction. In: Lichtenberg, Judith, ed. *Democracy and The Mass Media*. Cambridge: Cambridge University Press, pp. 1–20.

Livingston, Steven and Bennett, W. Lance (2003) Gatekeeping, Indexing, and Live-Event News: Is Technology Altering the Construction of News? *Political Communication*, 20(4), pp. 363–380.

Livingston, Steven and Eachus, Todd (1995) Humanitarian Crises and U.S. Foreign Policy: Somalia and the CNN Effect Reconsidered. *Political Communication*, 12, pp. 413–429.

Löffelholz, Martin (2004) Krisen- und Kriegskommunikation als Forschungsfeld: Trends, Themen und Theorien Eines Hoch Relevanten, aber Gering Systematisierten Teilgebietes der Kommunikationswissenschaft. In: Löffelholz, Martin, ed. *Krieg als Medienereignis II: Krisenkommunikation im 21. Jahrhundert*. Wiesbaden: VS Verlag für Sozialwissenschaften, pp. 13–55.

Lynch, Colum (2016) The War Over Syria's War Dead. *Foreign Policy* [online], 13 January. Available at: http://foreignpolicy.com/2016/01/13/the-war-over-syrias-war-dead/ [accessed 23 June 2016].

Lyons, John (2012) Bombs in Syria as Saudis 'Send Arms to Rebels'. *The Australian* [online], 19 March. Available at: http://www.theaustralian.com.au/news/world/bombsinsyriaas-saudissendarmstorebels/storye6frg6so1226303233997 [accessed 27 June 2015].

Mandel, Michael (2005) *Pax Pentagon: Wie die USA der Welt den Krieg als Frieden Verkauft.* Frankfurt am Main: Zweitausendeins.

Mansour, Ahmed (2009) *Inside Fallujah: The Unembedded Story.* Moreton-in-Marsh: Arris Books.

Marx, Karl (1904 [1859]) *A Contribution to a Critique of Political Economy.* Translated from German by Stone, N.I. Chicago: Charles H. Kerr & Company.

Marx, Karl and Engels, Frederick (1977 [1932]) *The German Ideology: Part One.* 2nd edn. Repr. London: Lawrence & Wishart.

McChesney, Robert W. (1997) *Corporate Media and the Threat to Democracy.* New York: Seven Stories Press.

McChesney, Robert W. (2003) The Problem of Journalism: A Political Economic Contribution to an Explanation of the Crisis in Contemporary Journalism. *Journalism Studies,* 4(3), pp. 299–329.

McChesney, Robert W. (2004) *The Problem of the Media: U.S. Communication Politics in the 21st Century.* New York: Monthly Review Press.

McChesney, Robert W. (2007) *Communication Revolution: Critical Junctures and the Future of Media.* New York: The New Press.

McChesney, Robert W. (2008) *The Political Economy of Media: Enduring Issues, Emerging Dilemmas.* New York: Monthly Review Press.

McChesney, Robert W. (2013) *Digital Disconnect: How Capitalism is Turning the Internet Against Democracy.* New York: The New Press.

McKee, Alan (2005) *The Public Sphere: An Introduction.* Cambridge: Cambridge University Press.

McNair, Brian (1991) *Glasnost, Perestroika and the Soviet Media.* London: Routledge.

McNair, Brian (2003) *News and Journalism in the UK.* London: Routledge.

McQuail, Denis (2010) *McQuail's Mass Communication Theory.* 6th edn. London: Sage.

McQuail, Denis and Siune, Karen (2001) *Media policy: Convergence, Concentration & Commerce.* Repr. London: Sage.

Mearsheimer, John and Walt, Stephen (2006) The Israel Lobby. *London Review of Books* [online], 23 March. Available at: http://www.lrb.co.uk/v28/n06/john-mearsheimer/the-israel-lobby [accessed 22 June 2016].

Medact (2003) *Continuing Collateral Damage: The Health and Environmental Costs of War on Iraq 2003.* London: Medact.

Meier, Werner A. (2003) Politische Ökonomie. In: Altmeppen, Klaus-Dieter and Karmasin, Matthias, eds. *Medien und Ökonomie. Band 1/1: Grundlagen der Medienökonomie: Kommunikations- und Medienwissenschaft, Wirtschaftswissenschaft.* Wiesbaden: Westdeutscher Verlag, pp. 215–243.

Meiklejohn, Alexander (1960) *Political Freedom: The Constitutional Powers of the People.* New York: Harper & Brothers.

Mermin, Jonathan (1996) Conflict in the Sphere of Consensus? Critical Reporting on the Panama Invasion and the Gulf War. *Political Communication,* 13, pp. 181–194.

Mermin, Jonathan (1999) *Debating War and Peace: Media Coverage of U.S. Intervention in the Post-Vietnam Era.* Princeton: Princeton University Press.

Merton, Robert K. (1968) *Social Theory and Social Structure.* Enlarged edn. New York: The Free Press.

Meyn, Hermann (2001) *Massenmedien in Deutschland.* New edn. Konstanz: UVK Verlagsgesellschaft.

Miliband, Ralph (1987 [1973]) *The State in Capitalist Society: The Analysis of the Western System of Power.* London: Quarted Books.

Mill, John Stuart (2009 [1859]) *On Liberty.* New York: Cosimo.

Miller, David and Dinan, William (2000) The Rise of the PR Industry in Britain, 1979–98. *European Journal of Communication,* 15(1), pp. 5–35.

Miller, David and Dinan, William (2008) *A Century of Spin: How Public Relations Became the Cutting Edge of Corporate Power.* London: Pluto Press.

Miller, David and Dinan, William (2010) Introduction. In: Klaehn, Jeffery, ed. *The Political Economy of Media and Power.* New York: Peter Lang, pp. 1–5.

Mills, C. Wright (1956) *The Power Elite.* Oxford: Oxford University Press.

Moeller, Susan D. (2004) *Media Coverage of Weapons of Mass Destruction.* Center for International and Security Studies. Maryland: University of Maryland.

Molotch, Harvey and Lester, Marilyn (1974) News as Purposive Behavior: On the Strategic Use of Routine Events, Accidents, and Scandals. *American Sociological Review,* 39(1), pp. 101–112.

Mosco, Vincent (2009) *The Political Economy of Communication.* 2nd edn. London: Sage.

Mullen, Andrew (2010) Twenty Years On: The Second-Order Prediction of the Herman-Chomsky Propaganda Model. *Media, Culture & Society,* 32(4), pp. 673–690.

Mullen, Andrew and Klaehn, Jeffery (2010) The Herman-Chomsky Propaganda Model: A Critical Approach to Analysing Mass Media Behaviour. *Sociology Compass,* 4(4), pp. 215–229.

Murdock, Graham (1982) Large Corporations and the Control of the Communications Industries. In: Gurevitch, Michael, Bennett, Tony, Curran, James and Woollacott, Janet, eds. *Culture, Society and the Media.* London: Routledge, pp. 118–150.

Murdock, Graham and Golding, Peter (1973) For a Political Economy of Mass Communications. *The Socialist Register,* pp. 205–234.

Murdock, Graham and Golding, Peter (1977) Capitalism, Communication and Class Relation. In: Curran, James, Gurevitch, Michael and Woollacott, Janet, eds. *Mass Communication and Society.* London: Edward Arnold, pp. 12–43.

Murdock, Graham and Golding, Peter (2005) Culture, Communications and Political Economy. In: Curran, James and Gurevitch, Michael, eds. *Mass Media and Society.* 4th edn. London: Edward Arnold, pp. 60–83.

Nacos, Brigitte L., Shapiro, Robert Y., Hritzuk, Natasha and Chadwick, Bruce (2000) New Issues and the Media: American and German News Coverage of the Global-Warming

Debate. In: Nacos, Brigitte L., Shapiro, Robert Y. and Isernia, Pierangelo, eds. *Decision-making in a Glass House*. Lanham, MD: Rowman & Littlefield.

Neuberger, Christoph, Nuernbergk, Christian and Rischke, Melanie (2009) Journalismus – Neu Vermessen: Die Grundgesamtheit Journalistischer Internetangebote – Methode und Ergebnisse. In: Neuberger, Christoph, Nuernbergk, Christian and Rischke, Melanie, eds. *Journalismus im Internet: Profession – Partizipation – Technisierung*. Wiesbaden: VS Verlag für Sozialwissenschaften, pp. 197–230.

Neuendorf, Kimberly A. (2002) *The Content Analysis Guidebook*, Thousand Oaks: Sage.

NGIC (2006) *Complex Environments: Battle of Fallujah I, April 2004*. U.S. Army: National Ground Intelligence Center.

Nichols, John and McChesney, Robert W. (2005) *Tragedy and Farce: How the American Media Sell Wars, Spin Elections, and Destroy Democracy*. New York: New Press.

Norris, Pippa (1995) The Restless Searchlight: Network News Framing of the Post-Cold War World. *Political Communication*, 12, pp. 357–370.

Obermeyer, Ziad, Murray, Christopher J.L. and Gakidou, Emmanuela (2008) Fifty Years of Violent War Deaths from Vietnam to Bosnia: Analysis of Data from the World Health Survey Programme. *British Medical Journal* [online], 336. Available at: http://www.bmj.com/content/336/7659/1482.full [accessed 20 August 2012].

O'Donnell, Patrick K. (2006) *We Were One: Shoulder to Shoulder with the Marines Who Took Fallujah*. Philadelphia, PA: Da Capo Press.

O'Neill, Onora (1990) Practices of Toleration. In: Lichtenberg, Judith, ed. *Democracy and the Mass Media*. Cambridge: Cambridge University Press, pp. 155–185.

Owen, Bruce M. (1975) *Economics and Freedom of Expression: Media Structure and the First Amendment*. Cambridge, MA: Ballinger Publishing Company.

Page, Benjamin I. (1996) *Who Deliberates? Mass Media in Modern Democracy*. Chicago: The University of Chicago Press.

Pape, Robert A. (1996) *Bombing to Win: Air Power and Coercion in War*. Ithaca and London: Cornell University Press.

Parenti, Michael (1993) *Inventing Reality: The Politics of News Media*. 2nd edn. New York: St. Martin's Press.

Parliament (1999) *Kosovo* [online], 18 January. London: Parliament, UK. Available at: http://www.publications.parliament.uk/pa/cm199899/cmhansrd/vo990118/debtext/90118-06.htm [accessed 11 May 2016].

Paterson, Chris (2011) Government Intervention in the Iraq War Media Narrative Through Direct Coercion. *Global Media and Communication*, 7(3), pp. 181–186.

Pearl, Daniel and Block, Robert (1999) Despite Tales, the War in Kosovo Was Savage but Wasn't Genocide. *The Wall Street Journal* [online]. Available at: http://www.wsj.com/articles/SB946593838546941319 [accessed 14 June 2016].

Philo, Greg and Berry, Mike (2011) *More Bad News From Israel*. London: Pluto Press.

Pilger, John (2015) From Pol Pot to ISIS: The Blood Never Dried. *JohnPilger.com* [online], 16 November. Available at: http://johnpilger.com/articles/from-pol-pot-to-isis-the-blood-never-dried [accessed 24 June 2016].

Pilger, John (2016) Inside the Invisible Government. *JohnPilger.com* [online], 27 October. Available at: http://johnpilger.com/articles/inside-the-invisible-government-war-propaganda-clinton-trump [accessed 22 November 2016].

Pohr, Adrian (2005) Indexing im Einsatz. Eine Inhaltsanalyse der Kommentare Überregionaler Tageszeitungen in Deutschland zum Afghanistan Krieg 2001. *Medien & Kommunikationswissenschaft*, 53(2–3), pp. 261–276.

Reese, Stephen D. and Ballinger, Jane (2001) The Roots of a Sociology of News: Remembering Mr. Gates and Social Control in the Newsroom. *Journalism and Mass Communication Quarterly*, 78(4), pp. 641–658.

Rehman, Javaid (2010) *International Human Rights Law*. 2nd edn. Harlow: Pearson.

Reuters (2004c) Iraq Tells Media to Toe the Line. *Los Angeles Times* [online], 12 November. Available at: http://articles.latimes.com/2004/nov/12/world/fg-media12 [accessed 2 December 2011].

Reuters (2013) *Anti-Assad Monitoring Group Says Syrian Death Toll Passes 130,000* [online], 31 December. Available at: http://www.reuters.com/article/us-syria-crisis-toll-idUSBRE-9BU0FA20131231 [accessed 23 June 2016].

Risse, Thomas and Sikkink, Kathryn (1999) The Socialization of International Human Rights Norms into Domestic Practices: Introduction. In: Risse, Thomas, Ropp, Stephen C., and Sikkink, Kathryn, eds. *The Power of Human Rights: International Norms and Domestic Change*. Cambridge: Cambridge University Press pp. 1–38.

Roberts, Hugh (2011) Who Said Gaddafi Has to Go? *London Review of Books* [online], 17 November. Available at: http://www.lrb.co.uk/v33/n22/hugh-roberts/who-said-gaddafi-had-to-go [accessed 8 June 2016].

Roberts, Les (2007) Iraq's Death Toll Is Far Worse Than Our Leaders Admit. *The Independent*, 14 February, p. 32.

Roberts, Les, Lafta, Riyadh, Garfield, Richard, Khudhairi, Jamal and Burnham, Gilbert (2004) Mortality Before and After the 2003 Invasion of Iraq: Cluster Sample Survey. *The Lancet*, 364(29 October), pp. 1857–1864.

Robinson, Piers (2000a) Research Note: The News Media and Intervention: Triggering the Use of Air Power during Humanitarian Crises. *European Journal of Communication*, 15(3), pp. 405–414.

Robinson, Piers (2000b) World Politics and Media Power: Problems of Research Design. *Media, Culture & Society*, 22(2), pp. 227–232.

Robinson, Piers (2004) Researching US Media–State Relations and Twenty-First Century Wars. In: Allan, Stuart and Zelizer, Barbie, eds. *Reporting War: Journalism in Wartime*. London and New York: Routledge, pp. 96–112.

Robinson, Piers (2006) The CNN Effect Revisited. *Critical Studies in Media Communication*, 22(4), pp. 344–349.

Robinson, Piers, Goddard, Peter, Parry, Katy and Murray, Craig (2009) Testing Models of Media Performance in Wartime: U.K. TV News and the 2003 Invasion of Iraq. *Journal of Communication*, 59(3), pp. 534–563.

Robinson, Piers, Goddard, Peter, Parry, Katy, Murray, Craig and Taylor, Philip M. (2010) *Pockets of Resistance: British News Media, War and Theory in the 2003 Invasion of Iraq*. Manchester: Manchester University Press.

Röper, Horst (2002) Zeitungsmarkt 2002: Wirtschaftliche Krise und Steigende Konzentration. *Media Perspektiven*, 10, pp. 478–490.

Röper, Horst (2010) Zeitungen 2010: Rangverschiebungen Unter den Größten Verlagen. *Media Perspektiven*, 5, pp. 218–234.

Sampson, Anthony (2002) Oilmen Don't Want Another Suez – Critics of US Policy Claim It Aims to Carve Up Iraq's Oil …. *The Observer*, 22 December, p. 17.

Schiller, Herbert I. (1973) *The Mind Managers*. Boston: Beacon Press.

Schiller, Herbert I. (1982) *Who Knows: Information in the Age of the Fortune 500*. 2nd ed. Norwood, NJ: Ablex Publishing Corporation.

Schiller, Herbert I. (1986) *Information and the Crisis Economy*. Oxford: Oxford University Press.

Schiller, Herbert I. (1989) *Culture Inc.: The Corporate Takeover of Public Expression*. Oxford: Oxford University Press.

SCHRD (2005) *Report on the Current Situation in the city of Fallujah Presented to the 61st Session of the United Nations Commission on Human Rights*. Baghdad: SCHRD.

Schwartz, Michael (2008) *War Without End: The Iraq War in Context*. Chicago, IL: Haymarket Books.

Shaik, Salman (2011) Libya's Test of the New International Order. *Brookings* [online], 26 February. Available at: http://www.brookings.edu/research/opinions/2011/02/26-libya-shaikh [accessed 22 June 2016].

Sherlock, Ruth (2011) Libya's New Rulers Offer Weapons to Syrian Rebels. *The Daily Telegraph* [online], 25 November. Available at: http://www.telegraph.co.uk/news/worldnews/middleeast/syria/8917265/LibyasnewrulersofferweaponstoSyrianrebels.html [accessed 24 June 2015].

Shoemaker, Pamela J. (1991) *Communication Concepts 3: Gatekeeping*. Newbury Park, CA: Sage.

Shoemaker, Pamela J., Eichholz, Martin, Eunyi, Kim and Wrigley, Brenda (2001) Individual and Routine Forces in Gatekeeping. *Journalism and Mass Communication Quarterly*, 78(2), pp. 233–246.

Shoemaker, Pamela J. and Reese, Stephen D. (1996) *Mediating the Message: Theories of Influences on Mass Media Content*. 2nd ed. New York: Longman.

Siebert, Fred S., Peterson, Theodore and Schramm, Wilbur (1984 [1956]) *Four Theories of the Press*. Urbana: University of Illinois Press.

Sigal, Leon V. (1973) *Reporters and Officials: The Organization and Politics of Newsmaking*. Lexington, MA: D.C. Heath and Company.

Sigelman, Lee (1973) Reporting the News: An Organizational Analysis. *American Journal of Sociology*, 79(1), pp. 132–151.

Silverstein, Brett (1987) Toward a Science of Propaganda. *Political Psychology*, 8(1), pp. 49–59.

Sinclair, Ian (2015) 10 facts the Government Doesn't Want You to Know About Syria. *OpenDemocracyUK* [online], 10 December. Available at: https://www.opendemocracy.net/uk/

ian-sinclair/10-facts-government-doesn-t-want-you-to-know-about-syria [accessed 24 June 2016].

Smythe, Dallas W. (1981) *Dependency Road: Communications, Capitalism, Consciousness, and Canada*. Norwood, NJ: Ablex Publishing Corporation.

Snider, Paul B. (1967) "Mr Gates" Revisited: A 1966 Version of the 1949 Case Study. *Journalism Quarterly*, 44, pp. 419–427.

Soontae, An and Jin, Hyun Seung (2004) Interlocking of Newspaper Companies with Financial Institutions and Leading Advertisers. *Journalism and Mass Communication Quarterly*, 81(3), pp. 578–600.

Sparks, Colin (1999) The Press. In: Stokes, Jane and Reading, Anna, eds. *The Media in Britain: Current Debates and Developments*. New York: St. Martin's Press, pp. 41–60.

Sparks, Colin (2007) Extending and Refining the Propaganda Model. *Westminster Papers in Communication and Culture*, 4(2), pp. 68–84.

Sparrow, Bartholomew H. (1999) *Uncertain Guardians: The News Media as a Political Institution*. Baltimore, MD: John Hopkins University Press.

Stepp, Carl Sessions (1990) Access in a Post-Social Responsibility Age. In: Lichtenberg, Judith, ed. *Democracy and the Mass Media*. Cambridge: Cambridge University Press, pp. 102–135.

Szukala, Andrea (2003) Medien und Öffentliche Meinung im Irakkrieg. *Aus Politik und Zeitgeschichte*, 24–25, pp. 25–34.

Taheri, Amir (2004) Events that Make Fallujah a Deadly Cocktail. *Arab News* [online], 10 November. Available at: http://www.arabnews.com/node/257897 [accessed 4 May 2017].

Thompson, Peter A. (2009) Market Manipulation? Applying the Propaganda Model to Financial Media Reporting. *Westminster Papers in Communication and Culture*, 6(2), pp. 73–96.

Tilford, Robert (2012) *US Helping to Train and Arm Islamic Mercenaries to Fight in Syria* [online], 9 March. Available at: http://www.examiner.com/article/ushelpingtotrainandarmislamic-mercenariestofightsyria [accessed 24 June 2015].

Trappel, Josef (2008) "Worldmedia Inc.": Vision oder bereits Geschichte? *Media Perspektiven*, 3, pp. 138–147.

Trettenbein, Harald (1994) Interventionsmöglichkeiten Gegen Medienkonzentration. In: Bruck, Peter A., ed. *Medienmanager Staat. Von den Versuchen des Staates, Medienvielfalt zu Ermöglichen. Medienpolitik im Internationalen Vergleich*. München: Verlag Reinhard Fischer.

Triebe, Benjamin (2005) Bundesrichter Werfen Schröder Unterstützung des Irak-Krieges vor. *Spiegel Online* [online], 8 September. Available at: http://www.spiegel.de/politik/deutschland/0,1518,373592,00.html [accessed 10 November].

Tuchman, Gaye (1972) Objectivity as Strategic Ritual: An Examination of Newsmen's Notions of Objectivity. *American Journal of Sociology*, 77(4), pp. 660–679.

Tuchman, Gaye (1973) Making News by Doing Work: Routinizing the Unexpected. *American Journal of Sociology*, 79(1), pp. 110–131.

Tuchman, Gaye (1978) *Making News: A Study in the Construction of Reality*. New York: The Free Press.

Tulloch, John (2007) Tabloid Citizenship. *Journalism Studies*, 8(1), pp. 42–60.

Tumber, Howard and Palmer, Jerry (2004) *Media at War: The Iraq Crisis*. London: Sage.

Tunstall, Jeremy (1996) *Newspaper Power: The New National Press in Britain.* Oxford: Clarendon Press.

Turse, Nick (2015) U.S. Special Ops Forces Deployed in 135 Nations. *TomDispatch.com* [online], 24 September. Available at: http://www.tomdispatch.com/post/176048/ [accessed 7 November 2016].

Ungar, Sanford J. (1990) The Role of a Free Press in Strengthening Democracy. In: Lichtenberg, Judith, ed. *Democracy and the Mass Media.* Cambridge: Cambridge University Press, pp. 368–398.

United Nations General Assembly (1974) *A/RES/3314 (XXIX). Definition of Aggression* [online]. Available at: https://documents-dds-ny.un.org/doc/RESOLUTION/GEN/ NR0/739/16/IMG/NR073916.pdf?OpenElement [accessed 4 May 2017].

United Nations Security Council (1998) *Security Council Demands All Parties End Hostilities and Maintain a Ceasefire in Kosovo* [online], 23 September. New York: United Nations. Available at: http://www.un.org/press/en/1998/19980923.sc6577.html [accessed 14 September 2016].

United Nations Security Council (2004) *S/RES/1546.* New York: United Nations.

United Nations Security Council (2011) *S/Res/1973* [online], 17 March. Available at: http:// www.nato.int/nato_static/assets/pdf/pdf_2011_03/20110927_110311-UNSCR-1973.pdf [accessed 8 June 2016].

United Nations Security Council (2012) *Security Council Press Statement on Attacks in Syria* [online], 27 May. New York: United Nations. Available at: http://www.un.org/press/ en/2012/sc10658.doc.htm [accessed 11 May 2016].

UNSMIS (n.d.) *United Nations Supervision Mission in Syria. Monitoring of Cessation of Armed Violence in All Its Forms* [online]. Available at: http://www.un.org/en/peacekeeping/missions/past/unsmis/ [accessed 8 June 2016].

UN Watch (2011) *Urgent Appeal to Stop Atrocities in Libya* [online], 21 February. Available at: http://secure.unwatch.org/site/apps/nlnet/content2.aspx?c=bdKKISNqEmG&b= 1330815&ct=9135143 [accessed 22 June 2016].

US Department of Defence (2004) *DoD Briefing – Iraq Security Forces and Multinational Forces Offensive Actions in Fallujah, Iraq* [online], 8 November 2004. Available at http://www. defenselink.mil/transcripts/transcript.aspx?transcriptid=2087 [accessed 11 April 2011].

Vautravers, Alexandre (2010) Military operations in urban areas. *International Review of the Red Cross,* 92(878), pp. 437–452.

Wallerstein, Immanuel (1974) The Rise and Future Demise of the World Capitalist System: Concepts for Comparative Analysis. *Comparative Studies in Society and History,* 16(4), pp. 387–415.

Wallerstein, Immanuel (2004) *World-Systems Analysis.* Durham: Duke University Press.

Warner, Malcom (1971) Organizational Context and Control of Policy in the Television Newsroom: A Participant Observation Study. *The British Journal of Sociology,* 22(3), pp. 283–294.

Weber, Robert Philip (1990) *Basic Content Analysis.* 2nd edn. Newbury Park, CA: Sage.

Weischenberg, Siegfried, Malik, Maja, and Scholl, Armin (2006) *Die Souffleure der Mediengesellschaft: Report über die Journalisten in Deutschland.* Konstanz: UVK Verlagsgesellschaft.

West, Bing (2005) *No True Glory: A Frontline Account of the Battle for Fallujah*. New York: Bantam Dell.

Whale, John (1977) *The Politics of the Media*. London: Fontana/Collins.

White, David Manning (1950) The "Gate Keeper": A Case Study in the Selection of News. *Journalism Quarterly*, 27, pp. 383–396.

Whitlock, Craig (2011) U.S. Secretly Backed Syrian Opposition Groups, Cables Released by WikiLeaks show. *Washington Post* [online], 17 April. Available at: https://www.washingtonpost.com/world/us-secretly-backed-syrian-opposition-groups-cables-released-by-wikileaks-show/2011/04/14/AF1p9hwD_story.html [accessed 22 June 2016].

Wikiwand (n.d.) *Casualties of the Syrian Civil War* [online]. Available at: http://www.wikiwand.com/en/Casualties_of_the_Syrian_Civil_War [accessed 22 June 2016].

Winter, James (1997) *Democracy's Oxygen: How Corporations Control the News*. Montréal: Black Rose Books.

Winter, James (2007) *Lies the Media Tell Us*. Montréal: Black Rose Books.

Wolfsfeld, Gadi (1997) *Media and Political Conflict: News from the Middle East*. Cambridge: Cambridge University Press.

Zaller, John and Chiu, Dennis (1996) Government's Little Helper: U.S. Press Coverage of Foreign Policy Crises, 1945–1991. *Political Communication*, 13(4), pp. 385–405.

Zenko, Micah (2011) Syria: Military Intervention a la Carte. *Council on Foreign Relations* [online], 28 November. Available at: http://blogs.cfr.org/zenko/2011/11/28/syria-military-intervention-a-la-carte/ [accessed 14 November 2016].

Zollmann, Florian (2008) Warfare as Remedy: How the Independent Framed the First US Assault on Fallujah. *Occasional Working Paper Series*, 1(1), pp. 1–15.

Zollmann, Florian (2009) Is It Either Or? Professional Ideology vs. Corporate-Media Constraints. *Westminster Papers in Communication and Culture*, 6(2), 97–118.

Zollmann, Florian (2010a) Falludscha: Muhamad Tareq Al-darraji gibt die Hoffnung nicht auf, dass die Geschichte eines Tages Recht sprechen wird und die Weltöffentlichkeit von dem Schicksal seiner Heimatstadt erfährt. *Publik-Forum*, 24(18), pp. 54–59.

Zollmann, Florian (2010b) Paper of Record or Paper of Power? How *The New York Times* covered the second US assault on Fallujah. *Z Magazine* [online], September. Available at: http://www.zcommu- nications.org/paper-of-record-or-paper-of-power-by-florian-zollmann [accessed 20 November 2010].

Zollmann, Florian (2012) *Manufacturing Wars? A Comparative Analysis of US, UK and German Corporate Press Coverage of the US Occupation of Iraq*. PhD diss., University of Lincoln, UK.

Zollmann, Florian (2014a) Unterm Brennglas: Libyen. *Publik-Forum Extra Leben*, December, pp. 28–29.

Zollmann, Florian (2014b) State-Ending: A Brief History of the Destruction of Iraq. *teleSUR* [online], 21 July. Available at: http://www.telesurtv.net/english/opinion/State-Ending-a-Brief-History-of-the-Destruction-of-Iraq-20140722-0024.html [accessed 7 November 2016].

Zollmann, Florian (2015a) Bad News From Fallujah. *Media, War and Conflict*, 8(3), pp. 345–367.

Zollmann, Florian (2015b) The Relevance of the Herman-Chomsky Propaganda Model in the 21st Century New Media Environment. In: Broudy, Daniel, Klaehn, Jefferey and Winter, James, eds. *News From Somewhere: A Reader in Communication and Challenges to Globalization*. Eugene, Oregon: Wayzgoose Press, pp. 143–162.

INDEX